1 MONTH OF
FREE
READING

at

www.ForgottenBooks.com

By purchasing this book you are eligible for one month membership to ForgottenBooks.com, giving you unlimited access to our entire collection of over 1,000,000 titles via our web site and mobile apps.

To claim your free month visit:

www.forgottenbooks.com/free563161

ISBN 978-0-666-34362-8
PIBN 10563161

This book is a reproduction of an important historical work. Forgotten Books uses
state-of-the-art technology to digitally reconstruct the work, preserving the original format
whilst repairing imperfections present in the aged copy. In rare cases, an imperfection in
the original, such as a blemish or missing page, may be replicated in our edition. We do,
however, repair the vast majority of imperfections successfully; any imperfections that
remain are intentionally left to preserve the state of such historical works.

29

THIRTY-EIGHTH ANNUAL REPO

WOMAN'S FOREIG
MISSIONARY SOCIET

METHODIST EPISCOPAL CHUR

1907

CONTENTS

MRS. CARRIE W. JOYCE.

OCTOBER 24, 1840—SEPTEMBER 27, 1907.

Corresponding Secretary of the Minneapolis Branch, 1901-1907.

"Lo, the Son of God is come!"

Motto: "SAVED FOR SERVICE."

THIRTY-EIGHTH ANNUAL REPORT

OF THE

WOMAN'S FOREIGN MISSIONARY SOCIETY

OF THE

METHODIST EPISCOPAL CHURCH.

ORGANIZED 1869.
INCORPORATED 1884.

GENERAL OFFICE:
Room 611, 150 Fifth Avenue, New York.

1907.

CINCINNATI:
WESTERN METHODIST BOOK CONCERN PRESS.

SESSIONS OF THE GENERAL EXECUTIVE COMMITTEE.

Date	Place	President	Secretary	Receipts
1870	Boston, Mass...............	Mrs. Dr. Patten...........	Mrs. W. F. Warren.....	$4,546 86
1871	Chicago, Ill...................	" Bishop Kingsley	" W. F. Warren.....	22,397 99
1872	New York City............	" Bishop Clark.....	" W. F. Warren.....	44,477 46
1873	Cincinnati, O..............	" L. D. McCabe......	" R. Meredith........	54,834 87
1874	Philadelphia, Pa.........	" F. G. Hibbard.....	" J. H. Knowles.....	64,309 25
1875	Baltimore, Md......	" F. A. Crook........	" R. R. Battee.......	61,492 19
1876	Washington, D. C........	" F. G. Hibbard.....	" W. F. Warren.....	55,276 06
1877	Minneapolis, Minn.....	" Dr. Goodrich......	" Delia Williams...	72,464 30
1878	Boston, Mass...............	" W. F. Warren.....	" J. T. Gracey.........	68,063 52
1879	Chicago, Ill.................,	" S. J. Steele...........	" L. H. Daggett......	66,843 69
1880	Columbus, O...............	" W. F. Warren.....	" J. T. Gracey.........	76,276 43
1881	Buffalo, N. Y...............	" F. G. Hibbard.....	" Mary C. Nind......	107,932 54
1882	Philadelphia, Pa.........	" W. F. Warren.....	" J. T. Gracey.........	195,678 50
1883	Des Moines, Ia...........	" L. G. Murphy.....	" J. T. Gracey.........	126,823 33
1884	Baltimore, Md.............	" W. F. Warren.....	" J. T. Gracey.........	148,199 14
1885	Evanston, Ill..............	" I. R. Hitt...........	" F. P. Crandon......	157,442 66
1886	Providence, R. I........	" W. F. Warren.....	" J. H. Knowles.....	167,098 85
1887	Lincoln, Neb............:	Miss P. L. Elliott......	" J. T. Gracey.........	191,158 13
1888	Cincinnati, O..............	Mrs. Bishop Clark......	" J. T. Gracey.........	206,808 69
1889	Detroit, Mich.............	" I. N. Danforth.....	" .T. Gracey	226,496 15
1890	Wilkesbarre, Pa.........	" W. F. Warren.....	" T. Gracey.........	220,329 96
1891	Kansas City, Mo.........	" J. J. Imhoff........	" T. Gracey.........	263,660 69
1892	Springfield, Mass........	" W. F. Warren.....	" T. Gracey.........	265,242 15
1893	St. Paul. Minn............	" W. Couch..........	" T. Gracey.........	277,803 79
1894	Washington, D. C........	" A. H. Eaton........	" T. Gracey.........	311,925 96
1895	St. Louis, Mo............	Miss E. Pearson........	" T. Gracey.........	289,227 00
1896	Rochester, N. Y...........	Mrs. S. L. Baldwin....	" T. Gracey.........	285,823 94
1897	Denver, Colo...............	" C. D. Foss...........	" T. Gracey.........	313,937 86
1898	Indianapolis, Ind........	" C. D. Foss...........	" T. Gracey.........	328,488 75
1899	Cleveland, O...............	" C. D. Foss...........	" J T. Gracey......	360,338 63
1900	Worcester, Mass..........	" C. D. Foss...........	" J. T. Gracey...	414,531 33
1901	Philadelphia, Pa.........	" C. D. Foss...........	" T. Gracey.........	426,795 28
1902	Minneapolis, Minn.....	" C. D. Foss...........	" T. Gracey.........	478,286 08
1903	Baltimore, Md.............	" C. D. Foss...........	" T. Gracey.........	491,391 75
1904	Kansas City, Mo........	" C. D. Foss...........	" H. Knowles.......	534,040 17
1905	New York City............	" C. D. Foss...........	" . S. Nutter.........	548,943 55
1906	Omaha, Neb.................	" A. W. Patten......	" J. W. Barnes......	616,457 71
1907	Springfield, Ill............	" C. D. Foss............	" C. W. Barnes......	692,490 07

Total since organization...$9,232,285 23

OFFICERS

of the

Woman's Foreign Missionary Society

of the

METHODIST EPISCOPAL CHURCH.

PRESIDENT.
MRS. C. D. FOSS, 2043 Arch Street, Philadelphia, Pa.

SECRETARY.
MRS. C. W. BARNES, Delaware, Ohio.

TREASURER.
MRS. J. M. CORNELL, 560 West 26th Street, New York City.

GENERAL COUNSEL.
LEMUEL SKIDMORE, 67 Wall Street, New York City.

CORRESPONDING SECRETARIES.
MISS MARY E. HOLT, 4 Berwick Park, Boston, Mass.

MRS. J. M. CORNELL, 26th St. and Eleventh Ave., New York City.

MISS C. J. CARNAHAN, Shady Ave. and Walnut St. E., E. Pittsburg, Pennsylvania.

MRS. E. D. HUNTLEY, "The Postner," Washington, D. C.

MRS. R. L. THOMAS, 792 E. McMillan St., Walnut Hills, Cincinnati, Ohio.

MRS. F. P. CRANDON, 1414 Forest Ave., Evanston, Ill.

MRS. W. B. THOMPSON, 1018 Des Moines St., Des Moines, Iowa.

MRS. F. F. LINDSAY, 25 Seymour Ave., St. Paul, Minn.

MISS ELLA M. WATSON, 1701 S. 17th St., Lincoln, Neb.

MRS. S. F. JOHNSON, 520 Oakland Ave., Pasadena, Cal.

MRS. A. N. FISHER, 214 Twelfth St., Portland, Ore.

GENERAL SECRETARIES.
German Work.—MISS LOUISE C. ROTHWEILER, 1190 Mozart St., Columbus, Ohio.

Scandinavian Work.—MRS. HANNA HENSCHEN, 2830 N. Hermitage Ave., Chicago, Ill.

Young People's Work.—MISS WINIFRED SPAULDING, Deaconess Training School, Wesley Ave., Cincinnati, Ohio.

Children's Work.—MRS. LUCIE F. HARRISON, Los Angeles, Cal.

LITERATURE COMMITTEE.
MRS. J. H. KNOWLES, 150 Fifth Ave., New York City.

MRS. L. T. M. SLOCUM, 2234 Kenmore Ave., Chicago, Ill.

MISS LULU HEACOCK, Pacific Grove, Cal.

3

EDITORS OF PERIODICALS.

WOMAN'S MISSIONARY FRIEND.
MISS ELIZABETH C. NORTHUP, 77 Crescent St., Waltham, Mass.

DER FRAUEN-MISSIONS FREUND.
MISS AMALIA M. ACHARD, 710 Bellevue Ave., Elgin, Ill.

CHILDREN'S MISSIONARY FRIEND.
MRS. O. W. SCOTT, 86 Highland Ave., Fitchburg, Mass.

THE STUDY.
MRS. MARY ISHAM, University Place, Lincoln, Neb.

GENERAL LITERATURE.
MISS ELIZABETH C. NORTHUP, 77 Crescent St., Waltham, Mass.

PUBLISHER.
MISS PAULINE J. WALDEN, 36 Bromfield St., Boston, Mass.

SECRETARY OF GENERAL OFFICE.
MISS ELIZABETH R. BENDER, Room 611, 150 Fifth Ave., New York.

OFFICIAL CORRESPONDENTS.

North China and South America.—Miss Holt.
Central China.—Mrs. Cornell.
Korea, Germany, and Switzerland.—Miss Rothweiler.
Mexico and Japan.—Miss Carnahan.
Foochow and South India.—Mrs. Huntley.
North India and South Japan.—Mrs. Thomas.
Italy, Bulgaria, and West China.—Mrs. Crandon.
Bombay and Burma.—Mrs. Thompson.
Malaysia and Philippine Islands.—Mrs. Lindsay.
Northwest India.—Miss Watson.
Africa and Bengal.—Mrs. Johnson.
Central Provinces and Hing Hua.—Mrs. Fisher.

TREASURERS IN FOREIGN FIELDS.

North India.—Mrs. R. C. Thoburn, Naini Tal, India.
Northwest India.—Miss Anne E. Lawson, Ajmer, Rajputani, India.
South India.—Miss Catherine Wood, Haiderabad, Deccan, India.
Central Provinces.—Mrs. Alma H. Holland, Hawa Bagh, Jabalpur, India.
Bombay.—Miss Christine H. Lawson, Telegaon, Dabahada, Poona District, India.
Bengal.—Miss Elizabeth Maxey, 150 Dharamtala St., Calcutta, India.
Burma.—Miss Luella Rigby, Methodist Mission, Rangoon, Burma.
Malaysia.—Mrs. W. T. Cherry, Singapore, Sts. Settlement.
Philippines.—Miss Marguerite Decker, 203 Calle Cervantes, Manila, P. I.
North China.—Mrs. Charlotte M. Jewell, Peking, China.
Central China.—Miss Clara E. Merrill, Kiu Kiang, China.

4

TREASURERS IN FOREIGN FIELDS.—Continued.

West China.—Miss Ella Manning, Tsicheo, China.

Foochow.—Miss Elizabeth M. Strow, Foochow, China.

Hing Hua.—Miss Lizzie Varney, Hing Hua, via Foochow, China.

Korea.—Miss Josephine O. Paine. Seoul, Korea.

North Japan.—Miss Mary S. Hampton, Hakodati, Japan.

Central Japan.—Mrs. Charles Bishop, Aoyama, Tokio, Japan.

South Japan.—Miss Elizabeth Russell, Nagasaki, Japan.

Mexico.—Miss Laura Temple, Appartado 2033, Mexico City, Mexico.

Buenos Ayres, S. A.—Miss Mary F. Swaney, 1449 Calle Laprida, Rosario de Santa
Fe, Argentine Republic, S. A.

Montevideo.—Miss Lizzie Hewitt, 257 Calle San Jose, Montevideo, Uruguay, S. A.

Peru.—Miss Elsie Wood, Lima, Peru, S. A.

Bulgaria.—Miss Kate B. Blackburn, Lovetch, Bulgaria.

Italy.—Miss Edith T. Swift, Crandon Hall, via Veneto, Rome, Italy.

Africa.—Miss Susan Collins, Malange, Angola, Africa.

East Africa.—Mrs. Virginia S. Coffin, Old Umtali, Rhodesia.

Switzerland.—Mrs. Anna Spoerri, Zeltweg, Zurich, Switzerland.

North Germany.—Mrs. C. Wunderlich, Tilsiter St. 14–15, Berlin, Germany.

COMMITTEE OF REFERENCE:

The President of the Society and the Corresponding Secretaries of the several Branches constitute a Committee of Reference.

All communications to be brought before the Woman's Foreign Missionary Society in the interim of the General Executive Committee, should be addressed to the Secretary of this committee, Miss Ella M. Watson, 1701 S. 17th St., Lincoln, Neb.

OFFICERS AND DELEGATES
OF THE
GENERAL EXECUTIVE COMMITTEE
OF THE
Woman's Foreign Missionary Society,
1907.

PRESIDENT.
MRS. CYRUS D. FOSS.

SECRETARY.
MRS. C. W. BARNES.

NEW ENGLAND BRANCH.
MISS MARY E. HOLT. MISS CLEMENTINA BUTLER. MRS. B. T. WILLISTON.

NEW YORK BRANCH.
MRS. J. M. CORNELL. MRS. RICHARD STEPHENS. MISS W. R. LEWIS.

PHILADELPHIA BRANCH.
MISS C. J. CARNAHAN. MRS. G. B. RICHARDSON. MISS E. A. FOWLER.

BALTIMORE BRANCH.
MRS. E. D. HUNTLEY. MRS. H. R. NAYLOR. MRS. S. A. HILL.

CINCINNATI BRANCH.
MRS. R. L. THOMAS. MRS. J. ELLINGTON McGEE. MRS. F. A. SCHUMANN

NORTHWESTERN BRANCH.
MRS. F. P. CRANDON. MRS. C. W. FOWLER. MRS. I. H. IRISH.

DES MOINES BRANCH.
MRS. W. B. THOMPSON. MRS. W. M. DUDLEY. MRS. J. T. MILLER.

MINNEAPOLIS BRANCH.
MRS. F. F. LINDSAY. MRS. W. H. LANDIS. MRS. R. J. SMART.

TOPEKA BRANCH.
MISS ELLA WATSON. MISS FRANCES J. BAKER. MRS. MARTHA REYNOLDS.

PACIFIC BRANCH.
MRS. S. F. JOHNSON. MRS. N. S. HANSON. MRS. C. E. BROWN.

COLUMBIA RIVER BRANCH.
MRS. A. N. FISHER. MRS. M. C. WIRE. MRS. J. P. MARLATT.

SECRETARY OF THE GERMAN WORK.
MISS LOUISE ROTHWEILER.

SECRETARY OF THE SCANDINAVIAN WORK.
MRS. HANNA HENSCHEN.

LITERATURE COMMITTEE.
MISS KATE MOSS. MRS. J. H. KNOWLES. MRS. L. T. M. SLOCUM.

COMMITTEES FOR 1907-1908.

COMMITTEE OF REFERENCE.
MRS. C. D. FOSS, Chairman, 2043 Arch St., Philadelphia, Pa.
MISS ELLA WATSON, Secretary, 1701 S. 17th St., Lincoln, Neb.

COMMITTEE ON LITERATURE
MRS. J. H. KNOWLES, 150 Fifth Ave., New York. Term expires 1908.
MRS. L. T. M. SLOCUM, 2238 Kenmore Ave., Chicago, Ill. Term expires 1909.
MISS LULU HEACOCK, Pacific Grove, Cal. Term expires 1910.

COMMITTEE ON BY-LAWS.
MRS. C. D. FOSS. MRS. C. W. BARNES. MRS. JOHN LEGG.
MRS. W. B. THOMPSON. MRS. S. J. HERBEN.

COMMITTEE ON REAL ESTATE AND TITLES.
MRS. W. B. DAVIS, Clifton, Cincinnati, O. MRS. C. D. FOSS.

COMMITTEE ON MISSIONARY EDUCATION IN METHODIST COLLEGES.
MRS. MARY ISHAM, University Place, Neb. MISS IDA V. JONTZ, Herkimer, N. Y.
MISS LOUISE MANNING HODGKINS, Winter Hill, Boston, Mass.

COMMITTEE ON GENERAL OFFICE.
MRS. W. B. DAVIS, Chairman. MRS. CYRUS D. FOSS. MRS. JOHN. LEGG.
MRS. J. M. CORNELL. MRS. F. P. CRANDON. MRS. J. E. LEAYCRAFT.

GENERAL STATEMENT FOR THE YEAR OCTOBER 1, 1906— OCTOBER 1, 1907.

RECEIPTS.

Balance on hand October 1, 1906,	$59,695	67
*REGULAR RECEIPTS,	677,668	88
Annuities,	4,843	78
Special gifts,	11,321	19
Total Receipts,	$753,529	52

DISBURSEMENTS.

†GENERAL DISBURSEMENTS,	$669,685	39
Transferred to Trust Fund,	1,784	00
" " Invested Fund,	1,700	00
" " Annuity Fund,	8,509	78
" " Nind Evangelistic Fund,	342	60
Total Disbursements,	$682,021	77
	$71,507	75
Deficit in one Branch,	1,122	31
Balance, October 1, 1907,	$72,630	06

* For receipts by Branches, refer to page 12.
† For Disbursements by Branches, refer to pages 194, 195.

OFFICIAL MINUTES

OF THE

General Executive Committee

OF THE

Woman's Foreign Missionary Society

OF THE

METHODIST EPISCOPAL CHURCH.

Thirty-Eighth Session.

THURSDAY, OCTOBER 24, 1907.

The Thirty-eighth Annual Session of the General Executive Committee of the Woman's Foreign Missionary Society of the Methodist Episcopal Church convened, on account of the burning of the interior of the First Methodist Church, in the First Presbyterian Church at Springfield, Illinois, on Thursday morning, October 24th, 1907, at 9 o'clock.

The meeting was called to order by the President, Mrs. C. D. Foss, who introduced Mrs. F. P. Crandon, the Corresponding Secretary of the entertaining Branch. Mrs. Crandon conducted the devotional service. After the singing of hymn No. 1, selections from the Thirty-third Psalm and the first chapter of Colossians were read, and prayer was offered by Miss Pearson, President of the Des Moines Branch. The devotional service closed with a song, "It was the Man of Gallilee," rendered by Mrs. C. H. Brown, Montpelier, Indiana.

Mrs. Crandon gave a brief, but cordial, welcome, and the President, Mrs. C. D. Foss, replied, expressing her satisfaction in again being present at an Executive Meeting. She briefly reviewed her trip among our Mission Stations, and gave hearty endorsement to the missionaries.

The roll was called by the Secretary as follows:

President—MRS. CYRUS D. ROSS.   *Secretary*—MRS. C. W. BARNES.

NEW ENGLAND BRANCH.	NEW YORK BRANCH.
Miss Mary E. Holt,	Mrs. J. M. Cornell,
Miss Clementina Butler,	Mrs. Richard Stephens,
Mrs. B. T. Williston.	Miss W. R. Lewis.

9

PHILADELPHIA BRANCH.

Miss C. J. Carnahan,
Mrs. G. B. Richardson,
Miss E. A. Fowler.

BALTIMORE BRANCH.

Mrs. E. D. Huntley,
Mrs. H. R. Naylor,
Mrs. S. A. Hill.

CINCINNATI BRANCH.

Mrs. R. L. Thomas,
Mrs. J. Ellington McGee,
Mrs. F. A. Schumann.

NORTHWESTERN BRANCH.

Mrs. F. P. Crandon,
Mrs. C. W. Fowler,
Mrs. I. H. Irish.

DES MOINES BRANCH.

Mrs. W. B. Thompson,
Mrs. W. M. Dudley,
Mrs. J. T. Miller.

MINNEAPOLIS BRANCH.

Mrs. F. F. Lindsay,
Mrs. W. H. Landis,
Mrs. R. J. Smart.

TOPEKA BRANCH.

Miss Ella Watson,
Miss Frances J. Baker,
Mrs. Martha Reynolds.

PACIFIC BRANCH.

Mrs. S. F. Johnson,
Mrs. N. S. Hanson,
Mrs. C. E. Brown.

COLUMBIA RIVER BRANCH.

Mrs. A. N. Fisher,
Mrs. M. C. Wire,
Mrs. J. P. Marlatt.

GENERAL SECRETARIES.

Miss Louise Rothweiler,
Secretary of German Work;
Mrs. Hanna Henschen,
Secretary of Scandinavian Work.

LITERATURE COMMITTEE.

Miss Kate Moss,
Mrs. J. H. Knowles,
Mrs. L. T. M. Slocum.

The seating of the delegates was next in order, and was arranged according to the usual custom; after which Miss Watson, Secretary of the Reference Committee, announced the following standing committees:

MISSIONARY CANDIDATES.

New England—Mrs. B. T. Williston.
New York—Mrs. Richard Stephens.
Philadelphia—Mrs. G. B. Richardson.
Baltimore—Mrs. H. R. Naylor.
Cincinnati—Mrs. F. A. Schumann.
Northwestern—Mrs. I. H. Irish.
Des Moines—Mrs. J. T. Miller.
Minneapolis—Mrs. R. J. Smart.
Topeka—Mrs. Martha Reynolds.
Pacific—Mrs. C. E. Brown.
Columbia River—Mrs. J. P. Marlatt.

PUBLICATION COMMITTEE.

New England—
Miss Clementina Butler.
New York—Miss W. R. Lewis.
Philadelphia—Miss E. A. Fowler.
Baltimore—Mrs. S. A. Hill.
Cincinnati—
Mrs. J. Ellington McGee.
Northwestern—Mrs. C. W. Fowler.
Des Moines—Mrs. W. M. Dudley.
Minneapolis—Mrs. W. H. Landis.
Topeka—Miss Frances J. Baker.
Pacific—Mrs. N. S. Hanson.
Columbia River—Mrs. M. C. Wire.

The Finance Committee, consisting of the Corresponding Secretaries. Memorials were presented as follows:

From the Cincinnati Branch.—WHEREAS, The German element of the Woman's Foreign Missionary Society is scattered among the eleven Branches of our Society, thereby causing many complications in the carrying on of the work; and

WHEREAS, We believe it would tend to the better carrying on of the work and larger results, therefore we memorialize the General Executive Committee to create a German Branch.

From the Baltimore Branch—We, the Baltimore Branch in annual session convened, memorialize the General Executive Committee to continue the terms of membership in the Woman's Foreign Missionary Society as they are now and have been from the beginning—two cents a week or a dollar a year.

We, also, do unanimously pray that in the proposed changes in the Constitution of the Woman's Foreign Missionary Society, the Presidents of the Branches be given recognition as members of the General Executive Committee by virtue of their office.

WHEREAS, We of the Baltimore Branch do earnestly desire to be represented by two delegates annually elected;

Therefore, we memorialize the General Executive Committee to so amend the Constitution that in the event of the Branch Presidents being made members of the Permanent Committee, each Branch be allowed four representatives at the General Executive Committee meetings.

We, the Executive Committee of the Baltimore Branch, also pray that the assessment of one per cent for general expenses be made upon the appropriations—not upon the receipts of each Branch.

From the Northwestern Branch.—We, the Northwestern Branch in annual meeting assembled, memorialize the General Executive Committee to change Section 1, Article IV, of the Constitution, which reads, "Branch Treasurers shall be required to publish quarterly reports in the Woman's Missionary Friend," to "Branch Treasurers shall be required to furnish quarterly reports for publication in the Woman's Missionary Friend."

These memorials were referred to a committee to be appointed by the chair, and announced later.

Mrs. J. H. Knowles presented the following resolution:

WHEREAS, The new Act of Incorporation of the Woman's Foreign Missionary Society includes the Literature Committee in the personnel of the General Executive Committee; and

WHEREAS, By an inadvertance, this fact was overlooked in the action of the General Executive Committee of 1906, eliminating the Literature Committee from Section 2, Article VI, of the Constitution; therefore,

Resolved, That we herewith revoke that action, and recognize the Literature Committee as a legitimate part of the General Executive Committee while the present Act of Incorporation remains in force.

Mrs. F. P. Crandon stated that we must be governed by the Act of Incorporation; and Mrs. Thompson failed to see any necessity of action on this resolution, and moved that the resolution be laid on the table. This motion was carried, and the members of the Literature Committee were therefore recognized as having votes in this session of the General Executive Committee. . ·

Mrs. Cornell requested that the Branch officers and missionary candidates and missionaries should be seated with their Branch delegations. Mrs. Thomas requested that Mrs. William Gamble be seated with the Cincinnati delegation.

The reports of the home work were presented by the Branch Corresponding Secretaries. Mrs. C. S. Winchell, Secretary Emeritus, read the report for the Minneapolis Branch. (See reports.)

The receipts for the year were read by the Recording Secretary as follows:

New England Branch	$84,320 88
New York Branch ....,..............	96,746 83
Philadelphia Branch	65,981 59
Baltimore Branch	18,814 87
Cincinnati Branch	88,695 53
Northwestern Branch	152,952 46
Des Moines Branch	67,420 97
Minneapolis Branch	28,209 63
Topeka Branch	42,066 96
Pacific Branch	33,329 00
Columbia River Branch	13,951 35
Total amount received	$692,490 07
Total amount received 1905-6	616,457.71
Increase	$76,032 36

"Praise God, from whom all blessings flow" was sung with thankful hearts on account of the success of the last year.

The following missionary candidates were presented: Misses Estie Boddy, Eugenia Norberg, Josephine Liers.

The program of this Executive Meeting, as presented by the Committee and printed, was adopted.

The report of the Reference Committee was read by Miss Ella Watson and accepted with the proviso that matters demanding action should be brought up later in the meeting.

On motion the reading of other reports scheduled for this session was deferred until Friday morning.

The following were introduced:

From India—Mrs. Bishop Warne, Miss Mary E. Williams, Miss Laura Bobenhouse, Miss Anna E. Elicker, Miss Isabel McKnight, Miss Fanny Fern Fisher, Mrs. Dr. Stevens, and Dr. Margaret D. Lewis.

China—Misses Effie G. Young, Fanny Meyer, Kate L. Ogborn, Dr. Mary Ida Stevenson, Phœbe C. Wells, and Grace B. Travis.

Japan—Mrs. C. W. Van Petten, Misses Jennie M. Gheer, and Mabel Seeds.

Korea—Misses Minerva Guthapfel and Lula A. Miller.

Mexico—Miss Laura Temple.

The Philippines—Miss Winifred Spaulding.

Branch Officers—Miss Wilhelm, Secretary of Young People's Work,

Philadelphia, Pa.; Mrs. C. H. Stowell, Secretary of Children's Work, New England Branch; Mrs. Chapel, Secretary of Children's Work, Topeka; Mrs. W. J. Clapp, Secretary of Children's Work, Minneapolis Branch; Miss Pearson, President of Des Moines Branch; Mrs. Dow, First Vice-President of Des Moines Branch; Miss M. V. Patten, Home Secretary of Des Moines Branch; Mrs. C. W. Fowler, Home Secretary of Northwestern Branch; Mrs. W. H. Landis, President of Minneapolis Branch; Mrs. A. J. Pichereau, Conference Secretary of Des Moines Branch; Mrs. J. E. McGee, Secretary of Home Department, Cincinnati Branch; Mrs. J. F. Fisher, Secretary of Children's Work, Cincinnati Branch; Mrs. A. W. Patten, President Northwestern Branch; Mrs. M. C. Wire, President Columbia River Branch; Mrs. W. A. Gamble, of Cincinnati Branch.

Mr. and Mrs. Soudam, of St. Paul, Minnesota, were introduced.

Mrs. Irish announced the literature, and Mrs. Kuhl, the General Chairman of the Committee of Arrangements, was introduced and gave announcements.

Rev. Dr. Lucas, of Lincoln, Illinois, led the closing prayer and pronounced the benediction.

Memorial Service.

On Thursday afternoon at 3 o'clock a service was held in memory of Mrs. Frank Gamewell, Misses Lois Buck, Susanna M. Stumpf, Mary Bell Tuttle, and Mrs. Carrie W. Joyce.

Mrs. A. W. Patten presided and announced the hymn, "O, mother dear, Jerusalem," No. 610. Prayer was offered by Mrs. W. B. Thompson, and Mrs. Patten read the selection, Rev. vii, 9-17, after which Mrs. C. H. Brown sang effectively, "Sometime We'll Understand."

A memoir of Mrs. Gamewell was presented by Mrs. J. H. Knowles, of the New York Branch. She spoke briefly of the life of Mrs. Gamewell, and paid high tribute to her character and service in this great missionary work.

A memoir of Miss Lois Buck, written by Prof. Clara Nelson, was read by Mrs. R. L. Thomas. It showed how thoroughly prepared Miss Buck was for the work in which she was privileged to serve for such a short time.

Mrs. A. J. Pichereau reviewed the life of Miss Susanna Stumpf, and spoke of her faithfulness and devotion to duty.

Mrs. Bishop Warne brought tribute to the memory of Dr. Tuttle, and read a letter from Miss Mary Means, which depicted the self-sacrificing character of this faithful missionary.

After the singing of the hymn, No. 470, "Lord, it belongs not to my care," Mrs. C. S. Winchell, as representative of the Minneapolis Branch, brought her loving tribute to the memory of Mrs. C. W. Joyce, who had served that Branch as both President and Corresponding Secretary. Mrs. Joyce had found and placed fifteen missionaries, and she was wont to say, "I have done what I can and now I leave it with Him." Her last words were, "I am going home to die no more." Mrs. W. B. Thompson spoke to her memory for the General Executive Committee. She stated that the center of Mrs. Joyce's work was her Christian character, and gave heartfelt tribute to this noble Christian woman. Miss Mary E. Holt added a few loving words, saying that Mrs. Joyce's very presence was a benediction to all who were with her.

After the singing of the hymn, "My Heavenly Home is Bright and Fair," Rev. W. A. Smith pronounced the benediction.

FRIDAY, OCTOBER 25.

The session opened at 9 o'clock, Mrs. C. D. Foss presiding, with Mrs. J. H. Knowles, of the New York Branch, in charge of the devotional hour. After the singing of the hymn, No. 354, "O, for a Heart to Praise My God," Mrs. Knowles read selections from St. Paul's letter to the Philippians and led in prayer, and the hymn, "I Can not Do Without Thee," was sung. The roll was called and the minutes of the Thursday morning meeting were read and, after corrections, accepted.

The President announced the Committee on Memorials as follows: Mrs. M. C. Wire, Mrs. W. H. Landis, and Miss E. A. Fowler.

The report of the German work was read by the Secretary, Miss Louise C. Rothweiler. Accepted and ordered printed. Mrs. Hanna Henschen presented the report of the Scandinavian work. Accepted and ordered printed. Mrs. Evelyn P. Marsh presented her report as Secretary of Young People's work. Accepted and ordered printed.

The reports of the Conference Secretaries on Home work as presented on Thursday, were accepted. Mrs. C. H. Brown again favored the meeting with an appropriate solo, "Let Them that Love Him be Singing."

Mrs. Foss announced that the report of the Constitutional Publication Committee had been included in the report of the Reference Committee as presented by Miss Watson on Thursday.

The report of the publisher, Miss Walden, was read, accepted, and referred to the Publication Committee. As this was the twenty-fifth anniversary of Miss Walden as the publisher of the Woman's Foreign Missionary Society, she gave an interesting summary of the progress of this department in this quarter of a century. A rising vote of thanks was given Miss Walden for the faithful service and the summary was ordered printed in the Annual Report.

Reports of the periodicals of the Society were read, accepted, and referred to the Publication Committee as follows: *Woman's Mission-*

ary Friend, by Miss E. C. Northup; *Children's Missionary Friend*, in the absence of Mrs. Scott, read by Miss Walden; *Frauen Missions Freund*, by Miss Achard; Zenana paper, by Miss M. E. Holt; The Study, by Mrs. Mary Isham; Tokiwa, by Miss Kate Moss.

The reporters of this meeting for the various Church papers were appointed as follows:

Zion's Herald, Miss Elizabeth C. Northup.

Northwestern Christian Advocate, Miss Frances J. Baker.

Epworth Herald, Mrs. R. O' Irish.

Christian Advocate, Mrs. J. H. Knowles.

World Wide Missions, Mrs. J. F. Fisher.

Central Christian Advocate, Mrs. Mary Isham.

Western Christian Advocate, Mrs. J. Ellington McGee.

Pittsburg Christian Advocate and Philadelphia Methodist, Miss E. A. Fowler.

Baltimore Methodist, Mrs. S. A. Hill.

Michigan Advocate, Miss Frances Baker.

California Christian Advocate, Mrs. N. S. Hansen.

German Apologete, Miss Olivia Heidel.

Methodist Advocate Journal, Mrs. William Gamble.

Iowa Methodist, Mrs. Oner S. Dow.

Northern Advocate Mrs. Richard Stephens.

Pacific Advocate, Mrs. M. C. Wire.

Missionary Review of the World, Miss Clementina Butler.

Mrs. S. A. Hill presented the following, which was adopted:

The Publication Committee offers the following resolution:

WHEREAS, The daily press reports, while written in the greatest kindness, might fail to present the most important points of our proceedings, and

WHEREAS, It has been stated that other religious bodies provide the reporters with material which they wish to be printed; therefore,

Resolved, That some members of the Society shall be appointed to prepare suitable reports to be offered to the daily press.

The report of the Special Committee on Mission Study in the Colleges was read by Mrs. Mary Isham. The report was accepted and the committee continued.

Mrs. Cornell, in behalf of the General Executive Committee and missionaries in attendance, presented to Miss Gheer twenty-eight chrysanthemums as a recognition of the twenty-eighth anniversary of her departure for work in Japan. Miss Gheer accepted the gift with thanks and a Japanese bow.

The following missionary candidates were presented: Miss Estella M. Forsyth, Dr. Lena Hatfield, and Dr. Margaret Campbell.

Mrs. William Butler, the Mother of Missions, was introduced and was greeted with the Chautauqua salute.

The following missionaries were introduced: *China,* Dr. Agnes M. Edmunds, Miss Ella Shaw, Dr. and Mrs. Lewis; *India,* Misses May Ruddick, Lucy Sullivan, and Anna E. Winslow; *South America,* Mrs. L. G. Craver and Rev. George P. Howard, Presiding Elder of the Buenos Ayres District; *Japan,* Misses Harriet S. Alling and Mary E. Melton.

Mrs. Iva Durham Vennard was also introduced.

Mrs. C. W. Fowler, of the Northwestern Branch, advertised the literature on sale. After announcements, Dr. C. P. Masden, pastor of the First Methodist Episcopal Church of Springfield, Illinois, led in a short prayer and pronounced the benediction.

SATURDAY, OCTOBER 26.

The session opened at 9 o'clock, with Mrs. Foss presiding, and the Baltimore Branch in charge of the devotional hour. Mrs. S. A. Hill announced hymn No. 336. Mrs. H. R. Naylor read a selection from Romans xii, and Miss Minerva Guthapfel offered prayer. The hour closed with a song by Mrs. C. H. Brown, "Send Out Sunshine as You Pass Along." The roll was called and the minutes of Friday morning's session were read and approved.

The report of the Literature Committee was presented by Miss Kate Moss and referred to the Publication Committee.

Mrs. Foss announced for Committee on Resolutions Miss Kate Moss, Miss Frances Baker, and Mrs. Hanna Henschen. Mrs. W. M. Dudley and Miss W. R. Lewis, were added to the Committee on Memorials.

Mrs. S. F. Johnson moved that greetings be sent to the Woman's Home Missionary Society in annual session at Brookline, Mass. Carried. The message was as follows: "Greetings to our co-workers in Christ Jesus. See 2 John iii."

Miss Pauline J. Walden presented the financial report of the Literature Committee. Accepted and referred. The report of the General Treasurer was read by Mrs. J. M. Cornell. Accepted.

The official correspondence was next in order. Malaysia and the Philippines, Mrs. C. S. Winchell, Official Correspondent, were represented by Miss Elizabeth Parkes, from Manilla. Japan, Miss C. J. Carnahan, Official Correspondent, represented by Mrs. Van Petten, Yokohama. Mrs. W. B. Thompson, Official Correspondent, represented Burma. Central China, Mrs. J. M. Cornell, Official Correspondent, was represented by Miss Kate L. Ogborn and Miss Ella E. Shaw. North India, Mrs. R. L. Thomas, Official Correspondent, represented by Dr. Margaret D. Lewis, Misses May Ruddick and Lucy Sullivan. Miss Rothweiler, Official Correspondent for Korea, reported the grant of land, which had been given us by the Korean Government for the "Lillian Harris Memorial Hospital" at the east gate of Seoul, Korea; and resolutions were adopted thanking the Marquis Ito and the Korean

Government for this land. Miss Lula A. Miller, of Chemulpo, and Miss Minerva Guthapfel spoke of the work. The written reports of the Official Correspondents were accepted and ordered printed in the Annual.

Mrs. Lucie Harrison read the report of the Children's work. Report accepted. On motion of Mrs. Harrison, the baby in the Governor's Mansion House was made a life member of the Little Light Bearers.

The following resolution was adopted:

Resolved, That the Woman's Foreign Missionary Society of the Methodist Episcopal Church sell to George Freedman, of Marion County, Indiana, for the sum of $............, the following described real estate in Marion County, Indiana, to-wit: Lot No. 46, except 75 (seventy-five) feet off the eastern side thereof, in the E. T. Fletcher Brookside addition to the City of Indianapolis, subject to all taxes and municipal assessments, and that Mrs. C. D. Foss, President of said Society, and Mrs. C. W. Barnes, its Secretary, be and they are hereby authorized and directed to deliver proper deed of conveyance therefor, in the name and on behalf of said organization.

Mrs. Lucy Ryder Meyer, Superintendent of the Chicago Training-school, was introduced and ably represented that institution.

Miss M. E. Holt, in behalf of a friend in the Middle West, presented to Miss Walden, in recognition of her twenty-fifth anniversary, a beautiful bunch of carnations. Miss Walden heartily responded.

Mrs. E. W. Utt, Chairman of the Hospitality Committee, Mrs. Ira D. Blackstack, Chairman of the Committee of Arrangements, and Mrs. N. E. Kenney, Chairman of the Lunch Committee, were introduced. Mrs. S. A. Hill stated that Mrs. Mary Isham would furnish material to the press concerning the morning sessions; Mrs. H. R. Naylor for the afternoon and evening sessions, and Miss Grace Todd would give a summary for the Associated Press. Announcements for the Sabbath services were read, and Mrs. J. H. Knowles spoke concerning the new book, "The Life of Mary Porter Gamewell," and offered the following resolution, which was adopted:

Resolved, That we hereby express our great pleasure in the fact that a record of the life of our beloved missionary, Mary Porter Gamewell, has been prepared by Dr. A. H. Tuttle; and also our sincere appreciation and thanks to Dr. F. B. Gamewell for his kind offer to give the proceeds that may come from the sale of this book to the Mary Porter Gamewell School in Pekin; and our assurance that as a Society we will endeavor to give the book a wide circulation, believing it will be a spiritual stimulus to all who read it.

Miss Grace Todd announced the literature on sale.

The following missionaries were introduced: Mrs. Mary Carr Curtis, formerly of Maylasia; Miss Anna R. Limberger, of Puebla, Mexico; Miss Carrie M. Foster, Rangoon, Burma. Mrs. C. H. Brown, of Montpelier, Indiana, was also introduced, after which Dr. Spencer Lewis offered a short prayer and pronounced the benediction.

2

MONDAY, OCTOBER 28.

The session opened at nine o'clock, Mrs. C. D. Foss presiding, and the Pacific Branch in charge of the devotional hour. Mrs. C. E. Brown announced the hymn, No. 653, and Miss Elizabeth Parkes read a portion of Psalm xcvi. Mrs. N. S. Hansen offered prayer, after which hymn No. 180 was sung, and Mrs. C. E. Brown offered a closing prayer. The roll was called and the minutes of Saturday morning's session were read and approved.

On motion of Mrs. S. F. Johnson, the publisher and editors were given the privilege of the floor, when the matter under discussion was one in which they were concerned.

Mrs. S. A. Hill presented a partial report from the Publication Committee. It was received and acted upon item by item.

First—Resolution regarding missionary illustrations in the daily press at time of the General Executive Committee meeting. Adopted.

Second—Regarding renewed efforts to place the Study in the hands of every member of the Woman's Foreign Missionary Society. Adopted.

Third—A recommendation that Branch workers place in the hands of the editor of the *"Friend"* helpful items. Adopted.

Fourth—A recommendation that the Secretary of Scandinavian work be authorized to draw $100 from the funds of the publishing house to be used in the interest of literature for her work. Adopted.

Fifth—Regarding salary of editors and publisher. Adopted.

The report of Miss Ida V. Jontz, Superintendent of Folts' Institute, was read by the Recording Secretary. Accepted and ordered printed.

The official correspondence was resumed. Mrs. W. B. Thompson, Official Correspondent for Bombay Conference, gave her time to Miss Mary E. Williams, of Baroda, and Rev. William Ayers impressed the need of more workers. South America, Miss M. E. Holt, Official Correspondent, represented by Rev. George P. Howard. Africa, Mrs. S. F. Johnson, Official Correspondent, represented by Bishop Burt. After the singing of hymn 503, Bulgaria was also represented by Bishop Burt. Hing Hua Conference, Mrs. A. N. Fisher, Official Correspondent, represented by Miss Phoebe C. Wells. South India, Mrs. E. D. Huntley, Official Correspondent, represented by Miss Fannie Fisher, Kolar. Mrs. Foss, Mrs. Crandon, and Dr. Ayers spoke of the necessity of comfortable conveyances for our missionaries. On motion, it was carried that the official reports be accepted and published as written.

The resignation of Mrs. J. T. Gracey as a member of the Central Committee for the Universal Study of Missions was presented and accepted with deep regret, and the Recording Secretary was instructed to send to Mrs. Gracey an expression of appreciation for her long and faithful service as Recording Secretary and as a member of the Central Committee. Miss Elizabeth Northup was elected to succeed Mrs. Gracey on the Central Committee.

Mrs. J. E. Leaycraft and Mrs. F. M. North were appointed auditors for the General Treasurer's report.

Mrs. Thompson presented the matter of constitutional changes, notices of which were given last year:

First—That the first sentence of Article III of the Constitution, which reads, "The payment of $1.00 annually shall constitute membership," be so changed as to read, "The payment of ten cents a month or $1.20 annually shall constitute membership." This proposed change was lost.

Second—That the word Scandinavian, in Article V, Section 1, be stricken out, and the word Swedish be inserted in its place. On motion this was tabled, as it would not be in accordance with our new Act of Incorporation.

Mrs. Thompson presented the following resolution, which was adopted:

WHEREAS, The action of the General Executive Committee of 1906 regarding the relation of the Literature Committee to this body was taken under misapprehension and was illegal; therefore,

Resolved, That the Secretary be instructed to restore to the Constitution the references to the Literature Committee, which by reason of the above mentioned action were omitted.

Miss Kate Moss advertised the missionary leaflets on sale.

By motion of Mrs. Crandon the report of the By-law Committee was made the first order of miscellaneous business on Tuesday morning. The following were introduced: Mrs. B. D. York, Treasurer of the Northwestern Branch; Mrs. H. E. Springer, missionary from Africa; Mrs. W. B. Davis, from Cincinnati; Dr. S. W. Thornton, pastor of the Kumler Church, and Rev. E. M. Jeffries, of the Illinois Conference.

After announcements the Rev. Dr. Thornton pronounced the benediction.

TUESDAY, OCTOBER 29.

The session opened at nine o'clock, with Mrs. Foss presiding, and the Columbia River Branch delegation in charge of the devotional hour. Mrs. J. P. Marlatt announced the hymn, "What a Friend We Have in Jesus," and read a portion of Acts viii; prayer was offered by Mrs. M. C. Wire and two verses of "Nearer My God to Thee" were sung.

The roll was called and the minutes of Monday morning's session read and, after corrections, approved. Mrs. S. A. Hill presented her second partial report from Committee on Publication.

Item 1, regarding appropriations for special contributions to our periodicals. Adopted.

Item 2, regarding issuing of 30,000 copies of the Secretary's Annual Report. Adopted.

Item 3, regarding the announcement of our books and leaflets in our Church papers. Adopted.

The official correspondence was resumed. Mexico, Miss C. J. Carnahan, Official Correspondent, represented by Miss Limberger. Foochow, Mrs. E. D. Huntley, Official Correspondent, represented by Miss Grace Travis. South Japan, Mrs. R. L. Thomas, Official Correspondent, represented by Misses Mary E. Melton, Mabel Seeds, and Jennie Gheer. Northwest India, Miss Ella M. Watson, Official Correspondent, represented by Miss Isabel McKnight and Miss Laura Bobenhouse.

Mrs. C. H. Brown sang "Hark, 'T is Jesus Who Calleth Thee." Return greetings were read from the Woman's Home Missionary Society.

The report of the Committee on By-laws was deferred, on motion, until Wednesday morning. Mrs. A. W. Patten read the Constitution prepared by a special committee for the Foochow College. A motion to accept it item by item was lost, and the Constitution was adopted as a whole. As a recommendation had been received from China that this college shall be incorporated in this country under the laws of the State of New York, authority was given to the officers of the General Executive Committee to proceed with the Act of Incorporation as soon as practicable.

Miss W. R. Lewis was appointed as the Methodist member on the Committee on Program for the Summer-school at Northfield.

Mrs. M. C. Wire presented the report from the Committee on Memorials, which was accepted and acted upon item by item.

First—Memorial from the Northwestern Branch regarding a change in the by-laws, which shall read, "Branch Treasurers shall be required to furnish quarterly reports to the Woman's Missionary Friend." Adopted.

Second item—Regarding the formation of a German Branch; was recommended by the committee for adoption, but on motion of Miss Fowler, the persons introducing this memorial were instructed to present the same as a proposed change in the Constitution.

Third item—A memorial from the Baltimore Branch regarding the matter of giving the Presidents of the various Branches recognition as members of the General Executive Committee, was not recommended.

Fourth item—Regarding the assessment of one per cent for expenses upon the appropriations, not upon the receipts of each Branch, was not recommended. Report accepted as a whole.

Miss Fowler ably represented the missionary literature. After announcements, the Rev. Mr. Schutz was introduced, and expressed the wish to present to each missionary present a book on Catholicism, which he had prepared.

The Rev. D. Ayers brought greetings from Mrs. E. B. Stevens, offered a short prayer, and pronounced the benediction.

WEDNESDAY, OCTOBER 30.

The session opened at nine o'clock, with Mrs. Foss presiding, and the Philadelphia Branch in charge of the devotional hour. Mrs. G. B. Richardson announced the hymn, No. 433; after the singing, Miss Mary Williams, of Baroda, read a portion of the first chapter of Joshua, Miss Carnahan led in prayer, and Mrs. C. H. Brown sang, "My Ain Countree;" the roll was called and the minutes were read and, after suggestions, approved.

Mrs. G. B. Richardson presented the report of the Committee on Missionary Candidates; Miss Helen Sante, Miss Aletheia. Tracy, Dr. Lena Hatfield, Miss Mary Richardson, and Dr. Melissa Manderson were recommended for acceptance. The case of Miss Jennie M. Gasser was referred to the Reference Committee; Miss Blanche Theresa Search was recommended for acceptance with the proposition that she shall take further training, and Miss Minnie Gardner was recommended for acceptance with her appointment deferred until next fall. This report was accepted.

Mrs. S. A. Hill presented a partial report for the Committee on Publication:

First—Regarding an endorsement of the management of our periodicals in this country. Adopted.

Secondly—An endorsement of the Tokiwa and our missionary literature published in Japan. Adopted.

Thirdly—An endorsement of the Zenana paper, and asking for fuller financial statements of the same. Adopted.

Fourthly—Regarding payment by the Branches of the expenses for publication of the pictures of the Little Light Bearers. After discussion this was not adopted. The report of the Publication Committee was adopted as a whole.

The official correspondence was resumed. North China, Miss M. E. Holt, Official Correspondent, represented by Miss Effie Young and Dr. Ida Stevenson; Bengal, Mrs. S. F. Johnson, Official Correspondent, represented by Mrs. Bishop Warne. West China, Mrs. F. P. Crandon, Official Correspondent, represented by Dr. Edmunds. Central Provinces, Mrs. A. N. Fisher, Official Correspondent, represented by Anna R. Elicker.

It was ordered that the reports of the Official Correspondents be received and printed.

Miss Fowler and Mrs. Lindsay were appointed tellers and votes were cast for President, Recording Secretary, and Treasurer.

After one verse of "Rock of Ages," Miss Harriet S. Alling, of Japan, gave a short address.

The report of the Committee on General Office was presented by Mrs. Legg; report was accepted and discussed item by item.

First item—Regarding copyrighting the badge. Adopted.

Second—The Committee recommended that the following by-laws be adopted: (1) That the Secretary of the General Office shall be nominated by the Committee on General Office and confirmed by the General Executive Committee. Adopted. (2) That the Secretary shall be authorized to receive money sent through the Board of Foreign Missions to the Woman's Foreign Missionary Society, and forward the same to the Treasurer of the Branch to which it belongs. Adopted.

Third—Regarding the salary of the Secretary of the Office. Adopted.

Fourth—Regarding rules for governing the New York Office, and the nomination of Miss Elizabeth Bender as Secretary. Adopted.

The report as a whole was then adopted, and by motion the report was ordered printed, in full, in the Annual. The Committee of last year on General Office was re-elected.

Mrs. S. F. Johnson presented the following resolution, which was adopted:

Resolved, That we present the following recommendation as a desired Article of Incorporation of our Society to the New York Legislature, providing that the wording of the same is acknowledged to be correct by the attorney of our Society, Mr. Skidmore:

"The management and general administration of said Society shall be vested in a General Executive Committee to consist of a President, Recording Secretary, and Treasurer of the Woman's Foreign Missionary Society, and the Corresponding Secretary and two delegates from each Branch, or such other persons as the Constitution of the said Society shall hereafter, from time to time, provide. The said Society by its Constitution may provide for the future composition and election of the General Executive Committee.

"The meetings of the General Executive Committee shall be held annually or oftener at such time and place as the General Executive Committee shall appoint, and such place of meeting shall be either within or without the State of New York. This act shall take effect immediately."

The Board of Directors of the Foochow College as nominated in China were confirmed, and are as follows:

For Foochow.—Miss Julia Bonafield, Miss Lydia A. Trimble, the Rev. Mr. Mains, the Rev. Mr. Lacy, Miss Carrie I. Jewell, Miss Jean Adams, Mr. W. S. Bissonette.

For Hing Hua.—Miss Elizabeth W. Varney, Miss Alethea M. Todd, Mr. W. R. Jones, Mr. Stanley Carson, and Miss Martha Lebeus.

The Northwestern Branch presented the following notice of change of Constitution: At the General Executive Meeting for 1908 the following change of Constitution of the Woman's Foreign Missionary Society will be asked for, namely, "That Article 7, Section 1, shall be changed by inserting in the first sentence immediately following the words, 'General plans for districting the Church,' the words, 'except the German Conferences;' also by inserting after the enumeration of Branches the words, 'German Branches—all German Conferences in the Methodist Episcopal Church.' "

Mrs. Thompson presented the matter of a change of Constitution, notice of which was given last year. That the portion of Article VI of the Constitution which is entitled "Constitutional Publication Committee be stricken out." Adopted.

Miss Fowler reported for the tellers as follows: For President, Mrs. C. D. Foss, 34 votes; Mrs. A. W. Patten, 2; Mrs. Bishop Warne, 1. For Recording Secretary, Mrs. C. W. Barnes, 36 votes. For Treasurer, Mrs. J. M. Cornell, 36 votes; Mrs. C. W. Barnes, 1. Mrs. C. D. Foss was therefore elected as President, and Mrs. C. W. Barnes as Recording Secretary, and Mrs. J. M. Cornell as Treasurer.

The Recording Secretary presented to Miss Walden, on behalf of the Woman's Foreign Missionary Society, a token of love and esteem. Miss Walden briefly expressed her thanks. After announcements the doxology was sung and the meeting adjourned.

THURSDAY, OCTOBER 31.

The session opened at nine o'clock, with Mrs. C. D. Foss presiding, and the Topeka Branch delegation in charge of the devotional hour. Mrs. Martha Reynolds announced hymn No. 398; after the singing, Miss McKnight led in prayer, and Miss Winifred Spaulding read a portion of the eleventh chapter of Hebrews. Mrs. Brown sang "The Homeland."

The roll was called and the minutes of Wednesday morning were read and approved.

Mrs. S. A. Hill presented a report from the Publication Committee, recommending the re-election of the editors of our periodicals, the publisher, and auditor. Report adopted. On motion of Mrs. Knowles, the Secretary was instructed to cast the ballot for these officers, which was done, and they were declared duly elected as follows: Editor of the *Woman's Missionary Friend*, Miss Elizabeth Northup; Editor of *Der Frauen-Missions-Freund*, Miss Amalie M. Achard; Editor of the *Children's Missionary Friend*, Mrs., O. W. Scott; Editor of *The Study*, Mrs. Mary Isham; Editor of Missionary Literature, Miss Elizabeth Northup; Publisher, Miss Pauline J. Walden; Auditor, Mr. George E. Whitaker.

Miss Watson, for the Reference Committee, nominated the following: Secretary of Young People's Work, Miss Winifred Spaulding, with headquarters at Cincinnati; Secretary of the Children's Work, Mrs. Lucie F. Harrison; Secretary of the German Work, Miss Louise Rothweiler; Secretary of the Scandinavian Work, Mrs. Hanna Henschen. The Secretary was instructed to cast the ballot for these officers, which she did, and they were declared duly elected.

Miss Watson also presented the following nominations for Trustees of Folts Institute, which were approved.

Trustees—Folts Mission Institute. For those whose terms expire

January, 1908.—Mrs. S. L. Baldwin, Rev. F. M. North, Miss Louise M. Hodgkins, Miss Mary E. Holt. January, 1909.—Mr. George R. Blount, Lacona, N. Y.; Mr. Charles S. Millington, Herkimer, N. Y. January, 1910.—Rev. Samuel D. Robinson, Herkimer, N. Y. January, 1911.—Mr. Geo. P. Folts, Herkimer, N. Y.; Mrs. Charles Gibson, Albany, N. Y.; Mrs. E. A. Pharis, Syracuse, N. Y.; Mrs. William Terhune, Waterville, N. Y.; Mr. George W. Sanborn, Utica, N. Y.; Mr. J. P. Lewis, Beaver Falls, N. Y.

Miss Lulu Heacock, Pacific Grove, California, was nominated and elected on the Literature Committee as the member from the Western section, the term of Miss Kate Moss having expired.

Mrs. R. L. Thomas invited the General Executive Committee to meet within the bounds of the Cincinnati Branch next year, the place to be determined later. The invitation was accepted.

The report from the By-law Committee was presented by Mrs. Thompson and was considered item by item. (See Report of By-law Committee.) As the duties of the Secretary of Children's Work had not been defined in the by-laws, the attention of the Committee was called to this omission. Mrs. Thompson presented the following resolution, which was adopted: "The acceptance of Assistant Missionaries or Native Workers as Missionaries shall be in the hands of the Reference Committee, who in reaching a conclusion shall take into consideration (1) the testimonials required in the regulations relating to candidates, including health certificate; (2) a certificate showing three years of service under the Woman's Foreign Missionary Society; (3) the recommendation of the Bishop in charge of the Conference."

Mrs. Knowles presented the following resolution, which was adopted:

WHEREAS, No radical change should be made in the Constitution without an opportunity being given to the Branches to consider it; therefore, I move that that part of the report of the Committee on By-laws, which involves important constitutional changes be referred to that Committee, which shall submit it to the Executive Committee of each Branch to be finally voted upon by the Branch Annual meetings; and that the delegates to the General Executive Committee of 1908 be instructed to vote on these changes in accordance with the action of the Branch they represent.

Mrs. F. P. Crandon nominated the following as a Committee on By-laws and also to revise the Constitution: Mrs. C. D. Foss, Mrs. C. W. Barnes, Mrs. John Legg, Mrs. W. B. Thompson, and Mrs. S. J. Herben. The above were appointed.

Mrs. S. F. Johnson presented the notice of a change in the Constitution in Article V, Section 1, "That the first sentence in Article V, Section 1, reading as follows, 'The management and general administration of the affairs of the Society shall be vested in a General Executive Committee, consisting of a President, Recording Secretary, Treasurer, the Corresponding Secretary and two delegates from each Branch, Secretary of German Work, and Secretary of Scandinavian Work,' shall be so changed as to read, 'The management and general administration of the affairs of the Society shall be vested in a General Executive Committee, consisting of a President, Vice-President, Recording Secretary, Treasurer, the Corresponding Secretary, the member of the Home Board and two delegates from each Branch, or such other persons as the Constitution of the said Society shall hereafter from time to time provide.'"

On account of the stringent condition of the money market in New York, and because $21,000 of the New York Branch funds were invested in the Knickerbocker Trust Company, which has recently suspended payment, Mrs. Crandon offered the following resolution, which was adopted: "The Woman's Foreign Missionary Society of the Methodist Episcopal Church in Executive Session in Springfield, Iilinois, October 31st, 1907, does hereby authorize the Treasurer of said Society to borrow a sum, not exceeding twenty thousand dollars, on a note of the Woman's Foreign Missionary Society and signed by the Treasurer."

The report of the Committee on Real Estate and Titles was read and adopted. Mrs. W. B. Davis and Mrs. C. D. Foss were reappointed as this Committee.

Mrs. B. T. Williston offered the following resolution, which, after discussion, was adopted:

Resolved, That we recommend that Branches, when organizing, observe the following age limit and dues. All under fifteen years of age shall pay twenty-five cents; all over fifteen and under twenty shall pay sixty cents; all over twenty shall pay $1.00.

Miss Kate Moss read the report from the Committee on Resolutions, which was adopted by a rising vote.

The Corresponding Secretaries read the appropriations as follows:

New England Branch	$42,978 00
New York Branch	95,000 00
Philadelphia Branch	60,382 00
Baltimore Branch	18,135 00
Cincinnati Branch	75,212 00
Northwestern Branch	145,000 00
Des Moines Branch	65,015 00
Minneapolis Branch	24,000 00
Topeka Branch	41,960 00
Pacific Branch	31,600 00
Columbia River Branch	13,000 00

Miss Spaulding was introduced as Secretary of the Young People's Work, with headquarters at Cincinnati.

The minutes of the morning session were read and accepted.

This concluded the business of the General Executive Committee; Mrs. J. H. Knowles conducted the closing devotional services in an impressive manner, and the thirty-eighth session of the General Executive Committee adjourned.

MRS. C. W. BARNES, *Recording Secretary.*

PROPOSED CHANGES OF CONSTITUTION.   ·

At the General Executive Committee meeting for 1908 the following changes of Constitution for the Woman's Foreign Missionary Society of the Methodist Episcopal Church will be asked for, namely:

That Article VII, Section 1, shall be changed by inserting in the first sentence immediately following the words, "General plan for districting the territory of the Church," the words, "Except the German Conferences." Also by inserting after the enumeration of Branches the words, "German Branches—All German Conferences in the Methodist Episcopal Church."—Northwestern Branch.

That the first sentence in Article V, Section 1, reading as follows, "The management and general administration of the affairs of the Society shall be vested in a General Executive Committee, consisting of a President, Recording Secretary, Treasurer, the Corresponding Secretary and two delegates from each Branch, Secretary of German work, and Secretary of Scandinavian work," shall be so changed as to read, "The management and general administration of the affairs of The Society shall be vested in a General Executive Committee consisting of a President, Vice-President, Recording Secretary, Treasurer, the Corresponding Secretary, the member of the Home Board and two delegates from each Branch, or such other persons as the Constitution of the said Society shall hereafter from time to time provide."

Mrs. S. F. Johnson.

RESOLUTIONS ADOPTED BY GENERAL EXECUTIVE COMMITTEE.

LITERATURE AT CONVENTIONS.

Whereas, There is a growing demand for the exhibition and sale of our literature at the various public gatherings and conventions held yearly throughout the country,

Resolved, That is shall be the duty of the Secretary of Literature within whose borders the convention is held to have the entire charge of all such exhibitions and sales, the expenses to be borne by the Branch where the convention meets. When, as frequently occurs, the Epworth League, Student Volunteer, or other convention is held outside of our country, this duty shall belong to the Standing Literature Committee, the expenses to be met from the treasury of the Woman's Foreign Missionary Society. (1901.)

OUR SPECIAL WORK.

Whereas, We, your representatives on the foreign field, recognize that close personal touch is necessary in order to awaken and continue interest in mission work, and

WHEREAS, The present method of carrying on one form of special work, namely, the attachment of individual givers at home to an individual protege on the foreign field is often productive of many harmful influences and results, both upon the givers at home and the proteges on the foreign field, aside from the great labor involved in the necessary correspondence, and

WHEREAS, This system is detrimental to the fundamental principles of our Christian service in that such gifts frequently prove to have been of a merely temporal and philanthropic character instead of being offerings made to the Lord Christ, and to the general advancement of His Kingdom; therefore,

Resolved (1) That the missionary be made the living link between the givers at home and the foreign field, whose support shall be assigned to the various Conferences and Districts, and whose duty it shall be to write regularly to her constituency, letters which may be multiplied and sent to each auxiliary.

(2) That Bible readers, teachers, and scholarships, so far as possible, be paid from the regular funds as apportioned to the different Branches and Conferences.

Signed by Missionaries. ·
Adopted by General Executive Committee. (1901.)

DELEGATES.

Resolved, That no woman, not elected delegate or alternate by her Branch to the General Executive Committee, shall be admitted as a member of said committee. (1902.)

REPORTS.

Resolved, That reports presented by the various committees and individuals authorized by the General Executive Committee shall be limited to ten minutes in time of reading. (1902.)

Resolved, That the literature on sale at the meeting of the General Executive Committee shall be under the supervision of the Literature Committee of the Woman's Foreign Missionary Society and of the Branch in the bounds of which it is held. (1902.)

FOLTS MISSION INSTITUTE.

Resolved, That we recommend that missionary candidates·shall be required to attend our Foreign Missionary Training-school, Folts Mission Institute, at Herkimer, N. Y., for at least one year. 'In exceptional cases the Branch Standing Committee on Candidates shall have power to suspend the rule.

Resolved, That we recommend that returned missionaries spend at least six months at the Institute. (1903.)

BUILDING.

Resolved, That no Branch shall pledge itself for any new building in the foreign field, without the consent of a majority of the Finance Committee; also, that every building project undertaken by the Society shall be paid for *pro rata* by all the Branches, assessment being proportioned to the receipts of the Branches. Exceptions may be made in the case of Memorial Buildings by vote of the Finance Committee. Reference Committee. (1905.)

DUES.

Resolved, That we recommend that Branches when organizing observe the following age limit and dues: All under fifteen years of age shall pay twenty-five cents; all under twenty and over fifteen, shall pay sixty cents, and all over twenty shall pay one dollar. (1907.)

ASSISTANT MISSIONARIES.

Resolved, The acceptance of assistant missionaries or native workers as missionaries shall be in the hands of the Reference Committee, who, in reaching a conclusion, shall take into consideration:

First—The testimonials required in the regulations relating to candidates, including health certificate.

Second—A certificate showing three years of service under the Woman's Foreign Missionary Society.

Third—The recommendation of the Bishop in charge of the Conference. (1907.)

DUTIES OF THE SECRETARIES OF HOME DEPARTMENT IN THE BRANCHES DEFINED.

The Secretary of the Home Department shall collect quarterly and annual reports from the heads of all departments of the home work to transmit to the Corresponding Secretary.

Present a report to the Quarterly and Annual meetings of the Branch.

Furnish the Corresponding Secretary with the annual statistical report.

Be ex-officio member of the Branch Missionary Candidates' Committee, of which the Corresponding Secretary is Chairman.

Perform such other duties as each Branch may define. (1905.)

TREASURER'S REPORT.

Mrs. J. M. Cornell, *in account with the Woman's Foreign Missionary Society.*

RECEIPTS.

October 1, 1906, balance on hand		$1,320 31
From assessment of 1 per cent on Receipts:		
New England Branch	$447 00	
New York Branch	950 00	
Philadelphia Branch	610 00	
Baltimore Branch	156 00	
Cincinnati Branch	711 00	
Northwestern Branch	1,688 00	
Des Moines Branch	588 00	
Minneapolis Branch	226 00	
Topeka Branch	354 00	
Pacific Branch	244 00	
Columbia River Branch	50 00	
Total receipts from Branch assessments..........		6,024 00
Total receipts		$7,344 31

DISBURSEMENTS.

Traveling expenses to General Executive Meeting, Omaha, Nebraska, October, 1906.

President	$30 50
Recording Secretary	46 50
New England: Secretary, 2 delegates, 4 missionaries..	544 14
New York: ——, 2 delegates, 5 missionaries	471 94
Philadelphia: Secretary, 2 delegates, 1 missionary	182 50
Baltimore: Secretary, 2 delegates, 1 missionary	242 89
Cincinnati: Secretary, 2 delegates, 3 missionaries	271 10
Northwestern: Secretary, 2 delegates, 1 missionary	128 10
Des Moines: Secretary, 2 delegates, 3 missionaries	70 98
Minneapolis: Secretary, 2 delegates	74 40
Topeka: Secretary, 2 delegates, 1 missionary	71 05
Pacific: Secretary, 2 delegates, 1 missionary	349 60
Columbia River: Secretary, 1 delegate	169 25
Secretary of German Work	28 00
Secretary of Swedish Work	85 10
Secretary of Children's Work	69 59
Railroad Secretary and railroad business	40 15

Traveling expenses to Executive Committee in Omaha. ——— $2,875 79
Expenses of officers, President, postage, printing, etc... 42 37
Expenses of Acting President 5 00
Expenses of Recording Secretary 3 59
Expenses of Secretary of Children's Work 36 60

$2,963 35

Traveling expenses of Acting President and nine Secretaries to Reference Committee Meeting at Boston, Mass., May, 1907.

Acting President	$27 85	Cincinnati	$50 30
New England		Northwestern	15 00
New York		Des Moines	75 00
Philadelphia		Minneapolis	84 00
Baltimore	24 60	Topeka	86 00

362 75

Cablegram to Tokyo, Japan 5 34

Expenses of General Office.

Rent of office, October 1, 1906, to October 1, 1907	525 00
Salary of Secretaries	905 00
Office running expenses, including office help	325 00
Typewriter	100 00

1,855 00

Total disbursements for year closing Sept. 30, 1907	$5,186 44
Balance on hand. Oct. 1, 1907	2,157 87

$7,344 31

Examined and found correct.

CAROLINE C. LEAYCRAFT,
LOUISE M. NORTH.

REPORT OF THE REFERENCE COMMITTEE.

Prior to the mid-year meeting of the Reference Committee consent was given for the appointment of Dr. Belle J. Allen, to Baroda, India; for a four months' vacation to Miss Elizabeth D. Marble, and for the appointment of Miss Mabel Crawford to the Philippines. The home coming was announced of Miss Frances O. Wilson, accompanied by Miss Ida Stevenson; and Miss Clara B. Dyer was accepted as a missionary.

Mrs. W. T. Cherry was appointed as Treasurer of Malaysia, and Mrs. Evelyn P. Marsh was appointed as Secretary of Young People's Work; to succeed Mrs. Cora O. Boyd, resigned.

An expression of thanks was voted to Dr. J. H. Kellogg, of Battle Creek Sanitarium, for his kind offer extended to all missionaries of our Society.

Power of Attorney was granted to the Rev. B. M. Jones, of Rangoon, Burma, to adjust all lands and other property owned or leased by the Woman's Foreign Missionary Society.

Five hundred dollars was granted for immediate repairs for Garibaldi Building at Rome.

Consent was given to the Des Moines Branch that a gift of $5,000 might be applied to the Vikarabad Building, and to the Cincinnati Branch that a gift of $400 might be used for the addition to the Moradabad School.

The committee pledged the Woman's Foreign Missionary Society to maintain the Foochow College on account of the acceptance of a gift of $15,000 for the Administration Building.

The following was approved: To exchange the Winchell Home in Penang, China, for a piece of property in the residential part of the city with more than an acre of land around the same, and on it a fine house for the Girls' Boarding and Day School.

The mid-year meeting of the Reference Committee convened in Boston, May 9th, 1907, with Mrs. A. W. Patten presiding, and all the Corresponding Secretaries present, except Mrs. A. N. Fisher and Mrs. S. F. Johnson.

The order for *ad interim* communications will be as follows: President, the Corresponding Secretaries in the most convenient order, leaving Miss Watson until the last, to Mrs. Barnes, to the general office, to the originator.

It was voted that the Committee on Real Estate and Titles be asked to append as a part of their report a list of endowments with star to indicate the same.

The two propositions of Mr. Ralph Leininger were accepted. One was a kind offer regarding the providing of $25,000 worth of bonds, bearing interest at the rate of 6 per cent, for the benefit of the Kiu Kiang Hospital; and the second related to the education in medicine of three Chinese girls.

It was voted to request the Branches having Home Secretaries to send that officer as first delegate to the next General Executive Committee.

The report of the Committee on By-laws was presented by Mrs. Thompson, and after discussion, recommendations were given to the committee for consideration before the presentation of the report to the General Executive Committee.

The following resolution was adopted:

WHEREAS, We wish to extend information of our work for the purpose of arousing interest and enthusiasm,

Resolved, That we recommend to the Branches that in electing delegates to the General Executive Committee, they select women who shall be able to give a full report of the meeting at Branch, District, and Auxiliary meetings as occasion demands.

Mrs. S. J. Herben, Miss Kate Moss, Mrs. W. B. Davis, and Mrs. John Legg were appointed a Committee on Plans for strengthening and enlarging our work in harmony with its rapid growth.

The payment of 1 per cent for expenses is to be estimated on receipts from October 1st to October 1st.

It was voted that since it has been proven impracticable for the Recording Secretary of the Woman's Foreign Missionary Society to act as Secretary of the Finance Committee, and it seems expedient to have one Secretary for both Finance and Reference Committees, therefore,

Resolved, That we do not ask the Secretary of the Woman's Foreign Missionary Society to serve as Secretary of the Reference Committee.

It was voted to grant the General Missionary Society the privilege of erecting a church on grounds belonging to the Woman's Foreign Missionary Society in Madras, the church to be named "Grace Stephens Memorial."

Miss Carnahan was given permission to apply thank-offering of the Pittsburg Conference Young People in paying for land and erecting temporary building at Bedar.

Resolution, That all missionaries seeking admission to the Woman's Foreign Missionary Society from other societies shall not be received until they have served not less than three years, and have been recommended by the Woman's Conference in which they are working.

Permission was granted Mrs. Huntley to use $500 for the erection of a building near Puna for school, chapel, and dispensary purposes.

The pro rata per cent for the various Branches was readjusted as follows:

	Per cent.		Per cent.
New England	7	Des Moines	9½
New York	15	Minneapolis	4
Philadelphia	10	Topeka	6
Baltimore	4	Pacific	4
Cincinnati	11½	Columbia River	2
Northwestern	27		

It was decided to discontinue work at Jagdulpur after this year.

A resolution was adopted to the effect that a missionary shall be required to refund money due to the Society for outgoing expenses at the time she severs her connection therewith.

Mrs. Patten, Mrs. Elizabeth Pierce, Miss Gay Doliver, and Miss Frances Baker were appointed a Committee to devise plans for the provision for superannuated and disabled missionaries.

Vacation was granted to Miss Stoers at Calcutta.

Des Moines Branch was granted permission to build a home for missionaries engaged in native work in Rangoon at a cost of $3,000, to be named the Hagerty Home. It was decided to purchase property at Lingayen, in the Province of Linzoon; also, to pay the debt on the Mary Porter Gamewell Memorial Building in Pekin, by July 1st, 1908. It was voted to recommend to the General Executive Committee the rescinding of the three resolutions, "Status of Native Workers," on page thirty-six of the Annual Report.

The Philadelphia Branch was given permission to erect a cottage for Dr. Pak, of Nampo, and the New York Branch a home for Miss Estey at Pyeng Yang, Korea, and it was ordered that the Hospital at Pyeng Yang be rebuilt as soon as possible.

Consent was given for the home-coming of Miss Wisner, Miss Blair, Mrs. Van Petten, Miss Griffiths, Miss Watson, and for the return to the field of Misses Rigby, Illingworth, Myer, Organ, Atkinson, and Miss Laura White; and Miss Lenora Seeds, if she can secure health certificate.

Miss Bender was appointed to represent the Woman's Foreign Missionary Society at the Silver Bay Conference; alternate, Miss Northup. Mrs. Thomas and Miss Watson were appointed to secure a suitable woman for Secretary of Young People's Work, as Mrs. Marsh can not retain it.

It was voted that Foreign Conferences and Missions, recommending Missionary Assistants for acceptance as Missionaries, shall accompany such recommendations with the testimonials required in the regulations to candidates, including health certificate, also a certificate showing three years' service in our Society, and favorable vote of a majority of the Woman's Conference.

The following candidates were accepted: Cincinnati Branch—Miss Ora May Tuttle, Mille May Albertson, Margaret Campbell, Mrs. M. L. Dutton. Northwestern Branch—Misses Edna Jones, Eugenia Norberg, Adeline Naomi Smith, Dr. Josephine Liers, Alvina Robinson. Minneapolis Branch—Misses Luella Huelster, Mary Anna Sutton, Jessie Brooks. Des Moines Branch—Miss Estie T. Boddy. Topeka Branch—Misses Jennie Borg, Minnie M. Gabrielson, Cora E. Simpson, Blanch A. Betz. Philadelphia Branch—Miss Edna Campbell. Columbia River Branch—Miss Rosa E. Dudley. The above and also Miss Lulu C. Baker were appointed to various fields.

Mrs. J. E. Leaycraft was made a member of the Committee on General Office.

A cable from Japan announced the destruction of the school at Nagoya, and $2,000 was ordered sent at once for the rebuilding.

The question of enlarging the General Executive Report and discontinuing the Branch Reports was ordered presented to the Executive Board of each Branch, and then to the Annual Meeting.

During the interim prior to the General Executive Meeting consent was given to sell the present site at Nagoya and purchase in a more desirable part of the city.

Miss Dudley was appointed to Tarlac, Philippines.

Mrs. S. F. Johnson and Mrs. Z. L. Parmalee were given authority to sell lot in San Jose, Cal., deeded by Mrs. A. T. Richardson to the Woman's Foreign Missionary Society, and Mrs. Foss and Mrs. Barnes were authorized to make the deed when the lot is sold.

Consent was given for the return of Miss Anna A. Abbott and for the home-coming of Miss Kidwell, Mabel Seeds, Elizabeth Russell, and Margaret Edmunds, M. D., and also for the furlough of Miss Robbins, of Korea.

A letter from Bishop Cranston announced that the Committee on Erection of the "Lillian Harris Memorial Hospital," Seoul, Korea, had decided that it shall be at the East Gate. Miss Payne, Miss Fry, and Dr. George H. Jones were named as the Building Committee.

The home and school building at Hakodate, Japan, having been burned, permission was given to use the insurance on the school, amounting to $3,000, for rebuilding kindergarten on the old site; and insurance of $500 on the home, to purchase heavy furniture for the new home.

REPORTS OF COMMITTEES.

PUBLICATION.

WHEREAS, The daily press reports, while written in the greatest friendliness, sometimes fail to present the most important points of our proceedings, and

WHEREAS, Other religious bodies provide the reporters with the material which they wish to have printed; therefore,

Resolved, That some member of the Society shall be appointed to prepare suitable reports to offer to the daily press.

Resolved, That the Publisher and Secretaries be requested to assist the local press committee by bringing to the General Executive Committee cuts or photographs (1) of missionaries who are to be in attendance; (2) of buildings that may be of special and timely interest.

WHEREAS, We appreciate the efforts of the Editors of the *Woman's Missionary Friend*, the *Children's Missionary Friend*, *Der Frauen Missions Freund*, and the *Study* to meet in their columns the requirements of our work in all its departments; therefore,

Resolved, That we endorse their management and pledge ourselves to redouble our diligence to increase the circulation of our valuable periodicals.

Resolved, That we recommend that Branch workers place in the hands of the editor of the *Friend* material setting forth new plans, bright ideas, and helpful suggestions for the development of the 'home base' of our work.

WHEREAS, The *Study* advertises our own publications connected with the *United Study of Mission*, and brings to our notice facts regarding our own work; therefore,

Resolved, That we urge renewed efforts to place it in the hands of every member of the Woman's Foreign Missionary Society.

Resolved, That we rejoice in the continued success of the *Tokiwa*, and in the growing usefulness of the miscellaneous literature published by our literary missionary in Yokohama.

WHEREAS, Great interest is felt in our Zenana papers, and many may turn to the Woman's Foreign Missionary Society Report for facts regarding them; and

WHEREAS, The reports of the Zenana papers this year present practically no statistical or financial statement; therefore,

Resolved, That we request the Editor of each Zenana paper to provide the Treasurer of the Zenana paper fund with a statement covering the number circulated and the general expense.

Resolved, That we take great pleasure in making the following nominations: As Editor of the *Woman's Missionary Friend*, Miss Elizabeth C. Northup; of the *Children's Missionary Friend*, Mrs. O. W. Scott; of *Der Frauen Missions Freund*, Miss A. W. Achard; of the *Study*, Mrs. Mary Isham; as Editor of Literature, Miss Elizabeth C. Northup; as Publisher, Miss Pauline J. Walden, and as Auditor, Mr. George E. Whittaker.

Resolved, That we recommend that the following salaries be paid for the ensuing year: To the Editor of the *Woman's Missionary Friend*,

$700; to the Editor of the *Children's Missionary Friend*, $300; to the Editor *Der Frauen Missions Freund*, $250; to the Editor of the *Study*, $100; to the Editor of Literature, $300; and to the Publisher, $700.

Resolved, That we recommend that the appropriations for special contributions be as follows: To the Editor of the *Friend*, $75; to the Editor of Literature, $75; to the Editor of the *Children's Missionary Friend*, $25.

Resolved, That we recommend that the Secretary of Scandinavian Work be authorized to draw one hundred dollars, in quarterly installments, from the funds of the publishing house, to be used in the interest of literature for Scandinavian work, and to be expended at the orders of a Committee to be composed of the Corresponding Secretary of the Northwestern Branch and the Secretary of Scandinavian Work.

Resolved, That we recommend increased effort in circulating the excellent literature published the past year.

Resolved, That we request Branch Secretaries of Literature to endeavor to announce our books and leaflets, especially new publications, at least once a month in the Church papers within their bounds.

Resolved, That we recommend the issuing of 30,000 copies of the Secretary's Annual Report to be distributed as free leaflets to Auxiliaries, pastors also being furnished with a copy.

MRS. S. A. HILL, *Chairman;*
MISS W. R. G. LEWIS, *Secretary.*

MISSIONARY CANDIDATES.

We have examined the testimonials of the following candidates and recommend them for acceptance and appointment.

Philadelphia Branch—Miss Helen C. Sante, W. Piston, Pa.
Northwestern Branch—Miss Lena Hatfield, M. D., Chicago, Ill.
Topeka Branch—Miss Mary Richmond, Peabody, Kan.
Northwestern Branch—Miss Melissa Manderson, M. D.
New York Branch—Miss Althea Tracy.
Miss Jennie M. Gasser, testimonials satisfactory, case referred to the Reference Committee.
Philadelphia Branch—Miss Blanch Theresa Search, appointment recommended with the proposition that she take further training.
Topeka Branch—Miss Minnie Gardner, acceptance recommended.

MISS ISABELLA H. IRISH, *Chairman,*
MRS. G. B. RICHARDSON, *Secretary.*

MEMORIALS.

Your Committee on Memorials submits the following report:

FROM NORTHWESTERN BRANCH.

We, the Northwestern Branch in annual meeting assembled, memorialize the General Executive Committee to change Section 1, Article IV, of the By-laws which reads, "Branch Treasurers shall be required to publish quarterly reports in the *Woman's Missionary Friend*," to "Branch Treasurers shall be required to furnish quarterly reports for publication in the *Woman's Missionary Friend*." Its adoption is recommended.

FROM CINCINNATI BRANCH.

WHEREAS, The German element of the Woman's Foreign Missionary Society is scattered among the eleven Branches, thereby causing many complications; and

WHEREAS, We believe the formation of a German Branch would help to develop the work in every department;

Therefore, We, the Cincinnati Branch, memorialize the General Executive Committee to create a German Branch.

Recommended to the consideration of the General Executive Committee.

FROM BALTIMORE BRANCH.

We, the Baltimore Branch in annual session convened, do unanimously pray that in the proposed changes in the Constitution of the Woman's Foreign Missionary Society, the Presidents of the Branches be given recognition as members of the General Executive Committee by virtue of their office. Not recommended.

FROM BALTIMORE BRANCH.

WHEREAS, We of the Baltimore Branch do earnestly desire to be represented by two delegates annually elected;

Therefore, We memorialize the General Executive Committee to so amend the Constitution that in the event of the Branch Presidents being made members of the permanent committee, each Branch be allowed four representatives at the General Excutive Committee meetings. Not recommended.

FROM BALTIMORE BRANCH.

. We, the Executive Committee of the Baltimore Branch, also pray that the assessment of 1 per cent for general expenses be made upon the appropriations, not upon the receipts for each Branch. Not recommended.

MRS. M. C. WIRE, *Chairman.*
MRS. FLORA S. DUDLEY, *Secretary.*

The report was adopted. It was further recommended that the Memorial from the Cincinnati Branch should be presented in the form of a proposed change of Constitution.

RESOLUTIONS.

WHEREAS, God in His wisdom has taken to Himself our beloved Mrs. Carrie W. Joyce, Corresponding Secretary of the Minneapolis Branch for six years.

Resolved, That while we are poorer without her, heaven is richer in her presence, and her memory will always be a stimulus to us for patient perseverance in this work of God. We welcome her successor, Mrs. F. F. Lindsay, among us.

WHEREAS, Mrs. Mary Porter Gamewell, one of our pioneers in China, has finished her earthly pilgrimage;

Resolved, That we express our appreciation of the scope and wisdom constantly manifested in her varied phases of work.

WHEREAS, Three of our missionaries have been transplanted from earth to heaven.

Resolved, That we recognize the unselfish spirit of Miss Susanna Stumpf in literally giving her life for India's womanhood; that in the homegoing of Miss Lois' Buck we bow in submission to the Father, who is "too wise to err, too good to be unkind;" that our work has sustained an irreparable loss in the death of Dr. Mary B. Tuttle, not alone because of her efficiency and consecration, but because of the great need of women physicians.

WHEREAS, God in His Providence has returned to us our President, Mrs. C. D. Foss, from her official visit to our missions in the Orient;

Resolved, That we thank our God for this favor and thus express our gratitude to Him and to her.

WHEREAS, Mrs. William Butler, one of the founders of the Woman's Foreign Missionary Society, has been present with us and on two separate occasions addressed our meetings;

Resolved, That we thank our Heavenly Father for her long life of eighty-eight years and useful service, and pray Him to continue divine love to "our mother."

WHEREAS, The devotional hour under Mrs. Iva Durham Vennard, of Epworth Institute, St. Louis, has been one of inspiration and profit;

Resolved, That we thank her for this assistance and we pray God to give her many years of service.

WHEREAS, The general representation of foreign work by our missionaries has been such a source of illumination; therefore,

Resolved, That we hereby make grateful mention of the fact, and of the presence of such a goodly number of the representatives of the Woman's Foreign Missionary Society and of the Board of Foreign Missions of our Church.

WHEREAS, Mrs. C. H. Brown has so willingly and sweetly furnished us with such appropriate music;

Resolved, That we express to her our appreciation of this ministration.

WHEREAS, Fire made it impossible for the First Methodist Church of Springfield to entertain this body in its own building, and as the First Presbyterian Church very generously offered their edifice for our use;

Resolved, That such an expression of Christian love and brotherhood touches our hearts and we realize anew we are "one in Christ Jesus."

Resolved, That we appreciate the untiring efforts of the ladies of Springfield for our comfort and welfare during our sojourn in their city, and for the brotherly help so cheerfully given by Mr. Frank Kuhl, for the enjoyable reception at the executive mansion, and the ride about their historical city.

Resolved, That we hereby thank the papers of the city for their excellent reports, recognizing as we do the power of the press.

MISS KATE E. MOSS,
MISS FRANCES J. BAKER,
MRS. HANNA HENSCHEN.

REAL ESTATE.

The Committee on Real Estate are encouraged to feel that in the next *ten years* the files of the deeds of property belonging to the Woman's Foreign Missionary Society will be in good business shape. There is more and more interest, both at home and abroad, in the subject of having the deeds of property deeded "in trust to the Woman's Foreign Missionary Society of the Methodist Episcopal Church of the United States of America." In few Oriental countries can land be deeded to women, but if "in trust" is added, we are secure. Tedious and expensive legal proceedings are required by law to secure recognition by the government as to our ownership of land, but with patience we trust in time to make all our deeds secure.

At home, a note of inquiry from one of the Secretaries has been encouraging. "Has there ever been an order about the real estate deeds of foreign lands? Should they be in the hands of the Conference Treasurers? I can find nothing to answer it in the Report of the Woman's Foreign Missionary Society."

We copy from the Journal of Central Conference, held in Madras, India, February, 1904, as follows: ·

"Section 1. Since great effort has been made by the officers of the Woman's Foreign Missionary Society to secure correct and complete statements in regard to property owned by the Society, we recommend that those in charge of such property keep on file a careful record of the value, and that corresponding entries be made when property increases or diminishes in value.

"Section 2. We recommend that the Treasurer of each Woman's Conference keep a complete record of all properties of the Woman's Foreign Missionary Society within her Conference and also a record of the deeds.

"Section 3. We recommend that the deeds of all the Woman's Foreign Missionary Society property be given into the custody of the Conference Treasurer and that a list of such deeds be given by him to the Treasurer of the Woman's Conference.

Mrs. Wm. B. Davis,
Mrs. Cyrus D. Foss.

GENERAL OFFICE.

Practical ideas are developing in our office work. We will not give you a detailed report, but call attention to the following items:

A fine typewriter has been added to the furnishing of the office—the gift of Mrs. Bishop Warren in memory of Mrs. Keen.

Many communications from various associations have been received, asking information in reference to the organization of the Woman's Foreign Missionary Society, especially about our publishing interests.

A request came from the Interdenominational Missionary Association of Brooklyn to use our badge as a mark of the Society. It is recommended by this Committee that, as the badge is the distinctive mark of our Society, it should be copyrighted.

The Committee *recommend* that the Secretary be paid $75 per month salary, and be allowed $300 for incidental expenses.

After considerable effort the Secretary has secured a list of the women student volunteers of our Church. This list comprises the names of those who were reported to have graduated in the years 1904-05-06, who have not yet gone to the mission field; also those who graduate from college this year, and those who are undergraduates. Will you remember this list when you are looking for missionaries and apply to Miss Bender?

Ten thousand copies of "Opportune Investments in China" have been mailed from the office, the Centennial Commission bearing the expense of mailing. Five thousand copies are still on hand to be had on application.

Much time has been spent in investigation of best methods of transportation, and a record is being made as to steamship companies, routes, accommodations, etc. The Committee recommend that the General Executive Committee decide as to how their missionaries shall travel, whether first or second class. The Secretary could make much better terms for outgoing missionaries, if they could arrange to go in parties, in the fall. Definite and early information should be sent to the office Secretary, as it is necessary to make the bookings not later than July.

A cable code has been placed in the office, and all communications by cable can be forwarded by the Secretary.

The Committee recommends that the following by-laws be adopted: That the Secretary shall be nominated by the Committee on General Office and confirmed by the General Executive Committee.

The Secretary shall be authorized to receive moneys sent through the Board of Foreign Missions to the Woman's Foreign Missionary Society, and forward the same to the Treasurer of the Branch to which they belong.

The Transit Committee—Mrs. Miller, Mrs. Leaycraft, Mrs. Der Nooy, Miss Lizzie Owens—have given kind and thoughtful attention to eleven outgoing and incoming missionaries.

Miss Julia F. Bangs and Miss A. A. Brennen are assisting the Secretary in arranging the card calendar, photo file, and the scrap book.

The Committee present the following rules to govern the general office for your confirmation:

Rules to Govern the General Office.

1. The Office Secretary shall thoroughly inform herself of the work of the Woman's Foreign Missionary Society both at home and abroad, that she may be able to give prompt and reliable information when called upon.

2. Each Corresponding Secretary shall be required to, inform the General Office as to the movements of missionaries, that the Office Secretary may arrange for outgoing missionaries in parties; plans for their sailing to be made by the Office Secretary and Transit Committee. The Secretary shall keep informed about incoming missionaries, reporting them also to the Transit Committee.

3. The Secretary shall keep the *Friend* notified of the movements of missionaries, Young People's Conventions, etc.

4. The Secretary shall inform herself as to all Student Volunteer Conventions, all Young People's Assemblies, summer schools or missions, etc., as to time and place of such Conventions; advising the Home Secretary of each Branch as to what Conventions meet within the limits of her Branch, and arranging with her for a representation of the Woman's Foreign Missionary Society at said Convention.

5. The Secretary shall be sent to Conventions under the direction of the General Office Committee.

6. When so desired, the Secretary shall, together with the Shipping Agent of the Board of Foreign Missions, arrange for the shipment of freight intended for our missionaries.

7. The Secretary shall refer all applicants for literature and supplies to Depository of their Branches, or to Office of Publication, 36 Bromfield St., Boston.

8. The Secretary shall keep a complete card catalogue of all missionaries of the Woman's Foreign Society up to date—also complete files of all periodicals published by the Woman's Foreign Missionary Society, as well as Branch and Foreign Reports.

9. The Office shall be closed only on legal holidays. Office hours, 9 A. M. to 5 P. M., with one hour for lunch. Saturdays, 9 A. M. to 1 P. M.

10. The Secretary shall have one month vacation.

Respectfully submitted,

Mrs. Wm. B. Davis, *Chairman*,   Mrs. J. M. Cornell,
Mrs Cyrus D. Foss,   Mrs. F. P. Crandon,
Mrs. John Legg,   Mrs. J. E. Leaycraft.

LITERATURE.

Again we come to the end of the year with an attempt to show something of the work done and are grateful for the showing of the year. Remembering "thou shalt know hereafter," we look with earnest desire to know something of the hearts stirred to deeper interest, to better work, and to larger giving as a result of material put out. The statistical part of the report can bring only gratification, for the increase of output is larger than usual; however, figures, so often a source of delight, are often trying, in that they tell so little.

The total output of the office has been 4,983,220 pages of matter. This includes reprints of forty-seven leaflets, eighteen of which are children's leaflets, amounting to 1,710,720 pages; 14,000 copies of the programs of last year, with 112,000 pages; 35,000 new programs, with 560,000 pages, and 40,000 Standard Bearer cards; also, nine new leaflets for the children prepared by Mrs. Scott and Mrs. Harrison, the new Junior Handbook, and the Missionary Gems for Juniors, totaling 906,500 pages.

Twenty-five thousand copies of the Leaflet Report, with 200,000 pages, 320,000 pages of Topic Slips, 80,000 of these being for the Children's Work, and 10,000 copies of the Treasurer's Palaver, with 60,000 pages, were furnished free to the Auxiliaries by the respective Branches, making a total of free literature from the office of 580,000 pages without cost to the Auxiliaries.

Five thousand calendars, with sixty-four pages each, aggregating 320,000 pages, were put out. The work on this really belonged to the year previous, but of necessity appears in this report. Twenty-three new leaflets, totaling 797,400 pages, have been put out for use in connection with the uniform study and for general use. We feel that less of passing value only has been put out this year than last. Some of this nature is a necessity in developing the text. To plan the work in connection with the Uniform Study text with no knowledge of that text was impossible—hence could not be done at the Executive Meeting—and handling it by correspondence was so unsatisfactory, a meeting of the Committee was called in the early spring, and in response to the generous invitation of Mrs. J. M. Cornell, was held in her home at Seabright, N. J. Pleas had come in to present the outline earlier than July, and we made our plans to have them go out in April. Some delays in getting out the text, and some changes by the author at the last made this impossible. Working on the outline kindly furnished by her, we planned the when and how of the accompanying leaflets, and made the program of the year, depending on the appearance of Gloria Christi as to final order. This made June the earliest possible date of appearance. The meeting was most satisfactory in its results. The members of the Committee, the Editor of Literature, the Publisher, were present throughout the session, beginning Friday morning and closing Tuesday noon. The Secretary of Young People's Work spent one day with the Committee planning the work for the young people the ensuing year. It is a comparatively easy matter to plan an amount of work, so while a few days sufficed for the thorough canvass of the subject, to execute the plans has taken much of effort, and we are often reminded of Burns' well-known—

"The best laid schemes of mice and men
Gang aft agley."

Hence if some leaflets do not reach you quite so soon as you expected, look for them later. They will surely come, despite illness of planned workers and striking printers. This latter belongs to the chapter of difficulties of the Publisher and Editor.

We trembled just a little when we knew the Publisher had ordered 20,000 copies of the official Auxiliary programs for this year, but thinking she knew her end of the work better than we, we bided our time. The report shows an additional 15,000, and we rejoice that the real output is greater than our greatest hope and meets a felt need; also, that they appeared much earlier than last year.

The reports from the Branch Secretaries of Literature bring us some items of great interest.

The sales of supplies at the Branch Annual Meetings totaled

$1,523.30, the Northwestern, as always, leading, and the Topeka Branch following. This shows a falling off of some $300 as compared to last year, but the lost boxes of the Des Moines Branch Department will account for at least half of that.

The total sales of all supply departments are $15,829.66, an increase of $2,590.75. This is certainly a very substantial increase. The Philadelphia Branch shows exactly the same sales as last year, the Columbia River a decrease, and all of the other nine show an increase.

23,100 Branch reports were printed, not including the Topeka Branch. The Columbia River Branch report is a booklet of forty pages, that of the Northwestern Branch one of 205 pages, with those of the other · Branches ranging between. Philadelphia, Cincinnati, Baltimore, and New England Branches give their reports away. Most Branches supply officers and workers with free copies and sell some at an average price of ten cents per copy.

Five Branches report 320,400 pages of free literature in the way of leaflets, appeals, letters printed, and if all had reported on this item the total would have certainly been more than one-half million pages.

Five Branches report 12,187 books in various Church libraries on missionary topics.

More than twenty thousand of the seventy-thousand issue of the Study Text—Christus Redemptor—were sold by our Supply Bureaus. As we know of many of our women who buy this book through agencies other than our own, we are gratified to know that so many of our women are using this text. Deepened knowledge must bring broadened interests, increased responsibility, and if Christ rules the heart larger effort is inevitable. So this work, while but one arm, is a potent factor in the advance of the cause. May it come to be more and more a power!

KATE E. MOSS,
Chairman Literature Committee.

FINANCIAL REPORT OF LITERATURE.

From October 1, 1906, to October 1, 1907.

By Cash Paid for—

Printing Leaflets	$2,583 85	
Cuts for Leaflets	8 75	
		$2,592 60
Printing Leaflet Report	58 20	
Postage on Leaflet Report	25 00	
		83 20
Printing Calendar		734 59
S. B. Supplies	594 55	
L. L. B. Supplies	312 08	
L. L. B. Mite Boxes	127 87	
K. H. Supplies	217 00	
K. H. Mite Boxes	183 06	
		1,434 56
Helps and Books	720 37	
U. Study Books (4,850)	869 77	
		1,590 14
Office Rent	300 00	
Office Help	920 25	
W. Paper, Twine and Envelopes	70 40	
Postage and Express	730 04	
		2,020 69

Editor's Salary and Postage 302 00
Preparing Children's Literature 100 00
                                                          402 00
Traveling Expenses of Committee 253 55
Postage of Committee 12 40
                                                          265 95

                                                          $9,123 73
To Cash Rec'd for—
Literature $5,749 82
Calendars 923 52
K. H. Supplies 426 91
L. L. B. Supplies 321 18
S. B. Supplies 520 25
Leaflet Report 81 90
                                                          $8,023 58

Cash Deficit $1,100 15

Bills due on Literature $672 50
Literature of 1906-07 on hand 1,585 00
                                                          $2,257 50
Cash Deficit 1,100 15

Net Balance $1,157 35

PAULINE J. WALDEN, *Publisher.*

REPORT OF GERMAN LITERATURE.

1906—1907.
Literature printed:

Annual Reports	4,000 copies,	40 pp.	= 160,000 pp.	$115 00
"Die Inselwelt"	1,500 "	40 "	= 60,000 "	44 50
Price Lists	500 "	2 "	= 1,000 "	1 50
Total	6,000 "	82 "	= 221,000 "	$161 00

Sales have been as follows:
German Reports, 1,877 copies $93 85
German Leaflets 107 64
English Leaflets, Books, Etc...................... 71 21
Pins, Mite Barrels, Etc.......................... 67 01

Total $339 71

Paid Out for—
English Literature $55 80
Pins, Mite Barrels, Etc.......................... 68 58
Postage, Expressage, Etc......................... 40 32
Balance on hand October 1, 1906.................. 9 59
Balance on hand October 1, 1907................. 23 60

                                                    $349 30 $349 30

Respectfully submitted,
LOUISA C. ROTHWEILER,
Secretary of German Work.

TABULATED REPORT OF BRANCH WORK IN LITERATURE DEPARTMENT, OCTOBER 1, 1907.

	NEW ENGLAND	NEW YORK	PHILADELPHIA	BALTIMORE	CINCINNATI	NORTHWESTERN	DES MOINES	MINNEAPOLIS	TOPEKA	PACIFIC	COLUMBIA RIVER	TOTALS
Sale of Literature at Annual Conferences	$74 00	$12 00	$28 04				$18 61	$19 90	$17 88	$62 91		$158 98
Sale of Literature at District meetings		315 48	98 32			$959 56	205 29	33 50	46 54	89 21	$12 36	1,834 56
Sale of Literature at Branch Annual Meeting 1907	101 36	177 31	126 21	$52 86		355 99	*158 32	27 89	*216 48	*702 98	84 00	1,528 80
Sale of Literature at Executive Meeting 1907					$175 00							250 00
Total receipts from all supplies	984 82	2,094 26	1,075 80	357 17	1,805 65	4,304 92	1,824 58	687 95	1,767 98	784 43	243 10	15,880 66
Number of gatherings at which Literature has been on sale	29	55	35	11	20	69	41	14	20	12	5	311
Total receipts from same	$454 14	$557 23	$239 87			$1,470 48	$642 53	$162 05	$585 80	$216 33		
Number copies Christus Redemptor sold	†1,200	2,425	735	264	2,475	3,783	2,080	800	1,771	750	275	20,108
Number Prayer Calendars for 1907 sold		465	248	290	400	710	300	75	156			
Number Branch Annual Reports printed 1906	‡2,500	2,500	‡2,500	†2,000	‡3,900	5,000	1,700	1,000		1,000	1,000	28,100
Number pages in each		158	124	100	160	205	152	90		64	40	
Number different leaflets, appeals, etc., printed	7	5		4			6	11		8	6	
Total issue of same		17,600						135,500		105,000	10,600	
Number leaflets, appeals, etc., sent free		5					6	5		7	6	
Total pages of same		98,100					86,000	24,900		69,000	42,400	320,400
No. missionary volumes in church libraries		608			596	2,230		494	494	8,459		12,187

* Not Included in total for year.

† By Publisher, 3,600.

‡ Branch Reports free.

42

BY-LAWS.

The following is the report of the By-law Committee, with the action taken on the same, item by item:

I. OFFICERS.

The officers of the Woman's Foreign Missionary Society shall be a President, Recording Secretary, a Treasurer, and such other officers as shall be deemed necessary for the efficient work of the Society. These officers shall be elected annually at the General Executive Committee. (Action deferred.)

II. DUTIES OF OFFICERS.

It shall be the duty of—

The President to—
(a) Preside at all meetings of the Society, and, with the Recording Secretary and Treasurer in the *interim* of the General Executive and Reference Committee metings,
(b) Have authority to transact all business that requires immediate action. Adopted.

The Vice-President to—
(a) Perform all duties of the President in her absence, and
(b) Render assistance when needed. Deferred.

The Recording Secretary to—
(a) Give notice of all meetings of the General Executive Committee.
(b) Keep a full record of all its proceedings, placing the same in the safe of the Publication Office.
(c) Present a report of the year's work at the anniversary of the Society, and
(d) Forward to Foreign Treasurers a copy of the appropriation for each Mission as soon as practicable after the adjournment of the General Executive Committee.
(e) To prepare and print the Annual Report of the Woman's Foreign Missionary Society, including the Minutes of the General Executive Committee.
(f) Prepare and present a Quadrennial Report to the General Conference. Adopted.

The Treasurer to—
(a) Receive all money from bequests, gifts, donations, or legacies made to the Woman's Foreign Missionary Society and, unless otherwise specified by the donor, shall pay the same to the Treasurer of the Branch within whose bounds the donor resides at the time of death.
(b) Receive all money paid into the General Fund by the several Branches, and disburse the same, subject to the order of the General Executive Committee. (Adopted.)

III. BRANCH CORRESPONDING SECRETARIES.

A. There shall be a Branch (Corresponding or Foreign) Secretary elected by each Branch at its annual meeting. These Secretaries shall constitute the Foreign Committee of the General Executive to have general supervision of all interests of the Woman's Foreign Missionary Society.
1. Make appropriations and estimates for the Foreign Work.
2. Assign official correspondence.

3. And give careful consideration to the requests of missionaries.
4. Examine and report upon all the testimonials of missionary candidates that are presented by the various Branches.
5. Consider all matters relating to native assistants and workers that may be brought before the Executive Committee.

B. It shall be the duty of each Branch (Corresponding or Foreign) Secretary to—

1. Superintend all interests of the Branch pertaining to the Foreign Field.
2. Conduct the correspondence of the Branch with—
    (a) Foreign missionaries and missionary candidates.
    (b) Missionaries in Missions assigned for official correspondence and present a full report of the same to the General Executive Committee.
3. Report to the General Executive Committee the number of missionaries, Bible women, boarding schools, orphans, and other work supported by the Branch, and furnish a copy of the same, together with a report of the receipts and disbursements by the Branch Treasurer, for publication in the reports of the Woman's Foreign Missionary Society.
4. Sign all orders on the Branch Treasury for foreign remittances in accordance with the appropriations.
5. Give to the Branch all Foreign communications, plans, and business of the Branch, essential to the furtherance of the work.
6. Attend and present a report of the foreign work at all Branch Annual and Quarterly meetings, and submit an annual report for publication in Branch Annual Report.
7. Perform such other duties as the Branch may define. (Deferred.)

IV. Branch Home Secretaries.

A. There shall be a Home Secretary elected by each Branch at its annual meeting. These Secretaries shall constitute the Home Department of the General Executive Committee to—

1. Superintend the interests of the Home Work, including all publications, the work of the General Office, and Field Secretaries, Secretaries of Young People's Work, Secretary of Children's Work, and all other interests not specified in the duties of the Foreign Committee.
2. Present to the General Executive Committee nominations for these offices, and in each case where salaries are paid shall designate the amount.
3. Present to the Foreign Committee their Annual. Report prior to its presentation to the General Executive Committee.

B. The Home Committee shall be divided into sub-committees on the various departments of its work.

C. It shall be the duty of each Branch Home Secretary to—
    (a) Endeavor to advance the interests of the Woman's Foreign Missionary Society "as the necessities of the work require."
    (b) Conduct the correspondence (1) with the General Officers in charge of Home Work, (2) with Conference Secretaries, (3) Branch Superintendents of Departments, and Chairmen Standing Committees, and present a report thereof at the Branch Annual and Quarterly meetings.
    (c) Sign orders on the Branch Treasury for Home Work authorized by the Branch Executive Committee.
    (d) Prepare a report of the Home Work for publication in the

Branch Annual Report, and as required for the Annual Report of the Woman's Foreign Missionary Society and for the *Woman's Missionary Friend.*

(e) Furnish a copy of the report of Home Work to the Branch Foreign Secretary.

(f) Serve as ex-officio member on all Branch Standing Committees.

(g) Assist in the preparation of the Branch Annual Report.

(h) Perform such other duties as the Branch may define. (Deferred.)

V. Branch Treasurers.

A. There shall be a Treasurer elected by each Branch at its annual meeting.

B. It shall be the duty of each *Branch Treasurer to—*

1. Receive all funds of the Branch.

2. Make and promptly forward the quarterly foreign remittances according to the appropriations upon the written order of the Branch Foreign Secretary.

3. Disburse other funds under the direction of the Branch Executive Committee upon the written order of the Branch Home Secretary.

4. Furnish quarterly statements of receipts and disbursements for publication in the *Woman's Missionary Friend.*

5. Present full items of receipts and disbursements annually and quarterly to the Branch and furnish a copy to the Branch Foreign and Home Secretaries.

6. Prepare an itemized report for the Branch Annual Meeting and for publication in the Branch Annual Report, and

7. Perform such other duties as each Branch may define. (Deferred.)

VI. Branch Secretaries of Literature.

A. There shall be a Secretary of Literature elected by each Branch at its Annual Meeting.

B. It shall be the duty of each Branch *Secretary of Literature to—*

1. Advance the interest and increase the sale of the literature and publications.

2. Have charge, in connection with the Branch Committee on Literature and the Agent of Supplies, of the exhibition and sale of Woman's Foreign Missionary Society publications at the various public gatherings and conventions throughout the country, the expenses to be borne by the Branch within whose bounds the public gathering is held.

3. Literature for meetings held outside the country shall be in charge of the Literature Sub-Committee of the Home Committees and expenses paid from the General Treasury. (Deferred.)

VII. General Secretaries.

There shall be a Secretary of the General Office, a Secretary of Young People's Work, and a Secretary of Children's Work, elected annually by the General Executive Committee. Field Secretaries shall be employed as required on the nomination of the Home Committee.

It shall be the duty of the *Secretary of the General Office to—*

(See report of Committee on General Office.)

It shall be the duty of the *Secretary of Young People's Work to—*

(a) Advance the interests of the Society in all possible ways.

(b) Conduct departmental correspondence with Branch Superintendents.

(c) Furnish material as required for publication in the *Woman's Missionary Friend.*

(d) Prepare annually a report of her department for the General Executive Committee and for publication in the Annual Report of the Woman's Foreign Missionary Society. (Deferred.)

VIII. Field Secretaries.

When, in the judgment of the General Executive Committee, Field Secretaries are employed they shall be under the direction of the Sub-committee of the Home Committee, and their expenses shall be provided from the Branches employing them. (Deferred.)

IX. Foreign Treasurers.

A. There shall be a Foreign Treasurer for each mission where the Woman's Foreign Missionary Society supports work.

B. It shall be the duty of each *Foreign Treasurer* to:

(a) Forward receipt immediately upon receiving remittances from the Branch Treasurer.

(b) On January 1st and July 1st of each year forward to the Branch (Corresponding or Foreign) Secretary itemized statements showing balance in United States currency.

(c) Apply the funds of the Society only for the purpose designated by the General Executive Committee. This rule shall be interpreted to mean that no expenditure shall exceed the appropriation.

(d) Pay appropriations for buildings and for salaries of missionaries on the basis of United States gold, and all other appropriations on the basis of the local currency of the country, any surplus therefrom by exchange shall accrue to the Treasury of the Branch remitting.

(e) Report in the semi-annual statements all surplus funds arising from unused appropriations, exchange or other source and hold said funds subject to the order of the Foreign Secretary from whose Branch said funds accrue.

(f) Forward estimates approved by the Field Reference Committee, and printed, to the (Corresponding or Foreign) Secretary of each Branch to insure arrival on or before September 1st.

(g) Pay money for buildings, on presentation of properly audited bills only. (Adopted.)

X. Missionaries.

Each missionary shall—

1. On acceptance by the Woman's Foreign Missionary Society, be under the control of the General Executive Committee, directly amenable to the (Corresponding or Foreign) Secretary of the Branch employing her.

2. Devote her entire time and attention to her appointed work.

3. When beginning service, be provided by the Society with not less than $100 for personal outfit and also, if necessary, $100 for furniture, which shall be the property of the Society.

4. Consider the regulations of the Society named in the Constitution and By-laws as binding as the terms of the contract, and failure to conform to them on the part of the missionary shall release the Society from all financial liability.

5. Enter into the following contract by and with the Woman's Foreign Missionary Society through the Foreign Corresponding Secretary of the Branch employing her:

CONTRACT.

"I, —— ——, Corresponding Secretary of the ——— Branch of the Woman's Foreign Missionary Society of the Methodist Episcopal Church, covenant and agree on the part of the Woman's Foreign Missionary Society to pay the traveling expenses of —— ——, a missionary in the employ of the ———Branch, from her home to her field of labor and her salary from the time of reaching the field at the rate of $—— for the first year, and thereafter at the rate of $—— per annum. I further agree to pay her return passage and home salary as provided in the By-laws relating to those matters."

"I, —— ——, a missionary, agree to give at least five years of continuous service as a single woman to the work of the Woman's Foreign Missionary Society in any field to which I may be sent, and, failing in this, to refund the amount of outfit and passage money. I also agree to conform to all the rules and regulations of said Society while in its employ."

6. Report each quarter to the (Corresponding or Foreign) Secretary of the Branch employing her, and to the Presiding Elder of the District in which her work is located.

7. Furnish the Official Correspondent with all facts as required.

8. Report and credit in financial statements made January 1st and July 1st, of each year, all sums received for the support of the work in her charge.

9. Medical missionaries shall keep an itemized account of all receipts and disbursements, and report them quarterly to the Treasurer of the mission, any surplus being remitted to the Woman's Foreign Missionary Society. Medical outfit provided by the Society shall be the property of the Society.

10. Each missionary shall send annual communications for patrons supporting Special Work.

11. Keep a clear record of all Special Work, including Bible women, scholarships, etc., in her charge under the Branches supporting, and on her removal or furlough transfer it to her substitute or successor.

12. Present estimates and all other matter requiring the action of the General Executive Committee through the Field Reference Committee of the Conference in which her work is located.

13. Include in her estimates for Bible women and zenana workers all expenses of conveyances, munshis, and teachers, and those for scholarships, the cost of fuel, lights, medicines, and the minor expenses necessary in the maintenance of the schools.

14. Attend the first session of the General Executive Committee held after her return from the foreign field, and her traveling expenses to and from the place of meeting shall be paid from the same fund as those of members of that body.

15. On furlough, if her home is not in the United States, shall receive full salary, in which case no furlough expenses will be paid by the Society. This provision shall apply only to missionaries in satisfactory relation to the Society, and for the term of furlough authorized by the General Executive Committee through the Branch employing her.

16. If she contemplates returning home for any other reason than ill-health, secure permission of the General Executive Committee through the (Corresponding or Foreign) Secretary of the Branch employing her, upon the recommendation of the Field Reference Committee.

17. Accompany her application for return to the field after home leave with a new medical certificate. The recommendation of the (Corresponding or Foreign) Secretary of the Branch employing her and a majority vote of the Reference Committee shall be authority for her return.

18. The *salaries of missionaries* going to the field after October, 1901, either as new or returned missionaries, shall include all expenses hitherto classed as incidentals, and shall be, in Africa, $500; Bulgaria, $600; Foochow and Hing Hua, $600; North, Central, and West China, $650; India, $600; Italy, Japan, and Korea, $700; Malaysia, $600; Mexico, the Philippines, and South America, $750. The first year's work of a new missionary shall be so planned by the mission that the major part of her time shall be given to the study of the languages, and the first year's salary shall be one-sixth less than the full regular amount, except in the case of those whose full salary does not exceed $500. Medical missionaries shall from the first receive full salary.

19. No missionary in the employ of the Woman's Foreign Missionary Society shall adopt any child as her own, nor bring foreign-born girls or helpers to this country except upon the recommendation of the Field Reference Committee of the Conference in which they reside, and with the permission of the Foreign Committee of the Woman's Foreign Missionary Society.

20. If proved manifestly unfit for missionary labor, receive three months' notice by the Foreign Committee, at the expiration of which, the General Executive Committee may cancel its obligation to the Missionary. Return passage will be paid by the Society only at the expiration of the three months. Adopted.

21. Each Foreign Conference or Mission shall have a Field Reference or Finance Committee, of not less than three nor more than seven representative members, who shall be elected by ballot by the missionaries of the Woman's Foreign Missionary Society. Wives of missionaries who are in charge of work of the Woman's Foreign Missionary Society shall be eligible to membership on this Committee. It shall be the duty of this committee to approve and forward the estimates to the several Branch Corresponding Secretaries, to approve of all contracts for new buildings and of all repairs on buildings which amount to more than ten dollars (gold) before such repairs are undertaken. It shall be the duty of this Committee to consider all matters of general interest arising in the interim of the annual meetings, and to communicate concerning them to the official correspondents.

Article X adopted, excepting Item 21, which was referred to the By-laws Committee.

XI. MISSIONARY CANDIDATES.

Each person who offers herself as a missionary candidate shall—

(a) Declare her belief that (1) she is divinely called to the work of a foreign missionary; (2) that she is actuated only by a desire to work in accordance with the will of God; and (3) that she intends to make foreign missionary work the service of her effective years.

(b) Be not less than twenty-five nor more than thirty years of age. A special facility in acquiring languages or a call to English work may be considered a sufficient reason for deviating from this rule.

(c) When accepted, be under the direction of the General Executive

Committee, and, if not sent out within the year, her case shall be presented for reconsideration at the ensuing session of the General Executive Committee by the Corresponding or Foreign Secretary in whose Branch she resides.

(d) Fill out required application blanks and sign the contract in duplicate for file record with the Branch Foreign Secretary and in the General Office. Adopted.

XII. PUBLICATION DEPARTMENT.

1. The periodicals of the Woman's Foreign Missionary Society shall be known as the *Woman's Missionary Friend, Children's Missionary Friend, Der Frauen Missions Freund,* and *The Study.*

2. The Literature of the Society shall include all other publications not specified in Section 1.

3. The Editors and Publisher of the periodicals and literature shall be elected annually at the General Executive Committee, when their reports shall be received, and a copy thereof submitted for publication in the Annual Report of the Woman's Foreign Missionary Society.

4. The Editors and Publisher shall be entitled to floor privileges on matters concerning their work.

5. In the interim of the General Executive Committee the management of the Society's publications shall be under the control of the Home Committee section assigned to that work.

6. Sample copies of all publications issued by the Society shall be sent to the President, Secretary, and Treasurer of the Woman's Foreign Missionary Society, and to such other officers and exchanges as may be deemed essential to the progress of this department. Adopted, excepting Item 5, on which action was deferred.

XIII. ZENANA PAPER.

1. The Foreign Committee shall take charge of the funds raised for the endowment of the Zenana Paper, and control of their investment and expenditure, and have the general supervision of the interests of the paper.

2. The (Corresponding or Foreign) Secretary of each Branch shall have the control of the investment of the funds raised for the support of the Zenana Paper within the bounds of her Branch with the approval of the Foreign Committee, the interest on investment to be paid semi-annually to the Treasurer of the Zenana Paper.

3. The Woman's Conference in India shall nominate a Committee consisting of five persons, three women and two men, one of whom shall be the Publisher, to supervise the interests of the paper and arrange with the Press Committee for editing and publishing the Zenana Paper in the various languages and dialects required; these nominations to be subject to the approval of the Reference Committee in America.

4. The Official Correspondent of the Woman's Foreign Missionary Society in India shall send an Annual Report of the Zenana Paper to the Chairman of the Foreign Committee, with the amount of circulation and items of interest, in time to be presented to the Annual Meeting of the General Executive Committee in America.

5. The Treasurer in India of the funds of the Zenana Paper shall furnish the Foreign Committee an Annual Report of the receipts and expenditures of said paper, in time to be presented to the General Executive Committee meeting in America.

6. A report of the Zenana Paper shall be published in the Annual Report of the Woman's Foreign Missionary Society.

4

7. The Treasurer of the Zenana Paper funds in America shall send the interest on the investments direct to the Treasurer of the Zenana Paper in India, only upon the order of the Chairman of the Foreign Committee. Referred to the Reference Committee.

XIV. Annual Meetings.

, The Annual Meeting of the General Executive Committee shall be held, beginning the fourth Thursday in October, in each of the Branches consecutively. The Foreign and Home Committees shall assemble not less than three days earlier, to consider the work of their respective departments. The mid-year meeting of the Foreign Committee shall be held at the time and place agreed upon by themselves. Deferred.

XV. By-Laws.

These By-laws may be changed or amended at any meeting of the General Executive Committee by a two-thirds vote of the members present and voting. Adopted.

XVI. Quorum.

A majority of the members of the General Executive Committee shall constitute a quorum for the transaction of business. Adopted.

XVII. Anniversary.

The date and arrangements for the Anniversary exercises of the General Executive Committee shall be made by the President, the (Corresponding or Foreign) and Home Secretaries of the Branch within whose bounds the session of the General Executive Committee is to be held. Adopted.

XVIII. Expenses.

Section 1. The traveling expenses of the President, Vice-President, Recording Secretary, Treasurer, Foreign Secretaries, and two delegates from each Branch, missionaries and General Secretaries, to and from each meeting of the General Executive Committee, shall be paid from the Treasury of the Woman's Foreign Missionary Society, as well as the traveling expenses of the President and Foreign Secretaries to the mid-year meeting, all to be taken from a fund which shall be assessed pro rata upon each Branch, according to the provision of the Constitution.

2. The postage and traveling expenses of Editors and Publisher, to and from the meeting of the General Executive Committee, shall be paid from receipts of the publication office. Deferred.

XIX. The Order of Business.

The order of business for the General Executive Committee shall be as follows:

1. Calling the roll.
2. Appointment of Committees.
3. Reception of Memorials, Petitions, and proposed changes in the By-laws.
4. Reports of Foreign Secretaries by Branches.
5. Reports of Home Secretaries by Branches.
6. Reports of Foreign Committee.
7. Reports of Home Committee.
8. Reports of Editors and Publisher.

9. Reports of official correspondents and presentation of information concerning foreign work.

10. Fixing place of next meeting.

11. Election of President, Vice-President, and Secretary, Treasurer, and General Secretaries, and other officers, who shall continue in office until the appointment of their successors.

12. Election of Editors and Publisher.

13. Notice of constitutional amendments.

DAILY ORDER OF BUSINESS.

1. Roll call.
2. Minutes.
3. Reports of Committees immediately after the reading of minutes.
4. Miscellaneous business.
5. Introductions.

Each session shall open and close with devotional exercises. All resolutions to be discussed shall be presented in writing. No member shall be granted leave of absence except by vote of the entire body. Deferred.

XX. FIELD REFERENCE COMMITTEE.

There shall be a Field Reference Committee elected annually in each Foreign Conference where the Woman's Foreign Missionary Society supports work, whose duty it shall be to—

(a) Prepare estimates and other matters requiring the action of the General Executive Committee.

(b) Consider all matters of general interest arising during the interim of their annual meetings.

(c) Consider the furloughs of missionaries and forward its recommendations concerning the individual cases to the Foreign Committee.

(d) And perform such other duties as the General Executive Committee, through its Foreign Committee, shall require. Referred to the Reference Committee of the General Executive Committee.

XXI. FOREIGN BUILDING COMMITTEE.

There shall be a Foreign Building Committee elected annually by a majority vote of the Board of Foreign Missions, and Woman's Foreign Missionary Societies in each foreign mission and Conference where the Woman's Foreign Missionary Society supports work, whose duty it shall be to—

(a) Superintend all matters relating to the purchase of property, erection of new buildings, and extensive repairs.

(b) Audit and order paid all bills for new buildings and extensive repairs. Referred.

XXII. FUNDS.

1. *All money* raised under the auspices of this Society belongs to the Woman's Foreign Missionary Society of the Methodist Episcopal Church and shall not be diverted to other causes.

2. Receipts from the publication office shall constitute the *Publication Fund* and be drawn on to defray the postage and traveling expenses of the Editors and Publisher to and from General Executive Committee.

3. The *Reserve Fund,* a capital of $5,000, shall be retained in the Treasury of the Society's publications, and in no case shall said amount be used in publishing interests or for any other demands.

4. Gifts, bequests, donations, and other moneys received from donors residing outside of the United States shall be paid into General Treasury, and credited as "received from the Society *at large.*"

5. Proceeds on the Foreign Field, accruing rates of exchange, surplus from remittances made under appropriations and other sources, shall belong to the Branch supporting the work, and shall be reported January 1st and July 1st of each year, and held subject to the order of the Foreign Secretary in whose Branch they accrue.

Item 2 amended by insertion of "Literature Committee" after "Editors and Publisher." Adopted.

XXIII. RULES.

All rules pertaining to the relations of the Woman's Foreign Missionary Society of the Methodist Episcopal Church with its· missionaries shall be published in the ˙general Annual Report. Adopted.

XXIV. DELEGATES.

Delegates to General Executive Committee shall be appointed to service on the Foreign ·or Home Committees ·on nomination of their respective Branch Secretaries. Deferred.

The following was also adopted as a by-law:

The acceptance of assistant missionaries, or native workers as missionaries, shall be in the hands of the Reference Committee, who, in reaching a conclusion shall take into consideration: (1) The testimonials required in the regulations relating to candidates, including health certificates; (2) a certificate showing three years of service under the Woman's Foreign Missionary Society; (3) The recommendation of the Bishop in charge of the Conference. ˙

MRS. W. B. THOMPSON,
MRS. S. J. HERBEN,
MRS. C. W. BARNES.
Committee.

MISSION STUDY IN COLLEGES.

Your Committee beg leave to submit the following report:

In advising with members of the University Senate of the Methodist Episcopal Church, it was ascertained that there would be no further conferences of that body until 1908, when it would seem eminently suitable to bring before it, as was advised by the Executive Committee of 1906, the proposition of making the study of missions a collegiate department ranking with other studies looking toward the college degree. As nothing could be done by the Senate, as requested by the Executive Committee, until the Senate convened in 1908, the Committee on their own initiative sent to twenty-two leading colleges the following questions, selecting the colleges thus interviewed from all parts of the country.

To twenty-two universities and colleges the following questions were put and ˙fifteen replies received: ˙

"Have you a Mission Study Class in your college? If so, what is the number of its members?

"Has work in this line ever counted toward a degree? If not, would you think it advisable, 'considering the present interest in the missions, to allow it to do so?"

It.was a pleasure to find that in each of the colleges replying to our inquiries there were Mission Study Classes, and in· four credits were given for the work done. These notable four were: Northwestern University, Evanston, Ill.; Lawrence University, Appleton, Wis.; Baker University, Baldwin, Kan., and Illinois Wesleyan University, Bloomington, Ill. Nearly all of the letters expressed the hope of˜ further work on these lines, and your committee would recommend that the original proposition to bring the matter before the College Senate of our Church, when it convenes in 1908, be carried out.

All the literature pertaining to this subject will be carefully preserved to be handed over to such committee, should you choose to appoint it. That the field is one to inspire hope is evident, while the results in finely fitted candidates for our mission fields would be incalculable could candidates for a degree make mission studies count towards a degree. Respectfully submitted,

LOUISE MANNING HODGKINS,
MARY ISHAM,
IDA V. JONTZ.

"WOMAN'S MISSIONARY FRIEND."

The report of a year's work on a periodical is necessarily a summary. The periodical speaks for itself and the "constant reader" does not need a detailed record. Certain points, however, should be noted:

Special Numbers.—Six special numbers have been presented, two of which were in harmony with the general observance of the centennial of the entrance of Protestant missions into China. The April number was especially rich in illustrations, statistics, and special articles on our work in China. The June number, with a new cover design, set forth a carefully prepared menu for young people. September was devoted to the work of our Chinese doctors. The cover in brown ink was a printer's error, and as great a surprise to publisher and editor as to the constituency. In October Burma was given precedence. November covered the first and second chapters of "Gloria Christi," with supplementary articles on evangelistic and educational missions, while the December number is to be divided between the Philippines and the General Executive Committee meeting.

Special Features.—While China has had the right of way with its accounts of the China Centenary Conference, the Central Conference (Methodist) of China, and news items, six articles have covered the jubilee aftermath. Special Branch interests have been touched upon in articles on the Taylor High School, Poona, the work in Puebla, and others. The department entitled "News from the Field," has had generous space, and space has been given regularly to Young People's Work, the literature, and Folts Institute.

Magazine Fund.—The Magazine Fund has had two hundred and eleven magazines and periodicals recorded in its card catalogue—the largest number in its history. Included in this have been the *Friend's* exchanges. The *Friend* maintains a reciprocal relation to our leading magazines, many of which are giving space to articles of missionary interest, and the brief reading notice that appears each month is only a fair return for the trade rates and exchanges that benefit our missionaries. The Magazine Fund is on a sound business basis and takes care of itself financially.

Correspondence.—The correspondence connected with the *Friend* shows an average of ninety-three letters per month. This is entirely outside the enormous correspondence maintained in the Boston office.

Subscriptions.—The subscription returns show a total of 24,657 subscribers—an increase for the year of 1,030. This indicates that the Branches have made an effort to reach the thirty-thousand mark that was set as the goal for 1906-1907. We have not attained, but the advance that has been made should be an incentive for the coming year.

The statistical returns by Branches show that there has been an advance in all save Philadelphia. The figures are as follows:

	Subscriptions.	Increase.	Decrease.
New England	2,074	64	..
New York	3,177	192	..
Philadelphia	3,055	...	58
Baltimore	814	81	..
Cincinnati	2,837	71	
Northwestern	5,830	233	
Des Moines	2,674	297	
Minneapolis	822	88	..
Topeka	1,365	2	
Pacific	812	95	
Columbia River	518	77	..

Last year a careful calculation was made of the advance required by each Branch, in proportion to membership, in order to reach the thirty-thousand mark. The figures on the basis of proportional increase are as follows:

New England	Required	628	Gained	64
New York	"	2,700	"	192
Philadelphia	"	255	Lost	58
Baltimore	"	129	Gained	81
Cincinnati	"	1,003	"	71
Northwestern	"	1,238	"	233
Des Moines	"	576	"	297
Minneapolis	"	94	"	88
Topeka	"	244	"	2
Pacific	"	183	"	95
Columbia River	"	87	"	77

The percentage of increase for the five Branches that comprise the *Friend's* honor list gives Minneapolis 93.6 per cent; Columbia River, 88.5 per cent; Baltimore, 62.8 per cent; Pacific, 51.9 per cent; Des Moines, 51.6 per cent. These are widely distributed sections of the country. If such good work can be done in five Branches, why not in all the coming year?

"Do It Now!" is the title of a little circular issued to help in the canvass for subscriptions. This may be had on application to the publisher, who will also be glad to furnish free copies of the *Friend* for canvassing.   Respectfully submitted, .

ELIZABETH C. NORTHUP.

TABLE OF SUBSCRIPTIONS TO THE WOMAN'S MISSIONARY FRIEND FROM 1869-1907.

Year	Subscriptions	Year	Subscriptions
1870	3,000	1889	19,834
1871	21,000	1890	19,236
1872	22,000	1891	20,401
1873	24,000	1892	21,512
1874	25,000	1893	21,529
1875	16,000	1894	21,617
1876	17,313	1895	20,411
1877	16,000	1896	19,146
1878	14,074	1897	19,026
1879	13,388	1898	20,858
1880	15,606	1899	21,812
1881	18,007	1900	22,720
1882	20,020	1901	21,447
1883	19,571	1902	23,538
1884	20,045	1903	24,120
1885	19,816	1904	24,184
1886	19,456	1905	23,402
1887	19,987	1906	23,627
1888	19,907	1907	23,978

"THE TOKIWA."

The Tokiwa is devoted to the interests of the home. Some one has said: "That which makes a people is domestic life. The loss of it degrades a people to a horde." To clarify the vision, to speak comfort to the heart, to widen the horizon, and to equip for Christian service the women in the home is the aim of our magazine, and we trust that it is a potent influence in preventing the Japanese from becoming a horde. During the year 11,400 copies have been printed, averaging forty pages each. We have had articles of general interest, and articles on religion; instruction on the care and training of children, helps for Bible women and the Sunday-school teacher, popular foreign cooking recipes, lectures on hygiene, lessons in knitting and crocheting, songs and exercises, and last, but not least in attraction, and also expense, illutrations. Nearly all were half-tones, but for the Christmas number we have a calotype of Murillo's beautiful Madonna, and for the January frontispiece a lithographed greeting in colors.

We have been gratified to learn of some of the uses to which *Tokiwa* is put. One subscriber uses it in her woman's meetings, and has found the religious articles of great help. Another makes it the basis of her talks at the Ladies' Aid Society. She has an article read and dwells upon the special points of interest. In this way the time that otherwise might be spent in idle gossip is turned to good account.

"I wish you great success and thank you for the splendid magazine." "It has many helpful features and my workers always welcome it." "The women and evangelists are so pleased with the paper, they say it is the best paper for women there is." These are some of the messages that have encouraged us during the year. Now a Korean lady has introduced *Tokiwa* to her associates in Seoul, and she says if we only had a Korean edition she could get many more subscribers.

During the absence of Miss Baucus and Miss Dickinson we have been having a sabbatic year in publications, the calendar for 1907 being our only issue, aside from a few reprints. The calendar proved to be quite a success. At this time when the Japanese are bending every energy to secure the things that will pass away, we wanted to present in an attractive form Bible verses on the things that will abide. We selected therefore for the design the pine tree, which means unchanging. After the calendar was out we were happy to learn that we had chosen the imperial subject for the year in the pine-tree.

We thank God for the success already attained by the *Tokiwa* and the Tokiwasha publications, and we pray for larger things to come that we may not be found wanting in making known His saving grace within the home. Respectfully submitted,

N. MARGARET DANIEL.

"FRAUEN-MISSIONS-FREUND."

We close the twenty-second year of the *"Frauen-Missions-Freund"* with gratitude to God, who has been our ever present help throughout this past year.

During the month of May it was our privilege to visit several German District Meetings in the West, as the sisters were anxious to meet their editor face to face. We were warned beforehand not to expect many new subscribers, as almost everybody was a subscriber now, and so we found it; but it encouraged us greatly to hear: "We love our little paper." "*The Study* has been so interesting—just what we like." And we were made to feel that our women pray for their editor.

Shortly after this trip the Editor was laid .on the sick bed for awhile, but she was wonderfully helped and carried along on the arms of prayer, that .were lifted up in her behalf.

It was a great disappointment to find at the end of the year that we had a decrease in subscriptions amounting to one hundred and fifty. We were surprised, because so many new subscribers had been gained during the year, especially in the Southern and Pacific Conferences. But when we found that in one charge all the thirty-seven subscribers had been dropped because there was no woman there who would take up the work of looking after the subscriptions and renewing them, we could see where the trouble might be found.

With one exception (in 1889) this was the only time we ever had a decrease. May it be the last time. The question may arise here if we have not almost reached the limit of our possibilities. By no means. In some Conferences only a small part of the charges have auxiliaries, and where we have no auxiliary we may get one, and where we get an auxiliary, we also get subscribers to the "Freund."

So we are not discouraged, but with the help of God we hope that the "Freund" will grow to double its size and usefulness.

Respectfully submitted,

AMALIA M. ACHARD.

"CHILDREN'S MISSIONARY FRIEND."

To the members of this Executive Committee, to missionaries, and friends, the *Children's Missionary Friend* extends greetings on this its eighteenth anniversary. Gratitude and praise fill our heart in view of its general success and its ever widening influence. Such is its advanced age to-day that many young mothers in our own land and several missionaries in the foreign field can say, "When I was a little girl I read that paper and learned to love missions." Perhaps there are young business men, too, who are giving more to the cause we love, influenced by the teachings of what was in their boyhood the *Heathen Children's Friend*. If its publication was begun in loving faith, have n't we a right to believe that God's promises concerning such ventures are really blossoming and bearing fruitage to-day?

You who have read the paper the past year have noted the excellence of its contributed articles. From Mrs. Emily Huntington Miller's bright and tender four-chapter story to the least little sketch from a weary missionary, all have been excellent. But O, if you knew how like the "widow's oil" our supply has often been, you would wish, with us, that the claims of the little *Friend,* like those of the Woman's magazine, might be presented at the Women's Conferences on the field, so that some child-lover may represent each country at least once a quarter. With sincere gratitude for past favors, we beg the missionaries who listen to these words to heed the poet's injunction: "*Sow in the morn thy seed,*" and send to the editor the stories and incidents which will prove good seed in many a young heart.

The coming year we are to gather up the glorious results of mission work in many lands as we travel around the globe "In Circles of Light." Shall we not pray that in studying the victories of Christ our children may give Him their hearts, and become in deed and truth His loyal heralds? Our Reading Course is commended to leaders, and the paper, as a part of it, will try to lead in the direction suggested.

Our General Secretary's Letter is a pleasant feature of the little *Friend,* and we wish it might be read in every monthly gathering of the Heralds, as it now is in many. The New England Branch mourns its loss, as Mrs. Harrison goes to make the Pacific Branch richer and happier. But they must keep the babies hidden unless they are willing to have them made life members!

Last December we began to report the children's thank-offering for an Industrial School in Mexico. Including the reports for the coming month (November) they have already given $972 toward the $1,000 pledge. However, it has been thought best by those most interested to continue this offering another year, as the need is great. It has also been thought wise to send reports of thank-offerings to the editor to avoid delay.

If you have counted the bright little faces which have appeared the past year, you know that we have had in the paper the pictures of two hundred and forty-seven life members! There are others, as Mrs. Harrison's report will show, but the number specified has certainly shown the widespread interest in this department, as well as the generosity of our people. Your Editor regrets the necessity of cutting down the items sent with photographs, involving most delicate surgical operations at the point of the pen, but if all the nice items were printed we would have space for but little beside. We believe, with the publisher, that the cost of these cuts ought not to fall entirely upon the paper, and hope a happy arrangement may be made by which each Branch shall bear a proportionate share of the expense.

This seems the more important as the fluctuating character of subsciption lists leads to financial variations not always in our favor. For instance, instead of reporting a gain of more than three thousand subscribers, as last year, we sorrowfully admit a decrease of more than one thousand. We shall recover from this, we feel sure, but the very low price of our paper and the very high price of material and labor calls for a watchful loyalty on the part of our friends to enable us to become and remain self-supporting. Let this be our aim as we reach the threshold of another year.   Respectfully submitted,

Mrs. O. W. Scott.

"THE STUDY."

For another year *The Study* has gone out upon its mission to the women of Methodism. It is such a very diminutive periodical that we wonder if it is worth while, and often wish that it might be larger. We take heart of courage, however, when we think that though its pages be few they are scattered far among the women of the Auxiliaries the unit of our sisterhood—and its price is so low that the Auxiliaries may send copies to the shut-in members and to the uninterested women of the Churches.

During the past year Christus Redemptor led us through the harvest fields of others, and the task was the pleasant one of bringing to the woman, whose library was the text-book and the *Friend,* a glimpse between the covers of less accessible books and magazines.

For the present year the need of a supplementary outline seems imperative. Gloria Christi is an encyclopedic review of the achievements of Christendom in a century. Our own work seems lost—indeed it can not be fully presented in such a text-book. Beside this composite picture of evangelistic, educational, and medical missions we need the clear photograph of our own work and workers—and we shall not be ashamed to see how well these workers have wrought when we remember that one in every six Protestant Christians in India, and one in every five in China, belong to our own communion.

We need also lists of references to books and magazines to be found in Methodist libraries, and especially we need to present the leaflets to be found in our depots of supplies.

Last year we were cheered by a large increase in subscriptions, and in April a further advance of 1,796 was reported by the publisher. It is, therefore, a disappointment to come to the close of the year with a decrease of 547.

The subscriptions by Branches is as follows:

New England	2,577	Topeka	2,754
New York	4,409	Pacific	1,029
Philadelphia	4,305	Columbia River	873
Baltimore	1,031	Scattering	3
Cincinnati	4,582	Foreign	1
Northwestern	8,385		
Des Moines	4,352	Total	35,644
Minneapolis	1,343		

This does not, however, indicate the entire circulation, since the copy is furnished to the editor of *Frauen-Missions-Freund,* and is published in that magazine also.   Respectfully submitted,

MARY ISHAM, *Editor.*

PUBLISHER'S REPORT.
(Covering her twenty-five years of service.)

Twenty-five years ago a telegram came to me from the Executive Committee in session at Philadelphia containing this message, "Will you accept the position of agent of *Heathen Woman's Friend?*"

Although I had been waiting before the Lord just at this time to know His will for the future, this came as a complete surprise, and I said, "Surely *this can not* be what He wants me to do, for I am inexperienced in this kind of work, and I *almost* begged to be excused."

I took the telegram to my room and laid it before the Lord, and while in prayer this sweet answer came to me, "I will strengthen thee and help thee," and I sent this reply, "By the help of the Lord I will take the position for one year," and I am here this morning after twenty-five years to testify that the Lord has not only fulfilled this promise, but also that "He is able to do exceeding abundantly above all that we ask or think."

I wish to bring before you *some* of the results of these twenty-five years, not what *I* have done, although there must necessarily be a few personal allusions. *We* have been workers together with each other, as well as with God, and are dependent upon each other for the opportunity of service. The beautiful work of the editors could not reach the people without the aid of the publisher, and the labor of all these could not extend so widely but for the faithful women in city and country who have made up the rank and file of this noble organization.

There were only seven Branches—New England, New York, Philadelphia, Baltimore, Cincinnati, Northwestern, and Western. At my first Executive Meeting in 1883, the Western Branch was divided into three—Des Moines, Minneapolis, and Topeka. At Cincinnati in 1888, the Pacific Branch, with sixteen Auxiliaries and six hundred members in their territory, and $1,100 asked to become a Branch and appropriated $2,400 that year. At Springfield, Mass., in 1892, Columbia River was received, and made its first appropriation of $4,118.

One editor, our first and well beloved, gave me a most cordial welcome, and was a tower of strength in my first year of experience. In the twenty-five years four editors of *Woman's Missionary Friend,* one of *Children's Missionary Friend,* three of *The German Friend,* four of *The Study,* and two editors of Literature—fourteen in all—have been associated with me.

The money value represented in these years has been small compared to the vast amount of labor in the detail of the office work, and given by the women all through the Society who have gathered the subscriptions one by one to all the periodicals and assisted in scattering the literature.

The total receipts have only been $408,486.19—the first year $10,041, the last $27,253, some gain, but not what it should be in comparison to the large membership and the contributions to our Society. But money value is not all that counts in the Lord's work, for seed has been sown without which the glorious harvest of $692,490 reported yesterday could not have been gathered. Leaflets, numbering 100,000,000 pages, have been scattered, and periodicals a billion of pages. Not only has our own Society been benefited, but the influence has been felt all through the Church. The leaflets were distributed and *read* in the families and the foundation laid for the present missionary interest.

In 1876, with an appropriation of $25 from each Branch, the new era of literature commenced, and in 1880 from surplus funds of *Heathen Woman's Friend* $300 was appropriated, increased each year, until in 1885 $1,100 was given, and the total for the six years was $4,000 for free leaflets. The first leaflet, issued in 1876, "Seven Reasons Why I Should Belong to the Woman's Foreign Missionary Society," written by Miss Belle Hart, has been reprinted from time to time, and is still in service, having been reprinted this last year.

Possibly some here do not know that for nearly ten years, from 1876, when the *Missionary Advocate* closed its career, to 1885, when *Gospel in All Lands* was adopted by the General Missionary Society, that the *Heathen Woman's Friend* was the *only periodical* in the Church devoted to Foreign Missions.

We have also extended our influence across the sea, for in 1883 $1,200 was given to start the *Zenana Paper* in India, and our total gift to that paper has been $2,276.56—"the first paper of its kind brought into existence by the help of that excellent periodical, the *Heathen Woman's Friend.*"

In 1884 it was voted to pay for our Annual Report from this fund, and we have paid $7,710.90 for the same to date. In 1885 the invested fund was drawn upon for Life Membership Certificates to the value of $1,531. In 1887, giving us a rest of one year, the surplus fund was again taxed, this time for the traveling expenses of missionaries, and at the same time the proposition was made to pay all the delegates' expenses conditionally, but the conditions were not met, and the sum for the traveling expenses of missionaries was $1,019.

In 1886 the *German Friend* was started, and the *Mother Friend* has paid for it $3,835.08. In 1884 the need of a children's paper was presented, but it was rejected. However, patience and perseverance conquered, and in 1890, after six years of waiting, the beautiful children's paper, which has been such a blessing to children, and mothers as well, was started on its career, and has cost $3,992.

In 1889 a real donation was given to the subscribers in the form of a supplement containing the Uniform Study, costing the *Friend* in the five years $2,500, until in 1894 *The Study,* as it is now printed, was started, and the amount expended, above the receipts, has been $1,490.64. In 1897, at the meeting in Denver, the Quarterlies were added to the paper at the additional expense of $1,200 *each year,* but with no extra cost to the subscriber.

We have given the Swedish Work $500.

SUMMARY FROM OCT. 1, 1882, TO OCT. 1, 1907.

Profits from Woman's Missionary Friend	$35,876 27	
Interest on Invested Funds	8,232 35	
Profits from other sources	1,536 30	
		$45,644 92

Donated for—

Zenana Paper	$2,276 56	
Life Membership Certificates	1,531 55	
Missionary Traveling Expenses	1,019 47	
Frauen Missions Freund	3,835 08	
Children's Missionary Friend	3,992 54	
The Study	1,490 64	
Literature	20,848 27	
Annual Reports	7,710 90	
Swedish Work	500 00	
		$43,205 01

The inventory passed over to me by my predecessor was sixteen varieties of leaflets, valued at $70.46. To-day we catalogue nearly 500 varieties, and the value of literature on hand October 1, 1907, was $6,625. The amount contributed for the output of literature, including Annual Reports, which are really a part of the literature, is $28,447.80. Twenty-five years ago we had only one periodical, with a subscription list of 19,645. Now we have four periodicals, with a combined circulation of 100,000. The first year 4,400 letters were received. Last year about 15,000 money letters and about one-half as many more with all kinds of inquiries.

Dear Sisters, we will praise the Lord for all that has been accomplished in this publication work, but it is small compared to what can be done in the future if we put forth earnest effort, with strong faith in the Lord and in the women of our Society. We ought surely to double our subscription lists. Will we make the effort?

I thank my Heavenly Father that He has kept me and given me the precious privilege of service. I am grateful for the love and confidence of the dear women from the Atlantic to the Pacific who through the years have helped me to carry on the work. A noble band (God bless them!) have been "workers together with Him," and some of the results are seen—the *full* record is written in Heaven.

There have been difficulties, but patient waiting, perseverance, and steady faith in ultimate success have conquered. Others might have done more. "I have tried to be faithful" to the trust committed to me.

Respectfully submitted,

PAULINE J. WALDEN, Publisher.

PAULINE J. WALDEN, *Publisher, in account with Woman's Foreign Missionary Society, from October 1, 1906, to October 1, 1907.*

To cash on hand		$3,125 36
Received for subscriptions to *Woman's Missionary Friend*	$11,800 48	
Received for subscriptions to *Children's Missionary Friend*	3,233 73	
Received for subscriptions to *Frauen Mission Freund*	1,122 16	
Received for subscriptions to *The Study*	912 20	
		$17,068 57
Received for Literature		8,023 58

Received for Annual Reports $894 73
Received for Woman's Foreign Missionary
   badges 666 91
Received for advertising...................... 323 49
Received for interest on loans and deposits...... 264 70
Received for sundries........................ 11 62   2,161 45

    Total receipts $30,378 96

By cash paid for—
Printing and mailing *Woman's Missionary
   Friend* $8,126 04
Editor's salary and incidentals............... 1,138 18
          $9,264 22

Printing and mailing *Children's Missionary
   Friend* $3,475 31
Editor's salary and incidentals.............. 313 85
          3,789 16

Printing and mailing *Frauen Mission Freund*... $895 21
Editor's salary and incidentals............... 255 25
          1,150 46

Printing and mailing *The Study* $801 62
Editor's salary and incidentals............... 101 50
          903 12

Printing and mailing Annual Reports $941 96
Editing Annual Reports..................... 50 00
          991 96

Literature expenses 9,123 73
Publisher's salary $700 00
Office expense 739 52
          1,439 52

Insurance $52 20
Woman's Foreign Missionary badges........... 417 40
Auditor 10 00
Incidentals 49 46
          529 06

Swedish translations $150 00
Traveling expenses to General Executive Com-
   mittee 199 65
          349 65
On hand 2,838 08

          $30,378 96

ASSETS.

Publishing Interests, October 1, 1907.

Five first mortgages............................ $3,000 00
Deposit in Five Cent Saving Bank................. 800 11
Deposit in Home Saving Bank................... 575 78
Interest due on loans and deposits............... 77 43
Cash on hand................................. 2,838 08
          $7,291 40

Less amount due on unexpired subscriptions on
   *Woman's Missionary Friend, Children's Mission-
   ary Friend, Frauen Mission Freund,* and *The
   Study* 6,475 50

          $815 90

I have examined the accounts of the Publishing House of the
Woman's Foreign Missionary Society for the year ending September 30,
1907, and find the same carefully kept, proper vouchers for all payments
and assets as given above.   GEORGE E. WHITAKER, *Auditor.*

ZENANA PAPER.

The Zenana Paper is published in five languages as follows: Abla
Hitkarak, Hindi; Rafiq, I., Niswan, Urdu, editor, Miss Lilavati Singh;
Mathar Mithiri, Tamil, editor, Miss Grace Stephens; Mahili Bandhub,
Bengali, editor, Mrs. J. P. Meik; Marithi, editor, Miss Helen E. Robinson.
These are published in Lucknow, Calcutta, Madras, and Bombày.

Mrs. L. H. Messmore, the former editor, reports for the Hindi and
Urdu editions.

The paper has no incident nor accident to report during the year,
and but few changes are noticeable. We have used our illustrations,
sent out six years ago, and are now using old ones lent us by the *Press,*
many of which have been used before. The Garhwal District Bible
women have given their Conferences essays as helps to the paper; each
essay has been good, and the subjects explained have been full of
variety, and evince an increasing interest in the mission of the paper.
One of the committee has written several articles for the Children's
Corner.

Miss Buck is giving a serial, the story of Christ, the first chapter was
published in October.

The present Christian Number contains the Jublilee calendar; this
is the love gift of Miss Waugh. It was her thought and plan, and our
thanks are due to her. We also appreciate and thank Mr. Meek of the
Press for his help and kindness given. We have received many notes from
Hindus and Mohammedans, commending and approving the paper. We
still need good and appropriate illustrations for the paper. For seven
years we have had to use what we could get. Scarcely ever what we
needed to make plain a teaching fact. We hope our successor will have
the help to improve the needy paper.

We leave our best wishes with and for the paper. We count it
among our best honors that we have been permitted to be the mother of
this growing evangel for a few years, and we ask that love and every
possible help may be given to our successor.

Miss Grace Stephens gives the following in regard to the publishing
of the Tamil edition:

We are very grateful to our publishing house for our *Mathar Mithiri,*
and for the large number of Bible booklets and tracts we received and
distributed during the year. These silent messengers have gone into many
hearts and homes, and are indispensable in our work. One of our
zenana women said: "After reading your *Mathar Mithiri* I give it to my
husband, who reads it to the friends who come to see him. We learn
much from it." Another said: "By having this paper we are kept from
laziness and also from reading vain stories; our thoughts are changed to
good things." Many have expressed their appreciation and have frequently said: "I have learned much from your papers; they are full
of good things. In our temples there is so much that is bad and false.
Your papers show us what is right, and how to live right." The children
look for what they call "The Picture Paper." We are glad we can use
it so much for God in this great heathen India.

The following is from Miss Helen E. Robinson's report of the
Marathi edition:

The output has been reduced this year from five hundred to four hundred copies of eight pages a month, which means ninety-six pages of reading matter to prepare by way of translation, 4,800 copies or 38,400 printed pages to circulate during the year. We have had a cut for a frontispiece nearly every month. On the front cover is a permanent illustration and the ten commandments are printed on the back.

Cuts are as difficult to obtain as ever, so the thought has come to have 400 copies of a Perry picture to insert each month as a frontispiece and an article telling all about the picture. This will help solve the problem of illustrations.

Among the articles prepared this year were three on the persecutions of the early Roman Christians, including especially women martyrs. These were intended to teach the Hindu women readers personal love for Christ. We were glad to share with our readers the interesting account of the baptism of the Parsee, Rev. Dhanjibhoy Nowrojee, who is well known in Bombay. Many selections adapted to native minds have been taken from the Indian Ladies' Magazine and translated into Marathi. A few, but very few, of the articles came to the editor's mind by inspiration.

The rates are 8 annas a year for a single copy. Subscriptions to the paper have amounted to Rs, 14/8 this year. The paper is circulated in all parts of the Marathi field by different missions, but mostly in Bombay by our zenana workers. Some are sent to Marathi readers in Baroda and Hyderabad.

The Gujarat missionaries are calling for a fund for such a paper for their women. There is just as large a field in Bombay for a Gujarati as for a Marathi paper.

FINANCIAL STATEMENT ZENANA PAPER FUND.

October 1, 1906, balance.....................		$1,535 36
Received from Baltimore Branch....................	$87 50	
Received from Northwestern Branch.................	220 16	
Received from Topeka Branch.....................	60 00	
Received from interest on deposits.................	35 50	
Total receipts		$403 16
		$1,938 52
Remitted to Lucknow for four editions..............	$470 00	
Remitted to Bombay for Marathi edition............	250 00	
Total disbursements ....·........		$720 00
October 1, 1907, balance...........................		$1,218 52

MARY E. HOLT, *Treasurer.*

Reports of the Home Work.

BRANCH OFFICERS.

I. NEW ENGLAND BRANCH.

NEW ENGLAND STATES.

President—Mrs. John Legg, 5 Claremont St., Worcester, Mass.
Corresponding Secretary Emeritus—Mrs. L. A. Alderman, Hyde Park, Mass.
Corresponding Secretary—Miss Mary E. Holt, 4 Berwick Park, Boston, Mass.
Secretary of Home Department—Miss Clementina Butler, Newton Centre, Mass.
Recording Secretary—Mrs. A. H. Nazarian, Chelsea, Mass.
Treasurer—Mrs. B. T. Williston, 3 Monmouth St., Somerville, Mass.

II. NEW YORK BRANCH.

NEW YORK AND NEW JERSEY.

President—Mrs. S. L. Baldwin, 1218 Pacific St., Brooklyn, N. Y.
Corresponding Secretary—Mrs. J. M. Cornell, Twenty-sixth St. and Eleventh Ave., New York City.
Secretary of Home Department—Miss W. R. Lewis, 83 West Washington Place, New York City.
Recording Secretary—Mrs. J. H. Knowles, Room 401, 150 Fifth Ave., New York City.
Treasurer—Mrs. J. Sumner Stone, 1895 Madison Ave., New York City.

III. PHILADELPHIA BRANCH.

PENNSYLVANIA AND DELAWARE.

President—Miss Susan E. Lodge, 1720 Arch St., Philadelphia, Pa.
Corresponding Secretary—Miss Carrie J. Carnahan, Shady Ave., and Walnut St., Pittsburg, Pa.
Recording Secretary—Mrs. Amos Wakelin, 200 Bullitt Building, Philadelphia, Pa.
Treasurer—Mrs. T. H. Wilson, Lawnhurst, Fox Chase, Philadelphia, Pa.

IV. BALTIMORE BRANCH.

MARYLAND, DISTRICT OF COLUMBIA, VIRGINIA, NORTH CAROLINA, SOUTH CAROLINA, GEORGIA, AND FLORIDA.

President—Mrs. A. H. Eaton, 807 Arlington Ave., Baltimore, Md.
Corresponding Secretary Emeritus—Mrs. E. B. Stevens, Baltimore, Md.
Corresponding Secretary—Mrs. E. D. Huntley, "The Postner," Washington, D. C.

Secretary of Home Department—Mrs. S. A. Hill, 2513 Madison Ave., Baltimore, Md.
Recording Secretary—Mrs. D. C. Morgan, Bloomingdale Road, S. Walbrook, Baltimore, Md.
Treasurer—Mrs. J. S. Rawlings, 206 Woodlawn Road, Roland Park, Md.

V. CINCINNATI BRANCH.

OHIO, WEST VIRGINIA, KENTUCKY, TENNESSEE, ALABAMA, AND MISSISSIPPI.

President Emeritus—Mrs. Wm. B. Davis, Clifton, Cincinnati, O.
President—Mrs. A. J. Clarke, 925 Main St., Wheeling, W. Va.
Corresponding Secretary Emeritus—Mrs. B. R. Cowen, Walnut Hills, Cincinnati, O.
Corresponding Secretary—Mrs. R. L. Thomas, 792 East McMillan St., Cincinnati, O.
Secretary of Home Department—Mrs. J. Ellington McGee, Pleasant Ridge, O.
Recording Secretary—Mrs. L. L. Townley, 237 Burns Ave., Wyoming, O.
Treasurer—Mrs. J. C. Kunz, 511 Broadway, Cincinnati, O.

VI. NORTHWESTERN BRANCH.

ILLINOIS, INDIANA, MICHIGAN, AND WISCONSIN.

President Emeritus—Mrs. Isaac R. Hitt, Washington, D. C.
President—Mrs. A. W. Patten, 616 Foster St., Evanston, Ill.
Corresponding Secretary—Mrs. Frank P. Crandon, 1414 Forest Ave., Evanston, Ill.
Secretary of Home Department—Mrs. Charles W. Fowler, 208 Fremont St., Chicago, Ill.
Recording Secretary—Mrs. L. H. Jennings, 1460 Graceland Ave., Chicago, Ill.
Treasurer—Mrs. B. D. York, 231 Hancock Ave., West, Detroit, Mich.

VII. DES MOINES BRANCH.

IOWA, MISSOURI, ARKANSAS, AND LOUISIANA.

President—Miss Elizabeth Pearson, 1100 High St., Des Moines, Ia.
Corresponding Secretary—Mrs. William B. Thompson, 1018 Des Moines St., Des Moines, Ia.
Secretary of Home Department—Miss May Villa Patten, 406 Iowa Ave., Muscatine, Ia.
Recording Secretary—Mrs. J. I. Compton, 400 Wabash Ave., Kansas City, Mo.
Treasurer Emeritus—Mrs. E. K. Stanley, 1102 High St., Des Moines, Ia.
Treasurer—Mrs. W. H. Arnold, 1032 West Twentieth St., Des Moines, Ia.

VIII. MINNEAPOLIS BRANCH.

MINNESOTA, NORTH DAKOTA, AND SOUTH DAKOTA.

President—Mrs. W. H. Landis, 1505 Clinton Ave., Minneapolis, Minn.
Corresponding Secretary Emeritus—Mrs. C. S. Winchell, 113 State St., Minneapolis, Minn.
Corresponding Secretary—Mrs. F. F. Lindsay, 25 Seymour Ave., S. E., Minneapolis, Minn.
Recording Secretary—Mrs. A. J. Thorne, 628 Eighth Ave., S. E., Minneapolis, Minn.
Treasurer—Mrs. C. W. Hall, 3206 Second Ave., S., Minneapolis, Minn.

5

IX. TOPEKA BRANCH.

KANSAS, NEBRASKA, COLORADO, WYOMING, UTAH, NEW MEXICO, OKLAHOMA, AND TEXAS.

President—Mrs. EMMA A. IMBODEN, 215 North Emporia Ave., Wichita, Kan.

Corresponding Secretary—Miss ELLA M. WATSON, 1701 South Seventeenth St., Lincoln, Neb.

Recording Secretary—Mrs. MARY M. TORRINGTON, 203 Clay St., Topeka, Kan.

Treasurer—Mrs. I. E. McENTIRE, 704 Taylor St., Topeka, Kan.

X. PACIFIC BRANCH.

CALIFORNIA, NEVADA, ARIZONA, AND HAWAII.

President—Mrs. GEORGE B. SMYTH, 2605 Hearst Ave., Berkeley, Cal.

Corresponding Secretary—Mrs. S. F. JOHNSON, 520 Oakland Ave., Pasadena, Cal.

Associate Corresponding Secretary—Mrs. CHARLOTTE O'NEAL, 1460 N. Marengo Ave., Pasadena, Cal.

Recording Secretary—Mrs. J. R. UMSTED, 3036 Hoover St., Los Angeles, Cal.

Treasurer—Mrs. Z. L. PARMELEE, South Pasadena, Cal.

XI. COLUMBIA RIVER BRANCH.

MONTANA, IDAHO, WASHINGTON, AND OREGON.

President—Mrs. M. C. WIRE, Eugene, Ore.

Corresponding Secretary—Mrs. A. N. FISHER, 214 Twelfth St., Portland, Ore.

Recording Secretary—Mrs. W. H. SAYLOR, 871 South First St., Portland, Ore.

Treasurer—Miss NETTIE M. WHITNEY, 704 South First St., Tacoma, Wash.

HOME WORK.

The New England Branch has cause for profound thankfulness. The debt of nearly ten thousand dollars, which had been gradually accumulating for years, has been lifted. It was heroic to undertake this task and to raise the appropriations in one year, but the zeal of Miss Clara Cusham, who led the campaign, and the faith of the women enabled us to close the year with every item provided for. To do this we have taken all our reserve funds, and must follow with a strong advance the coming year if we are to reach our appropriations. Another red lettered item in the year's record is the munificent gift of $37,700 for the buildings for our work for children. This, together with the sum from the Conferences, brings us up to the million dollar line of receipts since our organization. New England Branch, therefore, feels the uplift of a glad achievement. God has done great things for us whereof we are glad.

There has been a small loss of membership of all our organizations, but we have a small gain of subscribers to the *Woman's Missionary Friend*. A strong effort will be put forth to remedy this condition. New members have been recruited through itinerary work and also a new crusade, which happily called upon the workers to greet Mrs. William Butler with a welcome from three hundred and twenty-six new members, a very delightful presentation. During the year, the Misses Danforth, Organ, Harvey, Young, Kneeland, and Glover have given the inspiration which only the missionary speaker can bring. Several of the pastors have helped royally in our district meetings which have been very successful. Our work was represented at thirteen camp-meetings and at all Conferences.

The Literature interests are prosperous, and our Depot of Supplies is proving its worth. The Little Light Bearers Life Memberships, made under the inspiration of Mrs. Harrison's visit, place us on the honor roll. Thirteen secured at one service and thirty-one at the Anniversary sets a record for some other Branch to meet. Mite box distributions come with renewed interest as a topic, for New England claims the record in this for the year with its box, which brought fifty-two dollars.

It has been the custom in this Branch to observe Good Friday as a day of prayer for this work. Last Easter this was overlooked by some Auxiliaries, to their loss we are sure; but in one case, at Trinity, Worcester, Mass, a Union meeting of all the Woman's Missionary Societies in the city brought bright representatives from eight different denominations together for a very blessed season of communion. So helpful was it that request has already been made for another such opportunity. We trust that our sacred day will be more fully kept next spring, for it has resulted in a glorious blessing to some of our Auxiliaries.

Zion's Herald continues to grant us a column once a month for notes and frequent opportunity for missionary letters. The secular press can be used to greater advantage, as seen in the reports of the offerings of our sister Church, the Protestant Episcopal, which furnished a column-long article in one of the leading Boston dailies on the gifts of the women at their triennial Conference.

Our number of missionaries have been increased by two this year. Immediately after General Executive, Dr. Belle J. Allen, formerly of Cincinnati Branch, was accepted by us, and in January sailed for India to take up the medical work at Baroda and to superintend the erection of the Mrs. William Butler Memorial Hospital. The funds for her outgoing were furnished by a personal friend. The corner-stone of the hospital was laid in December last, and the erection of the building is now in progress.

In August, Miss Clara P. Dyer, a teacher of several years' experience and an earnest Bible student and Sunday-school worker, sailed for China. She has probably been appointed to Chang Li. Miss Glover returned to this place last spring after a year's furlough. We had expected that Dr. Terry would soon return home because of ill-health, but recent word has come that she may be transferred to Tai An in the hope that the change of climate will be beneficial.

Miss Ruddick, after six years in India, came home last winter and is now with us. Miss Young has also returned for a much needed rest, and Miss Knowles is still unable to take up the work in Darjeeling, which is her great desire. Miss Harvey, having regained her health and strength, will probably sail for India in November. Miss Organ expects to arrive in Bombay early in November, and will probably go immediately to Budaon to enter upon evangelistic work in that district. A friend has generously contributed the necessary funds to send Miss Kneeland to her old field of labor in Rosario, South America.

The great Juggernaut cars in India have immense ropes with which they are dragged forth in triumph procession. Not one score of men could pull these structures, nor one hundred, but everybody who can get near is allowed to take a hand, and the crowd rushes to pull till the great wheels creak and turn and the idol rides on in triumph. We need to secure the co-operation of every woman in Methodism to share in our great endeavor.

This is our Branch aim—not one Christian woman without a share in the magnificent toil which is to bring in the kingdom of our Lord and His Christ. MARY E. HOLT, *Corresponding Secretary.*

TREASURER'S REPORT, 1906-1907.

Balance, October 1, 1906	$676 73
Annuity Fund, previously reported	1,343 78
Receipts, October 1, 1906, to October 1, 1907	84,320 88
Total	$86,341 39
Disbursements	60,836 35
	$25,505 04
Investment of Annuity Funds	1,509 78
Balance, October 1, 1907	$23,995 26

BELLE A. WILLISTON, *Treasurer.*

NEW YORK BRANCH.

This past year New York Branch has come into closer touch with our work through the visits of some of its members to the foreign field. Our Branch Treasurer visited most of our missions in Eastern Asia as well as in India, while our Home Secretary gave five months to a study of missions in India.

It has made us half believe that our own eyes have seen the wonderful growth of God's Kingdom in the lands beyond the seas.

Early in the year the President of our Branch prepared a special appeal for the China Centennial, sending it with a personal note to every Auxiliary President. Through the kindness of Bishop Bashford interesting literature was circulated, which, together with the work of Miss Hughes and Dr. Stone, we hope will result in doubling, before July, 1908, the $8,000 already received.

The first quarter of our year was discouraging. In January two of our members prepared a Prayer Cycle, calling the Branch to united prayer every Thursday, giving a specific object for each week until midsummer, appealing for definite needs in the foreign stations in turn, as well as for the large needs in the home land, if we are to begin to measure up to our opportunities.

Our treasury shows a small increase; but as much of the money has been given for special objects, we close the year with a small balance in bank, but a large indebtedness to special Thank-offering gifts. Our Heavenly Father has wonderfully answered the earnest prayers and work for the last few months in granting us the largest receipts for this fourth quarter that have ever come into our treasury in any other three months in its history.

Our Field Secretary and ten missionaries at home have made 368 addresses, adding many new members and $5,000 to our receipts.

Our young women have come to realize that they can not live without intelligent leadership, and on March 14th gave themselves to united prayer for leaders. They rejoice in being able to report an increase in interest and, consequently, in members. There have been Young People's Rallies in connection with a number of District Meetings. The average contribution has risen in two years from seventy-eight cents to $1.08 per member. These young women now support seven missionaries and four assistants who have been trained in America. In Genesee Conference they have also given all the hospital supplies for their Dr. Li Bi Cu. To the $1,200 given last year for the Mary Porter Gamewell School in Peking, our young women have added through their Thank-offering another thousand dollars, including one hundred dollars to name a "Bashford" Room. Eight hundred copies of missionary letters have been distributed. District Superintendents are showing increased efficiency, giving watchful care to the new organizations.

The Secretary of *Children's Work* reports 112 King's Heralds and Junior League Bands and 118 Little Light Bearers Circles; eighteen new Life Members; five Societies on the Honor Roll.

At the Silver Bay Student Conference the Secretary of the Philadelphia Branch and the New York Branch Treasurer represented our Society. They found forty-four Methodist girls living within the bounds of the New York Branch, eight of whom were volunteers for foreign work.

Although our registration at Northfield Summer School for Missions was not large as compared with other Societies, we feel greatly encouraged by the impression made upon those who attended. The young women, under the leadership of the Branch Secretary of Young People's Work, gained a new vision of missions, and gave themselves in deeper consecration to the work.

Our missionary family has experienced some changes. Miss Davison, of Nagasaki, and Miss Deavitt, of Kiukiang, have changed their sphere of usefulness, while four new workers have entered our ranks. Immediately after the Executive Meeting in Omaha Miss Welthy Honsinger sailed for China and her work in the school at Nanchang. Miss Alice Powell followed in December, spending some months at Nanking until transferred in July to Peking, where her training was more needed for the new Union Nurses Training School.

The first of January Miss Sophia Coffin started for Africa to help Miss Swormstedt in the rapidly growing girls' school at Old Umtali, while in March Miss Alice McKinney joined the small corps of teachers in the big school in Callao, Peru.

During the early summer Miss Lula Miller from Chemulpo, Miss Grace Travis and Miss Phebe Wells from Foochow, and Miss Gheer from Nagasaki, came home for their needed furloughs.

Refreshed and strengthened workers have returned to their fields during the year, Miss LeHuray to Buenos Ayres to hunt for a new home for her disturbed school, Miss Estey to Northern Korea, Miss Linam to her Woman's Training School in Iong Bing, Miss Plumb to her Boarding School in Foochow, going with a lonely heart without the mother whose blessed companionship had meant so much to her in Foochow, Miss Atkinson to another department of work in Yokohama, as fire had consumed the old school at Nagoya and with it all her earthly possessions. New York also gladly claims Miss Baucus, who, with Miss Dickinson, has returned to their literary work in Japan.

Our Branch Annual Meeting was one of unusual power. Coming together for the first time as a delegated body, the women seemed to feel their responsibility and the trust reposed in them and gave themselves heartily to the work of the hour. The closing exercises were marked by deep spirituality and the delegates returned to their homes in a spirit of earnest determination to follow more closely than ever their God's command to carry the story of His love to the uttermost parts of the earth.   SARAH K. CORNELL, *Corresponding Secretary.*

TREASURER'S REPORT.

Balance on hand, October 1, 1906........................... $573 94
Receipts for the year, closing September 30, 1907............ 96,746 83

Total $97,320 77
Disbursements for the year............................... 97,288 17

Balance on hand, October 1, 1907........................ $32 60
                         KATE E. STONE, *Treasurer.*

PHILADELPHIA BRANCH.

"Thus saith Jehovah, Let not the wise man glory in his wisdom, neither let the mighty man glory in his might, let not the rich man glory in his riches:

"But let him that glorieth glory in this, that he hath understanding and knoweth me, that I am Jehovah, who exerciseth lovingkindness, justice, and righteousness in the earth: for in these things I delight, saith Jehovah."—Jer. ix, 23-24.

For another year it has been the privilege of the members of Philadelphia Branch to make the God "who delighteth in lovingkindness" known in the dark places of the earth, and in the habitations of cruelty.

Our hearts rejoice in the certain knowledge that God has been caring for us and our work through the year, and at times when our perplexities have been greatest His care has been most clearly shown and we praise Him for it.

The work of our missionaries—our representatives— has been blessed, souls have been won to Christ, and the coming of His kingdom brought nearer, while we on the home side have found it a privilege and a blessing to be co-workers with Him and them.

We rejoice that our Treasurer's report shows an increase over last year. This increase is due to bequests and money placed with us on the annuity plan. The growth of the work on the foreign field makes necessary a steady increase in our income.

Two of the sad things which have come to us during the year are the resignations of Mrs. W. H. Pearce, our Home Secretary, who, because of removal from our Branch territory, finds it impossible to continue in office; and Mrs. P. P. Stravinske, who for many years has been our faithful and efficient Secretary of Young People's and Children's Work. Frail health and many home cares do not permit her to retain this office. The good she has done this year is shown in part in the fine increase in organizations and membership among our King's Heralds and Little Light Bearers. At the recent Branch meeting Miss Ina Wilhelm, of Franklin, Pa., was elected in her stead.

Miss Minerva Guthaphel, who returned from Korea broken in health, has sufficiently recovered to be appointed Field Secretary for the Branch for the coming year.

One new missionary has gone to the field since last Executive Meeting—Miss Margaret D. Crouse, now stationed at Baroda, India.

We have three desirable candidates, two of whom will take additional training in Folts Institute. The third is prevented by the illness of her mother from going to the field at present.

We are glad to have Miss Mary E. Williams home again after her busy years in Baroda. The many patrons scattered throughout the Branch who support scholarships in the Orphanage will be glad to hear of the work through her.

* Dr. Rachel Benn is now en route home, stopping to visit mission stations along the way. And Miss Matilda Spencer will soon return. Both have well earned their furlough.

We sympathize with the Misses Cook, of Guanajuato, Mexico, because of the ill-health of Miss Celinda Cook, which makes necessary their resignation.

Our hearts have ached at the word which has come from our missionaries in Nagoya and Hakodate, Japan. Miss Soper, who was not well, was away from Nagoya at the time of the fire there, but lost all her possessions except the little she had with her in her steamer trunk. At Hakodate, in the last great fire, Misses Dickerson and Sprowles, and their co-worker, Miss Hampton, were even more seriously distressed by almost complete loss of all personal property.

All in attendance at our Branch meeting, held in Sewickley, were interested and benefited. The speaker of the first evening was Mrs. Mary Carr Curtis, who told us of the work in Malaysia. Miss Williams, of India; Miss Palacios, of Mexico, and Miss Guthaphel, of Korea, made an interesting program the second evening.

The review of the Branch Annual Report by a Conference Secretary impressed with all its value. The question drawer, conducted by the Editor of the *Branch Quarterly,* was helpful to us all. Among other interesting features of the meeting was the introduction of the President of the banner Auxiliary—in the matter of membership—in Philadelphia Branch. This President has been largely instrumental in bringing this increase to pass, and for quite a period of time was successful in getting five new members a day. When introduced, she stated that they had 274 members and twenty on her waiting list. When asked what was meant by her waiting list, she replied, "Twenty available women in the Church who are just waiting for me to ask them to join."

In Pittsburg Conference this is to be an anniversary year. Our well-beloved Conference Secretary, Mrs. Van Kirk, is entering on her twenty-fifth year of service for the Woman's Foreign Missionary Society. The battle cry throughout the Conference will be fifty thousand dollars this year—this will mean one hundred per cent increase in funds, and we hope to reach this rate of increase in our membership.

We enter the New Year with courage and looking unto Him who is able to make all grace abound toward us, and who will supply all our needs if we be willing and obedient workers.

CARRIE J. CARNAHAN.

TREASURER'S REPORT.

Receipts from Conferences	$57,565 40
Annuities	2,500 00
Bequests, special gifts, etc.	5,916 19
Total	$65,981 59
Balance, October 1, 1906	13,214 35
Grand total	$79,195 94
Disbursements	68,586 59
Balance, October 1, 1907	$10,609 35

MRS. THOMAS H. WILSON, Treasurer.

BALTIMORE BRANCH.

Ruskin says: "If you do not wish for the coming of Christ's kingdom, do not pray for it; but if you do wish it you must do more than pray for it; you must work for it!" The Baltimore Branch has worked and prayed and is steadily progressing, notwithstanding its decreased territorial limits.

The South land is giving to us its gold; from the coast States we have received the past year over $500. At each of our four Quarterly Meetings the appeals for patrons for special work have met with a generous response. The Lord has answered our prayers in opening the hearts of our people to their great privilege. During the year we have missed the counsel of our Secretary Emeritus, Mrs. E. B. Stevens, but before another Executive we will be richer in facts, because of the thrilling stories she will bring to us of India and its needs. Emerson says, "Nature arms each man with some faculty which enables him to do easily some feat impossible to any other." With that thought before us we have endeavored to put the right woman in the right place in our Branch work.

The young people are organizing themselves into District Associations with a full list of officers, a stepping-stone for the larger opportunity for the future.

The Little Light Bearers are doing good work, and the smiling faces of eight little Baltimore babies greet us from the pages of our *Children's Missionary Friend.*

The number of organizations has been slightly increased. It is refreshing to find pastors who wish you to come and organize the women of their Churches into Auxiliaries. Evidently those men know their Churches will be stronger and better equipped for all kinds of Church work, because of this company of consecrated, intelligent women.

The individuals supporting Special Work have increased, and much of this is due to the fact that our dear missionaries have been giving us such vivid pictures of the needs through their letters-that we have been compelled to help just a little more.

The home workers have been encouraged to larger activity, and they have listened to the thrilling words of Mrs. Mary Curtis who gave one month of the work on the Washington District; and the need as pictured by our dear Miss Harvey has put into our treasury many a dollar. The glimpse given by Miss Sullivan of the great work at Pithoragarh will not easily be effaced.

Miss Florence Plumb attended one meeting in the Washington District, and her appeal for day schools materialized in a financial way sufficiently to care for one school, and a typewriting machine was given to her for her use when she should return to Foochow.

The "Woman's College" of Baltimore had nine delegates at "Silver Bay Convention," and the Branch was well represented at "Northfield;" wonderful places for our young people to gather inspiration and needed information for intelligent work for the Master.

Our Church paper, the *Baltimore Methodist*, has offered to give the Woman's Foreign Missionary Society space every other week for one thousand words of missionary information. Through this medium we expect to reach the outlying districts and scatter the news that comes from the foreign field. Mrs. S. A. Hill has been elected editor.

Three bequests have come to us during the year, one of $500 from Mrs. B. F. Bennett, and another of $400, given in memory of Miss Ada Fowler by her father, and the third from Mrs. Robert Magaw. This last is not available at present. The gift includes three houses, to two of which the Woman's Foreign Missionary Society have the deeds. These two houses are to be sold when a purchaser can be found, and the proceeds to be devoted to a memorial for Mr. and Mrs. Robert Magaw. The third house is given in trust, the income to be paid to the legatee during her life, and the Woman's Foreign Missionary Society to inherit it at her death.

During the year we have sent out two missionaries to the foreign field, Miss Sarah B. Hallman to Pyeng Yang, Korea, as a trained nurse. She is adapting herself beautifully to conditions and will be able to assist by her practical ideas in the rebuilding of the hospital. Miss Edna Jones was accepted at the May meeting and sailed September 10th for Foochow, China, to take charge of the Mary E. Crook Memorial.

Miss Ruth Robinson has returned to India after a year of study in the home land. Mrs. Susan A. Tippet is still at home seeking health and strength, hoping she may some day return to the work she loves and the little ones who call her "mother."

> "Not to the strong is the battle,
> Not to the swift is the race,
> But to the true and the faithful
> Victory is promised through Grace."

TREASURER'S REPORT.

Balance, October, 1906	$5,463 85
Receipts for year closing October, 1907	18,814 87
Total	$24,278 72
Disbursements	19,396 06
Balance, October, 1907	$4,882 66

MRS. J. L. RAWLINGS, *Treasurer.*

CINCINNATI BRANCH.

The Cincinnati Branch began and closed the year with a deficit of more than five thousand dollars, and while we wish this deficit was a thing of the past and not a burden to be met this present year, yet we come with hearts full of praise and gratitude to our Heavenly Father for His goodness to us and for His blessing upon our work.

When we remember that we began the year with a deficit; that our appropriations were two thousand dollars less than the actual cost of our foreign work, leaving nothing for running expenses at home, nothing for emergencies, nothing for sending out new missionaries; that the natural increase of our work was very heavy, because of the increase of living in the mission fields; that we were morally obligated to assume about five thousand dollars on the pro rata plan; when we remember all this, then realize that God has enabled us to meet an increased appropriation and our home expenses; that we have sent out two new missionaries and met the emergencies caused by fire, disease, and famine, that we have paid more than three thousand dollars of our pro rata appropriations; that we have given outside of our appropriations, through the generosity of the members of the North Ohio Conference, more than eight hundred dollars to Mrs. Eddy, of Poona, for necessary repairs in the school,—and through the liberality of Mrs. W. A. Gamble, five thousand dollars to the new school building in Puebla, Mexico; five thousand dollars for a Rest Home for the missionaries of the South India Conference; one thousand to purchase the lot adjoining the Training School in Foochow and long coveted by our missionaries; that we have built the needed addition to our Moradabad School at a cost of four hundred dollars; that we have given five hundred dollars to Budaon, and have built the Gate House at Chemulpo, Korea; and that she has made it possible, by advancing money, to give a new home to our workers in Dwarahat and lifted the debt on the Nagasaki land, which was a heavy burden to Miss Russell; and when we come with an advance of more than seventeen thousand dollars, the largest amount, by far, ever raised, by the Cincinnati Branch, do you not feel like saying, "O sing unto the Lord a new song: for He hath done marvelous things: His right hand and His holy arm, hath gotten Him the victory." For indeed, "This is the Lord's doing; and it is marvelous in our eyes!"

The special meetings at headquarters will long be remembered, because of the power of the Spirit. Though both the Day of Prayer and Thank-offering Day were stormy, yet all who braved the rain were well repaid, and returned to their homes conscious of having been in God's presence. At the latter meeting we enjoyed having with us the Recording Secretary of General Executive meeting, but who still belongs to us—Mrs. C. W. Barnes—who delivered an inspiring address on China. Miss Hillman, of Korea; Miss Plumb, of China, and Misses Scott and Kemper, of India, made "our hearts burn within us" as they told of the needs and success of our work in their respective fields.

Our Branch Annual Meeting was one of the best for years. From the first session—the Standard Bearers' Meeting, with Dr. Theodore Henderson, of New York City, as speaker, which closed with an altar service, on one side of which were the workers, who were willing to give not "other people's children," but their own daughters to the Lord for foreign work, and on the other, the young people, who would dedicate their lives to God for service—to the closing session, which ended with a consecration service—it was a sweet, inspiring meeting. The anniversary address, unusually fine, was delivered by Dr. J. G. Vaughan, Secretary of the Chinese Centennial Fund, and the last evening we spent listening to the needs of Korea, China, India, Japan, and Malaysia, as told by returned missionaries.

The Week of Prayer and Self-Denial, while not observed throughout the Branch, was a great spiritual blessing to those Auxiliaries who gathered that week to pray for our work.

The loyal Conference Secretaries have been tireless in their efforts to advance the work, and were ably seconded by their District officers and their devoted constituency, and to these workers is due much of the success of this year.

Our new Secretary of Home Department, Mrs. J. E. McGee, coming to us an entire stranger, has won her way into our hearts by her faithfulness and the able way in which she has handled the home side of the work,—ever of growing importance to-day, when our income does not advance with the growth of our foreign work.

One important step that she has inaugurated is for the young people of the Cincinnati District. This is a complete District organization for the young people, corresponding to the District organization for Auxiliaries. She has also arranged for two contests for the young people. One, an amount of money, which will be invested in a scholarship or an evangelist teacher, to be given to the Young Woman's Society, whether Standard Bearer, Young Woman's Missionary Society, or King's Daughters, having the best exhibit at the next Annual Meeting: the other, a Missionary Study Reference Library of nine volumes, to be presented to the member writing the best article of not more than fifteen hundred words on the subject, "Why I Believe in Foreign Missions."

Mrs. C. R. Houston, the Branch Superintendent of Young People's Work, having worked until the last helping in the preparations for the Branch Annual Meeting, was taken ill, two days previous to the opening session, with typhoid fever. We missed her hearty welcome, and accepted her resignation with great regret. She loves young women, and there is no better society than the one she personally leads in her own Church. Miss Mary I. Scott, of Moundsville, W. Va., was elected to fill her place. We welcome her to our ranks and pray God to bless her, as she is called to assume charge of this most important part of our work with all of its latent possibilities.

Two of our Standard Bearers' Societies gave the first gifts to the Chinese Centennial Fund. The Westwood and St. Paul Standard Bearers, each giving one hundred dollars to the debt on the Peking School, thereby naming a room. There has been a gain of ten new Societies.

The Cincinnati Branch is favored in having Mrs. J. F. Fisher as Superintendent of her children. The indefatigable work of last year has been continued; several charming leaflets and letters having been prepared for the children. A missionary of their own—Miss Jessie Marker, of Korea—has been selected, and her name has become a household word, and her face seen upon the dollar, which was the happy thought of the leader to raise her salary, is a well-known picture to the little ones. She reports an increase of 75 new Societies, 31 new life members, and a gain of 243 new subscribers to the *Children's Missionary Friend.* Total number of children in *new* Societies, 1,275.

Miss Glenna Myers, in charge of our Special Work, has been most faithful and the work has constantly increased. We are indebted for this growth to our faithful missionaries, who have been prompt in sending the patrons' letters. We reluctantly accepted Miss Myers' resignation. We welcome to this office Mrs. Emma Moore Scott, of India, who thoroughly understands the importance of this work.

Mrs. Phillip Roettinger, who has so ably served the Branch as President for three years, felt compelled to lay down the work, but we know that she will have the same faithful interest in this work so dear to her heart. We welcome as leader of the Cincinnati Branch Mrs. A. J. Clark, of Wheeling, W. Va., who in the shadow of a great sorrow is putting aside her own grief to faithfully minister to other sorrowful ones across the seas. May the blessed promise given to the new leader, Joshua, abide with her all the year!

A great disappointment came to us in April when Miss Kemper, our Field Secretary, was compelled to resign, as we had counted upon her success as an organizer to make possible the increased income so much needed.

The Depot of Supplies has had the best year of its history: more letters received, more visitors, and increased sales of more than two hundred dollars over last year.

The number of missionaries remain the same—Miss McHose, because of continued ill-health has withdrawn from our ranks, and dear Lois Buck has been transferred from her work in India to her eternal work in the heavenly home.

Two new recruits, Miss Lulu C. Baker and Miss Millie May Albertson, have been sent to Hing Hua, China, and Seoul, Korea. The Branch is greatly indebted to Broad Street Auxiliaries, Ohio Conference, for the most generous outfit provided for Miss Albertson. Miss Eva Hardie has been very ill and will be returned as soon as she is able to travel. Miss Mary Thomas was seriously ill in our hospital in Foochow from October till March, when she returned to Hing Hua, and though far from well, undertook to remain until the close of the school, when she was hurried to Japan, where she still lingers, hoping to recover her health. Miss Cody has just passed through a serious operation in Tokyo, but the latest news assures us that she has passed the danger point and is on the road to recovery. Misses Fannie Scott, Luella Anderson, and Leonora Seeds still linger in the home land, waiting the necessary health certificate, which will permit them to return to their fields of labor. While waiting, as far as health and strength permitted, they did effective itinerant work in our Branch.

Miss Mary Hillman has given herself most steadily to the upbuilding of the work while she waits for opportunity to return to Korea. We have loaned her, during the year, to the Topeka, Des Moines, Philadelphia, and Minneapolis Branches. Miss Lucy Sullivan has been a willing helper during her furlough. She returns to India in November.

Cincinnati Branch reports 719 Auxiliaries with 19,199 members, and 2,837 subscribers to *Woman's Missionary Friend*, a gain of 24 Auxiliaries, 539 members, and 71 subscribers to *The Friend*, also a *Quarterly*, ably edited by Mrs. Chas. Burkam, which seems almost indispensable to the members of our Branch.

We close the year, realizing that our earnest efforts have not given us an income sufficient to meet the needs of our growing work, but we go forward, trusting God, who has helped us in the past, to bless and prosper us until we meet the sum given to us as our watchword—one hundred thousand dollars for Cincinnati Branch.

Mrs. R. L. Thomas, *Corresponding Secretary.*

TREASURER'S REPORT.

Balance on hand (Special Fund), October 9, 1906	$14,385	36
Total receipts	88,695	53
Grand total	$103,080	89
Total disbursement	97,235	64
Balance on hand (Special Fund), October 9, 1907	$5,845	25

Mrs. John C. Kunz, *Receiving Treasurer.*
Mrs. Chas. C. Boyd, *Disbursing Treasurer.*

NORTHWÉSTERN BRANCH.

A comprehensive view of the Home side of Northwestern's march of progress shows that the great bulk of influence is *forward.*

. Interdenominational mission study classes have multiplied, and serve to stimulate intelligent interest in world-wide evangelism. .

Summer Conferences have afforded not only bodily recuperation, but, sustained as they are, by all Boards, they help to fix serious life purpose, do things scientifically, and get *"key"* young people. These significant occasions merit emphasis, because leaders, competent and effective, are in demand everywhere, and seem to be essential to growth. Hence, the farthest reaching work is that which develops, unifies, and promotes the unlimited possibilities in our younger people.

The Standard Bearers have rallied splendidly and are especially well equiped by the *Standard Bearer's Handbook,* prepared and issued by Mrs. D. C. Cook, Secretary of Young People's Work. *The Mystery Box* is another item in *"First Things,"* to which Mrs. R. E. Clark, Secretary of Literature, has given a compelling persuasion to detailed reading of the *Woman's Missionary Friend.* At the Branch meeting, the *Daily Bulletin,* published under the direction of Mrs. R. O. Irish, gave unique and gratifying means of recording the progress of affairs at the largest gathering of women for religious work in the country. The *April Council* has become a fixture and, with a Wall Chart of Statistics, completes this year's list of *"First things."* .

The spiritual atmosphere was deeply felt in the appropriation and closing services, and particularly emphasized by the remarkable fact that the business was despatched with such celerity that an hour ahead of a full schedule marked the close of affairs and the blessed time thus gained was spent in earnest prayer.

At the beginning of the year the superintendence of Special Work, which fell from the hands of the sainted Mrs. H. B. Prentice, was undertaken by Mrs. John A. Scott. Scarcely had her devotion to the work been shown when an almost utter collapse made another transfer necessary. Mrs. William Bock, a former District Secretary in Illinois Conference, brings experience to her appointment to the arduous task. With this exception the ranks of officers have remained in service the entire year.

We must take occasion at this time to express our appreciation of the work done in the last two years by our retiring Home Secretary, Mrs. Stephen J. Herben. Notwithstanding the disability under which she has labored, she has given time and strength gladly and unreservedly to her duties. She has broadened the view of the world's needs by reports of the meetings of the Branch Executive Committee sent to Conference Secretaries and Treasurers; by thousands of foreign letters mimeographed and sent to the Auxiliaries, together with frequent interchange of letters with Branch, Conference, District, and Auxiliary officers. We rejoice that, though she may accept no official rank or title, she will still be ready with her willing heart and able pen to do whatever may come to her hands to do. Mrs. C. W. Fowler, who becomes Home Secretary, has been Rock River Conference Secretary for several years, · and will continue to bring her best gifts for service in the larger field to which she has been called.

The Committee on Literature has touched high water mark, and report through Mrs. Burke 3,722 Study Books sold, besides a vast amount of miscellaneous literature, representing an aggregate of $1,675.

Total organization number 2,345, a decided gain, while membership in all organizations is 60,619. The financial returns of $152,952 marks an increase of $17,000 over appropriations.

Five missionaries are at home on furlough—Miss Bohannon, Miss Heaton, Miss Mabel Seeds, Mrs. Van Petten, and Dr. Lewis. Miss Abbott expects to return early in October to her work in India.

The heart of Methodism is not stingy, but the controlling head is not yet filled with the facts that open wide the purses and increase provisions by making bequests and by proportionate gifts from the vast sums now controlled by Methodist women.

The day of small things is past, and the marvelous growth afar necessitates a decided advance in receipts, as well as an increase in the number of active working members, who will work and work hard.

But neither of these needs constitutes our greatest want. The ever present and most imperious need of our Society is for the prayers of all our members. Samuel Mills, in praying for foreign missions, took as his motto: "We can do it if we will." At the last meeting of the American Board, a company of India's missionaries sent this message: "We can and we will, if you will what you can to make India Christ's." The President of the Board, in his closing words, said: "Let us leave out the word 'and' and say, 'We will, we can.'" Are we ready to make this pledge?

"Then, by and by," says John R. Mott, "we shall have the vision of the great multitude, whom no man can number, out of all nations, from all tribes and tongues and kindreds, standing before the throne and before the Lamb, clothed with white robes or with palms in their hands, shouting with a loud voice 'Salvation unto God, and unto the Lamb that sitteth upon the throne.'"

> "For lo! there dawns a yet more glorious day,
> The saints triumphant rise in bright array,
> The King of Glory passes on His way,
>   Alleluia."
>   MRS. T. P. CRANDON, *Corresponding Secretary.*

TREASURER'S REPORT.

Balance in General Fund October 1, 1906......	$11,936 54	
Total Receipts for the year 1906-7.............	152,952 46	
Grand total		$164,889 00
Transferred to Annuity Fund	$6,000 00	
Transferred to Invested Fund	1,700 00	
Transferred to Nind Evangelistic Fund	342 60	
Total transferred		8,042 60
General Fund		$156,846 40
Total Disbursements for 1906-7		145,729 33
Balance in General Fund, October 1, 1907...		$11,117 07

                        MRS. BERTRAND D. YORK,
                        MRS. LAURA C. DUNN,
                                Treasurers.

DES MOINES BRANCH.

The brief twelve-month since our last Annual Meeting has been marked by cheering gains at every point—in membership, in subscriptions to *The Friends,* in the placing of Special Work, in receipts, and in new missionaries. The blessing of our Divine Leader has been vouchsafed to our loyal, hard-working, harmonious sisterhood in the Des Moines Branch. When one sees well-tilled fields covered over with golden grain one needs not to be told that not only has the diligent husbandman wrought early and late, but that the heavens have not withheld the sunshine and the showers. So has it been with our good field.

Two or three special gifts aggregating between seven and eight thousand dollars have cheered us. One of these, the gift of five thousand dollars from Mrs. Mary A. Knotts, of Kansas City, made possible the immediate inauguration of the building enterprise at Vikarabad, India, for school, which is to bear her name.

At this station a singular condition obtains. Instead of the usual slow-moving operations of the Orient, the push and energy of a business-like contractor are rather disconcerting us, and we find that we, too, must move promptly in the providing of funds. The experience is at least refreshing for its novelty.

Since the outgoing of new missionaries in immediate connection with last Annual Meeting, two others have gone—Miss Crawford, to Manila in the spring, and Miss Robinson, recently with Miss Rigby, to Burma. Two others will soon go—Misses Liers and Boddy, to Central Provinces, India, and to North China. The year has been one of strange vicissitudes as regards our missionaries in the field. The weariness wrought by long bearing of heavy burdens placed four of these upon the home-leave list for regular furloughs—Misses Ogborn, Bobenhouse, Elicker, and Dr. Edmonds—while immediate danger to health brought to us Miss Wilson, Dr. Stone, and Miss Newby. Dr. Stone, having accomplished already a good recovery, sailed in September to return to her inspiring hospital work in Kiu Kiang. Miss Hyde, of Jubbalpore, India, after several years of splendid service, chiefly in the Orphanage, was married in July to Dr. F. R. Felt, of the Missionary Society.

The Conference session last winter in this same city was marked by a deep sorrow in the death of one of our faithful missionaries, Miss Susanna Stumpf. Her first years had been spent in the work at Calcutta, and then at her own urgent request she was sent to Jagdalpur, far away in the jungle. She believed in her devoted heart that it was here the Lord of the harvest had appointed her for service. Her heart and her letters were weighted with the needs of the women and girls of this vast field. At the close of her brief year at this station she had gone to Jabbalpore for the Conference session, when, after a very few days of illness (which seemed at first not serious), she was suddenly translated. She sleeps in a beautiful spot in the English cemetery, but she will wake when it is morning.

This year has also recorded the death of her who was the earliest representative of the Society from the great trans-Mississippi region—Mrs. Gamewell, Mary Q. Porter, of Davenport, Iowa. Hers was a long and notable missionary career, dating back to 1871. The people of her long-ago Iowa home have been pleased to gather a goodly sum, which they are contributing to her memorial in Peking.

The Annual Meeting, always a rich feast, was at its recent session characterized by unusual blessing. The Secretary was compelled to miss the greater part of the meeting, but this refreshing note is furnished by one in attendance: "The presence of the Holy Spirit recognized from the first session. One service long to be remembered was that called to meet in the gallery at the close of an afternoon session. Its object, as stated, was prayer for the revival spirit upon the women of the Branch, to begin in our own hearts. All fell upon their knees before God and a real Pentecost came upon us. Hearts long burdened were able to cast all their care upon Him. Outgoing imssionaries 'received power because the Holy Ghost came upon them.' All saw anew the blessed Master's work and were anointed for renewed effort. Our hearts greatly rejoice."

The year, so filled with its varied experiences, its lights and shadows, is gone "as a tale that is told." Because its blessings were so rich, so bounteous, we look forward to the year to come with confident expectation of the mercies "new every morning and fresh every evening," "For this God is our God forever. He will be our guide even unto death."

MRS. WILLIAM B. THOMPSON,
Corresponding Secretary.

TREASURER'S REPORT.

Receipts $67,420 97
Disbursements 65,983 93

Balance October 1, 1907 .... $1,437 04

MRS. W. H. ARNOLD, *Treasurer.*

MINNEAPOLIS BRANCH.

The Minneapolis Branch stands to-day in the shadow of inexpressible grief and loss. Our beloved leader, trusted counselor, devoted friend, was suddenly called September 28th from service to reward. For six successive years Mrs. Carrie W. Joyce has led our forces through much of conflict, ever on to victory. From personal observation and · study of our various mission fields she knew the needs and sympathized with the brave workers at the front as few in the home land are able to do. And so when appeals for help came to us her great, loving heart could not but respond. She had seen the white harvest fields in many a land; had seen the few gleaners there breaking under the heavy burdens they were carrying, and so it came to pass that during her six years as Secretary of this small Branch she found and placed . fifteen new missionaries in the field, and although the annual receipts increased each year so as to be nearly doubled in the six years, yet they failed to keep pace with expenditures, and we come to the close of the year with an empty treasury and heavier indebtedness than we have ever known before.

Six new missionaries have been sent out the past year. Three of them left during the last session of the General Executive Committee. Miss Alice Brethorst was sent to our farthest outpost in China—so far that she was seventeen weeks and three days on the way. So few are the workers and so great the need there that even while studying the language she had to serve as nurse, doctor, and· evangelist. With her Miss Rank sailed‾ for Singapore to relieve Miss Blackmore, and Miss Ilien Tang to her beloved work in China. A few months later Miss Stixrud reached the Philippines and began her work in Dagupan, and September 13th, just two weeks before Mrs. Joyce went home, Miss Jessie Brooks and Miss Marianna Sutton sailed for Malaysia to re-enforce the work there.

We record with gratitude the fact that though the Death Angel has been busy in the ranks at home all of our .workers in the field have been kept in health and safety.

Miss Blackmore, who has given eighteen years of successful service, left in April for a year's furlough and rest in her Australian home. This is her third furlough since entering our service. All other members of our field staff have been· doing excellent work at various stations in India, Burma, China, Japan, Malaysia, and the Philippines.

At home we have prosecuted the work under many difficulties and close the year with serious losses of officers. Our Branch Recording Secretary has removed to California, our Agent of Supplies to Seattle, and Secretary of Standard Bearers to another State. Our Home Secretary has been obliged to lay down her work, as also has the Secretary of the Swedish Conference.

But the message to Israel after the removal of their great leader: "Have I not commanded thee? Be strong and of a good courage; be not afraid, neither be thou dismayed; for the Lord thy God is with thee whithersoever thou goest," was taken as our watchword, and under its inspiration and the help and guidance of our Divine Leader the Minneapolis Branch will keep step with you in the conquest of the world for Christ.

Especial mention should be made of the help given us during the year in the brief itineraries made by Mrs. Willma Rouse Keene, Misses Anderson and Hillman, of the Cincinnati Branch, and Miss Parkes, of the Pacific Branch. The last two were greatly appreciated at the recent Conference anniversaries and at the Branch Annual Meeting. We also gladly acknowledge our indebtedness to Dr. Mary Stone and Miss Jennie Hughes, who spent ten days in our Branch en route to the coast, and gave several addresses, thrilling their audiences with the wonderful story of the work being done for women at Kiu Kiang.

We rejoice to know that our greatly prized organ, the *Woman's Missionary Friend,* is reaching more readers than ever before, and shows an increase of eighty-eight subscriptions, lacking only six of our proportion of the number needed to make the desired thirty thousand.

The *Frauen Missions Freund* also shows a marked increase, while the *Quarterly Review,* our own Branch paper, has had much the best year in its history, not only maintaining itself and sending hundreds of free circulars of information through the Branch, but also paying expenses of its editor to the Branch meeting, and leaving a good balance in its treasury.

We published one thousand copies of the Branch Annual Report, containing ninety pages, at a cost of $106, which was nearly repaid by the advertisements and sales.

Our Secretary of Literature has issued leaflets, circulars, and letters of information aggregating about thirty thousand pages, the greater part of which were for free distribution.

The total receipts for the year have been $28,209. $3,500 of which was a special gift toward the Johnston Memorial Hospital, leaving $24,700 receipts from regular channels, an advance of $2,100, but as we began the year with a deficit, and our disbursements have exceeded $29,000, we close the year with $1,400 deficit in our treasury.

The year 1908 marks the twenty-fifth year of our Branch history, and we propose to celebrate it as a silver anniversary, and have already issued a call asking for a special silver offering from every member in our constituency, and with the blessing of God we hope to come to you one year hence with songs of rejoicing and notes of praise.

MRS. C. S. WINCHELL.

TREASURER'S REPORT.

October 1, 1906, to October 1, 1907.

Total Receipts	$28,209 63
Total Disbursements	29,331 94
Deficit	$1,122 31
Deficit October 1, 1906	345 35
Total Deficit	$1,467 66

MRS. C. W. HALL, *Branch Treasurer.*

6

TOPEKA BRANCH.

We began the year with the General Executive convening within our borders. The influence of that splendid meeting continues to abide, and we come to the end of another twelve months with songs of thanksgiving for health and wealth and opportunity to labor for Him. There has not been a time, however, in our connection when we have reviewed the year with such a consciousness that "Thus far the Lord has led us on." The burdens have seemed a little heavier, the problems more difficult of solution, the calls more numerous and urgent, but the One in whose name we labor has been better than all our fears—yea, than were our hopes.

The statistics indicate a growth in members, the receipts an increase of interest, larger sales of literature and copies of Christus Redemptor, a more intelligent working constituency. This advance is due not only to the effort of Auxiliaries, District and Conference officers, but the loving service of those who by experience know what it is to live in a land without a Christ.

Mrs. S. P. Craver, of South America; Mrs. Mary C. Curtis, Malaysia; Miss Mary Hillman, Korea, and Miss Fannie Meyer, of West China, itinerated in Kansas and Nebraska, instructing the people and strengthening the work.

Within a few weeks after the adjournment of our last Annual Meeting, seven of our representatives were outward bound—Miss Livermore returning, and Miss Lavina Nelson, Miss Lena Nelson, Miss Widney, and Miss Ericson going for the first time to India; Miss James to Burma, and Miss Dreisbach to the Philippines. A special reason for thanksgiving is that these young women reached their destination in safety, and the letters received during the year have been written in such confidence that each one is in the place of the Lord's choosing. The sending of so large a number of recruits has very greatly increased the financial output of the Branch, this and the natural growth of the work adding to the appropriations ten thousand over the previous year.

At the mid-year meeting of the Reference Committee the testimonials of four candidates were presented, all of whom were accepted.

Miss Cora Simpson, Guide Rock, Nebraska.
Miss Jennie Borg, Lindsay, Nebraska.
Miss Blanche Betz, Denver, Colorado.
Miss Winnie Gabrielson, Lincoln, Nebraska.

For lack of funds to send them, Miss Simpson and Miss Betz were transferred to the Northwestern Branch, the first going to China and the second to Mexico. Miss Borg sailed from Seattle September 12th, and is hastening on to that distant station, Chung King, West China. Early in the year news came that Dr. Ida Stevenson was en route home, her coming made necessary as caretaker and companion for a sick missionary. We are glad of her presence, and after seventeen years of service the privilege of welcoming her for the first time to the General Executive Meeting.

Miss McKnight, having completed her first term of service in Northwest India, reached the home circle in August, and following our usual custom for resting missionaries, we started her on a tour of the Conferences, four of which she has attended.

Miss Winslow tarries in the home land regaining health, and meanwhile a longing eye is turned toward India.

In May news came of the destruction by fire of the property at Nagoya and entire loss of the personal effects of Miss Watson. A plan inaugurated two weeks ago at the Annual Meeting, showing thoughtfulness of missionary women, is to give her a book shower before Christmas.

Each year marks the home-going of some one closely identified with us in service. Away in the Himalaya Mountains there lies a lonely grave that will be forever sacred to the women of the Topeka Branch. At the dawn of a June day, after a few hours of suffering from cholera, Dr. Mary Tuttle, of Pithoragarh, India, entered into Life. After nearly five years her ministry to the women and girls of India ceased, but the influence of her life will abide.

In early summer Mrs. H. E. M. Patten, at one time Corresponding Secretary of the Branch, heard the summons. Scarcely one remains who was in active relations, but her works do follow her, and we are building on the foundations that she helped to lay.

The thank-offering, the object being again Bangalore, was the largest in our history.

The Annual Meeting was one of the best, eight Little Light Bearer Life Mem e s ps secured being but one of the many things accomplished. b r hi

For our failures we are truly sorry; for our victories, humbly grateful, and for the future pledge more and better service.

As the representative of the Topeka Branch, and for the blessed women scattered over our vast territory, we can confidently say, "Lord, if we may, we'll serve another day."

ELLA M. WATSON, *Corresponding Secretary.*

TREASURER'S REPORT.

Balance October 1, 1906 .... $7,104 34
Receipts 42,066 96

Total $49,171 30
Disbursements 47,753 17

Balance October 1, 1907 .... $1,418 13

MRS. L. E. MCENTIRE, *Treasurer.*

PACIFIC BRANCH.

With real gratitude in our hearts we say, "O give thanks unto the Lord, for He is good." In His strength we will courageously begin the work of another year.

Last year we came with special rejoicing to the close of the year, because notwithstanding the dire disaster which had come to the largest city within our borders we still were able to announce a phenomenal increase in receipts. Some of us feared a reaction, but instead of that our receipts this year are $8,872 larger than last year. Truly God has honored the earnest and faithful efforts of the consecrated women of the six Conferences which constitute this Branch.

A few months ago a good friend of our work, Mr. J. D. Payne, of Los Angeles, asked his pastor to send some of our officers to him with information concerning special needs in China or Japan. After many interviews contracts were drawn for a gift of $15,000 to erect the Administration Building of our Woman's College in Foochow, China. Three thousand dollars of this amount has been paid, and the balance is to come in regular payments. Not long after the legal papers were signed, which conveyed the gift, the generous donor "was not, for God took him."

Our record of progress other than financial shows a larger gain than usual in Auxiliaries, Young People's Societies, King's Heralds, and Little Light Bearers. We also have an increase in subscriptions to the *Woman's Missionary Friend* of ninety-six; also an increase in the

Frauen Missions Freund, while our subscriptions to *The Study* have more than doubled.

During the year a book, entitled, "Missionaries of the Pacific Branch," has been issued; also, several leaflets for use in our Auxiliaries. In the preparation of these and in many other ways our Mrs. Charlotte O'Neal gave valuable assistance. The sales of literature for the year have increased 38 per cent.

On the 15th of January very many of our Auxiliaries met, either in groups or separately, for a day of special prayer for the objects to which our thank-offerings were to be applied. The following day at the Branch Quarterly Meeting, after an inspiring address by Mrs. Ada Lee, but without special appeal or plan of officers, the people present spontaneously offered almost $700 to pay the outgoing expenses of our two new missionaries. "Thus saith the Lord God: I will yet for this be enquired of by the house of Israel, to do it for them: I will increase them like a flock." Since then these missionaries—Miss M. Helen Russell and Miss Evelyn B. Baugh—have sailed for their new work in Japan and China.

Of our other missionaries only two have been home on furlough— Miss Elizabeth Parkes, of Manila, and Miss Elizabeth Dana Marble, of Meerut, India. After several months of itinerary work in some of the Eastern Branches, Miss Parkes is to return to the Philippines this fall. We greatly regret that Miss Marble finds it impossible to return to her work.

All the others of our missionaries have been rendering faithful service in their respective foreign fields—Africa, India, and China.

We are greatly indebted to very many of our pastors for their cordial support, and in many cases for special addresses from them. In one Church the pastor preached a missionary sermon on Sunday morning, following which he made the appeal for our annual thank-offering, the response being $1,100.

Much assistance was also given us by Mrs. Ada Lee and other visiting missionaries; also, by Mrs. A. N. Fisher, of Portland, Oregon, and Mrs. Lucie F. Harrison.

The hearts of our people have been touched by the appeals for famine relief in China, and more than $400 was given for that purpose. This amount, with contributions from other Branches, was used under the direction of our Dr. Gertrude Taft in Chinkiang, and served the double purpose of feeding hundreds of hungry people for many months and at the same time secured extensive improvements to our mission property by the employment of those who were able to work.

Our Branch Annual Meeting was held in First Church, Pasadena, and was more largely attended than any previous meeting. We greatly missed the presence of Mrs. H. E. M. Pattee, who has served as Secretary of the Southern California Conference for so many years. Tender and loving tributes were paid to the memory of her for whom none but loving thoughts could exist.

Rev. D. F. Howe and Rev. F. M. Dowling were the inspirational speakers at the evening services, while during the day sessions we were greatly assisted by Miss Wilson, of China; Miss Marble, of India, and Mrs. Corbin, of Mexico.

The spirit of the meeting was indicated by the fact that the Corresponding Secretary was authorized to make an advance in appropriations from $20,000 in 1907 to $30,000 for 1908, while our gain in membership in Auxiliaries only, has been 18 per cent this year, our motto for the coming year is "One hundred per cent advance in membership."

Mrs. S. F. Johnson, *Corresponding Secretary.*

TREASURER'S REPORT.

Receipts from Conferences	$26,925	00
Annuity	1,000	00
Special gifts	5,404	00
Total receipts	$33,329	00
Balance, October 1, 1906	3,107	00
Grand total		$36,436 00
Disbursements	$25,256	00
Transferred to Trust Fund	1,784	00
Transferred to Annuity Fund	1,000	00
Total disbursements		28,040 00
Balance, October 1, 1907		$8,396 00

MRS. Z. L. PARMALEE, *Treasurer.*

COLUMBIA RIVER BRANCH.

Columbia River Branch has not yet arrived at that mature age when one may cease caring to number· the passing years, hence the inclination to announce the fact that this is the fifteenth year of our history. Larger anticipations and plans than usual marked its beginning, and the deep conviction of Divine leading which enabled these has been our joy and stay through all the months since.

The special aim for the year was twofold—to ·double our membership and to increase our appropriations by more than one third those of the previous year. In each respect this was the largest proportionate advance determined by any Branch.

· The outcome as regards membership has not fully met the cherished hope, though the effort was fruitful both in increased numbers and in a firmer confidence for success in the near future. That it has proven so much greater task to win new adherents than added dollars is a subject for pondering which may be most helpful.

Our army of Little Light Bearers is recruited by goodly numbers from year to year, while the Little Light Bearer and King's Herald Life Members of the past three years have nearly doubled during the present. Among the latter is our second wee band of triplets.

Financially the aim has been more than realized, and the gain the largest of any year since organization. The ·total receipts very nearly reach $14,000. Consulting the records of other Branches for any possible encouragement in this direction, we find that this exceeds the amount reported by each of two Branches in their fifteenth years.

Our territory is so broad and towns are so separated by magnificent distances that all the wheels of the admirable machinery of the Society can not be set in motion. This is especially true of district associations. While the number of Conference Districts in the Branch is twenty, only· four of these are organized and holding district meetings, a serious obstacle to rapid progress which time alone can obviate. Four very successful district meetings were held this year. Three of these were stirred for China by our gifted resident missionary, Mrs. William Rouse Keene, while the fourth was so fortunate as to secure the services of Miss Mary Williams, returning on furlough from Baroda, India. We· are especially indebted to Miss Williams, who with great self-denial tarried a few weeks for the help she might give by the way as she journeyed homeward. Somewhat of the success of the year must be

attributed to her vivid presentation of the needs and the triumphs of
the Gospel in a field in which we are particularly concerned.

A wider, tenderer interest than ever was manifest in the Thank-offering, owing to the fact that its object was the erection of a Missionary
Home in India as a memorial of our former beloved Treasurer, Mrs.
Mary E. Whitney. Love for our dear friend and helpmeet combined
with love for the Master to supply a need in itself pressing, and the
result was the largest Thank-offering we have ever known.

Once again has that divinest seal been put upon our work in the call
of a young life to service in the mission field. Midway in the year the
testimonials of Miss Rosa E. Dudley were received and she was accepted
and under appointment, while there was no provision in the appropriations
for her outgoing expenses and support. Yet has there been no lack.
Special gifts have come so spontaneously for sending out the new missionary that the experience has been altogether most blessed. She goes
to the Philippine Islands.

Would that it need not be written over against this that one of our
missionaries on the field has been obliged to lay down her work. At
the close of the spring term in the Foochow Seminary, after months of
brave effort against failing health, Miss Parkinson returned home under
medical orders.

Our Annual Meeting was characterized by a spirit of loyalty and
devotion which argue well for the future. The papers and discussions
were of such merit as to make one justly proud of the noble women who
labor in that remote corner of the possessions of the Woman's Foreign
Missionary Society. One feature of the program was a Fifteenth Anniversary exercise on "Taking Stock." Under "Assets" were treated
"Membership," "Missionaries," "Receipts," followed by "Liabilities" and
"Profit and Loss." It was a happy setting forth of the progress of the
Branch. In the discussion of Profit and Loss our Recording Secretary
utterly refused to recognize any loss whatsoever, but by a stroke of
genius all her own, transferred every seeming loss of the years over to
the side of veritable profit. And why should it not be ever so with
those who link life and labor with the eternities. We praise God for
all the way in which He has led us.

Mrs. A. N. Fisher, Corresponding Secretary.

TREASURER'S REPORT.

Balance on hand, October 1, 1906	$3,233 56
Receipts from October 1, 1906, to October 1, 1907	13,951 35
Total	$17,184 91
Disbursements	12,288 21
Balance on hand, October 1, 1907	$4,896 70

Miss Nettie M. Whitney, Treasurer.

GERMAN WORK.

Although unable to report an increase in the receipts from our
German work we are not at all cast down or dismayed concerning its
general condition. The slight decrease of $166.75 is due not to any de-
crease of general receipts, which are larger than ever before, but to the
absence of any legacies such as we have had. There were also received
by two of the Conference Treasurers, just a little too late to get into the

reports, sums large enough to turn this deficit into an increase of like amount.

One Conference, the Southern, has doubled the number of. Auxiliaries and members, others have gained smaller percentages; California shows a good advance in Young People's Work; the Northwestern and St. Louis Conferences have each pushed Children's Work with much energy. While there is much in these lines yet to be wished for, and while we wish that the advances made by some had been equaled by all, still we feel that we have much cause for gratitude, and we praise Him who has been with us during the year, trusting Him for further help and guidance. The aggregate advance in Auxiliaries has been five per cent; in members, seven per cent. Owing to a decrease in one Conference there is very little advance in Standard Bearer work, but King's Heralds bands show an advance of eighty-five per cent, and an advance in membership of eighty per cent. Thirty little ones have been made life members; twenty-three of these are in one Conference, the Northwestern.

Our German Conferences comprise twenty-seven Districts; during the year thirteen District Conventions were held in the interests of the Woman's Foreign Missionary Society.

The difficulties under which we labor regarding German literature have been mentioned in former reports. They are not growing less, but rather increasing. In former years we were helped in this matter from the publication fund, but for a number of years we have tried to carry this matter without any such help. At the beginning of the year our treasury was so depleted that we have not been able to publish during the year more than our Annual Report and the Study Booklet, "Die Inselwent." Four thousand copies of the Annual Report were printed, of which 1,877 have been paid for. Altogether over $200 worth of German literature, beside quite a little English literature, has been sold. The demand for literature for children was in part satisfied by our German *Sunday-school Advocate.* The Editor kindly offered to put a certain amount of space at our disposal if we would furnish missionary material. This was furnished by one of our young women.

The Study Course is followed by many of our Auxiliaries and some Leagues have also taken it up.

The subject of a German Branch does not seem to have died out, as voices in demand of it are still being heard.

I am glad to report quite a number of German girls in different schools preparing for foreign service. Some of them will be ready to send in their applications during the year.

Inquiries have again come from girls in Europe as to the necessary qualifications and preparations for service. I have had to tell these, as heretofore, that there was no hope of their acceptance unless they could come to America and here finish their preparation. Many of us have felt, and Bishop Burt seems to share this feeling, that some of these merit our attention, and that there are women in Switzerland and Germany who can be used by our Society in the foreign field as well as those from this land. Can we not make it possible to utilize some of these and so enthuse and secure more support from our Church in those countries? With gratitude to God for His help in the past we look hopefully to the future, trusting Him for guidance and help in this work. Respectfully submitted,

LOUISA C. ROTHWEILER, *Secretary of German Work.*

STATISTICS OF THE GERMAN WORK.

CONFERENCES	CONTINGENT FUND	DECREASE	INCREASE	RECEIPTS IN 1905-1906	RECEIPTS IN 1906-1907	CHILDREN'S MISSIONARY FRIEND	WOMAN'S MISSIONARY FRIEND	FRAUEN MISSIONS FREUND	MITE-BOXES	LIFE MEMBERS	MEMBERS	KING'S HERALDS SOCIETIES	MEMBERS	STANDARD BEARERS OR BANDS	MEMBERS	AUXILIARIES
California	$20 45		$386 25	$858 50	$1,244 75	32	2	210	111	1	35	2	137	5	212	10
Central	68 04		444 74	2,559 43	3,004 17	186	18	369	534		18	1	140	7	972	34
Chicago	29 47	$275 75	1 84	1,400 36	1,402 20	183	5	315	51				245	9	501	17
Eastern	41 00	334 33		2,046 45	1,770 25	100	14	331	57		100	3	57	1	765	22
Northern	63 41	312 72		2,573 94	2,289 12	217	24	610	206		249	11	118	5	807	84
Northwestern	48 27		7 41	2,606 89	2,294 22	285	6	541	358	5	338	14	296	13	809	41
Pacific	8 45			227 89	235 30		9	122	34	27	66	3	58	2	138	7
St. Louis	48 54	59 06		1,806 40	1,247 84	61		367	53	2			21	1	762	29
Southern	58 80		112 90	543 65	656 55		21	87			87	3	46	3	200	13
Western	35 72	157 30		3,010 55	2,863 24	180		694	509	1					914	45
Scattering	1 40							375								
Total for United States	$93 55	$186 08		$17,133 17	$16,947 14	1,203	99	4,021	1,913	36	893	37	1,118	46	6,080	252
North Germany				$214 82	$239 30			110					35	1	596	28
South Germany				302 00	287 91			204							1,379	105
Switzerland				500 38	509 27			173							1,201	44
Total for Europe				$1,017 20	$1,036 48			489					35	1	3,116	
Grand Total	$408 55	$166 75		$18,150 37	$17,983 62	1,203	99	4,510	1,193	36	893	37	1,153	47	9,196	429

SCANDINAVIAN WORK.

Our Swedish work was started in 1901 by Miss Alma Jakobson, from Pakur, India, who, feeling the great need of more adequate buildings for the Orphanage under her care, conceived the idea of coming to America to secure help for the erection of the necessary edifice. She was promised that if she would organize Auxiliaries of the Woman's Foreign Missionary Society in the Swedish Churches the money thus secured would be expended for this purpose. She succeeded in organizing ninety-four Auxiliaries, with a membership of 2,278. The first year we had no General Secretary, consequently no report showing our standing at the end of the year.

Our first report is dated 1903 and shows an income of $2,755.44. The next year our membership had gone down and some of our Auxiliaries had ceased to exist, but our income was nevertheless larger than the preceding year. In 1905 we had the largest increase in our short history, the Auxiliaries having grown from eighty-seven to ninety-six, the membership from 2,110 to 2,414, and the receipts from $2,831.97 to $3,231.97. Last year our Auxiliaries were ninety-nine, membership 2,546, and receipts $3,922, showing that the increase in money received has been larger than that in membership. This year's membership I have not yet been able to ascertain with any degree of accuracy, but our receipts exceed those of last year's by $438.35. We have a few Standard Bearers' Societies, but owing to the need of our young women to supply the offices in our Auxiliaries, we have been glad to have them among us there. The coming year we hope to be able to push the work among the children better than heretofore. The Northern Conference leads in this work, having several King's Herald Societies. The different Conferences support some nine or ten girls in Pakur as well as several Bible women and widows.

Our work is divided among four Conferences, the Swedish Central, which lies well within the boundary of the Northwestern Branch; the Northern, which has work within both the Northwestern and the Minneapolis Branch, but has so far only reported to the Minneapolis Branch. An effort has been made this year to have the Conference work divided so that it may be reported in both Branches, but this has met a very decided opposition from the officers and the pastors, and a memorial will be presented to this meeting strongly urging that the work be left undisturbed and the Conference be allowed to report as before. Beside these three Conferences there is a Western, with Auxiliaries belonging both to the Topeka and Des Moines Branch. This Conference has been ahead of the others both in receipts and membership this year. The Eastern Conference has Auxiliaries in both the New York and the New England Branch. On the Pacific Coast we have two Districts belonging to American Conferences.

One great want has been and is still—the want of knowledge among our people of the mission work and its needs. It seems almost impossible to sell any literature, we have to distribute as much as we can free. We are allowed three or four columns in our Church papers thrice a month, and I have tried to fill them with what I thought would most interest our people—letters from our own and other missionaries and general information about the work both at home and abroad, beside the Mission Study. On the suggestion of one of our Conference Secretaries I have had the book, "The Cry Heard," by Ellen Perry Price, translated by one of our pastors and inserted as a serial in the paper, permission having kindly been granted by Messrs. Jennings & Graham, who hold the copyright. We have printed 3,000 copies of our Annual Report, but a great many remain unsold. Two tracts have been reprinted and some of them sold. During the year I have been allowed, through the kindness of the Literature Committee of the Northwestern Branch, to put in a desk and bookcase for our supplies at their headquarters, in 57 Washington Street, Chicago, which has been a very great convenience in the work.

Miss Hilda Swan's latest report from Pakur shows that on the building Miss Jakobson was so anxious to erect, and which was dedicated several years ago, and which cost $12,324.30, only $9,134.29 have been paid, leaving an indebtedness of $3,190.01. During these years the Swedish Auxiliaries have raised $17,102.47, according to the Annual Reports. As this last year's receipts show $4,360.72, and the remaining debt is only $3,190.01, we devoutly hope and pray that this debt may be canceled and the burden taken off our shoulders.

We have not been able to give much money, but we have given our girls at the rate of one a year, so we now have six in the work, one on the way, one will go out from this meeting, and three are preparing for the work.

Feeling that a blessed privilege is ours, we are so thankful for even the smallest share in the work, and hoping that we too some day shall grow and leave behind the small things, we commend ourselves for the future to the loving kindness of our Heavenly Father and to the patient forbearance and good fellowship of our sisters and co-workers.

Respectfully submitted,

MRS. HANNA HENSCHEN.

STATISTICS OF THE SCANDINAVIAN WORK.

CONFERENCES.	AUXILIARIES	MEMBERS	MITE-BOXES	SCHOLARSHIPS	SPECIAL GIFTS	THANK-OFFERING	COLLECTIONS	RECEIPTS	INCREASE	DECREASE	CONTINGENT FUND
Central	15	600		$215 00	$75 00	$15 50	$71 45	$1,109 20		$58 60	$30 00
Northern	19	710				225 76		1,071 72	271 62		73 96
Western Topeka	29	490	$170 00		213 60	53 00	180 20	1,170 25	401 95		42 45
Western Des Moines	9	175			19 00	12 85		213 50		21 95	16 40
Eastern	17	*486						509 78		163 29	49 25
California District	5	*174						283 30	65		18 30
Puget Sound District	4	65			40 00	4 00		115 67			9 17
Total	97	2,700	$170 90	$255 00	$311 60	$307 11	$251 65	$4,473 42	$789 80	$238 84	$239 53

* Last year's figures

YOUNG PEOPLE'S WORK.

BRANCH SUPERINTENDENTS.

New England—MRS. C. H. STACKPOLE, Waltham, Mass.
New York—MRS. CHARLES SPAETH, 94½ Meigs St., Rochester, N. Y.
Philadelphia—MISS INA WILHELM, 1212 Buffalo St., Franklin, Pa.
Baltimore—MRS. E. L. HARVEY, 1314 Thirteenth St., N. W., Washington,
    D. C.
Cincinnati—MISS MARY I. SCOTT, Moundsville, W. Va.
Northwestern—MRS. DAVID·C. COOK, 105 N. Gifford St., Elgin, Ill.
Des Moines—MRS. R. S. BEALL, Mount Ayr, Iowa.
Minneapolis—MRS. S. L. SHERWIN, Lake Crystal, Minn.
Topeka—MRS. J.. T. RINKER, 2636 North St., Lincoln, Neb.
Columbia River—MRS. E. E. UPMEYER, Harrisburg, Ore.

REPORT OF YOUNG PEOPLE'S WORK.

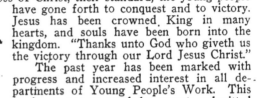

With "Love, Loyalty, and Victory," their watchword; "Thy kingdom come," their prayer; the cross of Christ, their standard, the young people have gone forth to conquest and to victory. Jesus has been crowned King in many hearts, and souls have been born into the kingdom. "Thanks unto God who giveth us the victory through our Lord Jesus Christ."

The past year has been marked with progress and increased interest in all departments of Young People's Work. This is shown not so much by reports submitted as by the sentiment of personal letters that have been received from all parts of the field.

Were success measured by numbers alone there might be cause for discouragement and criticism, but judging of the work from the standpoint of public sentiment, personal conviction, and the spirit of this great body of young people and its leaders, the work is to-day occupying a place in the Church never before realized.

During the year the General Secretary itinerated in New York, Cincinnati, Des Moines, and Northwestern Branches, and found certain conditions evident and very significant.

1. Our Young People are demanding recognition, and the great issues of the day are organization and leadership for the accomplishment of work. Where leadership is lacking the work without exception is on the decrease, and great losses are being sustained. We need to pray for trained leaders capable of guiding these young people.

2. The universal clamor for missionary literature and increased interest in missionary lectures and facts of missions, show an awakening sentiment among our young people that is extremely gratifying. The influence exerted by attractive leaflets and books is beyond our power to estimate, and is universally evident.

3. Our representation at summer Conferences is on the increase. This last year eleven representatives were sent to the several summer Conferences. Literature was distributed, and facts were presented in such a way that at Silver Bay, out of a total attendance of 143 Methodists, 45 young women signed the volunteer pledge for work in the foreign field. At Lake Geneva out of 40 volunteers 17 were Methodists; 62 of the young women were Methodists.

Without exception, the work among these young women of our

colleges, resulted in broadened sympathies, enlarged views, and deepened interests in the grandest theme of the ages—"the salvation of the world." This is of vital importance to our work and is the promise· of large fruitage in after years.

Plans should be devised by distribution of suitable literature, personal interviews, and · all other practicable methods; by which these Methodist young women in our schools and colleges shall gain more direct knowledge of the work of the Woman's Foreign Missionary Society, and be brought into communication with the Corresponding Secretaries of the various Branches. Only as this work is systematized and placed on a permanent basis can the results of this work be conserved.

4. While it is true that some organizations have disbanded, we must not forget that new companies have been formed by local leaders and not by a general organizer. Often a Sunday-school class has been the nucleus of a new company. This shows the significant fact that a conviction and desire to work have been the great motive power of the organization. Couple with this fact another—that the mother societies are beginning to feel the mighty force of this great army, and, if organization is lacking, are asking, "Why?" and feel apologies are necessary if the young people have not a part in the District Conventions and general public demonstrations, and we may safely say that our young people are well on the way toward taking their rightful place in the work. Not only are these facts general impressions of the work; they are supported by such statistical reports as have been received.·

The plan of the year was to increase interest and·numbers to stimulate mite box collections, help the missionaries to whom support was pledged, carry on special work as the different Branches were able, to support the *Friend,* and to liquidate the balance of the Peking debt of $5,000.

In order to accomplish the latter object, use was made of tracts, helps, and cards, printed by Miss Cushman for that purpose, and appeals were made through the *Friend* for the accomplishment of these results.

New York has responded nobly to the call and closes the year with a net gain of five organizations, with 438 members, against a loss of 1,000 last year, making a total of 310 Societies and 8,179 members, which leads all Branches in numbers. New York excels also in Thank-offering for Peking Girls' School, giving $1,200. Total gifts amount to $2,800. New York reports largest number of missionaries supported, there being eleven in all.

The naming of chairs, rooms, windows, etc., in Peking has met with· such success that Miss Jewell says she spent the summer endeavoring to place the many names upon windows, rooms, chairs, etc., in such a way as not to have a gingerbread effect.

Northwestern has given the largest totals into the treasury, as reports show the magnificent ingathering of $6,059.22. Northwestern supports ten missionaries, which is one less than New York Branch.

California supports the largest number of scholarships, having twenty-six. Des Moines paid $3,288 into the treasury this year and has· carried *large* special work.

While it is impossible to give a definite statement of totals in all· Branches, it is safe to say God has blessed the young people, and they have responded. ·

New York Special.—Dr. Li's Hospital, entire appropriation, including twelve beds, at $25 each; support of eleven missionaries; Mrs. Mary Porter Gamewell's room at Peking—also a Bashford room; several chairs at $10 each, etc.; box packed and Christmas supplies sent.

Northwestern Branch Special.—Ten missionaries.

Des Moines Special.—Sixty-eight girls; twelve Bible women; one hospital bed; three day schools; one Sunday-school; one woman in training school; twelve shares in salaries of missionaries; support of Elsie Reynolds, missionary.

California Conference Special Work.—Twenty-six scholarships; eight Bible women; two assistant teachers; two day schools; support of missionary, Miss Helen Russell, of Japan.

Baltimore Branch.—Life members, two; missionary, Miss Hallman, Penang, Korea.

In large giving, and for the increase in spiritual power and blessing, we praise and magnify His holy name.

·MRS. EVELYN P. MARSH, *General Secretary.*

STATISTICS OF YOUNG PEOPLE'S WORK.

BRANCHES.	YOUNG WOMEN'S SOCIETIES	MEMBERS.	STANDARD BEARERS' SOCIETIES.	MEMBERS.	TOTAL YOUNG PEOPLE'S SOCIETIES.	TOTAL MEMBERS.	THANK-OFFERING.	SUBSCRIPTION TO FRIEND.	TOTAL MONEY IN TREASURY.
New York	67	2,248	243	5,931	310	8,179	$1,200 00		
Northwestern	29	682	185	4,751	214	5,433	1,075 40	430	$6,059 22
Des Moines			143	1,430	143	1,430			3,288 00
Pacific	14	516	82	2,283	96	1,799			
Minneapolis	46	784			46	784			
New England	120	3,054			120	3,054	550 90		3,021 47
Baltimore	17	310			17	310			208 94
Philadelphia	25	2,540			25	2,540			
Totals	318	10,134	653	14,395	971	24,529	$2,826 36	430	$12,577 63

CHILDREN'S WORK.

BRANCH SUPERINTENDENTS.

New England—MRS. C. H. STOWELL, 99 Fairmount St., Lowell, Mass.
New York—MRS. H. C. LEARN, 600 Bedford Ave., Brooklyn, N. Y.
Philadelphia—MISS INA WILHELM, 1212 Buffalo St., Franklin, Pa.
Baltimore—MRS. WM. E. MOORE, 524 N. Caroline Ave., Baltimore, Md.
Cincinnati—MRS. J. F. FISHER, 11,427 Detroit Ave., N. W., Cleveland, O.
Northwestern—MRS. W. C. WHITCOMB, Rochelle, Ill.
Des Moines—MRS. ALICE F. FINTEL, Fort Des Moines, Iowa.
Minneapolis—MRS. W. J. CLAPP, 824 Fifth Ave., Fargo, N. Dakota.
Topeka—MRS. S. A. CHAPEL, Lincoln, Neb.
Columbia River—Mrs. J. H. Ryckman, Seattle, Wash.

REPORT OF THE CHILDREN'S WORK.

We are greatly indebted to the ladies of 'Springfield, who have extended the courtesy of entertainment to our Branch Superintendents of Children's Work this year. New England, Philadelphia, Cincinnati, Minneapolis, Des Moines, and Topeka Superintendents have accepted the invitation and are present to represent their Branches. In these noble women are found as gifted and consecrated a corps of workers as our Woman's Foreign Missionary Society possesses anywhere. "The Morning Light is Breaking" for the children.

Each day attention will be given to the children's work Profitable conferences, both public and private, will be held. This, our first opportunity to meet together, will, we believe, bring rich results in the year to come.

At the beginning of the year circulars were printed and sent to the various Branches, to be distributed among the Auxiliaries, giving the aim for the year. When able to meet these conditions the Auxiliaries were to fill out and return these blanks. They would then be placed on the *Honor Roll.*

To fulfill these requirements meant that an Auxiliary would be well developed on all lines of Children's Work, and that is just what we are striving for. This aim can be reached with a reasonable amount of effort. While this has been an incentive to many Auxiliaries, and scores are working toward it, too few have yet reached the goal. If a District Secretary or a Conference Secretary finds she has not even one Honor Roll Auxiliary reported, she has reason to feel that the fault may be partly her own. Remember, if a Children's Superintendent exists in any District, she acts simply as an Assistant, and the District Secretary is still responsible. Let us all fall into line with the plan, keep it before our Auxiliaries, and see what the next year will bring us.

Requests were sent to the Editors of the *Branch Quarterlies,* asking that they place in their columns the names of those Auxiliaries reported to them as on the Honor Roll.

Almost without exception favorable responses came cordial and hearty. We believe we shall continue to have their co-operation for another year in this effort. Fifty-four are reported on our Honor Roll: New England, 13; Philadelphia, 2; Northwestern, 17; Minneapolis, 3; New York, 5; Cincinnati, 5; Des Moines, 3; Pacific, 8.

The Banner for the Honor Roll belongs to the Pacific Branch.

There are children's missionaries now in New England, Philadelphia, Cincinnati, Northwestern, Topeka, Pacific, and Des Moines Branches. This is an inspiration to the children as they work for her, pray for her, and receive letters from her. A letter has been written by your Superintendent this year on "Our Children's Missionaries," telling of their fields of labor and their work. This may be used as an exercise personating the different missionaries if desired.

Topeka Branch Superintendent inaugurated a novel way of interesting the children in their missionary and gaining money for her support. She issued cards of invitation to a birthday party for Miss Widney. These could be used anywhere in the Branch. They asked as admission to this party as many pennies as those attending were years old. This proved a marked success and might well be copied in other Branches.

The Cincinnati Branch Superintendent, among many other things, prepared missionary dollars for the support of Miss Marker. These have been decidedly successful.

The Industrial School in Mexico continues to be our thank-offering for this year. New cards have been published called "Nickle Gleaners" for the use of the King's Heralds. On one side there is provision for a record to be kept of the nickles given, and on the other is a certificate of a dollar share in the school. These we believe will prove practical in raising money and also in awakening interest.

Two hundred and two new organizations gladden our hearts this year. While we are growing in so many ways, it is certainly surprising and serious to find a decrease in the subscriptions to our valuable little paper. We ask your prayers and sympathy as our Branch Superintendents attempt this year to gain 4,500 new subscriptions, apportioning it to the different Branches. The great solution of this problem is in each Auxiliary feeling a responsibility in placing this paper in the hands of the children entrusted to its care. They love and enjoy it so much. What can Auxiliaries be thinking of when depriving the children of this paper? Surely they are thinking not of the children.

We deeply regret that the Philadelphia Branch Superintendent, Mrs. Strawinski, has been compelled to resign on account of ill health. Miss Ina Wilhelm has been appointed to fill her place, one who well understands the work, having filled the office of Conference Superintendent.

Columbia River Branch has wisely separated its Young Women's and Children's Work, choosing a Superintendent for each. Mrs. Upmeyer retains the Young Women's Work, and while we shall miss her valuable help, yet we welcome Mrs. Wrightman, of Seattle, who takes her place. Mrs. Wrightman is already a successful worker among the children.

Mrs. Chappell, our new Superintendent for Topeka Branch, was elected during the year and has already brought a wealth of originality, enthusiasm, and devotion to the Children's Work of Topeka Branch.

Surely no person need to hesitate to take the leadership of a King's Herald Band for lack of helps. The new book, "In Circles of Light," by our own gifted Editor, presents a rich mine of material in addition to e lessons which appear each month in the *Children's Missionary Friend*.

A Junior Hand Book has also been prepared by your Secretary this year containing a full explanation of our methods and many suggestions for workers.

I would also call attention to a little poem published this year, entitled, "A Penny a Pound for the Baby," and ask every Auxiliary to have this year a Little Light Bearer Pound Party; enclose one of these poems; have scales at the party; collect the pennies and enlist the Little Light Bearers.

This has been the banner year in Life Membership. Where did you ever see a more beautiful collection of faces than that which greets us from month to month in the *Children's Missionary Friend?*

For the second time Columbia River Branch has presented its triplet life members. Are the Methodist triplets confined to this one Branch? Your Secretary asks other Branches to look around and gather them in. There was an occasion in Trinity Church, Worcester, on a recent Sunday evening, when, in response to a call from your Secretary, the names of thirteen child life members were given in twenty minutes. We hope many of the large Churches in our Branches will try this. Talk it up beforehand; then ask the pastor for a part of a Sunday evening.

Des Moines Branch made eight life members during the year in one Mission Church, thus showing what a small Church can do—thanks to the enthusiasm and faithfulness of Mrs. Irmscher, the Superintendent. Des·Moines Branch set a remarkable pace last year, with twenty-six life members made at their Annual Meeting. New England Branch thus stirred to good works, made twenty-nine life members at their Annual Meeting this year. We thus see the effect of a good example. Topeka Branch made at Branch Meeting eight life members, double the number made last year.

Four hundred and five life members have been reported: New England, 81; New York, 16; Philadelphia, 18; Baltimore, 6; Cincinnati, 31; Northwestern, 100; Minneapolis, 26; Des Moines, 60; Topeka, 27; Pacific, 20; Columbia River, 20.

We present the following aim for the new year. Each Auxiliary to have—

1. A Supervisor of Children's Work.
2. Both King's Heralds and Little Light Bearers.
3. A combined membership of King's Heralds and Little Light Bearers equal to that of the Auxiliary.
4. A copy of the *Children's Missionary Friend* in every family where there are King's Heralds or Little Light Bearers over two years of age.
5. A new life member.

In the words of Frœbel: "Come, let us live for our children."

Respectfully submitted,

LUCIE F. HARRISON, General Secretary.

STATISTICS OF THE CHILDREN'S WORK. OCTOBER, 1906-OCTOBER, 1907.

BRANCH	KING'S HER-ALD'S BANDS	MEMBERS	LITTLE LIGHT BEAR-ERS' BANDS	MEMBERS
New England	144	3,648	51	1,008
New York	122	2,318	75	1,274
Philadelphia	84	2,884	63	1,455
Baltimore	41	1,244	34	677
Cincinnati	125	3,100	98	1,808
Northwestern	264	5,955	230	4,591
Des Moines	64	1,800	32	588
Minneapolis	96	2,914	43	864
Topeka	58	1,180	27	371
Pacific	50	874	39	790
Columbia River	21	353	40	800
Total	1,069	25,770	732	14 171

FOLTS MISSION INSTITUTE.

During the year 1906-07 there were forty-four students enrolled in Folts Institute, with the best average attendance in the history of the school. Seven different foreign countries were represented—China, Japan, India, Korea, British West Indies, Germany, and Norway. A class of twelve received diplomas or certificates at the close of the school year. During the year most encouraging reports came from former students who are now on the field.

The Institute has now become better known through the *Folts Institute Record,* a twelve-page quarterly which has been published during the year.

The new year (1907-8) opens with a larger enrollment than ever before at the beginning of the year.

IDA V. JONTZ, *President.*

NOMINATIONS FOR TRUSTEES OF FOLTS MISSION INSTITUTE.

For those whose terms expire January, 1908—Mrs. S. L. Baldwin, Rev. F. M. North, Miss Louise M. Hodgkins, Miss Mary E. Holt.

January, 1909—Mr. George R. Blount, Lacona, N. Y.; Mr. Charles S. Millington, Herkimer, N. Y.

January, 1910—Rev. Samuel D. Robinson, Herkimer, N. Y.

January, 1911—Mr. George P. Folts, Herkimer, N. Y.; Mrs. Charles Gibson, Albany, N. Y.; Mrs. E. A. Pharis, Syracuse, N. Y.; Mrs. William Terhune, Waterville, N. Y.; Mr. George W. Sanborn, Utica, N. Y.; Mr. J. P. Lewis, Beaver Falls, N. Y.

HOME STATISTICS TABLE.

Branches	China Centennial Fund	Receipts	Subscribers to Study	Subscribers to Frauen Missions Freund	Subscribers to Children's Missionary Friend	Subscribers to Women's Mission Friend	Members	Little Light Bearers' Bands	Members	King's Herald Bands	Members	Young People's Societies	Members	Auxiliaries
New England	$16,700 00	$84,320 88	2,577	52	3,517	2,074	1,008	51	3,648	144	3,054	120	11,717	473
New York	7,656 55	96,747 83	4,409	253	4,740	3,177	1,274	75	2,318	122	3,179	310	25,546	997
Philadelphia		62,981 59	4,305	84	3,122	3,055	1,455	68	2,384	84	3,318	175	16,184	476
Baltimore	1,500 00	18,814 87	1,031	65	1,012	814	679	34	1,244	41	310	17	5,310	161
Cincinnati		88,646 63	4,582	219	3,420	2,837	1,808	98	3,100	125	4,448	190	19,199	719
Northwestern	13,450 00	162,952 46	8,385	911	7,788	5,880	4,591	230	5,956	264	9,886	299	40,178	1,552
Des Moines		67,420 97	4,352	747	3,512	2,674	588	32	1,800	64	1,564	65	9,961	415
Minneapolis		28,209 63	1,348	609	1,094	822	884	43	2,914	96	3,298	143	16,005	641
Topeka	1,500 00	42,066 98	2,954	704	1,819	1,365	371	27	1,140	58	784	46	6,496	302
Pacific	3,600 00	33,329 00	1,941	210	1,432	812	790	39	874	50	1,112	27	2,778	104
Columbia River		13,951 35	873	122	856	518	300	30	558	21	2,976	101	4,587	156
Total	$44,406 55	$662,490 07	36,557			23,978	14,171	732	25,770	1,069	38,923	1,493	158,111	5,996
*German		$17,983 62							868	87	1,156	47	9,196	429
*Scandinavian		4,473 42											2,700	

* These figures are included in the above table.

Report of the Foreign Work.

ASIA.

The Woman's Foreign Missionary Society commenced work by sending, in 1869, Miss Isabella Thoburn and Miss Clara M. Swain, M. D., to India.

November 29, 1859, the first Methodist Girls' Boarding School was opened by the Misses Sarah and Beulah Woolston, who had been sent to *China* by the Ladies' China Missionary Society. In 1871 the Woman's Foreign Missionary Society adopted them, and also sent Miss Maria Brown (Davis) and Miss Mary Q. Porter (Gamewell) to Peking.

The Woman's Foreign Missionary Society commenced work in *Japan* in 1874 by sending Miss Dora Schoonmaker (Soper) to Tokyo.

The Woman's Foreign Missionary Society commenced work in *Korea* in 1885 by sending Mrs. Mary B. Scranton to Seoul.

AFRICA.

The Woman's Foreign Missionary Society commenced work in *Africa* in 1874. In 1874 Miss Mary Sharp, who had been sent out by the Missionary Society that year, was adopted, and in 1879 Miss Emma Michener was sent to Monrovia.

SOUTH AMERICA.

The Woman's Foreign Missionary Society commenced work in 1874 in *South America* by sending Miss Lou B. Denning and Miss Jennie M. Chapin to Rosario.

MEXICO.

The Woman's Foreign Missionary Society commenced work in *Mexico* by sending, in 1874, Miss Mary Hastings and Miss Susan Warner (Dersmore) to Mexico City.

BULGARIA.

The Woman's Foreign Missionary Society commenced work in *Bulgaria* in 1874. A Boarding School for girls was opened by Rev. D. C. Challis in November, 1880. In 1884 the Society sent Miss Linna Schenck to Lovetch.

ITALY.

The Woman's Foreign Missionary Society commenced work in *Italy* in 1874, and in 1885 sent Miss Emma Hall to Rome.

PHILIPPINE ISLANDS.

The Woman's Foreign Missionary Society commenced work in *Manila* in 1899 by sending Miss Julia Wisner, Mrs. Annie Norton, M. D., Miss Cody, and Mrs. Cornelia Moots.

FOREIGN WORK.

OFFICIAL CORRESPONDENCE.

INDIA.

NORTH INDIA CONFERENCE.

Organized as a· Conference in· 1864.
Woman's Foreign Missionary Work commenced in 1869.
Official Correspondent, Mrs. R. L. Thomas.

The North India Conference embraces the Province of Oudh and
the Northeast Provinces ·east of the Ganges.

MISSIONARIES AND THEIR STATIONS.

BAREILLY.—*Margaret D. Lewis, M. D., Esther Gimson, M. D., Miss C.
Easton.
BHOT.—Martha Sheldon, M. D., Miss Brown.
BUDAON.—Laura S. Wright, *E. May Ruddick.
CHANDAG.—Mary Reed.
GONDA.—Elizabeth Hoge, *Francis Scott. ·
LUCKNOW.—Florence L. Nichols, *Eva M. Hardie, Helen Ingram, Lila-
vati Singh, *Ruth E. Robinson, Alice M. Northup, Ada Mudge,
Katherine L. Hill, Isabel T. Blackstock, Miss Widney.
MORADABAD.—Alice Means, Nora B. Waugh.
NAINI TAL.—Sarah Easton, Rue E. Sellers.
PAURI.—Mary E. Wilson.
PITHORAGARH.—Annie Budden, Lucy Sullivan, Mary Means.
SHAHJAHANPUR.—F. M. English, Clara M. Organ.
SITAPUR.—Ida Grace Loper.
WIVES OF MISSIONARIES IN CHARGE OF WORK.—Mrs. S. Knowles, Mrs.
L. S. Parker, *Mrs. J. H. Messmore, Mrs. J. H. Gill, Mrs. C. I.
Bare, Mrs. F. L. Neeld, Mrs. J. Blackstock, Mrs. L. A. Core, *Mrs.
J. L. Robinson, Mrs. J. N. West, Mrs. N. L. Rockey, Mrs. G. W.
Guthrie, Mrs. Florence Perrine Mansell, Mrs. G. C. Hewes, Mrs.
P. S. Hyde, Mrs. B. T. Badley, Mrs. R. C. Thoburn, Mrs. Jennie
Dart Dease, M. D., *Mrs. Flora Widdifield Chew, Mrs. C. M. Worth-
ington, Mrs. Wilson, Mrs. T. C. Badley, Mrs. Frey.

The missionaries of North India Conference, working to the utmost
limits of their strength, felt their force sadly depleted when two of
their number were suddenly called home. They had scarcely commenced the year's work, when Miss Lois· Buck, who had been appointed
to evangelistic work in Pauri, for which she was so well fitted,
after ·only two weeks in her new station, answered the call of the
Father for higher service. From all over the Conference came ex-
pressions of the love every one had for her, and of the purity of her
character. They can all be summed up in the words of Miss Budden,
who wrote her mother: "That blessed child lived more in Heaven than

---

⸪*Home on leave.

99

in earth, even when her purified spirit was tormented in her earthly tabernacle. I feel as if she had simply dropped this and gone where she belonged."

Dr. Tuttle, of Pithoragarh, gave her life in trying to save the lives of others in the mountain villages, where she had been so gladly welcomed only about a year before. Jesus said, "Greater love hath no man than this, that a man lay down his life for his friends."

BAREILLY DISTRICT.—From many places in the district come reports of revival effort and the awakening of the revival spirit. Mrs. Mansell says: "At Khera-Bajehera, so famous in the old days, as the village where General Gowan, a life-long helper of our Mission, was saved during the mutiny of '57 by two Hindu families, we found the people intensely interested in the message delivered.

"At our District Conference and the Dasehra Meetings held in Bareilly, many of our workers were wonderfully blessed and helped."

Mission Zenana Hospital.—Dr. Gimson reports: "The past year has been marked by more changes and difficulties than we have ever before experienced, yet, withal, more encouragement and joy and, as we review the work as a whole, we feel that the Lord has indeed been with us, and has cared for His work and His workers. One little girl after having treatment for months without benefit, was sent to us, and it was feared that only an amputation of her leg would save her life. But three operations, the last a skin-grafting, resulted in her perfect recovery, and she was sent back to school rejoicing. After this it was proposed to send her to another school, but those who had sent her to us asked for her return that they might show her to the people who had said the leg must be amputated."

A hand, also considered incurable, was saved in the same way. Quite a number of stones have been removed, one as large as a hen's egg. One Mohammedan woman, who came to us after two years of total blindness, received her sight by removal of cataracts, and after a few months, having had religious teaching day by day from the hospital Bible-reader, came and asked to be baptized, and is to-day our hospital matron, and having herself received both physical and spiritual sight, is rejoicing in Christ and telling others of His power to save. Our hospital Bible-reader spends a part of each day in the hospital, teaching the patients individually and collectively and then goes to the city for her zenana work. We believe that none of our work is bearing richer fruit than this. The total number of patients treated this year was 31,578; amount of fees and donations, $347.53.

Orphanage.—Two hundred girls have been in the Orphanage this year, and show, as Mrs. Widdifield says, what true love can accomplish in His name. There has been no epidemic of sickness among the girls, and they are making progress in their studies and learning some new industries.

Training School.—The women, as a rule, did unusually well in their examinations and won many words of praise from the examining committee. There have been forty-five women on the roll, five of whom completed the course. One new feature has been introduced this year. Instead of receiving their certificates when their husbands received their diplomas, they had a "closing" of their own, the day previous, furnishing the program, which consisted of an essay, dialogues, and songs. In the morning a thorough inspection was made of the forty houses to see which housewife had most fully followed the teaching regarding cleanlines in housekeeping, and in the evening a prize was awarded to the successful one, as well as a prize for the best sewing.

SHAHJAHANPUR.—Miss English is in charge of the school and reports a very prosperous year with very little sickness. Their roll has numbered 117, and they have raised the standard of the school another grade, and hope to send up a class for the next examination. There has also been spiritual improvement. The girls have done some industrial work and earned something for the Jubilee thanksgiving. They also helped in the benevolent collections, and are developing in their Christian character.

City and Village Work.—There is an increase in the number of zenanas visited. One hundred and fifty girls are enrolled in the four Hindu schools. The Bible-women received a great spiritual uplift during the District Conference, and start the new term with greater zeal and love in their hearts for their work than they ever had and feel a greater responsibility than ever before.

The Home for Homeless Women has had nineteen women enrolled, who work to earn part of their living. They go every morning to the Mission House for prayers and religious instruction. A Missionary meeting is held every month, which they attend, contributing what they are able.

Circuit Work.—In seven circuits, consisting of about one hundred and fifty villages, our faithful Bible-women are carrying the Gospel to many women. The spiritual condition of the Christian women is improving, while the non-Christian women are convinced that the Gospel teaching is right, and are giving heed to the Word of God and are inquiring into it.

BIJNOUR DISTRICT.—The Girls' Boarding School under the charge of Mrs. Gill has had an enrollment of eighty-three, twelve of whom were day-scholars. They have a hard time in the school, fighting itch, and, having no room where the children could be successfully isolated, were unable to entirely control it. They have the best staff of teachers they have had for years, all of whom are earnest Christians. The result of their Christian lives was, seen when Bishop Warne came to hold special services. The girls were ready to accept the truth, and many were converted, and are living Christian lives, and so anxious to testify that there is not time enough for all. They have prayer every evening and become so absorbed in prayer that they do not realize when it is bed-time. They have a very interesting Junior League and a good Missionary Auxiliary for the older girls.

City and Village Work.—Mrs. Gill also has supervision of the city and village work. In the city work there are two Bible-women and two teachers of Mohammedan schools. One Bible-woman visits in about fifty homes, and the other works from house to house. In the district work, we have workers in twenty-nine and nine circuits.

BUDAON DISTRICT.—Miss Laura Wright is in charge of the Sigler Girls' Boarding School. Three years ago the enrollment reached seventy; this year one hundred, four of whom are day pupils. Heretofore the girls have had to go to other schools for their middle examination, but from this year they hope to prepare them here for it. Miss Wright says: "As we review the year's work all other items sink into insignificance, when we consider the blessed work the Holy Spirit is doing in the hearts of our girls. For three weeks ten or fifteen girls had been praying that the Holy Spirit might come to our girls as He had come to the girls in the Moradabad school. One week ago the 'showers of blessing' began. Night after night they pray often for hours. Some hearts have been changed, others wonderfully blessed. Many have been given the spirit of intercession and are praying for their families and the prayers are being answered. Our school and boarding department are in very cramped quarters. We can not accommodate girls, and there is no more room to build. Then the railroad has come and the station is only a few hundred yards from our school. What we need is money to buy land for a new site and money for new buildings. May God move some one to send us this money."

The money for the land has been given; who will furnish the much needed buildings?

City and Village Work.—Miss Waugh has had charge of this work. Miss Waugh and her Bible-women have been hindered a great deal in their work by the plague and small-pox. All over the many circuits belonging to this district the people are hungry for salvation. God is working in the hearts of His people and the revival is spreading. In one circuit of one hundred and fifty villages, our eight Bible-women are able to visit but fifty of these villages. Who will carry the Gospel to the other hundred villages? This has been the Jubilee year in our zenana work, and our workers are unable to reach the many who want to hear the "good news." Our city schools, nine in number—four for Hindu girls, three for Mohammedan, and two for Christian girls—have had an unusually successful year. When Miss Waugh visited one of these schools, one of the little girls said, "Miss Sahib, that catechism you sent us is in Roman Urdu; we can't read it; please send us one in Hindi. A school *without a catechism is no good.*" It is certainly encouraging to hear from the lips of a Hindu girl that a school without daily Christian teaching is no good.

GARHWAL DISTRICT.—This district, comprising a small part of the Himalayan Mountain range, is densely populated with Indian people of different castes, many of whom have never heard of Jesus, and the majority still uninfluenced by the Gospel message. Faithful, conscientious work has been done, but the laborers are so very few. Mrs. Messmore, in charge, writes: "Early in the year, with my Bible-woman, I began my itineracy. We were busy early and late, and many women listened to the Bible story, but said their husbands, who were controlled by the priests, would not allow them to accept the teaching, although they believe the words true. But a school of fifteen girls has been opened, and the preacher's wife is now visiting in the Mohammedan zenanas, and in the evening the Hindu women come to her house for religious inquiries. We believe these beginnings will deepen into a great interest for all the women."

PAURI.—In the Girls' Orphanage, Miss Wilson gives thanks for general good health of the girls; for protection during the anxious days when the cholera raged in adjacent villages; for good harvests, and for a blessed revival. Four of these girls are in the Muttra Training-school, and two in the Ludhiana Medical School, and one of these girls is now a graduated doctor.

HARDOI DISTRICT.—Mrs. Tucker is Superintendent of the Girls' Boarding School, and reports as follows: "There have been sixty girls in the school, who have made good progress in their studies and other daily work. The school has been accepted as a school to be aided by Government, and a small monthly grant has been received since April. The girls do all their own cooking and grinding. They have grown spiritually, and some were greatly blessed during the evangelistic services held in connection with the District Conference. The great design of the school is to furnish well-equipped workers for the district, and each year some go out into the needy fields to teach others what they have learned."

Circuit Work.—In the Hardoi Circuit, on account of the plague, not so much itinerating has been done as usual, yet thirty-two women have been baptized during the year. Special evangelistic services have been held, and the Christians have received new blessings. In the other fifteen circuits of this district the Bible-women are teaching in 467 homes and holding eighteen Sunday-schools with about six hundred girls in them, besides the hundreds of women in non-Christian homes and the multitudes to whom they talk as they stop to rest under trees and along the roadside.

KUMAON DISTRICT.—At our last Annual Conference the Bareilly-Kumaon District was divided, and the old Kumaon District came into existence again, after five years' amalgamation with the Bareilly District. It is now a mountainous district with the Bhabar and Terai, the land at the foot of the mountain, and reaches from here way up to Bhot on the border of Tibet. Mrs. Neeld says: "A new feature of our district is the Branch Theological Seminary in Dwarahat, with Dr. and Mrs. Dease in charge. Mrs. Dease has a training school for the women workers of the district; the women will do better work in their villages having had this help. The hill work is hard, distance great, and idolatry most intense; the people are generally well to do, hence quite contented with themselves and the grand mountains 'round about them; they worship them and make long, weary pilgrimages to their snowy peaks. Our workers are few, but our hopes are large, and we have the satisfaction that comes from the fact that something has been, and is being, done to help these people to a better knowledge of God, and what it is to live for Him. Scattered over these hills are one thousand one hundred and eleven Christians of our Church, and in our schools are two thousand and seventy-six boys and girls.

Wellesley Girls' High School.—From Wellesley, where are Miss S. A. Easton and Miss R. A. Sellers, comes the following report: "Behind us are twenty-four milestones. The first six were set without tools by Miss Knowles. On her first milestone one boarding pupil was inscribed, and on the twentieth, one hundred and six, the highest number of boarders in the house any year. A full staff of efficient teachers, who love Wellesley, and, what is rarer, matrons and housekeeper devoted to their duties, the year has passed quickly, and we have come again to the final examinations. Of the 134 enrolled during the year, twenty-five have been entered for the Government examinations, the remainder received their class promotions before the prize distribution on November 24th, which this year had more than ordinary interest to us all. The staff and girls had decided to commemorate the anniversary by presenting Wellesley with a library fund. The committee reported more than Rs. 300, and the effort to add to this fund will continue next year. From the first music has been well to the front. In nine years one hundred and seventeen Trinity College music certificates have been obtained. This year fifteen candidates were presented for the practical examinations, both in violin and piano, and sixteen have been entered for the theory of music. To the fixed Government grant of the last seven years Rs. 100 was added this year, and later a supplementary grant of Rs. 1,200, making in all Rs. 4,950, or about $1,650."

Hindustani Work.—Mrs. Worthington has charge of the Hindustani work, and reports three day schools with an average attendance of 107 girls, and all the teachers being Christians. Some of the girls have made remarkable progress, having done nearly two years' work in nine months. The early marriage of our girls is the most discouraging feature. Many of these girls marry into homes in Naini Tal, and we follow them wherever we are allowed to go. The girls have had very earnest teaching and prayerful teaching from the Word of God, and we are sure that good seed has been sown, and impressions have been made that must, in the years to come, tell in their lives. Of the zenana work she says: "The zenana work has been carried on under difficulties, as I have had no Bible-reader to help me; but with few interruptions daily visiting has been done, and the Word has been given to ninety women. Our visits to the zenanas are always welcome, and in some houses eagerly looked forward to. One woman said to me, 'When you come in, our hearts revive, and we feel there is brightness in our home.' Another, when she was leaving Naini Tal, said with tears, 'Do not forget me, but pray for me. I love to hear what you teach,' and then she added with a smile, 'My husband says he will become a Christian when his old father dies.' So the work goes on slowly but surely."

DWARAHAT CIRCUIT.—*Girls' Boarding School.*—Twenty-four girls were enrolled when school reopened in March. Miss Seymore has been all alone since her sister's death, and is rejoicing over the transfer of Miss Oram from Pithoragarh to help her with this school. The Home for these workers, so badly needed, was granted during the year.

Village and District Work.—The village and district work is under the charge of Mrs. Neeld. A woman's school has been opened, and the regular Bible-reader's course has been taken up. After school the women go to do religious work among the women of the various villages or by the wayside wherever they meet them.

PITHORAGARH CIRCUIT.—While Miss Lucy Sullivan has been enjoying a well-earned furlough in the home land, the work at Pithoragarh has moved successfully forward, with Miss Conoly at the head of the school of seventy-three girls, Miss Budden in charge of the evangelistic work, Dr. Tuttle in charge of the medical work, and Miss Mary Means, with her faithful assistant, Miss McMullen, at the head of the Woman's Home. Dr. Tuttle was fast getting hold of the people, and had treated nearly six thousand patients. Miss Budden supervises fifty Bible-women, and takes them out on tours through many villages. In answer to many prayers, God visited first the school and then the home in a wonderful manner, and the girls and the women received great blessings, which prepared them for the dreadful trial which came to them after school opened June 3d, when cholera invaded Rai, just at the border of the farm. Then began a six weeks' siege; the girls were moved to Chandag, and fifty of the women sent away. The Hindu women fled and the coolies demanded exorbitant prices. June 13th brought added anxiety, when a woman died in the Home from small-pox. Soon cholera reached Chandag, and the girls had to be brought back; and on June 18th cholera reached the Mission, and two women, one little girl and Dr. Tuttle, who had come over to help them in this time of trouble, went home. No words can tell of these dreadful six weeks. In the burial of all these, the Hindu servants dug the graves, and our devoted missionaries and their faithful women did all the rest that was needed—were their own undertakers and preachers by turn. The faithfulness of the volunteer nurses, some of them Miss Budden's Bible-women, and others from our own home, and of the servants will not soon be forgotten. Miss Means writes: "God has indeed been good to us. I think we, who have gone through this trial, will never, never forget the sense of peace and security He gave us in the very face of death, when we did not know from hour to hour who might be the next to be stricken down."

CHANDAG HEIGHTS.—From her mountain home Miss Mary Reed sends greetings to her many friends. She writes: "I am practically lone-handed in this blessed service which so engrosses my thoughts. In addition to the care of more than eighty suffering ones, I also have the pleasure of teaching about seventy village boys with the help of a corps of four young teachers. This day school, attended by boys from the villages round about, is a great strain on my heart-strings, the sight of such suffering as must be endured by my poor patients. We have a very interesting and well attended Sunday-school with these dear, bright boys, whose growth toward the light delights my heart."

BHOT.—Dr. Martha Sheldon is happy in being again in her chosen field. During her absence Mary Reed had charge of the work. Dr. Sheldon reports: "Medical work has been carried on as usual. At the house we have taken patients in our servants' quarters or tents. Our busiest time with the sick is when they come up from the plains or malarious valleys below in the spring or early summer. We have also had several cataract cases. The time has come to build special rooms or wards for these patients, and a friend has already given the first donation towards this object. A suitable field has lately been purchased for the building. Medical work, too, is always a feature of our evangelistic tours. Itinerating this year has been largely carried on by my colleague, Miss Browne. On her longest tour she was away from Chaudas, July 10th to September 15th. While this year, by special order of the Government, all Europeans were kept out of Thibet, except special Government agents, Miss Browne's trip was full of interest and adventure, as she crossed a notoriously high and difficult pass between Biyas and Darma Bhot, on August 13th, which she calls (to her) 'the longest day in the year!' She was accompanied by our pastor, Umrao Singh, and two Christian servants. Miss Browne was well equipped with medicines fresh from America, and a beautiful series of pictures illustrating the life of Christ. She dispensed much medicine, in the use of which she has become quite an adept. The rice and flour, etc., received for medical services were a great help in supplying the needs of herself and party in the expensive villages she visited. Meanwhile I remained alone at Chaudas, taking up the services usually conducted by our preacher, looking after the Epworth-League, teaching, etc. Our fields and gardens have contributed to the support of ourselves and children. The fruit trees set out ten or eleven years ago are beginning to bear well. We exchanged a good deal of fruit for rice and flour. We encourage the people of the villages to plant vegetables, etc. In villages 11,000 feet above the sea, Miss Browne had fine cabbages brought to her with the remark, 'These are owing to you!'

"Sundays.—After Sunday-school on our verandah, five bands visited as many villages and held Sunday-schools in the villages; other services being held in the evening at the bungalow. With the help of Mr. W. E. Blackstone an entirely new roof has been put on our buildings; and we rejoice in the thought that we have a comfortable place of worship in a central location, near the road which goes up to Biyas and Tibet, over which literally thousands wend their way up and down in the course of the year."

MORADABAD DISTRICT.—Mrs. Core has been at the head of the evangelistic work of the district. She writes: "Our greatest cause for rejoicing has been the great revival which has visited our schools. Our District Conference was a blessed season to all. Many of our workers were filled to overflowing and went back to their work new men and women. The memory of the last wonderful Sunday in the grove will always live in the memories of those privileged to attend. There was a wonderful morning meeting where sins were confessed, and enemies of many years'. standing embraced each other and wept and begged forgiveness. The noonday communion service was to many the most impressive and beautiful service of the day. Village Christians, workers, laymen, boys and girls and missionaries—all gathered around the Lord's table with hearts overflowing with Father's love. In awed silence we felt the presence of the Holy Ghost. The last meeting of the day went on for hours and could not be stopped. There were literally showers of blessing. All night long could be heard the sound of prayer and praise in different parts of the grove. After seeing and hearing and feeling these things, it does not take much faith to believe that the Lord will do great things in our district the coming year. There have been about 1,600 baptisms in our district this year."

MORADABAD CIRCUIT.—The evangelistic work of the Moradabad Circuit is under the charge of Mrs. Faucett. Many of the villages lying near have been visited by the Bible-women. They carry the "good tidings of joy" through song and prayer and Bible teaching. They have Sunday-schools in several places where the children are taught about Jesus. The work is not confined to Christians, but many non-Christian homes are visited and the women taught the way of salvation.

City Schools and Muhalla Work.—Mrs. Parker, in charge of this work, reports: "On account of much sickness, the schools have not done as good work as usual, but some changes have been made which promise to add to the efficiency of the work. The Sunday-schools have been kept up, and the girls never tire of our Christian songs, and as they sing these in their homes the Christian truth is carried to all the inmates. The schools are centers of influence and are important auxiliaries in the work we are trying to do for the women of the city. In five of the Muhallas visited we have small schools, where the children of Christians and non-Christians are being taught. The number of listeners in the Muhallas varies from time to time. Sometimes ten or fifteen gather as *bhojans* are sung and explained. Sometimes fifty or sixty come. Often they bring their work and sit and work while they join in the singing. This is especially true in the Chamar Muhallas. These meetings are held in the shade of trees, in some courtyard, or in front of some friendly woman's house, where not only the women and girls, but often the men and boys sit down to listen. The old, old story never loses its charm."

Training School.—This school is for teaching and training Bible-readers especially for Muhalla and village work. There have been twenty names enrolled during the year. One of the advanced students is an assistant teacher in the school, another has commenced work by accompanying the missionary in the work in the city, and five are teaching Muhalla schools. Those who were able to attend the evangelistic services in connection with the District Conference were greatly blessed and returned to their work with renewed zeal.

Girls' Boarding School.—Miss Alice Means, in charge of the Boarding School, reports that "The past year has been one crowded with blessings. The accommodations of the school have been taxed to the utmost, and twenty girls have been turned away for lack of room. As to health, the record has been better than I have ever known it. As to educational results, of the six girls sent up for the Government Middle examination all passed. The Government Inspectress is much pleased with the work of the girls. But best of all is the spiritual advance. The revival has changed everything. The atmosphere of the place is so different. March 8th, the anniversary of the coming of the revival, the school was closed, and the day spent in prayer and thanksgiving by the request of the girls. We have had 131 pupils enrolled during the year, and have a nice kindergarten of over thirty children." Conference transferred Miss Nora Waugh to open a Normal Department, of which she took charge October 1st.

OUDH DISTRICT.—This year has been the best in the history of the Oudh District, and the work done by the Bible-women among the women and girls shared this general prosperity. Schools are scattered over the district, and many have been baptized into the new faith. Mrs. Robinson, who has charge of this work, has a great deal of sickness in the family, but her husband, though burdened with work, has kindly gathered and forwarded the letter from the Bible-women. The circuit work is growing, and we have not enough workers to go to all who call them. God has blessed the work of the Bible-women, and many women and girls have been baptized.

Lucknow City Schools.—Mrs. Badley, in charge, writes: "These little schools, situated in the midst of the native city, are attended by the little Mohammedan girls, who, were it not for the teaching given in the schools, would be left entirely without knowledge of Christ, and would grow up unable to even read or write. Better teaching and more careful supervision have made much improvement in these schools this year. The large Government grant makes it possible to have more than the present number, and arrangements are made to open one, and perhaps two, the coming year.

Deaconess Home and Home for Homeless Women.—The number in the Home for Homeless Women is larger than since 1902. The aim of the Home is to help these women to a better place in life, to help them develop and improve. A new feature in the work this year has been the coming of two widows from Lucknow, who applied for admittance because they felt the need of the protection of a Christian home. With their help a sewing class has been started to help the poor Christian women. Receiving a family of children for daily teaching is another new feature; this family belongs to a Mohammedan mother who was willing to have them receive both secular and religious teaching, but was not willing to place them in a regular school. Miss Hardie was in charge of this work all year, but in vacation was taken very ill, and, after being in the hospital some weeks, was obliged to return home. Miss Ingram has carried on the Deaconess visiting among the English-speaking, special attention being given those who were sick or in trouble. Many children, sick and crippled, have been taken to the hospital and helped, and many similar acts of kindness marked the year's work. A great advance has been made in the zenana work; all fancy work teaching has been dropped, and the whole time is devoted to religious instruction, or teaching the girls and women to read. Some of the less hopeful houses, where, after years of instruction, there seems to be so little interest, have been dropped, and the new doors entered. Some speak confidently of their faith in Christ, and others are almost ready to accept Him, yet none ask for baptism, but the break will come sometime and these secluded ones will acknowledge their Savior, whom they have learned to love. The registers show the largest number of calls for the year since the work was commenced. For the zenana workers about two thousand, and for the English and native Christian work over three thousand. Over three hundred and sixty people have been in the Home, and about four thousand five hundred papers, Testaments, etc., have been distributed.

Isabella Thoburn College.—The old College building has been greatly improved by the addition of a second story, and the two buildings have been made one by adding new verandas to the old buildings, and even the Government engineers say that it is one of the finest buildings in Lucknow. Miss Singh has had charge of the garden, and, while it has not been an easy task, yet the compound has been cleared, and now all the corners are as attractive as the center garden, and in turn chrysanthemums, roses, pansies, violets, nasturtiums, and sweet peas have made the garden beautiful. The great need now is a new High School building which will properly house the High School, the Normal Department, and the Kindergarten. Miss Nichols reports: "During the past five years Government has increased the yearly grant from Rs. 1,740 to Rs. 5,940, and has given special grants to the amount of Rs. 11,800. These grants are conditional on improvement in teaching and accommodations. The quality of the teaching staff has greatly improved. Seven of the twelve school teachers are our own students. The results of the Government University examinations in the Isabella Thoburn College were so phenomenal that we quote a paragraph from the *Star of India* as to their success:

"'It is no new thing for the Isabella Thoburn College to stand well in the regular Government University examinations. Indeed, so uniformly is it successful that it would be a surprise to have it occupy anything but a high place in its tuitional results. But the marks of the past year, recently published in detail, show that this well-known Woman's College has even surpassed its usual results, and has had really phenomenal success. In the B. A. examinations the number of candidates sent up from the provinces was 375, and in results Miss Lucy Bolton, of the Isabella Thoburn College, heads the list. In the First Arts examination a total of 641 candidates went, and Dorothy Bolton, of the Isabella Thoburn College, heads the list. In the Entrance examination there was a total of 1,367 candidates, and among this number twelve scholarships were to be distributed in order of merit. Emmie Moore and Vidyaviti Singh, of the Isabella Thoburn College, are among the successful twelve. In the Middle School examination the Government distributed sixteen scholarships among the seventy-seven girls who took the test. Of these sixteen, five come to the students sent up by the Isabella Thoburn College. The fact that this success is distributed so evenly among the various classes of the college and school shows that the high standing of the students is the result of all-round hard work and good preparation. We most heartily congratulate the principal and her efficient staff on the good results of their labors, and venture to hope for them as high success in the future.'

"The chief missionary interest of the year was the Jubilee. In school and college and among the teachers the work of our Mission in India has been constantly in mind. Rupees 1,300 have been paid in, and some more will be given before the close of the year. The enrollment in the college is nineteen, nine European and Eurasian girls and ten Indian girls. The college class-day was a great success. The Lieutenant-Governor presided, and after the exercises he and Lady La Touche inspected the college buildings and were greatly pleased with the new rooms. The special training in calisthenics, elocution, and music enables the students to give good programs on class-day and other occasions. The interest in music is growing. The enrollment in the Normal School is twelve—ten of these are Europeans or Eurasian. In the High School department the enrollment is 133; the great majority (120) of the girls are Indian. There are twelve resident teachers and a munshi. The cooking class continues to justify its existence, and the girls cook very good Saturday breakfasts. The sewing classes have been busy preparing a complete school outfit to send to the Jubilee exhibit. Each year we realize more fully that our success depends upon the spirit with which we work, and upon united efforts. Our family now numbers twenty-one, and our interests and ambitions are the same— American and Eurasian, Indian and English. We are all working together to train the girls of India to become earnest, true Christian women."

GONDA CIRCUIT.—Mrs. Hewes writes: "God has been in our midst, and has greatly blessed His own people. We believe woman has done her work faithfully and well, realizing that this work is of God, and that her reward is from Him. The number of zenanas is increasing, and the visit of the Bible-reader is looked forward to with pleasure. The work among the village people is most interesting and hopeful. God's Word is touching the hearts of these simple people. In places where they would not receive us formerly, the people now look for our coming with pleasure, and some say they have been thinking and wondering when we would come again. Once some of them said, 'We did not formerly give a thought to falsehoods, petty thefts, and such things which you tell us are sins, and we had never been told that we ought not to do them.'"

Girls' Boarding School.—Miss Celesta Easton had charge of this school until Conference, when she was transferred to Bareilly and Miss Elizabeth Hoge was appointed principal. Miss Hoge reports that her assistants are of the best; that her girls are like all girls—sometimes good and sometimes naughty, but on the whole are nice girls. Five of them took the Government examination. They had special meetings in April, during which the spiritual life of the school was quickened.

SITAPUR CIRCUIT.—The work on the circuit has had its encouragements and discouragements, but the work is progressing, though at times it seems hard to those in charge of the work to see so few taking a stand for Christ, yet they know that God is working in the hearts of the women, and that some would confess Christ if they could.

Girls' Boarding School.—Miss Soper reached India from her vacation in the homeland in March and found the work for the year well in hand, and everything progressing. After the summer vacation, although two of the teachers left to continue their studies and one was married, yet the school opened in July with a full corps of trained teachers. Ninety-two girls were enrolled, the largest number the school has ever had. The girls are doing well in lessons, sewing, and calisthenics. The Epworth Leagues, Class-meetings, and Missionary Society are doing good work. The results of the Government examination for the year were good, four out of five of the candidates having passed.

PHILIBHIT DISTRICT.—Mrs. Frey reports for the district a very successful summer school and a blessed revival, and for the circuit work progress everywhere. About five hundred houses are regularly visited, hundreds of women are under instruction, and 178 have been baptized.

NORTHWEST INDIA CONFERENCE.

Organized as a Conference in 1892.
Official Correspondent, Miss Ella M. Watson.

The United Provinces of Agra and Oudh south and west of the Ganges, the Punjaub, and such parts of Rajputana and Central India as are north of the twenty-fifth parallel of latitude, are embraced in the Northwest India Conference.

Missionaries and Their Stations.

AJMERE.—Anne E. Lawson, Lavinia Nelson.
ALIGARH.—Mary A. Hart, Julia R. Kipp.
BRINDABAN.—Emma Scott, M. D.
CAWNPORE.—Lydia S. Pool, Bessie F. Crowell.
MEERUT.—Melva Livermore, Lena Wilson.
MUTTRA.—Mary Eva Gregg, Agnes E. Saxe, Mary A. Parkhurst.
PHALERA.—Lilly D. Greene, C. E. Hoffman, *Annie S. Winslow, *Ida Ellis, *Laura Bobenhouse, *Isabelle McKnight.
WIVES OF MISSIONARIES AND DEACONESSES IN CHARGE OF WORK.—Mrs. P. M. Buck, Mrs. G. F. Matthews, Mrs. Rockwell Clancy, Mrs. W. W. Ashe, Mrs. D. C. Clancy, Mrs. H. R. Calkins, Mrs. Bensen Baker, Mrs. T. S. Molesworth, Mrs. J. B. Thomas.

AJMERE.—Miss Hart, after doing much to raise the standard of the school, was called to Aligarh at the last Conference. Miss Lawson and Miss Lavinia Nelson are now holding the fort here.

In the Boarding School satisfactory progress is recorded, much of which is due to the faithful work of the teaching staff. A normal class and kindergarten have also added to the success of this year's work. The girls pledged a rupee each to the Jubilee Fund, most of which was saved by drawn thread and embroidery articles which they made and sold at the Jubilee. Best of all, the girls are on a higher spiritual plane, and through the prayer band have gained new blessing. Of the district Miss Lawson writes: "The grim specter of famine still lurks in the background; for, although we had some rain, it has been quite inadequate to meet the need, and food prices continue abnormally high. Within the sphere of British rule great relief works have been established, employing thousands. In native states the arrangements were not so effective, and many migrated to other regions, deserting their villages. To aid the many hundreds of Christians throughout the Ajmere District our Mission opened grain shops in the large centers where the people could buy grain at reasonable prices, or receive it gratuitously if unable to work. These centers of grain distribution have been a great blessing to many. They have been made possible by the generous help of friends in America and elsewhere."

PHALERA.—Our forces at Phalera have been strengthened by Miss Hoffman, who has proved a very efficient worker. Thus Miss Greene has been relieved of some responsibility in the Orphanage and has been able to go into the villages to tell the eager waiting people of the love of Christ.

The work in the Orphanage is progressing, and the girls developing and entering larger fields of preparation and usefulness. Four have been sent to Muttra to take the training school course. Two of these are doing work in our own Mission. One girl is teaching lace-making in the Ajmere Girls' School.

The industrial work continues to be an important feature of the training of these famine children. The girls have woven hundreds of yards of cloth during the year, besides blankets and mats. Some of the most faithful and efficient were rewarded by being allowed to attend the Jubilee meeting and there demonstrate the beautiful lace-making, embroidery, and drawn thread work. The school benefited

---

*Home on leave.

financially by the sale of about two hundred rupees' worth of fancy articles at the Jubilee meeting.

Miss Greene writes of the district work: "My first trips after Conference were to the villages round about us. A fleet-footed pony carried me swiftly across· the sandy plains, where I was able to visit large villages and tell the Gospel story to great crowds of eager listeners. At Bichun an old fakir came with his school boys, and at the close of my talk received the Gospels which I gave to all who could read."

TILAUNÍA.—Dr. Edna Beck Keisler has left our ranks, but she will always be a medical evangelist among the women wherever she may be stationed. The work in this section of Rajputana is greatly in need of a doctor. Besides the sanitarium, an hour's distance by rail is the large Orphanage at Phalera. All who have been connected with work for famine orphans know that in cases of disease prompt measures are necessary, as frequently the constitution is already undermined by early privation and suffering. In addition to these two needy lines of work, the surrounding district, with its many villages where no medical work is being done, furnishes unlimited opportunities for winning the people to Christ through the ministry of healing.

ALLAHABAD.—Mrs. Dennis Clancy reports: "The past year has been our best. The girls ·have been wonderfully good throughout the year. The revival meant so much to them. Some had their consciences so awakened that they confessed their faults and returned even tiny pieces of cloth which they had stolen. One girl who always seemed so unhappy has entirely changed, and had such a wonderful experience she was almost beside herself for joy. As far as possible an itinerary of the district has been made."

CAWNPORE.—(Girls' English High School)—Miss Pool and Miss Crowell report a very successful year. Miss Pool says: "The school can boast of an excellent staff of teachers who are all trained and are not only efficient in the class-room, but are in loving sympathy with all the work of the school. The results· of last year's Government examinations were a great cause for encouragement.

"Finances are sometimes a problem, still in this respect the school has held its own during the· year. We are indebted to the Woman's Foreign Missionary Society for part of our support—some money comes from fees. Besides this, we have the Cooper Fund donated by Sir William E. Cooper, C. I. E., thus making it possible for some to receive an education.who otherwise would be denied the privilege. The Government grant-in-aid for the year was Rs. 2,953. A further grant of Rs. 3,000 was given for extensive repairs, provided an equal amount be duplicated by the school. This amount was furnished by the Woman's Foreign Missionary Society, and has been applied on the new roof and other needed repairs."

This large grant from the British Government shows certainly the esteem in which the school is. held. The missionaries are still struggling with heavy financial burdens, but God has been with them in the past and they have confidence for the future.

The Hindustani Girls' School has been supplied by Miss Leach, whose report is a thanksgiving for the Father's care. She writes: "The older girls and teachers have organized a prayer circle. This has done much for our school. Every Friday the teachers meet to talk and pray over the successes and failures of the week's work. These teachers' meetings have·helped us all greatly. At the close of a very busy year in the district with insufficient workers Mrs. Calkins writes:

"We had not even time to be discouraged. The needs and God Himself pushed us on through the year. Now at its close we are filled with praise."

KASJANG DISTRICT.—Here our faithful Bible-readers have been carrying on their work under the supervision of Miss Holman, who is rejoiced to be in India again. The District Conference, with Bishop Warne presiding, marked a definite advance in the spiritual life of many of our people.

MEERUT.—The past year has brought many changes here. It has been a grief to Miss Marble and her co-workers that unexpected circumstances have called her to the home-land. Miss Livermore has resumed her work in the school, bringing with her from America Miss Lena Nelson, who is proving to be a great help in the work. We read of their year's work: "The best time of the year was that of the revival. Almost every girl in the school testified to having been blessed. Certainly a new and more Christ-like spirit was found among us."

Mrs. Buck is as enthusiastic as ever in the district work. She writes: "Our field covers three civil districts in which are about 21,000 converts, largely untrained, living in more than a thousand villages. There are also a great number of inquirers calling on every side. It is India womanhood, consecrated to Christ, that is to do the greater part of the work of uplifting the down-trodden women of this land.

"I would like specially to mention the wives of our preachers in charge. Some of them as regular Bible-readers, others only receiving an allowance for itinerating, have, as a rule, stood nobly by their husbands, making the work of the whole circuit their own, visiting the distant villages as able, teaching the evangelist teachers, helping Bible-readers in their studies, supervising the work, and leading on the younger and more inexperienced workers. I can only mention one among so many.

"Sophia Haqq was rescued by Bishop Thoburn as a little waif out in the fields among the goat herds. She was given to Mrs. Parker and soon became one of the brightest and best among the Moradabad School girls. She married a son of Zahur ul Haqq, the first convert of our Mission, and together they have built up a home worthy of Christianity, with children stepping out into the service of the Master, with the blessing that comes to 'children's children' abiding upon them. In her plain, quiet dress, Sophia goes out with her husband in the simplest kind of bullock cart from village to village. Once when her husband brought in a long list of villages visited, I said, 'But these are the places you have gone.' With a smile he answered, 'But she always goes with me.' She has often said, 'The children are all settled or in school, and now I am free to serve.'"

MUTTRA DISTRICT.—AGRA.—Miss Holman is in charge of the Medical Home, city and zenana work. This is a very difficult field and needs your special prayers, for as has been well said, "There is no class of young women in India in whom there is the possibility of doing so much good as there is in these Christian medical girls, if their lives are consecrated to the service of the Master. There are none who can bring greater reproach upon the cause of Christ in this land if they fail to live the religion they profess."

ALIGARH.—After years of faithful service in building up the Orphanage on every side, Miss Bobenhouse has gone home for a much-needed furlough. Miss Hart and Miss Kipp are carrying on the work, and are kept busy supervising the school, gardening, plain and fancy sewing, and many domestic cares that arise in a family numbering one hundred and forty-five. The Bible work done by these girls is excellent, no girl having ever failed in the Scripture examinations. With such a basis it is no wonder that the revival which has reached the school too has left permanent results.

In the Woman's Industrial Home, Mrs. Matthews has had a good year. She writes: "In every department of the work there has been progress. The girls and women have grown in knowledge and grace." The girls and women of the Home received much commendation for the capable way in which they served at the tables and did the entire baking for the Jubilee Celebration at Bareilly.

BRINDABAN.—Miss Scott has been kept busy caring for the sick here and in the whole district, as far as she has time and strength to go. She has had efficient helpers in the zenana work, and writes that the work among the Christian women and children is more encouraging than it has been.

MUTTRA.—*Blackstone Missionary Institute.*—Muttra has had both cloud and sunshine during the past year. Illness has necessitated the absence for some time of Rev. and Mrs. Clancy, who have always been most helpful in sharing our burdens and advancing our work. Now we are rejoicing in the return of Miss Gregg to resume her old duties with new strength and enthusiasm; and the coming of Miss Parkhurst, the long prayed-for third missionary, who is so much needed in this heavy work

Our Deaconess Home family has numbered from sixteen to eighteen throughout the year—missionaries, assistants, and students in the English Department. The Boarding School is overflowing its dormitories, and the Training School has had an unusually good attendance of women and girls.

We must not forget to mention our kindergarten, an advance move in which Miss Saxe is greatly interested and which will mean much to the little folks in Summer School, as well as to our own boarding school gir s.

MUTTRA DISTRICT.—Mrs. Clancy has been detained in the hills on account of Mr. Clancy's illness during a greater part of the year. She writes: "In this time of enforced absence from Muttra, it has been a great comfort to know the work has not suffered, but has been carried on faithfully by Miss McLeavy and our beloved native helpers. Miss McLeavy is the only lady itinerant in a district of over 15,000 Christians. She is finding much to encourage, and also much to discourage. The principal cause of discouragement is the lack of efficient workers to teach these hosts of Christians, but it is very encouraging to find how anxious they are to be taught, and how readily they respond to kind and patient teaching."

ROORKEE DISTRICT.—Mrs. Lyons writes: "On taking up work early in the year we found the state of the workers low spiritually, so at once started revival services. On the fifth day of our meetings we had victory—such a time of heart searching and true blessing we had never seen before. Many proved this by having power to lead others to Christ.

"We have had three hundred and fifty baptisms of women and girls this year. Our hearts rejoice as we go around our circuits, and the best of all is, God is with us."

PUNJAB DISTRICT.—Mrs. Butcher is supervising the work in this great district alone. There are thirteen circuits, most of which are very large. Mrs. Butcher tells us: "It would hardly be possible for me to visit all the places covered by these circuits. That would be the work

8

of several ladies who could put in all their time. I hope we can have an evangelist who can learn the Punjabi language right away, and another lady to start our Boarding School. We have no buildings, but a house could be rented if we only had some money, and the missionary to run it. While we are waiting for it, the girls who could have come last year have many of them been married and their chance is gone forever. There will, of course, be other girls this year and in all the years to come, but the girls of *now* are losing their chances. Pray, dear sisters, who read these lines, that the time of waiting may not be long."

SOUTH INDIA CONFERENCE.

Official Correspondent, Mrs. E. D. Huntley.
Organized as a Conference in 1876; reorganized in 1886.

The South India Conference includes all that part of India lying south of the Bombay and Bengal Conferences and the Central Provinces' Mission Conference.

MISSIONARIES AND THEIR STATIONS.

BANGALORE.—Urdell Montgomery, Ary J. Holland, Elizabeth M. Benthein.
BIDAR.—Norma H. Fenderich.
HYDERABAD.—Catherine A. Wood and Alice A. Evans.
KOLAR.—*Fannie F. Fisher, Florence Maskell, Harriet A. Holland, and Judith Ericson.
MADRAS.—Grace Stephens.
BELGAUM.—Grace M. Woods.
VIKARABAD.—Elizabeth J. Wells and Mildred Simonds.
WIVES OF MISSIONARIES.—Mrs. A. E. Cook, Mrs. C. W. Sharer, Mrs. Buttrick, Mrs. P. V. Roberts, Mrs. Batstone, Mrs. Tindale, Mrs. M. C. Ernsberger, Mrs. Parker, Mrs. Anderson, Mrs. Hollister, Mrs. Schermerhorn, Mrs. Grose.

BANGALORE.—Since 1902 the Woman's Foreign Missionary Society has had the entire responsibility of the Baldwin Girls' School at Bangalore. The rent of the buildings and salaries of principal and associate principal have been paid by the Woman's Foreign Missionary Society. The Government has allowed a grant of 200 rupees a month toward teachers' salaries, and apart from this the school has paid its own way. The debt on the property is a great embarrassment, but Government has at last sanctioned a grant of 10,000 rupees, which is about one-third the amount we had hoped for. With the $4,000 that Topeka Branch will give as their thank-offering, we will have about one-half the amount needed to give us a clear title. When once free from this burden this will practically be a self-supporting institution.

A wall is greatly needed around the Compound, as the cattle and natives go through the place in throngs. The latest report gives a fine increase in the number of boarders. Miss Holland and Miss Benthein have the responsibility of this work, leaving Miss Montgomery free to do zenana and village work and superintend the day schools. As this is her chosen field of labor, she is very happy in it. Her home is about two miles from the Baldwin Girls' School at St. John's Hill. She is

*Home on leave.

occupying the parsonage, which is vacant, as the last Conference did not send a preacher to this place. We are not asked to pay any rent, but keep up the taxes and repairs. There is some furniture in the house, and only a few things needed to make it comfortable and cozy. She says, "I have a real home."

BIDAR.—The work at Bidar' was started by Mrs. A. E. Cook, who opened a Day School for Christian women and children and employed several Bible-women to go into the near villages. Later Mrs. Batstone continued the work and opened up three other day schools, since which time Miss Fenderich has had charge of the work.

As we did not own any property at Bidar, she has been obliged to share the home of the resident missionary of the General Society.

They are paying interest on the money borrowed for their buildings and have decided to ask the Woman's Foreign Missionary Society for $100 rent. This request was deemed fair, and should be granted. This is a promising field; this ancient capital city must be taken for Christ.

Within a short distance are thirty villages where day schools could be opened and good work done. During the past year we have had three day schools with an enrollment of forty-five. The attendance is very irregular, as the children are obliged to do work in the fields and tend the cattle. A siege of cholera necessitated closing for a time two schools, and the heavy rains following closely made it impossible to continue them, as we had no buildings in which to gather the children.

We have now several orphans who are children of Christian parents, and we need a boarding school and orphanage.

HYDERABAD.—The Stanley Girls' Boarding School has received a grant from Government to meet the salary of a new teacher for the more advanced classes and also to purchase a conveyance and a yoke of cattle to bring the Hindu and Mohammedan girls who come as day scholars. There has been no increase asked for scholarships in the last four years, and this is largely due to the work being limited to the Hyderabad District. Miss Catherine Wood has charge of the evangelistic work and the day schools, and has for two years had a very successful industrial school with Miss Hitchens as the assistant. Good results have been obtained. At first they intended only to teach darned network, but plain sewing has been added. The school work has gone on as usual, and in addition to the regular routine work, the Golden Text of the Sunday-school lessons, Catechism questions and answers, Lord's Prayer, Ten Commandments, Bible Stories, and Hymns have been committed to memory. Miss Wood writes: "During the devotional hour from eleven to twelve o'clock every day the women have learned the first Psalm, twenty-third Psalm, and are now learning the nineteenth Psalm by heart. The Life of Christ has been read to them, and most of them know the way of salvation. Many of them have not yielded and given themselves to Christ, but they all have a better standard of morals, and may we not hope that this line upon line, precept upon precept, may yet bear fruit in their lives. During the two years since this work opened we have sold 400 rupees, equal to $125, of work made by these women. We now have about fifteen women. While their hands have been growing skilled, we have seen the faces grow thoughtful and a new light come into the eyes as new truths have been explained to them."

Fourteen thousand seven hundred and two visits have been made this year, and three thousand three hundred and thirty-three women have heard the gospel regularly, and many of them have been taught every week. Fifty-four women on the circuit have been baptized, and there are many thoughtful listeners. Add to this the care of twenty-three

Sunday-schools with an average attendance of five hundred and fifty, and you can judge whether Miss Catherine Wood has much spare time on her hands.

KOLAR.—Kolar is beautifully situated 2,500 feet above the sea. Here we have a fine Orphanage, a Boarding School, a Widows' Home, and a Deaconess Home, and when Cincinnati erects the Ellen Thoburn Cowen Memorial the group will be complete. Miss Fisher secured the permit before coming home and a grant from the Government. Too much can not be said of the work done in this field.

Miss Ericson has charge of the Deaconess Home, the Widows' Home, the Orphanage, and the care of the girls outside of school hours; while Miss Holland has the educational side of the work.

There have been 176 enrolled in the Orphanage this year, and there are now 156 under the care of one matron. The general health of the school has been good. Tamil has been introduced in the school for the Tamil children.

Three of our girls have been married and gone out as Bible-women under Miss Maskell; two have become teachers in the day school, and one is teaching in our own Orphanage. Miss Holland writes: "My! what a privilege is this character-building and helping in the work of fitting these India girls for useful women workers in the harvest field among their own people."

The eight day schools for Hindu children continue to do well. These schools are a power for good. Miss Maskell since her return has devoted her time to the zenana and village work and the day schools. A local preacher writes: "Before you opened a day school in our village it was a dreadful place; if we tried to have street preaching we were stoned and in danger of our lives, but now all is different; the people listen gladly."

About four hundred Hindu homes are visited by Miss Maskell, the Bible women, and young lady assistants. The women receive gladly the Gospel message. There have been seven baptisms among the Hindus the last two months and several more will be baptized shortly.

Mohammedan men all over the Mysore Province are offering strong opposition to the Christian teaching. At Kolar great gatherings have been held in their mosques, and many of the men have signed a paper to the effect that they will not allow the missionary to enter their homes, nor will they allow their children to attend our schools. Miss Maskell writes: "The Mohammedan women in Kolar are very loyal. We went to some of the homes and the women received us lovingly, telling us they loved and trusted us, and they besought us not to give them up. In our Mohammedan school, where there was an attendance of forty-five, only three girls now come, but our faith is strong in God." All this was caused by two or three coming out on the Lord's side in Bangalore and Mysore. A woman who was herself baptized here some time ago had her two children baptized June 23d.

The new work for Mohammedan women which Miss Maskell hopes to open will be an untold blessing to both their souls and bodies; just a little industrial school to which they can come to sew, write, and learn to pray, and thus build each other up in faith.

MADRAS.—The work at Madras is so great that one hardly knows where to begin to report. The Orphanage has had a successful year. The 150 girls housed there have been remarkably free from contagious diseases. School duties are well done; sewing, lace work, and gold and silver embroidery are taught as well as religious instruction given. The Christian experience of these girls is quite the same as that of the mature

Christian at home. Well-chosen teachers and assistants have been a factor in this showing. The work has crowded so rapidly that an assistant was needed and Miss Young has been assigned the care of the home work, leaving Miss Stephens free to oversee city and village schools, Zenana work, and colony work.

In a letter just received from Miss Stephens, a note of rejoicing is all the way through it except in one thing which is weighing very heavily on her heart. I will give you her own words. "You will be very grieved to know that our High Caste Girl's School is entirely broken up. The heathen are raging there and will not allow one of our girls to attend the school. The Hindus have got up two opposition schools right near, and as the children come to our school they are pulled and dragged away. The Hindus are going from house to house and making the parents sign documents that they will not send their girls to our Christian school as they will all become Christians, and that they *must* send them to them. In fact, they have gone so far that they have threatened the parents, most seriously that if they send their girls to us they (the parents) will be put out of caste and will be disgraced in a public way. They are collecting large sums of money to keep up their schools."

There seems to be an unrest among the natives all over Madras and we are contending with a great deal of opposition in all our work. Many of them gave up their idol worship and many testified for Christ. We always had our missionary meetings with them and they used to go through the service very beautifully. Now my poor girls are made not to look at us. They are really dragged away from us on the streets, and my teachers are abused and stoned. They have threatened to pull down or injure the building and I have to keep a night watchman here all the time. When I go there I put on a lot of bravery, but my heart quakes with fear when I see all the people with sticks and stones. My heart yearns for those girls who were so brave for Christ. The other day twenty-five came to school (we had about three hundred pupils) in the midst of great difficulty; it was heart-rending to hear the punishments they got. But God is good; blessed are those who trust in Him. I thank God for the fidelity and courage of my dear workers, native and English. In spite of all this opposition and tumult and all the hardships they receive, they go as usual to school, open the building and take their places. They are very much abused and taunted, and although the children do not come they are at their post.

I wish to turn you to the bright side now. God is with us, and while we sorrow for our High Caste Girls' School, He is opening up the work for us in other directions. The other Sunday I had such a concourse of people from my new village. Many are under instruction and eighteen of them were baptized that day. Some are very notable cases, one man especially who was a great idolator. He is now a leader among the Christian people. Even in the Zenanas, while some of the Hindus are opposing us very greatly and would have every door closed against us, yet the women welcome us with smiles, and instead of sticks and stones I receive garlands and flowers from them.

The pioneer worker, Joseph, is reaching where Miss Stephens could not go, and during the past year he has been in many villages and hundreds have been converted. This necessitated buying land and building churches and school houses. The work is a great colony, and as money from the Woman's Foreign Missionary Society was not available the work has been supported by the General Society. It was given to Bishop Oldham.

On Easter there were ten baptisms in one of these villages all because of the effort of this one man.

RAICHUR.—The work at Raichur City until the last Conference was under the care of Miss Grace M. Woods. She has charge of our boarding school and evangelistic work. Since that time she has been moved to Belgaum and Mrs. Cook has resumed the responsibility of the primary boarding school and evangelistic work. The missionary lives in a rented building, but we have now received permission from the Nizam's government to buy land and erect mission buildings. This work is not new, but it is largely a division of work with other parts of the District.

The estimates that have come in to us show that the time is coming when we will be asked for increased help. This year we are asked to continue the support of ten scholarships that were left at Raichur when the school was moved to Belgaum; also the support for Bible women and conveyance and the support of the assistant.

Needed at this place, for total in round numbers, $200.

BELGAUM.—When Miss Grace Woods moved to Belgaum she took with her twenty scholars. She is living in rented quarters and asks that the appropriations for the buildings be granted this year. Philadelphia, New York, and the German Conference have at different times appropriated money for buildings. The request comes that these appropriations shall be made available this year. Miss Woods says in reference to her work in Belgaum that a conveyance allowance is greatly needed as she has to bring outside teachers to the school, and when the day schools in this District are given to the Woman's Foreign Missionary Society the missionary who has charge of the boarding school will find that a conveyance is an absolute necessity.

Mrs. Ernsberger's work has been evangelistic. The work carried on by the Woman's Foreign Missionary·Society the past year has supported Bible women, day schools, and conveyance, and there are two schools doing good work that have no patrons. Three schools have received Government grants, and that this money may be available we must reach the acquired standard of scholarship. The Scripture examinations have been fine, the Catechism well learned, and the Gospel portions assigned have been carefully taught and thoroughly learned. In some cases, as the lesson was taught tears would run down the girls' faces, and though they were opposed at home they loved their Scripture lesson. The fruits of the Scripture teaching in the schools are now being seen in some of the homes where there are some very earnest inquirers. Mrs. Ernsberger writes: "On a recent trip to the center of one of our circuits, sixty miles from the railway station was made in country carts. As the trip was necessarily a hurried one we could not stop in all the villages where we have Christians. In one village several Christians, hearing that we were passing through, came down to talk to us where we were having our dinner by candle light under a tree. As we talked one dear woman bore beautiful testimony to the saving power of Christ. She said: 'For three years I have completely left off idol worship and I know that truly, truly all my sins are washed away. I have the witness in my heart.' And so the Gospel is spreading among the people. 'Line upon line, precept upon precept. Here a little, there a little,' and every year souls are being born into the Kingdom. During the past year in the entire District we have had 275 baptisms, in spite of being badly handicapped for workers. True, we have our little band, but they are all too few among the 3,000,000 people in the District."

VIKARABAD.—In a territory of 4,000 square miles, containing 1,500 villages, ours is the only mission at work, and what is one missionary for a half a million of souls. Opposition at first was strong, but it has now given way, and many are eager to know the truth and have abandoned their idols and are trying to live up to the light they have. Hundreds have confessed Christ openly and received baptism, while many are still secret disciples. This is the result of a few years labor; the outlook for the harvest of souls was never more encouraging.

The methods employed here are two; evangelistic and educational. In the evangelistic work the Bible women go to the villages far and near and give the news of the Savior to their heathen sisters. In this way they reach many hundreds of women each week with the Gospel story. The educational work is carried on chiefly in the Girls' Orphanage, located at Vikarabad, and in three day schools in different villages. The number of girls this year in the Orphanage is averaged at forty-five; the present number in school is fifty-four, and recently they have had to refuse many for lack of room. Miss Wells asks for twenty-two new scholarships.

If the history of these girls could be written you would read sorrow, degradation, and dense ignorance, but after a year of home life in the Orphanage in most cases you find them earnest Christian girls. That some one cares for and loves them opens a realm entirely unknown in the old life.

The news that $5,000 has been given for buildings causes great rejoicing to our poorly housed missionary.

With the increased work Miss Wells asks that we provide for two day schools and an assistant. This assistant seems absolutely necessary that she may know the work when Miss Wells is ready to come home on furlough this year. A missionary should be sent, if possible, to take her place.

CENTRAL PROVINCES CONFERENCE.

Organized as a Mission Conference in 1905.
Official Correspondent, Mrs. A. N. Fisher.

The Central Provinces, with their feudatory states. Berar, a section of the Southern part of Central India, and a section of the Northern part of the Nizam's dominions, are included in the Central Provinces Conference.

MISSIONARIES AND THEIR STATIONS.

JABALPUR.—Mrs. A. H. Holland, Elsie Reynolds.
KHANDWA.—*Anna R. Elicker, Mabel Lossing, Miss Liers.
RAIPUR.—Ada J. Lauck, Emily L. Harvey.
SIRONCHA.—Mrs. Maud A. Turner, Bessie E. Galbreath.
WIVES OF MISSIONARIES IN CHARGE OF WORK.—Mrs. Louise Blackman Gilder, Mrs. W. D. Waller, Mrs. Martha Day Abbott, Mrs. V. G. McMurry, Mrs. F. C. Aldrich, Mrs. H. A. Musser, Mrs. Nettie Hyde Felt.

The latest Annual Report of the Woman's Conference of Central Provinces is illuminated with groups of bright-faced girls of its five

*Home on leave.

Orphanages and boarding schools, and its pages are filled with heart-stirring records of faithful work and of crying needs for which there is very inadequate provision.

MARATHI DISTRICT.—BASIM.—Mrs. McMurry reports that the work in all departments of the Orphanage was never more encouraging. Great advancement has been made in school work, as attested by the credits received in the Government examinations, while at the same time a steady spiritual growth has been maintained. Several of the girls have requested special training for the Master's work. Some have married and gone to found Christian homes. The present enrollment is eighty. Miss Sprague has proved herself an excellent assistant.

The evangelistic work has suffered, owing to the prevalence of the plague for a few months, yet the Bible women have met some very interesting cases where families are renouncing idolatry and seeking after God.

KAMPTI.—The following is transcribed from Mrs. Waller's report: "The work in Kampti has been carried on under very many difficulties this year, chief of which has been an appalling outbreak of plague. The year opened with as bright prospects as we could have desired, but the first cloud came in the death of one of our Bible-women. Beemabai was a Brahman convert, a fruit of our evangelistic work, and was baptized about twenty years ago. Hers was a remarkable conversion. She had been on some twelve weary pilgrimages, vainly seeking pardon and. rest of soul. While attending some of the sacred places of pilgrimage she heard the Gospel and was arrested by the truth, although with others she showed outward hostility to the preachers and even pelted them with stones. The singing of Christian hymns, especially those telling of the cleansing to be found in the precious blood of Christ, and describing the uselessness of pilgrimages, attracted her attention. For two years she resisted the truth, but finally coming to Kampti, one of our workers brought her to Mrs. Stephens, through whose instrumentality she was brought into the light and shortly afterward became a Bible woman. Her knowledge of Sanscrit, her grasp of the Hindu religion, and her experiences at the different places of pilgrimage, gave her a good influence over the Hindu women, and she was listened to with great attention and interest. She died in sweet peace and with a blessed assurance of salvation."

NAGPUR.—Would that it were possible to so present the remarkable opportunities for woman's work in this large circuit as to win the support lacking! This territory covers sixteen hundred square miles and contains cities and villages aggregating a population of 400,000, and outside of Nagpur, the capital, no Christian worker has ever been placed nor mission school ever started. Mrs. Musser writes: "One of the greatest sources of annoyance in the mission field is the dependence of the religious upon the material. It seems almost impious to have to say so many thousands must remain unsaved because of the lack of funds."

Generally the Woman's Foreign Missionary Society has kept pace with the Foreign Board of our Church in entering open doors, but we are lagging in this instance. While they are rapidly pushing the work here, we are investing only a pitifully small amount in Bible women and a couple of day schools. Little girls beg to be allowed to attend the boys' schools and have to be refused. An indication of the opportunities awaiting may be noted in the fact that at one place the district inspector of police offered the missionary a dozen little girls under ten whom he had found in the house of a public woman. Must we leave such to perish?

GODAVERY DISTRICT.—JAGDALPUR.—The only missionary of our Society to labor in this jungle city has been Miss Susanna Stumpf. For one short year she wrought with might and main and then suddenly slipped away to her eternal rest. She is mourned as one peculiarly fitted for pioneer work, whose heroic plans reached far into the future for the mission to which her heart was given.

SIRONCHA.—"Since the establishment of the work of the Woman's Foreign Missionary Society in Sironcha there have been many ins and outs, ups and downs in its history, but God has been watching over it all. Especial interest has attached to it from the beginning. The first building was erected by Cincinnati Branch as a memorial for Mrs. Bishop Clark, their early President. Later Miss Fuller laid down her life there and witnessed her love for its people by bequeathing what property she possessed for strengthening the mission. But not until the past year have we been able to supply two missionaries to be associated in its development. Mrs. Turner has been re-enforced by Miss Galbreath. Something of the loneliness of the situation prior to that may be gathered from a sentence in Mrs. Turner's report, "God is always giving us pleasant surprises and before the Conference year ended I had seen three white faces."

In a summary of the work we find twenty-four girls in the Orphanage. These take an active part in the League and other meetings and also in the village Sunday-schools, of which nine are maintained. The day school is flourishing, with one of the orphan girls as assistant, and a new school building is greatly needed. There are Bible-women in eight out-stations, the best of whom are girls trained in the Orphanage. The Widows' Home is growing so rapidly as to occasion perplexity for its maintenance. This is a very important part of the work thrust upon the missionaries and calling for large support.

JABALPUR DISTRICT.—JABALPUR.—Mrs. Holland and Miss Reynolds report a year of successful work in this large Girls' Boarding School. The results of examination in the advance grades are very satisfactory. Miss Harriet Ram, B. A., a graduate from the Isabella Thoburn College, is head mistress of the English department, while all of the primary schools are taught by their own girls. Bible training is given by Mrs. Holland, who also superintends the village evangelistic work. The city zenana work is cared for by Mrs. Felt, better known as Miss Nettie Hyde, through her nine years of service as a Singh missionary.

KHANDWA.—Miss Elicker, after seven years in Khandwa, the last of which she pronounces best of all, has returned home on furlough. The work of the Girls' School is accomplished with greater ease and satisfaction since the completion of the new buildings, and the girls are becoming more trustworthy each year. Miss Lossing writes: "A busy, happy, rather uneventful year! But character has been building, young minds have been expanding, and many a girl who will some day be a power in her land has had her feet established more firmly in the rock of India's salvation."

Mrs. Abbott and her nine Bible women and two assistant helpers are faithfully carrying the evangelistic work.

NARSINGHPUR.—The zenana and village work are superintended by Mrs. Aldrich. She reports that "The Bible women seem encouraged to press forward. A weekly meeting with them, which has sometimes taken the form of a Bible reading, sometimes of a prayer meeting, and often a consultation meeting for reporting and discussing the work, has proven helpful to all."

RAIPUR.—Life in the mission in Raipur has taken on a higher meaning in the past year. The four new buildings erected by Baltimore Branch have finally replaced the decaying abodes which were so long a menace to the health and life of their inmates. Under Miss Lauck all departments of the Orphanage and Widows' Home of the zenana and village evangelistic work have advanced. A Government grant attests the success of the school. Sixty-four zenanas—more than double the number at the beginning of the year—are regularly visited, and into all of these the Bible goes with the worker. Several small zenana parties have been held in the Mission Home, where the shut-in women have been made happy by a glimpse into a brighter life which Christ offers to all.

The most imperative need for Raipur is a medical missionary.

Mrs. Gilder still superintends the large district evangelistic work. She says: "The work in general is increasing and the seed sowing of the pioneer goes on in faith and patience, looking for abundant harvest in the Master's good time."

BOMBAY CONFERENCE.

Organized as a Conference in 1892.
Official Correspondent, Mrs. Wm. B. Thompson.

MISSIONARIES AND THEIR STATIONS.

BARODA.—*Mary E. Williams, Laura F. Austin, Margaret D. Crouse, Belle J. Allen, M. D.
BOMBAY.—Elizabeth W. Nicholls, Helen E. Robinson, Joan Davis, Mrs. Harriet L. R. Grove.
NADIAD.—Ada Holmes, Cora Morgan.
GODHRA.—*Anna Agnes Abbott, Kate O. Curts.
POONA.—Mrs. S. W. Eddy.
TELEGAON.—Christina H. Lawson.
WIVES OF MISSIONARIES IN CHARGE OF WORK.—Mrs. Bancroft, Mrs. Butterfield, Mrs. Clark, Mrs. Fisher, Mrs. Hill, Mrs. Parker, Mrs. Stephens.

Our centers of English work in this Conference are three. Bombay with its three English churches, Poona with its Girls' High School, and Kirachi, where the work is in English and vernacular. The relation of our society to the English churches in Bombay is through the deaconesses, Miss Davis and Mrs. Grove, who serve Bowen and Taylor Churches respectively. Bombay being one of the chief gateways to India, great numbers of missionaries and mission friends arrive and depart at this city. To provide these with needed care and assistance falls to the lot of the resident missionaries, entailing prodigious labor. This year, owing to the Jubilee, the number of visitors was great. The need of provision for these comers and goers was discovered by some of the Jubilee visitors, and it will be a good day when the plans suggested for relieving the missionaries are worked out.

Bowen Church supports its own deaconess and has contributed one hundred rupees a month to the Anglo-Indian Orphanage at Poona, has supported two native teachers in the city school, and a native preacher in Lanonli and built a little school and church in the central provinces, one of its Sunday-school classes supporting the native preacher. This is certainly good missionary work, and Miss Davis is said by the pastor

*Home on leave.

NAMES OF STATIONS.												Total
W. F. M. S. Missionaries				1	1			3	2		1	8
Wives of Missionaries in Active Work	1	1	1						1	1	1	6
Foreign or Eurasian Assistants	1	1		1	1						3	7
Native Workers		1		1	1				1		1	5
WOMEN IN THE CHURCH—Full Members	60	25	26		19	3	5	156	40	26		360
Probationers	32	15	4		26			52	260			389
Adherents	10		10		1			10		9		40
Women and Girls Baptized During Year								1	22	5		28
No. Christian Women Under Instruction	15	15	25		14			218	300	15	8	610
Non-Christian Women Under Instruction		*55	*100			*20	*40	*800	*90	*405	*6024	7,584
No. Bible-women Employed	6	5	4	12	19	3	4	13	9	10	36	121
BIBLE INSTITUTES OR TRAINING CLASSES												
No. of Institutes		1							1	1		3
No. Missionaries Teaching		1								1		2
No. Native Teachers									1	1		2
Enrollment		2							3	3		8
SCHOOLS FOR TRAINING BIBLE WOMEN—												
No. Schools								1				1
No. Missionaries								†1				1
No. Native Teachers								1				1
Enrollment								17				17
Receipts for Board and Tuition												
VERNACULAR AND ANGLO-VERNACULAR BOARDING SCHOOLS—No. Schools								1	1			2
No. Foreign Missionaries								†1	2			3
Foreign or Eurasian Teachers								2				2
No. Native Teachers								2				2
Self-Supporting Students								15	5			20
Wholly-Supported Students								20				20
Partly-Supported Students								§5				5
No. Day Students												
Total Enrollment								40				40
Receipts for Board and Tuition								$100				$100
Government Grants and Donations												
ORPHANAGES—No. Orphanages	†1			†1	†1			†1	†1		†1	7
No. Foreign Missionaries				1	1			†1	2		1	6
Foreign or Eurasian Teachers	1										2	3
No. Native Teachers	5			1	2			8	6		4	26
Total No. Orphans	75			22	25			200	109		60	491
Receipts for Board and Tuition												
Government Grants and Donations	$200			$24				$863	$83⅓			$1170⅓
HOMES FOR WIDOWS AND HOMELESS WOMEN—No. Homes											1	1
No. Foreign Missionaries												
Foreign or Eurasian Teachers												
No. Native Teachers												
No. Women											6	6
Receipts for Board and Tuition												
Government Grants and Donations												
DAY SCHOOLS—No. Schools		1	2	1	1	1		1				7
No. Teachers		2	2	1	1	1		1				8
Total Enrollment		42	96	24	18	14		14				208
Average Daily Attendance		42	96	24	18							180
Receipts for Tuition												
Government Grants and Donations												
KINDERGARTENS—No. Kindergartens								1	1			2
No. Foreign Kindergartners												
No. Native Kindergartners								1	1			2
Native Kindergartners in Training												
Total Enrollment								6	12			18
Average Attendance									10			10
Receipts for Tuition												
Government Grants and Donations												
INDUSTRIAL SCHOOLS—No. Schools								1	1		1	3
No. Ind. Depts. in Other Schools												
No. Foreign Missionaries												
Foreign or Eurasian Teachers												
No. Native Teachers												
No. Pupils												
Receipts for Tuition												
From Sale of Products								$38	$16⅔		$15	$69⅔
Government Grants and Donations												

*Owing to different interpretations, the figures are not quite correct. †All these orphanages receive boarders and day scholars. This missionary also had charge of this work. ‡The same missionary is represented. She had charge of both boarding school and orphanage. §A part of orphanage.

to be its chief inspiration.   She accomplished a vast work of visitation among the people.

Taylor Church has located near the slum districts, where the poor English-speaking people live under desperate conditions, morally and physically.   The efforts of the Church, however, meet with encouraging response, the newly recognized Church being eagerly attended by numbers of children.   The Church is having a steady growth, and Mrs. Grove is doing the work, which the mention of the deaconess' name always suggests to our minds.

POONA.—Taylor High School has had a most happy year, amply justifying the decision of the Society to clear it of encumberance.   Mrs. Eddy recites the following points as calling for special thanksgiving: The increased number in the boarding department with good prospects of further increase in the near future; increase of regular financial income, enabling us to make substantial improvements upon our bungalow; also a special gift from the Cincinnati Branch, which has given us good sanitary stone floors in our recitation building, over 2,500 square feet. Examination results—three sent up for matriculation examination, all of whom passed; six sent for Senior Cambridge Examination, three passed, one of these being a native Christian girl, thus giving our school the honor of passing the first native girl in this English examination. Music and drawing results are good.   Marvelous and Divine protection of our large family during the ravages of the plague and other diseases prevailing in Poona, and finally harmony and helpful Christian influence among the members of our family.

Karachi work is both English and vernacular.   This is an important field and fast developing.   Already some work among women is being done, and a small appropriation is asked for.

Vernacular Work.—Gujrat District has been divided.   The work is growing so fast and the Kathiawa region was so far to one side that it has been set off as a new district.

BARODA.—Here are the Girls' Orphanage, the Florence B. Nicholson School of Theology, with its women's department, and the Mrs. Butler Memorial Hospital, now in process of erection.   The Orphanage has been a large work for the new missionary, Miss Crouse, who realized, only after Miss Williams' departure, what a responsibility was upon her, but the good assistants, matron and helpful girls, have made it possible for the work to go on happily.   A large number of the girls have married and gone out to live the Christian life in the midst of heathendom. Several are studying in the Nicholson School.   Among the favors of the year are unsual good health, a growing industrial work, and an increased grant, but the new missionary has had no time under such circumstances as these for language study.

The missionaries' department of the theological school reports through Mrs. Parker a good year.   Seventy-four women have been enrolled, representing all grades from the beginning up, and most of them have made good progress.   Two have been able to take an advanced step and are studying in the regular theological school, taking the course with their husbands.

GODHRA.—The report of the Orphanage by Miss Curtis sounds much like a letter from the happy mother of good girls and incidentally answers the familiar question, "What becomes of our Orphanage girls?"   During the year a number of girls have married native pastors or Christian teachers, and are now working as Bible women in other parts of the district.   They are happy in their work, and report that many are re-

ceiving the Gospel. A call comes for two of our girls to be trained
in a mission hospital in Jansai. Three have been placed on our Godhra
staff and are doing good work, while two go to Bombay to work among
the Gujarati people of that city. This year three passed the Government
training college entrance examination. You may be sure that this Orphanage missionary mentions our three girls who are taking the regular
course in the theological schools side by side with their husbands. When
we consider that six years ago these Godhra girls had not even commenced their education, this speaks well for them. They have raised
two hundred rupees for the Jubilee fund. This was earned partly by
extra work after school hours and partly by doing without one article
of clothing from their small outfit received yearly. We have succeeded
in getting a Government grant also. One of five thousand rupees has
been promised for school buildings. The spiritual tone of the school
has improved, there is less quarreling, and the girls appear grateful for
what is being done for them. They even speak of their American mothers
as they call their patrons. Pray for our girls who have gone out in
the lonely places, for they have many difficulties and sometimes persecutions.

Evangelistic Work is carried on by Misses Holmes, Austin, and
Morgan and Mrs. Bancroft, from Baroda, Nadiad, and Godhra as
centers. Nearly one hundred native women are assisting in this work in
their humble way. This line of work is in direct contact with heathenism.
One method is to itinerate among the villages, spending five or six days
on a circuit, making our headquarters at the circuit center and working
out from there among the villages. We have gone first to the villages
where we have women workers, next where there are Christian women
but no women teachers, and lastly to the untouched places. With such
a large territory to cover, we can do little besides encouraging workers
under our charge and doing what we can in our short visits to help
them teach the people who have been baptized or who still have much
to learn about Christian life. The untouched villages have to be passed
by, but our audiences are always made up of a large per cent of non-
Christians in these other villages, when the meeting is public. Our aim
also is to reach the women and girls especially, but we nearly always
have a goodly number of men and boys in the meetings. We have found
much joy in the season's work, for we have never failed to have good
times with the simple village people. Of course, we get tired without
the conveniences of home, and of course we would like to see the
people develop faster, but there is nearly always the humorous side of
the inconvenience that saves the day, and results are not in our hands,
so we do our best and find much happiness in it.

One journey included a visit to a number of villages hitherto untouched. One was the residence of a native prince. We went into the
Bazaar as usual and told some men there that we had come to speak to
them of our religion; would they like to hear us? They began to call the
people, and in a few moments over two hundred stood crowding around.
They listened most attentively while we told them of Jesus and His
power to save from sin. At the close of the meeting a man brought
an invitation from the prince to come to his house to tea. We went,
and were kindly received and allowed to see his wife, who was a
Purdah woman. He urged us to come again, assuring us of a welcome
and entertainment in any of the eighteen villages in his jurisdiction.
There have been six hundred baptisms in the district this year among
the women and children, and there are nearly six thousand Christian and
non-Christian women under instruction. Not only the Bible teaching,
but the daily living of these native Christian women counts for much

among the people about them. Their houses, though all mud, are neatly kept, and by their kind acts they win the friendship of the people; then they teach them about Christ.

Gujarat has felt very keenly the need of an appropriation, medicines, and the maintenance of a dispensary. Miss Nunan, who is loved and trusted by the native people, kept bravely on with the work as long as, such funds as she could command made it possible. She even used some of her own small salary, but she was compelled to close the doors and turn away scores of people. You may be sure it was hard to hear them pleading for medicine and have none to give. Ever since then she has not been idle, but has many calls into the city and has cared for many. We have tried as far as possible to attend all the Christians who come for treatment, but have had aching hearts many a time as we have said, there is no medicine, we can do nothing for you, to scores who have been truly needy, and more than once we have been tempted to wish that our hearts might grow harder to suffering, which we have not the power or the means to relieve. What a glad day it will be when the new hospital is ready and Dr. Allen is installed to begin with strong hand, the medical work of the great and needy field!

Now to the Marathi Bombay City Schools. Miss Robinson has schools in three locations in the city, and through these agencies the good seed is being sown. In connection with one of these is an afternoon reading and prayer circle, attended thus far only by boys. In another school is a large group of girls, whom she calls her Gospel Band, as they follow her in her house to house visits and join in the singing, repeat the verses, etc. Two Bible women work among the Gujarat Christian women of the city. The *Gujarat Women's Friend*, in Miss Robinson's charge, has this year had the largest subscription list in its history. This is a useful appliance, but it is a difficult work and requires a great deal of plodding.

TELEGAON.—The school here has gone on as usual, and our own girls are doing good teaching in the lower standards. One who went to Poona for teacher's training passed first in her class. The industrial class has increased and has done some beautiful work. We hope for a Government grant for this class.

POONA.—The evangelistic work here is promising. A new school among high caste people has recently been begun. Sorrowful stories are told of the suffering caused by sin, which wears the name of religion, with its terrible wrecking of the lives of young girls.

IGATPURI, PUNTAMBA CIRCUITS.—In this region work is systematically carried on by native women in eleven villages, and there are indications of blessings on the work, although it is a long and tedious task to bring a Hindoo woman to the sense of sin and the need of a Savior. However, recently in this new field several have told Mrs. Fisher that they were ready for baptism. This missionary has been very successful and urges that the items asked for in her estimates are imperative. The principal needs of this Conference at present are four new missionaries, to supply the places of those who must soon furlough, and two deaconesses for Kathiawa. The new buildings already completed or now in process of erection at Baroda, Nadiad, and Telegu are cause for rejoicing.

NAMES OF STATIONS.	Bombay-Bowen Church	Karachi (Eng. & Vern.)	10a											Total
W. F. M. S. Missionaries	1	1	...	1	2	1	2			2	...	1	1	12
Wives of Mis'aries in Active Work	1	1	1	1	3	1	1				1	1		11
Foreign or Eurasian Assistants					4	2	2			3			1	12
Native Workers			3		1									4
WOMEN IN THE CHURCH—														
Full Members	50	28	36											114
Probationers	3	3	58											64
Adherents	100	30	25											155
Women and Girls B'zed during Year,		5	8				605	25	10	22	60			735
No. Christian Women under Inst'n.		60	36				4776	463	86	100	105	18		5,644
Non-Christian Women under Inst'n,			40				1116		12					1,168
No. Bible-women Employed			3				89	25	14					131
BIBLE INSTITUTES OR TRAINING CLASSES—No. of Institutes														
No. Missionaries Teaching														
No. Native Teachers														
Enrollment														
SCHOOLS FOR TRA'G BIBLE WOMEN—														
No. Schools				1										1
No. missionaries				1										1
No. Native Teachers				4										4
Enrollment				42										42
Receipts for Board and Tuition														
ENGLISH BOARDING SCHOOLS—														
No. Schools			1											1
No. Foreign Missionaries			1											1
Foreign or Eurasian Teachers			8											8
No. Native Teachers			1											1
Self-Supporting Students			35											35
Wholly-Supported Students														
Partly-Supported Students			20											20
No. Day Students			18											18
Total Enrollment			55											55
Receipts for Board and Tuition			$2.524											$2.524
Gov'ern't Grants and Donations			$506											$506
ORPHANAGES—No. Orphanages				1	1								1	3
No. Foreign Missionaries				1	1								1	3
Foreign or Eurasian Teachers				1	2								2	5
No. Native Teachers				10	13								7	30
Total No. Orphans and Others				248	237								54	589
Receipts for Board and Tuition														
Gov'ern't Grants and Donations				$425	$300								$104	829
HOMES FOR WIDOWS AND HOMELESS WOMEN—No. Homes														
No. Foreign Missionaries														
Foreign or Eurasian Teachers														
No. Native Teachers														
No. Women														
Receipts for Board and Tuition														
Gov'ern't Grants and Donations														
DAY SCHOOLS—No. Schools							59		9					68
No. Teachers							59		11					70
Total Enrollment														
Average Daily Attendance							518		252					770
Receipts for Tuition														
MEDICAL WORK—No. Hospital				1										1
No. Foreign Physicians				1										1
Eurasian or Native Physicians														
No. Medical Students														
No. Foreign Nurses				1										1
Eurasian or Native Nurses				1										1
No. Nurse Students														
No. Hospital Beds														
No. Hospital Patients				42										42
No. Hospital Clinic Patients														
No. Out-Patients														
No. Out-Dispensaries														
No. Dispensary Patients				3,113										3.113
Dispensary Receipts														
Hospital Receipts														
Fees and Donations from Fo'ners				$33										$33
Government Grants														

BENGAL CONFERENCE.

Organized in 1886. Reorganized in 1893.
Woman's Foreign Missionary Society Work opened in 1882.
Official Correspondent, Mrs. S. F. Johnson.
The Province of Bengal is all included in the Bengal Conference.

MISSIONARIES AND THEIR STATIONS.

ASANSOL.—
CALCUTTA.—Elizabeth Maxey, Nianette Henkle, Hilma A. Aaronson, Fannie A. Bennett.
DARJEELING.—*Emma L. Knowles, Bertha Creek, Julia E. Wisner.
MAZAFFARPUR.—Jessie Peters, Grace A. Bills.
PAKUR.—Pauline Grandstrand, Hilda Swan.
TAMLUK.—Kate A. Blair, *Jennie E. Moyer.
WIVES OF MISSIONARIES IN CHARGE OF WORK.—Mrs. J. Culshaw, Mrs. W. P. Byers, Mrs. Ada Lee, Mrs. J. P. Meik, Mrs. Bessie Robinson Beal, Mrs. Byork, Mrs. C. H. Shaw, Mrs. F. B. Price, Mrs. M. B. Deming.

*1 address —
Perry. Ohio*

New missionaries are greatly needed in this Conference. A very · urgent appeal is made for at least four new workers. Several of our noble band of women are in great need of a furlough. Some must leave, and there are none to take their places.

ASANSOL.—In no part of our work has God given stronger evidence of His approval than at Asansol. It was there that the great revival began and the fruits abide.

Since the home-going of Miss Forster, our school has been in charge of her sister, Mrs. Byers; but now she and her husband must take their much-needed furlough, and there is no one ready to take care of our work. There are one hundred girls in the Boarding School, where good progress has been made in class work. All were converted during the recent revival, and now a number are being trained to do work as Bible women.

The village and zenana work is full of encouragement.

CALCUTTA.—The Girls' High School building is being remodeled and enlarged. So necessary were these improvements that the civic authorities demanded that the work be done or the school closed. In a few months all will be in fine condition again, but the necessary funds must be appropriated, though the Government gives liberal assistance.

Miss Henkle and Miss Aaronson are much encouraged over the prospect of these enlarged quarters. Miss Storrs, who has rendered such valuable service so many years without remuneration, is now away for a vacation. Miss Bennett is doing much to build up the Orphanage. One who writes of her says, "She loves those girls too well to spoil them."

Miss Maxey, who has been in charge of the *Deaconess Home* so many years, pleads earnestly and fairly for some one to be sent to help in her work, and thus be prepared to take her place when she of necessity must be relieved of such responsibility. She writes: "I do not want money so much as that which is far more difficult to get—women who are willing to come to India. O! if they could only taste the joy of working in this land, I am sure that many would be eager to offer them-

*Home on leave.

selves. Surely we who know the Master need no other assurance than to know that He says, *I need thee in India."* A leaf from her diary shows truly that, like her Master, she is going about doing good.

While our English work in Calcutta is of such great importance, the Hindustani work is being carried on successfully also. At *Kidderpur* Mrs. F. B. Price is in charge, and has just opened a dispensary which will do much good. A lady physician who has been a student at our High School goes three days a week to assist. Mrs. Price with her Bible women teach the women while they wait for treatment. At *Beg Baaan* Mrs. Meik supervises a prosperous day school and the work of a Bible woman.

The work under Mrs. Ada Lee continued to grow as cared for by Misses Eddy and Cooper during the absence in America of Mrs. Lee, who has recently returned to her loved India with some recruits for her work.

DARJEELING.—Queen's Hill School sends the good news that during the recent revival all of our girls who were not already Christians began this life of loving service. Ninety-three girls are enrolled, of whom sixty-seven are boarders. Another missionary teacher is needed here, her salary being guaranteed there if we send a well-qualified teacher.

Seven thousand dollars have been received from the Government for the building fund, and Miss Wisner and Miss Creek are greatly encouraged, though a burden of debt must still be carried for a time. Miss Knowles, who is now home on furlough, writes: "As I correspond with the girls out there I realize how much of myself I have left in India. I do trust that this year may be one of great spiritual benefit throughout our schools."

MAZAFFARPUR.—Miss Peters writes thus encouragingly of her work: "Besides the zenana homes which we visit regularly, there are the villages on the outskirts of the city, where a group of listeners can always be obtained. If one could only be a ceaseless voice that could go on and on telling the good news of salvation all day long, and even into the night, there would be always those who would listen." In seven months she and her sister have visited 615 Burgali, Behari, and Mohammedan homes; and she adds: "How I long for just the right message for each one!"

Plague has hindered somewhat and has even entered our school, causing the death of one child.

Miss Bills was gladly welcomed here, where she has been in charge of our school of fifty girls; so the fact that she has announced her engagement to marry is greeted with real sorrow by those who wonder what will become of our work.

PAKUR.—Miss Swan finds her time fully taken between the care of a large school and the preparation necessary for her own language examinations. One of our school girls has just received a Government certificate which enables her to teach as a trained kindergartner. More widows with their little ones have come into the school, requiring additional money for support.

Miss Grandstrand looks after the work among the Santali women and girls, and accompanies the Bible women to the villages. Wagons and ponies have been secured for this work, and now a barn in which to care for them must be built, for which $300 is asked. She writes: "I often think what a treat it would be to our people at home if they could see these crowds of people who are listening to the simple story of Christ."

9

Besides helping in the evangelistic work in this district, **Miss Ruth Culshaw** has had to take again the supervision of the work at **Balpur,** where we have four Bible women and two day schools sending out their helpful influences.

TAMLUK.—Here Miss Blair still works alone far from other than native workers. Three faithful Bible women assist her. After twenty years of faithful service in India, she hopes to return to America on furlough next year. Who will take up her work? Two are really needed.

Surely we must rally to the relief of the many tired workers in this Conference. Money, of course, is needed, but missionaries—new, strong, courageous missionaries who have heard the Master's personal call—for these we plead for Bengal Conference.

BURMA.

Started work in 1879,
Organized as a Mission Conference in 1907.
Official Correspondent, Mrs. Wm. B. Thompson.

MISSIONARIES AND THEIR STATIONS.

RANGOON.—Misses Josephine Stahl, *Carrie Foster, M. Lotte Whittaker, Grace L. Stockwell, *Luella Rigby, Phebe James.
THANDAUNG.—Misses Fannie A. Perkins, *Charlotte J. Illingworth.

Present address— Diagonal, Ia.

In this interesting "Land of the Pagoda" our society has a good footing at Rangoon and Thandaung, with a small beginning at Pegu.

In Rangoon we have the Girls' High School (English), the Burmese Girls' School, and evangelistic work. The high school is now in its twenty-sixth year. It has all standards from kindergarten to high school, and is almost entirely self-supporting. It has a building finely adapted to its work and in every way convenient. When this school site on Lewis Street was selected twenty-five years ago, it was on the edge of the city, but Rangoon has grown so marvelously that business blocks are now but one street away. The Charlotte O'Neal Institute, the boarding department of the school, has also a fine property which is located in the best residence part of the city. Both these properties have vastly increased in value, and are now worth many times their original cost. At present the number of pupils in the school is two hundred and seventy, forty being boarders. The number of boarders is far less than in schools of the same grade in India, because of the fact that women in Burma are almost as free to go and come as European women. Girls can therefore freely go to and from school as day pupils. In efficiency the school stands well with the educational department of the Government and compares favorably with other schools in the same province. The twelve teachers are all certificated, except those now in training. We have special teachers for singing, calisthenics, and for piano. The greater number of teachers on the staff are from the school, and their interest in and devotion to their work could not be surpassed. Among those who have passed out of the school we find the following: A missionary of the Women's Foreign Society, a lady assistant surgeon,

*Home on leave.

lady principals at St. Phillip's School, Rangoon, and the European Railway School at Inseian, also kindergarten teachers in the Girls' School at Rangoon, and the Queen's Hill School, Darjeeling. A large number of others are teaching in various schools in Burma and India. Under the present inspector of European schools in Burma, new ideas that have revolutionized educational methods in Western lands are fast finding their way to us. Besides the regular work in the Government Normal School, there are plans for a course of lectures for teachers during the school holiday, for evening classes for teachers, etc.

Miss Foster, who came to the school in 1902, had had experience and training in school methods that were of great value to the school, so that her enforced furlough on account of ill-health was a great loss. The class of pupils in the boarding department is very satisfactory, and their development in the Christian life is beautiful to see. During this year they have maintained a daily prayer-meeting, conducted by themselves. In this, as well as in the Junior League meetings, they learn to lead in prayer, to offer testimony, and to conduct the meeting. The Junior League is supporting a girl in the Burmese School.

The continued good health of teachers and pupils is cause for sincere thankfulness, yet the plague came very near.

Miss Stahl has had marked success in her position. She is now greatly needing a furlough, which should come at once. She has had the assis ance of Miss James, who is preparing meanwhile for native work. t

The Burmese Girls' School has been advancing by leaps and bounds. The building erected a few years ago so large as to elicit the question, "What are you going to do with so much room?" is already outgrown, and an addition, thirty feet by fifty feet, has been made. This provides for two new school rooms and a large dormitory, which is also used for physical culture classes. Even now the crowded condition of the building necessitates the sending out of nearly the entire staff of teachers to live elsewhere, so an urgent appeal is made for a residence building. This is an important and pressing need. The inconveniences and discomfort of the present situation make serious demands upon strength, all of which is needed in the work. It is expected that this need will be supplied in the near future. The attendance is about two hundred and ten, including fifty boarders. Encouraging results have been achieved in the annual examinations, but the need of and difficulty in securing well-trained teachers is in evidence here, though the work has improved. To quote: "Even in long-established schools it has been found almost impossible to get women teachers qualified to teach Burmese in the high school year. The Burmese people are unwilling to send their daughters to men teachers. On the other hand, the Government regulation is such that no Burmese or natives may attend English school unless by special permission of the authorities, and they must change their own simple, beautiful, and healthful costume for the unlovely English dress. Burmese women are independent, but they are slow to change customs. They love their natural garb, and what sensible people would not? and alas! their daughters do not continue their education beyond the seventh standard. To me this is a grave state of affairs and one of wide reach, for in a certain sense every nation has most to do with shaping its own destiny. Even in India, where women are so degraded, it is she who keeps the nation what it is. So in Burma the women have been taught to think that they can not think, and they have believed what they have been taught. When once the schools have a fair chance at these women, a new era shall have dawned. You say a new era has dawned. Yes, and it is amazing that in a land where but a few years ago everything western was persecuted, to-day the Burmese of their own accord send even their daughters to school, but we must look into the future, and that future must stand for higher education for women, and this school must have a place in shaping that future. The Scriptures are taught in all classes of the school, chiefly in Burmese. There is a Sunday-school made up largely of the children of the boarding school. Good work is done here, the teachers being very faithful. A Sunday-school is conducted in another part of the city by members of this school and help is given by the girls in other Sunday-schools. There is a strong religious influence emanating from this Burmese school. The greater number of the boarders are Christians, and even some of the day pupils have confessed His name. One girl who lives with her Buddhist parents is securing her education with the avowed purpose of becoming a Bible woman. The fact that Buddhist parents allow their children to become baptized Christians is one of the most encouraging features of the work. Sometimes these girls win their parents to Christ. One little girl of seven knelt at the altar for baptism. She looked so tiny that a question arose in my mind whether she understood what she was doing, but as I turned to leave the church I had my answer. A Burmese man met me at the door saying, 'Did you see that little girl that was baptized to-night? That was my little daughter.' I asked if he were a Christian. 'No, we are a divided household now. My little girl is a Christian; the rest of us are Buddhists.' I told him he ought to be a Christian. "That is just what my little girl tells me every time I see her. Father, why do you worship idols, they have eyes, but they do not see when you bow before them. They have ears, but they can not hear your prayers. They have hands, but they can not help you.' With sudden energy he brought his fist down and said, 'It is true; there is nothing in Buddhism to help a man.' He needed help, for Satan had bound him with the opium habit and a fearful temper. Years ago he had murdered a man and had spent some time on the Andama Island because of his crime. Now his little daughter was teaching him that Jesus could break these bonds. 'When she talks to me that way, I can not sleep. I lie awake all night thinking of her words.' He did finally come into the Church with his wife and children, and I have often heard him in our prayer-meeting tell the story of how his little daughter brought him to the Lord Jesus."

Miss Whitaker, the principal, is greatly needing relief and rest.

Evangelistic Work.—Miss Stockwell in charge. She says: "Our field is a large one, as we are the only evangelistic workers of our society in all Burma, and it is often hard to decide where we should expend our efforts. Rangoon being our center and our school located here, it seems wise to centralize our evangelistic work. On the other hand, the village work is very interesting and in some ways more encouraging than that in the city. The people have fewer counter attractions, and are willing to listen and seem more easily impressed with truth. We can not begin to respond to all the invitations for village work. We have visited eleven villages and worked regularly in five quarters in the city. In city, village, or country place we work in the homes, in the bazars, on the streets, trains, and steamers. In fact, we work wherever we can find people to listen to our message, buy our books, or accept our tracts. Leaving home at 6.30 in the morning, we often work until the sun is high and we are driven home by the heat and by hunger. When in the villages, the early hours are given to street meetings, and later those who wish to learn more are invited to the place where we stay, and sometimes we talk with them until a very late hour. Sunday is given up to Sunday-schools, of which we have five. When sorrow and death enter the homes, they are learning to turn to us for sympathy and help, and even strong Buddhists have requested us to hold a Christian service in their home, in the midst of heathen funeral festivities. Strange it seems, and strange it is, but thus we sow beside all waters. On the streets or in the bazars we sing, and then preach to those who come to hear. A little telescope organ helps, as well as do the Berean Leaf Cluster pictures, illustrating the miracles and teaching of Jesus. We always take Scripture portions for sale and tracts for free distribution. During the year hundreds of Gospels and thousands of tracts pass through our hands.

"In our Sunday-schools it is most interesting to see a Buddhist boy or girl repeat the Golden Text for the quarter and proudly take one of the pictures from the roll to decorate the wall of the home. Some of the tiniest astonish us by their good memories.

"We are obliged to say 'no' to many invitations to visit the villages. One man said, 'Why do you not come oftener? If we could hear your preaching often, we would soon understand and follow.' How shall they hear without a preacher?" We need a training school for Burmese women workers. Steps in this direction will probably soon be taken.

THANDAUNG.—The scene recently of building operations is again assuming the appearance of ordinary life. The new building, Elizabeth Pearson Hall, houses a happy family, affording home, school, and church privileges. The activities in this institution relate themselves to the supply of training in practical self-helpfulness.

Miss Perkins says: "School work has been carried on faithfully by the teachers and results have been excellent. The teachers deserve the highest commendation for their cheerful faithfulness under the most trying discomforts. They have been ready to share every burden and responsibility. No hours have been too long, no task has been too menial. Devoted followers of Jesus Christ, they strive to be workmen who need not to be ashamed. I count myself exceedingly favored in having such co-laborers. The preaching service, Sunday-school, and Thursday Evening Epworth League have been faithfully carried on. The most of us are seeking to live a Christian life and take an active part in the services. I have been much delighted and encouraged by visiting some of our girls, who now have homes of their own, clean and well kept, with a real home atmosphere, which is a joy and comfort. If there ever came to me a question of the value of our methods here, it would be dispelled forever by these delightful homes. Our boys, too, who have gone out are doing well. The unusual beauty and healthfulness of this hill situation make it an inviting, refreshing place of resort for the missionaries of Rangoon in their brief periods of rest. In the Burma number of the *Friend*, the issue for this month, are pictures of Thandaung and other glimpses of Burmese people and places.

"Miss Turrell has been holding regular vernacular services on Sunday afternoon in Thandaung. There is singing of hymns, each singing in his own language, their hymn books provided by us; then the Scripture portion selected to suit the picture on the leaf clusters is read in each language represented. Another hymn follows, after which the lesson on the Scripture is repeated in English and interpreted in Hindoostani, which most of those present understand. We close with another hymn and a prayer. Scripture portions, tracts, and picture cards are distributed, and by special request Bibles in Hindi, Oryia, and Tamil have been procured for individuals.

"At Pegu there are a few women members of the Church and a promising opening for work if we had but the workers. Miss Rigby, accompanied by Miss Illingworth and a new missionary, Miss Robinson, sailed late in September. Their arrival is eagerly anticipated. Plenty of work awaits their coming."

SUMMARY OF WORK IN BURMA MISSION CONFERENCE.

NAMES OF STATIONS.	RANGOON AND VICINITY.		TAMIL.		TOTAL.
	Burmese	English	Pegu Sittang Circuit.	Thandaung	
W. F. M. S. Missionaries	2	1		1	4
Wives of Mis'aries in Active work					
Foreign or Eurasian Assistants					
Native Workers	2				2
WOMEN IN THE CHURCH—					
Full Members	30		20		50
Probationers	15		10		25
Adherents	20		10		30
Women and Girls B'zed during Year,			5		5
No. Christian Women under Instr'n,	7				7
Non-Christian Women under Inst'n,					
No. Biblewomen Employed	2				2
ENGLISH BOARDING SCHOOLS—					
No. Schools		1		1	2
No. Foreign Missionaries		1		1	2
Foreign or Eurasian Teachers		14		4	18
No. Native Teachers		1		Nil	1
Self-Supporting Students				14	14
Wholly-Supported Students		3		12	15
Partly-Supported Students		Nil		16	16
No. Day Students		230		Nil	230
Total Enrollment		270		42	312
Receipts for Board and Tuition		$4,667 00		$2.539 32	$7,206 82
Govern't Grants and Donations		{ G$2,350 00 D–Nil }		{ G$9,098 32 D–Nil }	{ $11,448 32 }
VERNACULAR AND ANGLO-VERNACULAR BOARDING SCHOOLS—					
No. Schools	1				1
No. Foreign Missionaries	1				1
Foreign or Eurasian Teachers	5				5
No. Native Teachers	3				3
Self-Supporting Students					
Wholly-Supported Students	21				21
Partly-Supported Students					
No. Day Students	158				158
Total Enrollment	211				211
Receipts for Board and Tuition	$618 00				$618 00
Govern't Grants and Donations	{ G$3,545 30 D $16 09 }				$3,561 39
DAY SCHOOLS—No. Schools			1		1
No. Teachers			1		1
Total Enrollment			28		28
Average Daily Attendance			18		18
Receipts for Tuition			$39 82		$39 82
Govern't Grants and Donations			{ G$61 90 D$50 00 }		$111 90
KINDERGARTENS—					
No. Kindergartens		*1			1
No. Foreign Kindergartners		2			2
No. Native Kindergartners					
Nat. Kindergartners in Training,					
Total Enrollment		50			50
Average Attendance		43			43
Receipts for Tuition		$400 00			$400 00
Govern't Grants and Donations		{ G $250 00 D–Nil }			$250 00

List Government Grants and Donations separately, one above the other, marking Grants (G) and Donations (D)

* Included in Report of English Boarding School.

MALAYSIA.

Organized as a Mission in 1887; as a Mission Conference in 1893; reorganized as a Conference in 1904.

Official Correspondent, †Mrs. Carrie W. Joyce.

The Malaysia Conference includes the Straits Settlements, the Malay Peninsula, French Indo-China, Borneo, Sumatra, Java, Celebes, and the adjacent islands inhabited by the Malay race.

MISSIONARIES AND THEIR STATIONS.

SINGAPORE.—*Sophia Blackmore, Mary Olson, Minnie Rank, *Luella Anderson, Mariana Sutton, Jessie Brooks.

PENANG.—Clara Martin, May B. Lilly.

KUALA LUMPUR.—Edith Hemingway.

TAIPENG.—C. Ethel Jackson, Evelyn Toll.

MALACCA.—Ada Pugh.

WIVES OF MISSIONARIES IN CHARGE OF WORK.—Mrs. Marie Oldham, Mrs. Emma Ferris Shellabear, Mrs. G. F. Pykett, Mrs. S. A. Buchanan, Mrs. W. T. Cherry, Mrs. W. H. Rutledge, Mrs. H. L. E. Luering, Mrs. J. M. Hoover, Mrs. W. E. Horley, Mrs. R. M. Avery.

The past year has marked a good advance in our work along several lines in Malaysia. Our missionaries have been kept in health and thus able to remain at their posts through all the year in spite of the effects of the tropical heat. Misses Blackmore and Anderson, of *Singapore,* after spending part of the year there, are taking well-earned furloughs. In their absence Miss Rank has taken Miss Blackmore's place as superintendent of the Mary C. Nind Home, and Miss Olson, in addition to her duties as principal of the Methodist Girls' School, has had supervision of the large Telok Ayer Day School among the Chinese.

Miss Olson believes it possible to raise the standard of the Girls' School, and in the near future place it where the boys' school has been from the beginning—upon a largely self-supporting basis. To this end she has this year asked for two American teachers whose support she promises to secure on the field. These have been found in the persons of Miss Mariana Sutton, a finely equipped experienced teacher, and Miss Jessie Brooks, of Minneapolis, a graduate of our State University with special normal training, both of whom left with the party of missionaries sailing September 13th from Seattle.

At KUALA LUMPUR, Miss Hemingway reports the growth of the work such as to emphasize the need of added buildings for the Boarding School.

At TAIPENG, Misses Jackson and Toll have had a good year of successful blessed services.

MALACCA is developing rapidly under the wise management of the workers there. It is only three years since Dr. and Mrs. Shellabear were sent to open a Methodist mission in this, one of the oldest cities on the peninsula. Now, besides the work of the General Society, we have a large day school and a rapidly growing boarding school in the care of our one representative, Miss Ada Pugh, besides a Bible woman's training school cared for by Mrs. Shellabear. Miss Pugh has been

---

*Home on leave.

†Deceased, succeeded by Mrs. F. F. Lindsay.

seven years on the field, and an urgent plea comes to us to send some one to take her work that she may have a well-earned furlough.

Iрон is another strategic point which would pay large dividends in souls saved had we the means and missionaries to invest. Here the General Society has its representatives who have already opened a girls' school and year after year send urgent appeals to us to come and enter this open door.

In Penang a wise exchange of our property has been effected during the year, so that our Deaconess Home and Boarding School with its day school adjunct have been moved away from the crowded Chinese quarter with its noise and commotion and indescribable odors to a large, desirable location in the midst of quiet and pleasant surroundings. There has been no loss in numbers, and the change has proven beneficial to all concerned. Miss Lilly has carried on the school, and Miss Martin with three Bible women has been earnestly engaged in evangelistic work among both Chinese and Malays. She was sent as a delegate to the Chinese Centennial, and was much benefited by the trip and the days spent in that great convocation.

Mrs. Pykett's Home for Homeless Women, then her Orphanage grown to such proportions as to need a building of its own, and her Bible training school, all the outgrowth of one woman's faith and labor of love, well deserve our prayers and our support. Would that the little she asks for could be granted.

In days of old the prophet wrote, "The Isles wait for Thy law." Alas, they still are waiting.

Borneo, with an area exceeding the whole of Great Britain and Ireland, with intervening seas, *Java,* with its hidden mines of untold wealth and its teeming population, *Sumatra, Celebes,* and the *Spice Islands* all ready to welcome the Gospel, are waiting the prayers of a woman's heart and the touch of a woman's hand to flood their shores with light.

PHILIPPINE ISLANDS.

Organized as a Mission in 1904.
Official Correspondent, †Mrs. Carrie W. Joyce.
The Philippine Islands Mission Conference embraces that part of the Island of Luzon included between a line drawn east and west through the city of Manila and a line similarly drawn through the city of Vigan, two hundred and twenty-five miles north.

MISSIONARIES AND THEIR STATIONS.

DAGUPAN.—Louise Stixrud.
MANILA.—*Winifred Spaulding, Louise M. Decker, *Elizabeth Parks, M. M. Crabtree, Rebecca Bowman, Rebecca Parrish, M. D., Gertrude I. Driesbach.
WIVES OF MISSIONARIES IN CHARGE OF WORK.—Mrs. M. A. Rader, Mrs. C. S. Lyons, Mrs. D. W. Klinefelter, *Mrs. A. E. Chenoweth, Mrs. Peterson, Mrs. Harper, Mrs. J. S. McLaughlin, Mrs. Huddleston.

*Home on leave.
†Deceased, succeeded by Mrs. F. F. Lindsay.

In the *Philippines* the marvelous change that has been wrought in the past few years fills our hearts with thanksgiving and our lips with praise. The difficulties met at first have been mostly surmounted, the wall of prejudice broken down, the foundations laid for good work by the training school established and hospital work begun. Our missionaries are learning how to care for their health in that treacherous climate, and we are prepared to do something and may do what we will toward the solution of the nation's problem in these, our new possessions.

CHINA.

NORTH CHINA CONFERENCE.

Woman's work commenced in 1871; organized as a Conference in 1893.

Official Correspondent, Mary E. Holt.

The North China Conference includes the Provinces of Shentung and Honan and all north of these.

MISSIONARIES AND THEIR STATIONS.

CH'ANG-LI.—Edna G. Terry, M. D., Ella E. Glover, Clara P. Dyer.

PEKING.—Mrs. Charlotte M. Jewell, Anna D. Gloss, M. D., *Effie G. Young, Gertrude Gilman, L. Maude Wheeler, Emma M. Knox, Alice M. Powell.

TIENTSIN.—Emma E. Martin, M. D., *M. Ida Stevenson, M. D., *Frances O. Wilson.

SHAN TUNG.—Lizzie E. Martin, Sue L. Koons, M. D., Rachel Benn, M. D.

WIVES OF MISSIONARIES IN CHARGE OF WORK.—Mrs. Maria B. Davis, Mrs. M. G. Headland, M. D., Mrs. Agnes Brown, Mrs. Irma R. Davis, Mrs. Elma E. Keeler, Mrs. Emily H. Hobart.

PEKING.—At the meeting of the Reference Committee in May last it was voted to cancel the entire debt on this school in 1908 and to name the school in honor of one of its founders, Mary Porter Gamewell. This news was received on the field with great satisfaction, and the reports will hereafter come under the head of Mary Porter Gamewell and Lucy A. Alderman Memorial Combined School. The latter name is included until this memorial can be rebuilt in Ch'ang-li and while the girls from this city attend the school.

The eight girls who graduated last year promised to go wherever their services should be required, and Mrs. Jewell reports that each has faithfully kept her pledge. Two went to Fai An School, which to them was a far-off place, and the reports of their work are most satisfactory. A third, selected as the one of best poise and efficiency for work for women, was sent to Ch'ang-li -to teach in the Training School. She was threatened with tuberculosis, and it was hoped that the air of this place might arrest the disease. She grew worse and returned to Peking, where she was very happy visiting the patients in the hospital, praying with them, and reading from the Bible. In less than a month she went to be with her Master whose teaching she had faithfully followed. Three girls are teaching in day schools. One has married and is living in a home of her own. The eighth girl has been taking a course in the Union School for Nurses, and has assisted Dr. Leonard, of the Presbyterian Mission, in her hospital work. At present she is assistant to Dr.

*Home on leave.

Chin, a Chinese physician, who has been appointed matron of an orphanage in Tientsin for the care of stray children.

The fall term the past year opened with 231 boarders and six day pupils. $410 (gold) was received for board and tuition. The day pupils are all from non-Christian families, and, with one exception, are from important families, one of which is genuinely friendly and invited our household to dine with them. Hospitality and entertainment were abundant. Two other day pupils, sisters, came to ask admittance to the school dressed in full European costume. They wanted English and music. They were advised to return to their native dress which they, at first, were not willing to do, but in about ten days they returned transformed in their own becoming Chinese dress and were accepted. The father is a high official in Tibet. The father of another of the day pupils was formerly a student in the United States and afterwards was an attache of the Chinese Legation.

Of the boarding pupils three have been expelled and two have died. One of our girls successfully passed the Government examination for entrance to the Normal School in Tientsin, but, as as she was unwilling to conform to the requirement to worship Confucius, she soon left, and is now in our school again, better satisfied for the experience she has had.

At the last Conference the course of study was somewhat extended and adapted to the changed sentiments of the people. It covers twelve years and has added botany, drawing, plain geometry, elementary chemistry and five years of English, while to the small children repeating from memory the moral philosophizings of the Sages are given reading books which are more appropriate to their age. The course is now as extensive as the majority of the girls will require for years to come, and, to the few who may desire further study, the Woman's Union College will be open.

Christmas celebrated merrily as in former years, and the gifts from America were much appreciated by the girls as showing that some one is helping and loving them. There have been nineteen class meetings on Sundays with volunteer leaders from the teachers and girls. Twenty-three girls have taught in the Sunday-school. The Standard Bearers still keep up their interest and enthusiasm and have contributed $36.97 (gold) this year. Two girls have been baptized, and two have joined the church on probation.

In April Miss Young left Peking for a much-needed furlough. In June five girls were graduated.

Mrs. Jewell closes her report of the school in these words: "Above every other request that we have to make of our supporters in the homeland is for their prayers that now, when China is putting all emphasis upon the new education and new methods, we may be able to impress upon our students that a renewed heart, a God permeated spirit is the only leaven that can transform their country; and more, that God will make them this leaven if they are willing to hide self away."

The Tartar City Day School has kept up well and numbers thirty-four in attendance. The teacher writes that God has been manifested among the pupils and He has richly blessed the work. There have been more children from heathen homes than during any previous year, and they have been willing to study the Christian teachings. The parents of some objected to their children praying or singing, but after awhile they not only were willing, but even gave the children money with which to buy hymn books.

The Bible women are doing faithful work in the hospital and wherever opportunity comes to them.

'Dr. Gloss writes that the new hospital in which the work has been going on for nearly a year is such a blessing. As nurses and patients are now in the same building, much better work can be done. The little class of nurses has been learning many things. Several have entered the school and have given it up. One girl, who disliked the work, tried to leave, but returned to try again, feeling that it was her life work. One girl has been splendid help all the year, and a new one who entered in February promises well. The coming of Miss Powell into the hospital will mean much to the department of nursing and to the large field for evangelistic teaching which the medical work affords. There have been more house patients this year than could be accommodated before. There are always some of the school girls in the wards and some charity patients, but most of the patients pay their board and a number of wealthy patients have paid for their medicines and treatment also. A number of patients have come from towns not far from Peking. These have to come in as house patients, and thus an opportunity is afforded to teach them as well as to treat them, but it is a matter of regret that the workers are so few that these cases can not be followed up and the teaching continued. The seed planted often bears fruit most unexpectedly. A heathen lady was in the hospital for some weeks last year with her only child of two years and a nurse. She left to accompany her husband, who was appointed to some official position in Manchuria. Later she returned to Peking, but without the baby, who sickened, and, with no foreign doctor to care for it, had died. When the mother was asked about it she replied that he had been taken to heaven. "I thought my heart would break," she said, "until I remembered what I had heard in the hospital about little children going to heaven when they died. Then I kept saying to myself, 'My little one has gone to heaven,' until my heart was comforted."

Other incidents related by Dr. Gloss show that the hospital and the medical work are means not only of bodily healing, but of blessing spiritually, and many have, through these instrumentalities, been led to know the one true God. The average attendance at the clinic has been about forty, though there have been seventy in one afternoon. It has been noticeable that a number of well-to-do and official people have come to the clinic for aid and treatment. A charge is made, but this is so small that it almost means charity. There has been a gratifying number of out-calls during the year. This work is very hard, but through it financial help is secured for the hospital and by it more is learned of the lives and interests of the people. One call may be in the palace of a prince, while another is in a mud hut, and there are many between these extremes.

It is now planned to open the medical school for girls next February with three pupils, one from Peking and two from Nanking. The desire is to educate young women in medicine without running the great risk of sending them to America. Thousands of dollars will be needed to build and equip a medical college. The school is a union school, and other missions will send their students and help with the teaching, but the equipment must come from us, as Dr. Gloss writes, and she begs that this cause be kept in mind and pleads that some one may be moved to build up this department of the Lord's work. The statistical report is as follows: House patients, 150; visits to patients, 360; dispensary treatments, 10,525; dispensary patients, 2,973; fees and donations, $600 (gold).

TIENTSIN.—Those of the visitors to the great Conference in Shanghai who were able to visit Tientsin were much disturbed as they looked upon the unoccupied compound and closed buildings of our Society. Dr. Martin arrived in Tientsin in September and reopened the hospital and home which have been closed for nearly two years. She should not long remain there alone, and it is hoped that Dr. Stevenson will soon be able to resume her work in this city. A teacher should also be found to open the Sarah L. Keen School, which still is closed. An Anglo-Chinese school in this city with up-to-date teachers and methods is still the ideal of our missionary workers, and we hope that they may not be disappointed.

CH'ANG-LI.—At the last Conference Dr. Terry, the sole missionary of our Society in this station, was appointed to have supervision of the woman's work and day schools on the three districts of Shan-Hai-Kuan, Lan Chou, and Tsun Hua; also to have charge of the Woman's Training School and medical work in Ch'ang-li. It goes without saying that Dr. Terry has broken down under the strain of all this work, and a strong appeal is made for a doctor and other workers in this important and most needy field. Miss Glover returned from her furlough last spring, and Miss Clara P. Dyer, a well-equipped teacher and earnest Bible student, sailed in August and reached Peking early in September. She will probably be appointed to Ch'ang-li, and it is hoped that she may be able, after acquiring the language, to teach in the Lucy A. Alderman Memorial School to be rebuilt as soon as practicable.

Dr. Terry reports that the Catherine E. Thompson Memorial Training School opened November 20th, with some of the old pupils and several new ones in attendance. One young woman coming to the school for the first time found a new world opened up to her and returned home with a new purpose in life. Her husband, who is a student in the Peking University, is preparing for the ministry. Not being accustomed to habits of study, the wife found it difficult to remember the characters, but by patient effort she finished the first small book of the course. Before coming into the school she would not allow her husband to teach her any religious truth, but now, she says, all will be different when she returns home, for her heart is changed.

Another woman in the school is the widow of one of the martyr preachers of 1900. There have been enrolled twenty-three women, of whom nine are widows. We look to these widows for our future Bible-women and helpers, but all do not have the necessary qualifications for evangelistic work. There are, however, places for all. One, who has finished the course, has been teaching in the school this year and, in the transition from pupil to teacher, she has shown remarkable good sense, · thus commanding the respect of all. The industrial work has been looked after as heretofore by Mrs. Davis, into whose plans the women entered most heartily. For a half-hour each day both the women and the children of the day school are drilled in calisthenics. This exercise is enjoyed most by the oldest woman in the school, the daughter of a military official.

When the Tientsin school was closed, three women came to this school and have proved valuable additions. A monthly missionary meeting has been organized, and one topic discussed was the story of the beginning and subsequent history of the Woman's Foreign Missionary Society. "Two cash a week and a prayer" was adopted as the standard, and five Mexican dollars have been collected. Dr. Terry attributes the success of the school this year to the efficient help and leadership of Mrs. Chou. Many have received, as they express it, "much of the Lord's grace," and have returned, we trust, to their homes to be witnesses for the Lord in the little communities in which they live. ·

It has been utterly impossible for. Dr. Terry to supervise personally the country work this year. She gratefully acknowledges the assistance of Dr. Hobart and Dr. Taft, who have looked after the pay-roll and various other matters on the districts. On the Tsun Hua District there is one regularly appointed Bible-woman who, with the day school teachers and pastors' wives, attends to the evangelistic work as opportunity arises. On the Lan Chou District another Bible-woman carries the message of the Gospel to her sisters in their homes. Interesting incidents are given of the work of these women and of the pastors' wives. One of the latter has gathered about her a little self-supporting school for the women who are too old to go to the Training School at Ch'ang-li. Another, in a large market town, has succeeded in getting the farmers' wives to attend church on Sundays, and they fill the woman's side of the little chapel. There are immense possibilities for the spread of the Gospel in this district work if only workers can be secured to carry it on.

The three day schools already established have been continued and two new ones have been started. One of the new ones is in the city of Tsun Hua and opened with eight pupils. Three boys have graduated from the Ch'ang-li day school, and soon three girls will be ready to enter the Peking school.

The number of patients coming to the dispensary for treatment has been about the same as last year, but there has been an increase in the number of hospital patients. One man came from a village ten miles away, bringing a child with bad eyes. The child cried so that it had to be taken home before the treatment could be finished. Medicine was given, however, and the child recovered. A reputation was thus established, and patients from that village have been coming to the hospital for help. One poor woman walked two and a half days, hoping to receive treatment, but her trouble was of such a nature that an operation was necessary. She could not consent to this without first consulting her husband, and she walked all the way back again, saying that she would return later if he was willing. As the station could not be left alone, no country medical work has been done this year.

SHANTUNG.—In this school, in which are nearly one hundred girls, Miss Martin is bravely struggling on alone in the midst of most trying difficulties. The old, worn-out building is so crowded that when the girls once get into the rooms they must stay until all are ready to leave at once. They are so packed into one room that to move about is like a game of checkers.

After being in these crowded school rooms it is especially comfortable and restful for Miss Martin to go into the new home, recently built, of which she writes with such grateful appreciation. She also mentions with gratitude the new hospital, the training school, and the church, which last is so well filled every Sunday.

Dr. Benn, before leaving for home in the early summer, made several country trips, doing the work which she greatly enjoyed. The lack of workers has been so great and the needs so many that Dr. Benn has been forced to remain on the field long after she should have been at home to regain lost health and strength.

The need for a new building in this most promising field is very urgent and must be supplied in the near future, or a great opportnuity for the advance of our work in this section will be lost. A strong appeal is also made for workers—medical, evangelistic, and educational—or those now at work will break irretrievably.

CENTRAL CHINA.

Central China Mission was opened in December, 1867, by missionaries belonging to Foochow, and was set apart as a separate Mission in 1869. Woman's work organized in Kiukiang, 1874; in Chinkiang, 1884; in Nanking, 1887; in Wuhu, 1897; in Nanchang, 1903. Official Correspondent, Mrs. J. M. Cornell.

MISSIONARIES AND THEIR STATIONS.

CHINKIANG.—Girls' Boarding School—Miss Grace A. Crooks (N. W. 1904). Medical and Evangelistic Work—Dr. Lucy H. Hoag (N. Y. 1872). Dr. Gertrude Taft (Pac. 1895).

NANKING.—Girls' Boarding School—*Miss Ella C. Shaw (N. W. 1887). Teacher of Music and English—Miss Alice Peters (N. W. 1904). Bible-woman's Training School, Day Schools, City and District Evangelistic Work—Miss Sarah Peters (N. W. 1888).

WUHU.—City and District Evangelistic Work and Day Schools—Miss Edith M. Crane (N. W. 1904).

KIUKIANG DISTRICT.—Girls' Boarding School—Miss Clara E. Merrill (N. W. 1896). Miss Thirza M. Pierce (N. W. 1902). Music in Girls' Boarding School—Mrs. F. G. Henke. Women's Bible Training School, City Evangelistic Work and Day Schools—Miss Jennie V. Hughes (N. Y. 1905). Elizabeth Skelton Danforth Memorial Hospital and Dispensary—Dr. Mary Stone (Des Moines 1896).

NANCHANG.—Stephen L. Baldwin Memorial School.—*Miss Kate L. Ogborn (Des M. 1891). *Miss Alta L. Newby (Des M. 1905). Miss Welthy B. Honsinger (N. Y. 1906). Assistant—Miss Ilien Tang (Minn. 1906). Medical Work—Dr. Ida Kahn (N. W. 1896). City Evangelistic Work, Day Schools and Translating—Miss Gertrude Howe (N. W. 1872).

January, 1907, Miss La Dona Deavitt married Mr. A. Rosenburg, of Shanghai. Miss Laura White (Phila., 1891), November, 1907, to Nanking School. *Nanking*

CENTRAL CHINA has had its share of good things this year. Our President with Bishop Foss took the long trip overland from Peking and down the Yangtse River that she might bring to us at home direct word from each station and a clearer vision of its individual needs. Her patient, thorough study of each question as it came, makes all the work dearer as well as clearer to us.

Bishop and Mrs. Bashford spent their midsummer vacation at Kuling, in the mountains above Kiukiang, where many of our Central China Missionaries have little bungalows for breathing places during the intense heat in the cities. The presence and careful, comprehending sympathy of these wise friends coming into closer contact with many of the problems, meeting our missionaries in their various fields, is proving as great a blessing to those who work on this side of the great ocean as to those in the field.

In the summer of 1906 our New York Branch Treasurer, with her husband, Dr. Sumner Stone, also had a little glimpse of our Missions on the Yangtse.

CHINKIANG.—*School*—Miss Grace Crooks who took last year the school-work which Mary Robinson had so long and faithfully cared for, reports that the year has been a happy though a busy one, and despite

---

*Home on furlough.

all her misgivings, now that the school year is closing, she feels that God has indeed been better than all her fears. Seventy girls have been enrolled, ranging in age from three to twenty; of these thirty orphans and five other girls are supported entirely, five are self-supporting, and the rest partially so, paying from five to twenty dollars a year. There are six young teachers (native), all graduates, capable and loyal Christian women. At this time when such teachers are in demand and these women could get five times their present salary in the Government Schools, we should congratulate ourselves that they feel impelled to recognize the obligation they are under to those to whom they owe their western education.

February 6th a class of seven received diplomas. It was a perfect day; invitations, with a program, had been sent to Chinese friends and all who understood the native language; every one was happy. "How Miss Robinson had looked forward to and planned for this day!" writes Miss Crooks. "Her picture hung above us and we almost felt that she was present. Perhaps she saw and knew from the Better Land, who shall say?" Bible Study has been upon the International Sunday-school Lessons one hour each day. Dr. Li's earnest, straight-forward preaching during his ten days in the city was a blessing to all.

"An opportunity (long sought for) has come to add a narrow strip of land to our property on the north, which will not only give a back yard, but furnish an opportunity (our only one) of enlarging our present buildings. We are asking money to aid us in paying for and walling in this addition.

Thirty thousand famine refugees have gathered around Chinkiang. Relief funds sent from home have given two months' employment to two hundred men who have carried the earth to fill our insatiable gully, until now the land is level and ready for our building.

Hospital.—Dr. Hoag writes: "The deep railway cutting spanned by a foot-bridge is just as it was and there has been rain more abundant by far than was desirable for any known purpose. We have never stopped in our efforts to buy more land. · The railway is unfinished and so is our new building site for the hospital, which lies near and parallel to it, though we are working near its completion and should certainly be encouraged by the progress we are making, though seemingly slow. Cut off from the city by the railway excavation, a few more women have learned the devious ways to our compound and the total number of patients for the year has been *five thousand four hundred and nineteen.* We have met with a great loss in the death of our Bible reader, Miss Hü. She entered the Boarding School when eight years of age, graduated in 1900 and for six years was our most loyal and faithful helper. Her health had been failing for some time, but the end came suddenly and with only a few hours of suffering. Words fail to tell how much we depended on her in a variety of ways, and especially in the work of an evangelist. We thank God for giving her to us so long and that hundreds and even thousands have listened through her to the story of the Savior, and that they have heard it from the lips of one who lived in the sunshine of His presence. We miss her while glad in her hapiness, and pray that her mantle may fall on the shoulders of her successor."

NANKING.—*School*—A class of four girls graduated in February, 1907, giving to our needy work four more trained Christian workers. Miss Pei went to the help of Miss Crane in Wuhu. Miss Cheo, having had some training under Dr. Gaynor and Dr. Ketring, is acting as the school nurse. Miss Chu and Miss T'su are teaching in this, their own school. At Commencement time the school as well as the graduating class gave proof of good musical ability and training. The gift of an organ would be much appreciated by some of the girls, as they go out into broader work as the wives of young preachers in the city or out on the districts. The girls have much Bible Study and besides their school work make their own clothes and do their part in the domestic work of the house. Since Miss Shaw left in the spring for her needed furlough, Miss Alice Peters has had entire charge of the school with her seven Chinese teachers, three of whom have been giving good service for many years.

Miss Powell spent nearly six months in Nanking helping in the household and with the care of the girls, organizing a basket-ball team that will make their much neglected physical exercise more attractive to them. In July she was transferred to Peking, where her training in nursing was more especially needed. The school course corresponds to Grammar grade and High School work at home. The best pupils are apt to be those who come to us when six or seven years of age and remain until they are over twenty.

A piece of adjoining land connecting the present property with the street has been purchased, filled in, and made level for the new school building.

Evangelistic Work.—Miss Sarah Peters, who began her work in this Conference in 1896, writes most enrouragingly of country work on Nanking District. She had just made a three weeks' trip. The party consisted of Mrs. Chi, Miss Peters, and a servant; four donkeys carried them with their beds and other necessaries and there were two donkey drivers. The nearest station was twenty miles distant, a weary ride, but that first night Miss Peters says, "The chapel at Mu-ling-kwon was packed with women and the sight of this large expectant company put life into us; we had an impressive meeting; the people seemed unusually receptive." From this point a trip was made to the home of an intelligent Christian farmer in a village in which the people had suffered greatly from the famine. "A service was held and afterward a combination picture was put up with five illustrations from the text, "Come unto Me all ye that are weary and heavy laden, etc.," representing a man with a great burden on his back and how he was finally relieved of it. Mrs. Chi spoke effectively from it. The word with illustrations found entrance into some hearts. There are two other Christian homes at like distances which are also used as preaching centers. A new station has been opened at Ia Hong, five miles distant. God's Spirit is working about Mu-ling-kwon." At Sia-Tan-Yang, twenty-two miles farther, a nice chapel, to cost about $300, is being erected, also a parsonage. "We found the Church in a thriving condition. Mr. Lin first rented a building himself and kept it three years, securing the help of the friend who had led him to Christ to preach. For three years there was little result, but now he rejoices in the precious harvest. Our audiences at this place were mostly intelligent women of the better class. After a stay of five days we left with Mr. Lin for home three miles distant, where he has a large guest hall which is used as a preaching place. After dinner this hall was filled with women, Mrs. Chin exhorted and prayed with power. We noticed that the Christians here and at Sia-Tang-Yang prayed for the Holy Spirit and for a revival, and felt it was coming. Seven miles farther on was another place where Mr. Lin preaches regularly. How our hearts went out in praise to God for this willing worker whom God Himself has raised up in this beautiful region! At Poh-Tang also there was life; since my last visit a little church has been raised up here. We spoke in a tea-house; they will soon build a house of reeds and mud for a little chapel; we were wonderfully helped in speaking."

Miss Peters writes that in her Bible School this year among the twenty-six enrolled she has a number of very promising young women, and has just started a most interesting Workers' Class with eight of the most advanced girls. The Day School at Kiu-I-Lan has sixty-one pupils after turning away ten who were less promising, and we have to add a third teacher. We hope soon to have four or five schools in our building there and we have a fine Sunday-school. Twelve of our trained Bible-women are constantly at work in the city and districts, besides those who are married and give their services as they are able.

WUHU.—The question of land for our Missionary's Home is still unsettled, but Miss Crane hopes to have possession of the new Day School building before Christmas. The beginning of the year's work was delayed, but she visited the women in their homes, teaching them personally. In March, Union Revival services, conducted by Dr. Li, the young Chinese evangelist from Soochow, resulted in a wonderful quickening in the life of the pastors and the people, a marked earnestness of prayer among the native workers. Miss Crane herself received an uplift from these meetings and from that time "the tide seemed to change and she took up her difficult labors with new courage." During the spring, accompanied by two of the Bible-women, she visited four of the stations on the District. They found eager listeners, women, who, recalling the former visits of the missionary, begged them to come more frequently that their good words might be better remembered.

KIUKIANG.—*School—The new Sarah A. Rulison Fish High School,* strongly and beautifully built, ready to comfortably accommodate one hundred girls, opened to receive them September 11, 1907.

The Mulberry Hill School opened a week earlier for the Primary grade girls under Miss Pierce's care. The old building has been thoroughly repaired and everything is ready for a good year of work. The schools registered seventy-six girls last year.

· Miss Merrill has patiently worked in this school for eleven years and at last has hope of graduating her first class, in which are three very promising young women who will be thoroughly trained and well equipped to take responsible positions as teachers and helpers. It is always difficult to keep the girls in school long enough to train them to be efficient workers. We congratulate Miss Merrill that she may soon reap some of the blessed fruits of her years of work.

Elizabeth Skelton Danforth Memorial Hospital has been necessarily closed for everything but some Dispensary work, since the first of January. Dr. Stone has performed several difficult major operations during the past few years and after a very serious one in December she herself had a severe attack of appendicitis. Dr. Hart found that an operation was very necessary for her safety, and although prepared to perform it in China, he strongly urged her coming to America for much needed rest and recuperation and for the best hospital advantages; after a fortnight's deliberation she was sent to the United States early in February, going immediately to Chicago to Dr. Danforth's care. After her recovery she was given opportunity to visit many clinics in New York and Chicago and to give close inspection to operations which she had been performing only through the aid of illustrated books and written descriptions, yet the Heavenly Father had guided her skillful hands and blessed her work, so that she had lost not one of her surgical cases. She sailed for Kiukiang in early September, followed by the prayers of many friends that God would richly bless her added skill and knowledge for the healing of many Chinese women during the coming years, helping her to bring peace to their souls as well as to their bodies.

10

The Woman's Bible Training School and City Day Schools have been under the care of Miss Deavitt since Anna Stone was called away in March, 1906. Early in the year Miss Deavitt married Mr. Rosenburg, of Shanghai, and Miss Hughes was appointed to the work. Her brief experience with the language was supplemented by three good teachers, and she had two happy, busy months with her twenty-one Bible students. After Dr. Stone's illness, when the trip to America was decided upon, the patient could not travel alone and it seemed best that Miss Hughes, the newer missionary, should leave her work to give the care needed during the long journey. The months at home were busily employed telling the needs of China's womanhood to men and women in many States, winning new friends and large gifts for the broadening of the work in Central China.

NANCHANG.—*Baldwin Memorial School*—After six years of faithful, successful work in the building up of this school, Miss Ogborn came home for needed furlough in the late autumn of 1906, leaving Miss Newby in charge. Although she had only been in China a little over a year, she carried the work alone for two months, until Miss Honsinger and Miss Tang were able to reach her the last day of the year. It had been too heavy a burden, illness came, and in the summer it became necessary for Miss Newby to come to America in search of health.

Miss Honsinger gave herself enthusiastically to the work, but could not have made progress with the school had not Miss Tang been at her side with her command of the two languages and her knowledge of the people. There was no possible opportunity for her to start her Kindergarten, for her presence in the school was indispensable. The dearth of Christian teachers, indeed of any good teachers, is the great hindrance. After a most profitable visit to the Centennial Conference with Miss Howe and some happy holiday weeks in Kuling, Miss Honsinger stopped in Kiukiang to search for teachers; one man recommended to her as a personal teacher, seemed so splendid that she decided the school must have him. She writes, "Of course he is not a Christian, but he stayed for the Sunday-school class and was very much interested." An educated young woman who had a small school of her own has been engaged to teach the children, and they are earnestly begging and hoping that their staff may be increased by a competent helper from Nanking. School opened September 6th. The first week brought them forty-seven pupils and they are expecting to humber seventy very soon. The school is now definitely graded and they start their new year full of hope and courage. Tennis courts have been laid out, but they need a good gymnasium.

Evangelistic Work—Miss Howe writes that Sunday, July 21st, several probationers of long standing were baptized and admitted to Church membership and other probationers received, many of them women. The "Yonkers Day School" has had a properous year, requiring two teachers besides Miss Howe. Chinese women of the better class are becoming ambitious to be educated. After a time they lose their fear of being forced into Christianity and take an intelligent interest in the Scripture lessons. They love to sing hymns and are willing to attend the Sunday-school in their day school building, which is superintended by Mrs. Cheng. Miss Howe herself has charge of two other Sunday-schools. Since New-Year they have had in the Dispensary the help of an excellent Bible-woman from Kiukiang. She finds that most of the women love to hear the Gospel story and those who can read gladly accept copies of the Scriptures. On their return visits they give evidence of having read and accepted many of the truths.

Medical Work—Dr. Kahn writes: "My practice has increased steadily

SUMMARY OF WORK IN CENTRAL CHINA CONFERENCE.

NAMES OF STATIONS.	Nanchang.	*Kiukiang.	Wuhu.	Nankin.	Chinkiang.	Yungchow.	Total.
W. F. M. S. Missionaries	4	5	1	2	3		15
Wives of Mis'aries in Active Work		1					1
Foreign or Eurasian Assistants							
Native Workers	10	20	‖4	19	12		65
WOMEN IN THE CHURCH							
Full Members	50	†100	§35	†150	26		361
Probationers		†25	†§8	†65	3		101
Adherents		160	†§30	200	150		540
Women and Girls B'zed during Year,		19					19
No. Christian Women under Instr'n,	20	50	20	60	40		190
Non Christian Women under Inst'n,	30	20	‡5	15			70
No. Bible-women Employed	2	4	1	6	2		15
BIBLE INSTITUTES OR TRAINING CLASSES—No. of Institutes							
No. Missionaries Teaching							
No. Native Teachers							
Enrollment							
SCHOOLS FOR TRAINING BIBLE WOMEN—No. Schools		1		1			2
No. Missionaries		1		1			2
No. Native Teachers		3		2			5
Enrollment		30		25			55
Receipts for Board and Tuition		$24 00		g$33 00			$57 00
VERNACUL'R AND ANGLO-VERNACULAR BOARDING SCHOOLS—							
No. Schools	1	1		1	1		4
No. Foreign Missionaries	2	2		2	1		7
Foreign or Eurasian Teachers					2		2
No. Native Teachers	5	6		7	6		24
Self-Supporting Students	15	4		24	5		48
Wholly-Supported Students	10	16		20	31		77
Partly-Supported Students	32	86		45	34		197
No. Day Students	†	11		5	2		18
Total Enrollment	57	106		90	71		324
Receipts for Board and Tuition	g$448 00	g$594 00		g$430 00	$344 77		$1,816 77
Govern't Grants and Donations							
ORPHANAGES—No. Orphanages		‡					
No. Foreign Missionaries							
Foreign or Eurasian Teachers							
No. Native Teachers							
Total No. Orphans		16					16
Receipts for Board and Tuition							
Govern't Grants and Donations							
DAY SCHOOLS—No. Schools	1	3	-1	3			8
No. Teachers	2	4	1	3			10
Total Enrollment	30	75		80			185
Average Daily Attendance	25	60		60			145
Receipts for Tuition	$30 00		$1 00	$9 00			$40 00
Govern't Grants and Donations							
MEDICAL WORK—No. Hospitals		1			1		2
No. Foreign Physicians		‡			2		2
Eurasian or Native Physicians	1	1					2
No. Medical Students		‡					
No. Foreign Nurses		‡					
Eurasian or Native Nurses	2	5					7
No. Nurse Students							
No. Hospital Beds		24			19		43
No. Hospital Patients		†164			237		401
No. Hospital Clinic Patients							
No. Out-Patients	315	†145			109		569
No. Out-Dispensaries	1						1
No. Dispensary Patients	7,988	8,000					15,988
Dispensary Receipts	g$784 87	g$525 00					$1,299 87
Hospital Receipts					g$621 00		$621 00
Fees and Donations from Fo'ners,							
Government Grants							

Column "Yungchow" marked "No W. F. M. S. Work."

* Hospital closed 5 months.　† Approximate.　‡ These figures do not include work on district.　‖ This includes Mrs. Tung, not paid apart from her husband's salary.　§ This is simply Wuhu City.　There are probably nearly as many more in the district.　g indicates gold.

among the foreigners and Chinese until now we have patients come to us from all the large interior cities, even to the boarders of Fukien, yet I have not even a microscope. You would be quite surprised if you knew how many foreigners I treat in this out-of-the-way .place, yet in my last case I had to send specimens of the patient's blood to the Wesleyan Hospital at Hankow for examination. My work is pre-eminently missionary and I am helping the greater majority of my patients .free of charge. It is not even missionary work among Christian people, but among those living in the utmost darkness, who need every bit of loving care and light which may be given them. During the year we have treated over eight thousand patients. The evangelistic work among them has been better undertaken than ever before and I am sure we shall see the results in the near future; several inquirers have been accepted, seven women have been taken in as probationers."

The Chinese have given Dr. Kahn her Dispensary Building and land for a hospital in the midst of the city. Ten thousand dollars is needed for the hospital building. There is fear that the free Dispensary which treats from forty to fifty patients every day will have to be closed for lack of money to pay its expenses.

Miss Howe and Dr. Kahn will be comforably settled in their new home before the first of January, we hope. It has been a long waiting, but the opportunity for gracious Christian hospitality will be wisely used and much appreciated by many neighbors.

After twelve years of consecutive work on the field we hope to welcome both Miss Howe and Dr. Kahn to our land next spring, and where the Doctor will have opportunity to increase her efficiency for relieving the sufferings of her own people by a personal experience of the advance in medicine and surgery during the past decade.

Dr Kahn reports from July 1, 1906, to June 30, 1907: Dispensary visits, 7,988; Out visits, 318; total number of visits, 8,306; money received from patients, $1,374.21.

SUMMARY OF WORK IN CENTRAL CHINA CONFERENCE.—
Continued.

	CONTRIBUTIONS OF WOMEN AND GIRLS FOR BENEVOLENCE.	TOTAL RECEIVED ON FIELD FOR SUPPORT OF WORK.	VALUE OF REAL ESTATE.	DEBTS ON REAL ESTATE.
Nanchang				
Kiukiang				
Wuhu			$15,000 gold is about the present valuation.	
Nankin, $20 gold	D. $160 gold. $505 gold for Church.		$18,000 about original cost price of real estate, now worth more.	$2,000 gold on land and wall. $350 on repairs and additions to home.
Chinkiang	$150		$16,000	

WEST CHINA.

Began in 1882. Discontinued in 1885. Reopened in 1894.
Official Correspondent, Mrs. F. P. Crandon.
The West China Mission is confined almost entirely to Szchuen
Province.

MISSIONARIES AND THEIR STATIONS.

CHUNGKING.—Miss Helen R. Galloway,* Dr. Agnes Edmunds, Dr. Mary
Ketring, Miss Annie M. Wells, Miss Winifred Stout.
CHENTU.—Miss Clara Collier, Miss Mary A. Simester, Miss Dorothy Jones,
Miss Frauces Hitchcock.
TSICHEO.—Miss Ella Manning, Miss Alice Brethorst.
WIVES OF MISSIONARIES IN CHARGE OF WORK.—Mrs. M. M. Canright,
Mrs. F. B. Manly, Mrs. M. J. Curnow, Mrs. L. A. Myers, Mrs. J.
F. Peet, Mrs. J. A. Beech.

_____

The booklet so generously issued by our Missionary Board describes
West China as follows:
"The West China Mission occupies the Chentu · Plain, the garden
spot of China, and in some measure of the world. It sustains a denser
population than any equal territory on earth, except perhaps the county,
in which London is located. It embraces an area 'of 218,480 square
miles and has a population of 68,725,000.'
"The missionaries of our Church were the first in the field, and thus
were able to select this most fertile part of the province for their location. We have but one-seventh of the territory, and about one-third of
its people. The problem is that of holding the territory we already
have. Other societies are supplying their territory more rapidly than
we are, and now have two or three times as many missionaries in proportion to their population as we have. The expression of our missionaries in West China is that we must increase the number of our missionaries, or else yield to others a part of our territory."

CHUNGKING.—The Boarding School in Chungking was transferred last
spring to Chentu. The reasons therefor were the crowded condition
in Chungking and the impossibility to purchase more ground; consequently sickness prevailed almost continually among the girls. Chentu
is a much more healthful locality and we have abundance of room.
Furthermore it is destined to be the educational center for our mission.
A day school will be maintained in Chungking and of course our medical
and evangelistic work will be continued.
Dr. Ketring reports concerning the Gamble Memorial:
"The Hospital has been full of patients, the majority, as usual, being
surgical cases, requiring operations more or less serious. Not only
are the wards full, but every corner is full. We have neither vacant
bed or bedding, so can not admit another patient without discharging
one already under treatment, no matter how great the need of either may
be. There is another disadvantage in being so crowded beside the hygienic one; that is, we are obliged to put all kinds of cases together.
"Now that the Government is stopping the sale of opium, we are
beginning to be overwhelmed with patients who must break the habit,
but who can not endure the torture without our help. We should have
a ward for them where they would be more comfortable, and have
more outlet for their restlessness. I feel that we are not doing justice

_____

*Home on furlough.

to our other patients when we subject them to the sight of these sufferings and the sound of the moans night and day.

"We greatly need more private rooms. Gentlemen of wealth often, and officials occasionally, wish to place their wives or daughters under our care. Such will gladly pay for a private room, but will refuse to leave the patient in a ward even if it costs the life of the loved one. Too often our private rooms are all occupied, and such patients are taken back home to die. These rooms would help greatly toward the support of the hospital, to say nothing of the humanitarian standpoint.

"To summarize, we need more room to prevent overcrowding, to help us in self-support, to improve hygienic conditions, to admit a better classification of patients, and for general convenience.

"Had we a trained nurse from home who could superintend the girls whom we are training and form them into classes, giving them instruction in books as well as in the practical work, I believe that they would make as fine nurses as any in the world. All that is needed is some one to be superintendent of nurses and Principal of the Nurses' Training School, to raise their work to the dignity of a profession. A trained nurse who could do this, relieving the physician of the responsibility of the nursing, and taking charge of the special cases, would take fully half the burden of the work."

How her heart must have rejoiced when the news reached her of the coming of Miss Borg, the trained nurse!

Miss Wells has been conducting two Day Schools, one for women, the other for girls, having the care of the house, and incidentally making strides in the acquisition of the language.

Miss Witte, having transferred her relations to the Baptist Mission, Miss Stout, who not only is a graduate of Northwestern University, but has had long experience as well as training in normal work, was appointed to Chentu; but as the home in Chungking was less crowded, has remained in Chungking while prosecuting her studies, but will probably be appointed to Chentu at the next conference. Miss Stout writes: "I am so happy to be in China. Christ is very near and I pray that I may be a missionary such as the Lord would have me be."

Two new workers for evangelistic work are greatly needed at this station.

TSICHEO.—Mrs. Manly writes from Tsicheo: "My request for one or two new ladies was more than granted by the coming of Miss Manning and Miss Brethorst. Miss Manning already had a command of the language, and could take up immediately the evangelistic work in which she had had five years' experience. Miss Brethorst is rapidly becoming prepared for effective service." Our thanks are due Mrs. Manly for the faithful work that she has done for us for many years.

There is a good Day School in Tsicheo which is registered in the educational union of West China, with an enrollment of about fifty bright little girls.

Only fifteen women have been in the Woman's Training School because the rooms have been so restricted. Three of these will be ready to be licensed as Bible-women, and receive an appointment at the next Annual Meeting. Several of the others will become helpers, either as the wives of native helpers, or will be able to begin gratuitous service. Miss Manning says, "We do not encourage the idea that every woman who serves the Lord must receive cash for doing it."

The neglected condition of the women and girls in our districts is a very burden on the hearts of our missionaries, and while the laborers are few, we rejoice that from the newly established Training School women will go forth better equipped for service.

CHENTU.—The transfer of the Chungking Boarding School of over thirty girls five hundred miles by boat was no small undertaking. Miss Jones wrote upon her arrival in Chentu: "It was a journey that one would not care to make but once in a lifetime. Our living-room was eleven by twenty-two. Sardines in a box was nothing in comparison, for they are dead, while our party was very much alive."

The new buildings not being completed, they are temporarily in a Chinese house which is fairly comfortable. The school now numbers sixty and is doing good work. Miss Collier reports concerning the new buildings:

"The land that was necessary to be purchased for the new buildings was owned by five different families or clans. It has required time and patience to combat the avarice and trickery of all the members of these different clans. When the last deed was written we proceeded to tear down the old buildings and clear the land for the new ones. Contracts have been let for the brick and lumber for the building, and work on the foundations is already begun.

"Our Day School is thriving under the care of Miss Simester. We had not thought of opening a Woman's School at this time, but the women came determined to study and we could not turn them away, so we secured a teacher for them. Several of the women have already become earnest Christians and are eager to help Miss Simester in teaching others."

"The country work is really neglected. The Chentu District embraces three thousand square miles in a densely populated portion of the province. Miss Collier has been able, besides contending for the new buildings, to make a few trips to the other stations, and finds the women eager to learn to read the Bible, and seven have recently joined the Church. At the stations where our school girls have gone as wives of pastors there are much more thriving Churches. They have opened schools for the girls and classes for the women, and are lights set in a dark place."

Concerning the need for reinforcements, Dr. J. F. Peat, Presiding Elder of Chungking District, writes:

"Chinese etiquette requires that the women remain away from services unless there is either a foreign woman or preacher's wife to act as hostess. And as many of our preachers are young men and unmarried, it is rather exceptional to see women at many of our chapels. Our married women can and do lead meetings and have classes in the city, but have seldom had strength or time to do itinerating. Again, several of our older workers' furloughs will be due soon, thus taking from the city some able workers, so all things considered, unless more workers are sent to us soon, the work will be much crippled. Not only will we be not able to advance, but we can not hold what we now have.

"We have great hopes that the China Centennial Movement will inspire both givers and candidates for China missions. Send to us more workers and be assured that there are the greatest possible opportunities for work for the Master."

Much interest has been aroused because volunteers from the West China Conference have offered to go over into Thibet to take the land for Christ. Not forgetting that our own Dr. Sheldon was first pioneer in work in that country, we are admonished that in the near future West China must furnish her quota for Christian service in "foreign fields." To do this she must be adequately provided not only with Churches, but with schools and hospitals and other departments of denominational activity. Denominational? Yes, for Methodism, acting in accord with the comity of missions, has undertaken alone to spread the gospel in a territory of twenty million souls. Yet the women and girls

SUMMARY OF WORK IN WEST CHINA CONFERENCE.

NAME OF STATIONS.	Chungking	Chentu	Tsicheo	Sui Ling	Jang Bt	Total
W. F. M. S. Missionaries	3	5	2			10
Wives of Missionaries in Active Work		2	1	1		4
Foreign or Eurasian Assistants						
Native Women	6	7	5	2	1	21
WOMEN IN THE CHURCH—						
Full Members	62	27	62	*	*	151
Probationers	24	17	20	*	*	61
Adherents	700		500	*	*	1,200
Women and Girls Baptized During Year	18	10	18	*	*	46
No. Christian Women under Instruction	45	38	19	*	*	102
Non-Christian Women under Instruction	60					60
No. Bible-women Employed	4	1	2			7
BIBLE INSTITUTES OR TRAINING CLASSES						
No. of Institutes	1	2	1			4
No. Missionaries Teaching	1	3	1			5
No. Native Teachers						
Enrollment	20					20
SCHOOLS FOR TRAINING BIBLE WOMEN—						
No. Schools			1			1
No. Missionaries			1			1
No. Native Teachers			2			2
Enrollment			19			19
Receipts for Board and Tuition						
VERNACULAR AND ANGLO-VERNACULAR BOARDING SCHOOLS—						
No. Schools		1				1
No. Foreign Missionaries		2				2
Foreign or Eurasian Teachers						
No. Native Teachers		4				4
Self-Supporting Students		1				1
Wholly-Supported Students		63				63
Partly-Supported Students						
No. Day Students						
Total Enrollment		64				64
Receipts for Board and Tuition		$25 00				$25 00
Field Donations		$80 00				$80 00
DAY SCHOOLS—						
No. Schools	1	1	1			3
No. Teachers	2	3	3			8
Total Enrollment	50	45	40			135
Average Daily Attendance	34	38	24			96
Receipts for Tuition	$9 70	$8 00	$5 00			$22 70
Government Grants and Donations						
MEDICAL WORK—						
No. Hospitals	1					1
No. Foreign Physicians	1					1
Eurasian or Native Physicians						
No. Medical Students						
No. Foreign Nurses						
Eurasian or Native Nurses						
No. Nurse Students	4					4
No. Hospital Beds	50	12				62
No. Hospital Patients	240					240
No. Hospital Clinic Patients	5,890					5,890
No. Out-Patients	377					377
No. Out-Dispensaries						
No. Dispensary Patients	5,890	3,000				8.890
Dispensary Receipts	$89 00					$89 00
Hospital Receipts	$251 57					$251 57
Fees and Donations from Foreigners	$150 00					$150 00
Government Grants						

* Not reported.

are almost entirely neglected except in the four cities where we have resident women missionaries. Plainly we must either reach these women with the gospel or surrender, to some more efficient agency the territory which on good authority is said to contain the most thrifty, intelligent and cultured people of China.

Arise, let us go over and possess the land.

FOOCHOW CONFERENCE.

Organized as a Conference in 1877.
Woman's Work commenced by Baltimore Ladies' China Missionary Society in 1858.
Woman's Foreign Missionary Society commenced work in 1871.
Official Correspondent, Mrs. E. D. Huntley.
The Foochow Conference includes the Fuhkien Province, except what is now the Hing Hua Conference.

MISSIONARIES AND THEIR STATIONS.

FOOCHOW.—Carrie I. Jewell, Julia A. Bonafield,* Ella Lyon, M. D., Hu King Eng, M. D., Phœbe C. Wells,* Phœbe C. Parkinson,* Florence J. Plumb, Jean Adams, Mrs. S. A. Tippet,* Elizabeth M. Strow, Ruby Sia, May Hu, L. Ethel Wallace, Cora E. Simpson, Edna Jones.
MING CHIANG.—Mary Peters, Mary E. Carleton, M. D.
NGU CHENG & HOKCHIANG.—Lydia A. Trimble, Carrie M. Bartlett, Li Bi Cu, M. D.
HAI TANG.—Mamie F. Glassburner.
KU CHENG & KU-DE.—Grace B. Travis,* Frieda V. Lorenz.
NORTH AND SOUTH YEN PING.—Mable C. Hartford, Alice Linam.

FOOCHOW.—The educational work at Foochow includes all the grades from Kindergarten to College work. For many years the highest work done was in our Seminary under Miss Parkinson, and the girls graduating in the Boarding School took the advanced English course with her. Good work has been done here and many of our native Christian workers will remember her with gratitude. We are sorry that she has been obliged to return to the home-land because of ill-health.

A friend in the Pacific Branch has given $15,000 to erect the Administration building for the Woman's College of South China. The present site for the college is hardly large enough for the group of buildings, and negotiations are pending for an added plot of ground.

In the Foochow Boarding School the highest attendance ever reached was during the term just closed, when 175 were enrolled and scores of applicants were refused for lack of room. Children are taken from the Kindergarten at the age of ten and are required to be self-supporting for the first two years, after which time scholarships may be granted to the very needy. In the graduating class this last year two girls have been self-supporting throughout the course.

The much needed dining-room and kitchen are in process of erection, the gift of the New England Branch.

They have had a summer school for teachers with an enrollment of thirty. It has been a trying year for Miss Bonafield with the care of the Boarding School and the heavy responsibility connected with the

*Home on leave.

remodeling of said school. With Miss Plumb's return she will take her needed furlough.

Mary E. Crook Memorial.—The reports from our Mary E. Crook Home and Kindergarten are very encouraging. Miss Strow was appointed here at the last Conference and she has cared for these two schools in addition to her regular work. It seems as if each worker in the Foochow Conference was doing the work of two or three people. The Kindergarten has a force of five native teachers and they have been paid from the money of the Home.

Prices of food have increased to such an extent that it was necessary to raise the salaries of the teachers or loose them. Then add to this the advance in rice and provisions, and you will find that the bills are about double what they were a year ago. It is almost an impossibility to carry on this work with the appropriation of last year. Repairs are needed in Kindergarten rooms and the three houses. Among the words of admonition that have come from our Secretary Emeritus, Mrs. E. B. Stevens, are these: "Do not cut any repairs, it is poor economy: I have seen it here in India. It will cost you double later on."

In the school the children do all the work of the houses and make all of their own clothes, shoes, and everything that belongs to the home. Last Chinese New-Year's vacation they made one hundred pairs of shoes and they will make all the clothing for next winter.

Our older children attend the Boarding School which is directly opposite, and the little ones attend the Kindergarten. Miss Strow writes: "I wish you could just step in and see our Kindergarten. We have ninety-three enrolled and they come from our very best Christian families. People say it is the most interesting place in Foochow. It has been such a blessed year, and I praise our Father for letting me serve Him in this place."

Foochow Woman's Training School.—The enrollment for the year has been twenty-six, seven of these entering from the Romanized School. Four of the women have been teaching half of each day, which necessitated a longer period for their study course. The women in training go out with the Bible-women on Saturday afternoons and tell the old, old story of Jesus and His love. While the fruit of this work of soul-saving is not apparent to any great degree, still a number of those visited have become regular attendants at Church; some have become interested and are now students in the Romanized School. During the year they have received twenty-five mex., for board, and $4.50 for the rent of two little veranda rooms, and part of the money was for board for two children who come with their mothers, and part was for two women who were brides. When brides are recommended for admission we will receive them if possible, but require the husband to support his wife.

Miss Jewell writes: "The reports of the famine in Central China had become very distressing; collections to aid the sufferers were taken up in many parts of this province, and we were asked to do our share. The pastor asked for subscriptions in the different schools; we gave $17.90 in money. Then the women asked to be allowed to do without their solid rice at dinner time for the remaining five weeks, and have instead the rice with considerable water in it three times a day. Then the cost of the small supply of vegetables netted five dollars more. The servants gave $2.50, thus enlarging the check to the amount of $20.65, which was sent to the starving people." This giving is true sacrifice.

The Romanized School.—The largest enrollment has been twenty-two during the year. Here the women get their first School instruction fitting them for the Training School, which is the stepping-stone which gives us our trained Bible-women. If these two, the Romanized School and the Training School, are not supported, we are going to lack for Bible-women. There has been no special religious movement in the school during the year though earnest work was done. among the women by the older ones, and some of the Sunday meetings were very interesting. Two of the women joined the church on probation, three were baptized, and these and one other joined in full connection.

YEN PING.—From the Girls' School we received news of a prosperous year. They have had thirty girls the past term and only twenty-one scholarships where forty are needed. The girls come long distances, from twenty-five to ninety-five miles. Their homes are from six different districts, and if we expect continued good work we must see that the full estimates are granted.

The women at Inka have had a year of careful training in spite of lack of funds. The question that presents itself to-day is where do we expect to get our Bible-women if we withhold our money to train them? There is a fine teacher at this place and the gifts from three Branches have enabled Miss Hartford to meet the obligations. These women in training go out with the Bible-women as they go from house to house, thus receiving practical instruction as a part of their work.

KU CHENG.—At the beginning of the year, Miss Travis and Miss Lorenz were caring for our work at Ku-Cheng. *Two women,* where three are needed to look after a Boarding School with an enrollment of 96 pupils, a Romanized School, a Training School, 40 Day Schools, and 40 Bible-women. A big problem for two missionaries, and one of them new in the work. What happened? The inevitable! Miss Travis was taken ill and obliged to return home, "and then there was one." What next? Miss Lorenz made a brave fight alone. but with a like result, "and then there was none."

At the last Estimating Committee the subject of the need for a worker at Ku-Cheng was brought up and it seemed imperative that a missionary of experience should be sent there, and Miss Peters volunteered to go and was appointed. This leaves added work for Miss Longstreet at Ming-Chiang.

MING-CHIANG TRAINING SCHOOL.—During the past year the Training School had its first graduates. It was a memorable day. These women will all be employed in the work as teachers or Bible-women.

In the Romanized Class most of the women that come are Church members; those that were not have accepted Christ. At the close of the first term the women could repeat some Scripture, a few hymns, the Ten Commandments, Apostles' Creed, and read very well in the new Reader, and best of all knew Christ as their Savior.

On this District are fifteen Bible-women all doing faithful work. Miss Peters and a helper visited the outlying villages during the vacation and held services. At one place the people compelled them to come and hold preaching services. Miss Peters writes: "One of my helpers has been teaching a class of ten women during the summer vacation and also studying the Chinese National Reader for her own education. She has written for ten Romanized Readers and the same number of National Readers. Our Bible-women greatly rejoice that they can now buy the whole Bible in Romanized, and willingly pay the sixty cents."

NGU CHENG.—Miss Bartlett, writes: "Here we have had between forty and fifty women enrolled in our Training and Romanized School during the year. It has been a great year to many of them. While minds have been developing and expanding, souls have been opening

⎯toward God. Miss Trimble held a week· of special service and God gave us a gracious revival. The women listened eagerly and step by step the way was explained and made clear to them. About the fourth or fifth day when we went to prayer they all broke out praying almost as one·voice; such calling upon God to forgive their sins, and in that very hour several claimed the special blessing and knew the joy of peace and pardon. At the close of the service all had accepted Christ, and O, the joy in their faces; some were like sunshine, and we did not need words to tell us that they had met Jesus by the way and talked with Him. Much was due to the three teachers who day by day did such faithful personal work with the women. Again in the spring the spirit of revival was in our midst. We all came back from the Centennial Conference greatly burdened for a revival, and at once started a little workers' prayer meeting in which we prayed definitely for this. After two weeks the time seemed ripe for a public meeting, and accordingly the pastors and teachers of the Boys' School invited all the Ngu-Cheng District to unite in service. The pastors and teachers have services during the day, the schools joining in the evening. God poured out .His Spirit upon the people; sins were confessed, wrongs made right, and lives rededicated to God and His service. Mr. Caldwell says he never witnessed anything like it in China, and what is better, it is still going on."

They have organized an evangelistic company of theological students, who during the summer months are going from charge to charge on the Ngu-Cheng District. It is marvelous the way God is pouring out His Spirit upon the people. One thing they are emphasizing, and that is, that Christians shall keep the Sabbath holy unto the Lord. This may sound easy, but any one that is acquainted with the customs of the Chinese people can readily understand.

The girls and women have been factors in these meetings. The Bible-women are doing noble, faithful service on the District. There are not enough of them, but if these schools are well supported we will have well equipped women to supply the needs as fast as they come. We are asked repeatedly for a woman to go into a village, but the reply must be "We have no one to send." A District Conference was held, over which Miss Trimble presided, giving instruction in the Bible.

Miss Wells has had charge of the Liang-au hospital in Foochow during Dr. Lyons's home leave in America. Her work has been arduous. Her special work has been among the lepers, and the gifts from the friends at home have enabled her to bring the light and the Gospel into the homes of hundreds of these suffering ones. She has won the hearts of these poor people and they have shown their love for her in many ways. When she started for the home-land they presented her with a banner and other tokens of their appreciation.

They have a little church and she holds services with them, and many of the children have learned to read and sing.

DR. SITES' MEMORIAL.—*Good Shepherd Hospital.*—Nearly twenty years ago Dr. Carleton came to China, and this is her sixth year of a third period of service. She has been able to help, not only their bodies, but has given much time in assisting in revival services, visiting the Church members, and dispensing medicines. As one result of the year's work, a church has been built about three miles from the hospital. Two small buildings, long needed, have been put up this year: One is a stable, a place for sedan chairs, a room for the caretaker, and a native kitchen with two rooms in the upper story. The second building is a morgue, a small one-story, two-roomed building, so situated that one door opens directly through the wall into the street so they do not need to go through the Compound. The building cost 300 mex. I think it would be wise to send Dr. Carleton to look after the construction of some of our other buildings. She evidently is a good manager. Dr. Carleton writes: "These two upper rooms in the first building, I have long wanted for the use of men who come for short treatment and are refused lodging in the inns. It is not in any sense a men's hospital, for I could not conveniently take cases who are confined to the bed. Neither I nor my students go to these rooms, but the men come to the dispensary to us. These men attend prayers in the chapel and go with the caretaker to Church and are, during their stay with us, under religious instruction. When we are able to purchase the lot next to us, I would like this building for an isolation ward, which we do not now have, but greatly need. A greater need here is another trained helper. While I have a native helper, Dr. Yong, still he can not treat women when I am away and am necessitated to close. This last year we had an epidemic of smallpox and some of the school girls took the disease. One of my students has been a great help to Miss Longstreet in caring for some of her sick during an epidemic of mumps, which occurred during the time that the hospital was closed. Probably ninety-five of these would have been in the hospital wards had it then been opened. She says it is a losing game to try and run a hospital with one physician; not only is it a losing game for the hospital and the physician, but also to the society. No one person can combine in herself the post of matron, housekeeper, nurse, general superintendent, mason, carpenter, general and optical practitioner and surgeon, and I am convinced that a new state of affairs will need to be arranged. Either there should be a foreign physician and a trained nurse, or a foreign physician and a native trained physician.

The following is a list for six months' work:

6 months—Ward patients	65.	Prescriptions,	260
6 months—Visiting out-patients	230.	Prescriptions,	460
6 months—Office visits	50.	Prescriptions,	100
2 months—Students visiting	30.	Prescriptions,	60
12 months—Dispensing	2,436.	Prescriptions,	4,872
Record ending July, 1907	2,711.	Prescriptions,	5,752

Woolston Memorial Hospital.—Supported by Philadelphia, Baltimore, and Minneapolis Branches. The hospital statistical report is as follows:

Receipts	$1,775.56
Hospital in-patients	408
Attendance and friends	126
Total in hospital	534
Dispensary patients	21,305
Patients seen at visits	834
Total patients seen	22,139
Total prescriptions written and filled	21,986
Total prescriptions written and not filled	57

Lau Sing Sang, Mrs. Lau, and Huang's report is as follows:

Morning services, attendance	17,120
Sunday afternoon services, attendance	3,607

Patients who heard the Word and received it with joy........... 265
Hearers at said dispensary ....,..................... 24,360
Prayer-meetings held in homes 53
Attendance at said meetings 2,620
Prayer-meetings held in hospital 282
Attendance at said meetings 8,460
Days visiting 204
Hearers 5,290
Total number of hearers 61,457

Dr. Hu, in giving us the statistics, says some of the items seem to show a decrease, particularly in the number of prayer-meetings that have been held in the homes. She says that one reason for this is that we have not had a suitable Bible-woman to do this work. It is difficult to find one in Foochow City who can speak the Foochow dialect without a brogue. She should be over thiry years of age, of a good character, and well versed in the Bible. This is very important, because the hospital Bible-woman is obliged to go out by herself, as we do not furnish a missionary to accompany her as they do in the Church of England Mission. The Bible-woman in the hospital is taxed so heavily looking after the in-patients that she has but little time to do outside work. There have been a large number of very ill patients that have stayed for longer periods of time than formerly, and as the hospital is small we have been obliged to refuse many patients. The outlook for the new hospital is very bright, and she is hoping for the 10,000 mex. that will enable her to build. The cost of maintaining the hospital is more than formerly, and rice and all the necessaries are almost double what they were last year.

The past year the hospital patients had their Christmas entertainment in the church. The students were the speakers and singers.

In April two young women finished their course of study in medicine; one of them is now the hospital matron.

The great need here is an evangelistic worker to visit in the homes of the patients. Oftentimes they hear the Word and believe, but do not stay long enough to become thoroughly familiar with our doctrines.

Dr. Hu closes her report with this: "Now, who will give us stereoscopes and nice views. I want my patients to know a little of the pretty parts of the world and of other homes besides their own dirty ones. We need a good-sized organ for our new hospital. The baby organ we have used for so many years is sick with chills and fever. I can not find a doctor who can cure it; not even Dr. George S. Miner was able to cure it, on account of its great age."

HAI TANG.—The Hai Tang Boarding School did not open at the beginning of the year, but will have a half-year's work. It was impossible to do so with the amount of money first pledged, but with the promise of added scholarships it is hoped that the school building secured to us through the gifts of the children will be occupied and good work done. During the first of the year Miss Glassburner did evangelistic work, and at one place a room was rented and services were held. These women are willing to stay hour after hour. They are so anxious to hear and know of the doctrine that ofttimes they are not willing to let a single word slip, and if they do not understand the missionary they stop her and ask her to say it over again. The Leaf Cluster Pictures of the life of Christ were used and were very helpful in leading these women to the light. The hymns that they sing are full of Scripture teaching, such as "He comes to save sinners," "He bore our sins," "It is Jesus who saves," and "We are His people." These truths come to them in a new way—through song! Miss Glassburner writes: "The song that we usually try to teach them is, 'I Have a Savior ·Who's Mighty to Keep,' or 'Precious Name.' They do not always get the time or the tune. In their eagerness and care to get in every strange, new word, some fall behind the others and we sometimes have to stop at the end of a measure for them to catch up; but if there is discord down here· on earth, we are sure that it is pure melody to Him whose praises they are singing."

The year has been a remarkable one in that many have been brought to Christ all over the island. In the Woman's School they have had a full attendance all the year notwithstanding that the appropriations were very small; twenty have been in attendance.

The Romanized School has made good progress; two women who three months ago could not read a character, have read the Primer, Catechism, Commandment Sheet, Apostles' Creed, Lord's Prayer, a little book of Bible verses, a health tract, the Ritual of Baptism and Reception of Members, and are using the Romanized Hymnal in their Church services. All this will make different women of them, and if they should never have any more training they have gotten a vision of a higher life, and with the ability to read for themselves we feel sure they will bless others wherever they go. The Romanized School is to be one of the great factors in lifting the womanhood of the Chinese people to a higher plane.

The day schools are doing good work. While there are hindrances and obstacles to overcome, still they are reaching where any other department can not.

The new church will be dedicated this fall, and with the new school building and the splendid hospital at Ngu-cheng, we feel that there is little else needed.

The Hai-tang workers went to the mainland this year for the teachers'' institute.

WORK IN THE FOOCHOW CONFERENCE.

NAME OF STATIONS.	Foochow	Hok Chiang	Hai Tang	Ming Chiang	Ku Cheng	Gu De	Yen Ping	Totals
W. F M. S. Missionaries	10	2	1	3	2		1	20
Wives of Missionaries in Active Work							1	1
Foreign or Eurasian Assistants								
Native Workers	54	45	31	32	44	34	19	259
WOMEN IN THE CHURCH—								
Full Members								
Probationers								
Adherents								
Women and Girls Baptized during Year								
No. Christian Women under Instruction								
Non-Christian Women under Instruction								
No. Bible-women Employed	16	19	14	15	15	16	8	108
BIBLE INSTITUTES OR TRAINING CLASSES.								
No. of Institutes				1	1			2
No. Missionaries Teaching				2	2			4
No. Native Teachers				2	3			5
Enrollment				25	36			61
SCHOOLS FOR TRAINING BIBLE-WOMEN—								
No. Schools	1	1	1	1	1		1	6
No. Missionaries	1	1	1	1	1		1	6
No. Native Teachers	3	2	3	1	2		1	12
Enrollment	26	23	21	20	23		20	133
Receipts for Board and Tuition	$5.00			30.00				$35.00

NAMES OF STATIONS.	Foochow	Hok Chiang	Hai Tang	Ming Of.	Ku Cheng	Gu De	Yen Ping	Totals
ENGLISH BOARDING SCHOOLS—No. Schools	1							1
No. Foreign Missionaries	1							1
Foreign or Eurasian Teachers								
No. Native Teachers	5							5
Self-Supporting Students								
Wholly-Supported Students								
Partly-Supported Students	7							7
No. Day Students								
Total Enrollment	36							36
Receipts for Board and Tuition	$270.00							$270 00
Government Grants and Donations								
VERNACULAR AND ANGO-VERNACULAR BOARDING SCHOOLS—No. Schools	1	1		1	1		1	5
No. Foreign Missionaries	3	2		1	1		1	8
Foreign or Eurasian Teachers								
No. Native Teachers	11	5		4	7		2	30
Self-Supporting Students								
Wholly-Supported Students								
Partly-Supported Students	98	57		34	76		24	299
No. Day Students	37	3						
Total Enrollment	170	60		34	96		24	384
Receipts for Board and Tuition					$91		$36	$127 00
Government Grants and Donations								
ORPHANAGES—No. Orphanges	1							1
No. Foreign Missionaries	1							1
Foreign or Eurasian Teachers								
No. Native Teachers	3							3
Total No. Orphans	44							44
Receipts for Board and Tuition								
Government Grants and Donations								
HOMES FOR WIDOWS AND HOMELESS WOMEN—No. Homes	1							1
No. Foreign Missionaries	1							1
Foreign or Eurasian Teachers								
No. Native Teachers								
No. Women	200							200
Receipts for Board and Tuition								
Government Grants and Donations								
DAY SCHOOLS—No. Schools	17	19	14	10	20	16	8	104
No. Teachers	17	19	14	10	20	16	8	104
Total Enrollment	250	190	140	100	300	279	100	1,359
Average Daily Attendance								
Receipts for Tuition								
Government Grants and Donations								
KINDERGARTENS—No. Kindergartens	1							1
No. Foreign Kindergartners								
No. Native Kindergartners	2							2
Nat. Kindergartners in Training								
Total Enrollment	93							93
Average Attendance								
Receipts for Tuition								
Government Grants and Donations								
MEDICAL WORK—No. Hospitals	{ 1 1	1		1				4
No. Foreign Physicians	1 1	1		1				3
Eurasian or Native Physicians	{ 3 2			1				6
No. Medical Students	{ 5 10			3				18
No. Foreign Nurses								
Eurasian or Native Nurses								
No. Nurse Students								
No. Hospital Beds								
No. Hospital Patients	681	150		112				943
No. Hospital Clinic Patients	{ 3,956 19,800	2905		3,854				30,015
No. Out-Patients	828	143		395				1,366
No. Out-Dispensaries								
No. Dispensary Patients								
Dispensary Receipts								
Hospital Receipts	{ $428 02 1,429 11			$402 93				$2,250 06
Fees and Donations from Foreigners								
Government Grants								

HING HUA CONFERENCE.

Hing Hua Mission Conference was organized in 1896.
Official Correspondent, Mrs. A. N. Fisher.
The Hing Hua Mission includes the Hing Hua prefecture and adjoining teritory where the Hing Hua dialect is spoken, and the Ing Chung prefecture and adjoining territory where the Amoy dialect is spoken.·

MISSIONARIES AND THEIR STATIONS.

HING HUA.—*M. E. Wilson, L. W. Varney, P. E. Westcott, M. M. Thomas, Lulu Baker.
TEK-HOE.—Althea M. Todd, Jessie A .Marriott, Gertrude Strawick.
SIENG IU.—Martha Lebeus, Martha Nicolaisen, Emma J. Betow, M. D., Frances L. Draper, M. D.
WIVES OF MISSIONARIES IN CHARGE OF WORK.—Mrs. E. F. Brewster, Mrs. H. G. Dildine, and Mrs. Carson.

The evidences of the dawning of China's new day are witnessed in every district in Hing Hua Conference. Miss Westcott and Miss Varney write from Hing Hua: "Already we feel the uplift of the rising tide of Western ideas that are filling the minds of progressive Chinese. Our Christians are beginning to realize the necessity of intelligence of those who are to become the wives and mothers of the land, consequently are seeking school advantages for their daughters."

From the westernmost outpost in Ing Chung District, Miss Todd writes: "It was suggested by the Government that the girls should have an easier course than the boys, but girls in Christian schools will not listen to that. It is difficult to believe that this is the same old China. They have very surprising ideas and make queer mistakes, but that matters not as long as China moves on."

HING HUA.—The necessary furlough of Miss Wilson, early in the year, and the continued illness of Miss Thomas left very heavy burdens and responsibilities on Miss Westcott and Miss Varney. One must wonder how they have managed to keep all the wheels moving in boarding school, Woman's Training School, day schools, city and district evangelistic work. Three more missionaries are greatly needed. One has been pledged in the outgoing of Miss Baker. Miss Westcott has been about six years on the field and should be relieved without delay.

Owing to the advance in the course of study and lengthening of the required time, there were no graduates from the girls' boarding school this year. Marked progress has been made in industrial work and many girls are thus learning to help in their support. The city day school has been adopted as the primary department and the little ones are making rapid progress under favorable conditions.

In the Woman's Training School five finished the four years' course. A four weeks' institute was held with the Bible women of the district in May, which was most helpful in new thoughts, new inspiration, and special blessing for the work of the coming year.

SIENG IU.—The Isabel Hart Girls' School increases year by year in numbers and efficiency, under the faithful care of Miss Nicolaisen. Including day scholars, seventy-three pupils are enrolled, which is the limit of the school accommodations. Miss Nicolaisen writes, "I thank God

*Home on leave.

11

for entrusting me with so many precious souls, and with His help the girls are daily making progress in forming Christian character."

Miss Lebeus reports a glorious year in the Woman's Training School and the district evangelistic work. The number in the training school has reached forty. Her itinerating trips are of thrilling interest.

The medical work in the Margaret E. Nast Hospital, under Drs. Betow and Draper, is a blessed boon to hundreds, both physically and spiritually. Dr. Betow writes, "I have reason to believe that many have found their Savior in the hospital and, after their return home,'serve Him to the best of their knowledge." She tells of two women, neighbors, who listened eagerly to the Gospel story and gave up their charms and idols while in the hospital. After returning home they walked back several times, a distance of six miles, on tiny, bound feet, to attend Church. When the hot weather began, they swept and cleaned a room for their chapel, decorated it with a couple of pictures from the Berean Leaf Clusters, and every Sunday they take their little boys there for worship, which consists of repeating the Lord's Prayer and talking about Jesus.

TEK-HOE.—Miss Todd and Miss Marriott have been made happy by the provision for a new school building, so long greatly needed. So many new pupils have come into the school that it has been necessary to use every possible device for increasing space, such as shortening beds and using wash-rooms for classes. The little kindergarten is a wonder to the people and attracts crowds of admiring fathers, mothers, brothers, and sisters. The children's church is another attractive feature. Formerly only a few children attended the services in the large church, and then only to play. Now twenty-five come regularly to their own little meeting and then sit quietly through the other meeting.

Miss Todd and Miss Marriott spend their vacation days in itinerating for evangelistic work in their large districts.

KOREA.

Women's Work commenced in 1885. Organized as a Conference in 1904.

Official Correspondent, Miss Louisa C. Rothweiler.

MISSIONARIES AND THEIR STATIONS.

CHEMULPO.—Josephine O. Paine, Gertrude Snavely.

PYENG YANG.—Mrs. Rosetta Sherwood Hall, M. D., Henrietta P. Robbins, Emily I. Haynes, Mrs. Esther Kim Pak, M. D., †Sarah B. Hallmann.

SEOUL.—Mrs. M. F. Scranton, Lulu E. Frey, Jessie Marker, M. J. Edmunds, Mary M. Cutler, M. D., Emma Ernsberger, M. D., †Millie Albertsen.

YENG BYEN.—Ethel M. Estey, *Lulu Miller.

WIVES OF MISSIONARIES IN CHARGE OF WORK.—Mrs. G. H. Jones, Mrs. W. N. Noble, Mrs. D. A. Bunker, Mrs. E. D. Follwell, Mrs. E. M. Cable, Mrs. W. C. Swearer, Mrs. J. Z. Moore, Mrs. C. Critchett, Mrs. A. L. Becker, Mrs. F. C. Williams, Mrs. C. Taylor, Mrs. C. D. Morris, Mrs. H. Miller.

Never has the door of opportunity been so wide open in Korea as at present, never have our missionaries been so embarrassed, yes, appalled, by the work confronting them as at present. The number of members

---

*Home on leave.   †Students of the language.

and adherents has more than doubled during the past year, an increase of 21,506 being reported. But of far more importance than this increase in numbers has been the wonderful outpouring of the Holy Spirit which has come to the Church, resulting in conviction, confession, and cleansing. Missionaries, native helpers, members, inquirers, pupils in the schools,—all had a share in the great blessing. Miss Miller wrote: "Ten days of revival meetings have closed. It is impossible to tell on paper what we saw and heard. The Spirit was poured out with manifestations of power. Strong men and women and even the school children cried out in agony as they became convicted of sin. All sorts of terrible sins were confessed; they felt that they must spew everything out of their hearts or they would be lost. Such agony in prayer, such wrestling with God! But the victory was as glorious as the confession had been terrible. The heathen had no part in this; the work was confined to the Christians. You can know the result of this on the Church. The Christians are preaching in power and the result is the same as in the early Church. This movement has passed over a great part of Korea, and the manifestations and results have been the same everywhere. There will be a still greater ingathering of souls, but what shall we do? Just a turning from heathenism with no teaching is almost worse than not coming at all."

If the need for more trained workers, both Bible-women and teachers, was great before, it is far greater now. Our fourteen workers have done all they possibly could do, but they stand dismayed. Their number should be doubled.

SEOUL DISTRICT.—The meetings in our large Chong Dong church, which holds nine hundred or more people, have become so crowded that it is necessary to hold services for the men at one hour and for the women at another hour. At Sang Dong, another large church, 166 women have been taken into the church during the year. The Bible-women under Mrs. Scranton's care report 4,000 homes visited and 12,000 people instructed.

At last the oft-repeated, urgent request for some one to take charge of the Training School for Bible-women has been answered by Cincinnati Branch in the sending out of Miss Albértsen. While she is studying the language, Mrs. Scranton, with the assistance of Mrs. Ha, a graduate of Ohio Wesleyan University, is doing what she can to train women.

The Girls' Boarding School reports one hundred boarders. Of these, one was entirely self-supporting, seventy-seven partly self-supporting, and only twenty-two were entirely supported. Certainly a very good showing as compared with a few years ago, when we had to be thankful to get a child, we furnishing everything free of cost. The standard of the school is being raised; an admission fee is charged, besides that all new girls are required to furnish their own clothing, bedding, rice bowl, and chopsticks. This insures the entrance of only such as come for the sake of an education and not merely to be taken care of. Additional teachers will be needed.

During the summer a Normal School was held here in order to help meet the great need of better trained teachers.

There are nine day schools reported on this district, with an average daily attendance of 240. One of these Mrs. Scranton reports as having seventy scholars packed into a room 8 x 16 feet.

Medical Work.—This has been carried on in Seoul, as heretofore, under very adverse circumstances. In the Chong Dong Hospital, with its cramped quarters and the constant repairs necessitated by the condition of the buildings, Dr. Cutler has cared for 188 ward patients and has seen 2,194 dispensary patients, besides 400 out-calls. Miss Edmunds has carried on the work of training native nurses and reports a class of nurses whose services are appreciated by natives and foreigners. One of their most promising ones died in service. Dr. Ernsberger has been bravely holding the fort at East Gate. Turning the chapel into a waiting room, the waiting room into a ward, and sending the girls' day school into a room of the Scranton home, she has been able to care for 120 ward patients and has seen 7,974 dispensary patients.

The location of the Lillian Harris Memorial Hospital, having been finally decided upon, we look forward to a near future when better equipment and less crowded quarters will make more and better work possible.

Just here it is in place to record the gratitude of all connected with our work for a most generous grant of land adjoining our East Gate compound, thus giving ample space and convenient access for the new hospital. The land in question adjoins our own grounds and the city wall and comprises 3,000 meters, being valued at $8,000 to $10,000.

CHEMULPO DISTRICT.—The work of our ladies here took in a part of Hai-ju, a part of the Pyeng Yang District, and Kong-ju, a district in the south, besides the large district of Chemulpo, a territory so immense that it is no wonder that Miss Miller was utterly discouraged when she compared what Miss Marker and she *could* do with what was waiting to *be* done. The ten country classes, held for a week or ten days each, were well attended. In some cases the women left their work in the harvest field in order to attend the class and have the opportunity for study. The revival wave spread over a large part of this district. New churches are springing up faster than they can be taken care of. At one place the women told with pride how they themselves had carried stones for the foundations, water for the mortar, and rafters for the roof of their church. In many places parents are begging for the children, and the children themselves are begging for day schools. At one place they had built a schoolhouse, but nothing could be done for them because of a lack of teachers and of a lack of money to support them if we had them. In the city of Chemulpo there is in regular attendance a membership of 632 women. The Holy Spirit came upon this church in mighty power and all experienced such a cleansing as they had never before known.

The day school numbers almost one hundred pupils. A second teacher had to be engaged. A night school for women was held by the Sunday-school superintendent and pastor.

Since Mrs. Sharp was obliged to return to America, after the death of her husband, the people of Konju and vicinity have felt as sheep without a shepherd. There are over one hundred groups of Christians here. Miss Miller went down last fall and held two classes for the women. We are thankful that one lady is under appointment for this place.

PYENG YANG DISTRICT.—Here the wonderful revival touched the hearts of missionaries and natives alike, giving to them a wonderful baptism of the Spirit and power which has manifested itself in increased zeal and earnest activity.

Nine Bible Institutes or classes were held, with a total attendance of over six hundred women, the one in Pyeng Yang City being attended by 287. These women carried the revival fires with them to their country homes.

Medical Work.—The total destruction in November last of the Woman's Hospital, with all the instruments and supplies, was a great blow to Dr. Hall and her co-workers. The insurance, of course, covered but a part of the original value, and as the price of building has increased very much during the last few years, at least $8,000 will need to be sent

NAMES OF STATIONS.	Seoul	Chemulpo.	PyengYang*	Yeng Byen†	Kong Jul‖	Hai Ju†	Total
W. F. M. S. Mi sionaries	6	2	4	1			13
Wives of Missionaries in Active Work	2		3	1			6
Foreign or Eurasian Assistants.							
Native Workers							
WOMEN IN THE CHURCH—Full Members							§1,500
Probationers							§8,575
Adherents							§6,000
Women and Girls Baptized during Year							§1,600
No. Christian Women under Instruction							§1,000
Non-Christian Women under Instruction							
No. Bible-women Employed	15	7	4	1			27
BIBLE INSTITUTES OR TRAINING CLASSES—							
No. of Institutes	2	10	9	2			23
No. Missionaries Teaching	3	2	5	1			11
No. Native Teachers		1	3	2			6
Enrollment	40	300	600	70			1,010
SCHOOLS FOR TRAINING BIBLE WOMEN—							
No. Schools	1						1
No. Missionaries	1						1
No. Native Teachers	1						1
Enrollment	10						10
Receipts for Board and Tuition							
VERNACULAR AND ANGLO-VERNACULAR							
BOARDING SCHOOLS—No. Schools	1						1
No. Foreign Missionaries	3						3
Foreign or Eurasian Teachers							
No. Native Teachers	2						2
Self-Supporting Students	1						1
Wholly-Supported Students	22						22
Partly-Supported Students	77						77
No. Day Students	4						4
Total Enrollment	104						104
Receipts for Board and Tuition	$48 00						$48 00
Government Grants and Donations							
DAY SCHOOLS—No. Schools	9	7	6	2			24
No. Teachers	11	3	9	2			25
Total Enrollment	381	203	460	25			1,069
Average Daily Attendance	240	150	350	20			760
Receipts for Tuition		$6 00	$50 00	$10 00			$66 00
Government Grants and Donations							
KINDERGARTENS—No. Kindergartens							
No. Foreign Kindergartners							
No. Native Kindergartners							
Native Kindergartners in Training							
Total Enrollment							
Average Attendance							
Receipts for Tuition							
Government Grants and Donations							
INDUSTRIAL SCHOOLS—No. Schools			1				1
No. Industrial Depts. in other Schools							
No. Foreign Missionaries							
Foreign or Eurasian Teachers							
No. Native Teachers			1				1
No. Pupils			8				8
Receipts for Tuition							
From Sale of Products			$35 00				$35 00
Government Grants and Donations							
MEDICAL WORK—No. Hospitals	1						1
No. Foreign Physicians	2		1				3
Eurasian or Native Physicians			1				1
No. Medical Students	1		2				3
No. Foreign Nurses	1		1				2
Eurasian or Native Nurses	1						1
No. Nurse Students	5						5
No. Hospital Beds	23						23
No. Hospital Patients	308						308
No. Hospital Clinic Patients	3,046						3,046
No. Out-Patients	490						490
No. Out-Dispensaries	1						1
No. Dispensary Patients	7,974						7,974
Dispensary Receipts	$350 00						$350 00
Hospital Receipts	$430 00						$430 00
Fees and Donations from Foreigners	$89 45						$89 45
Government Grants							

* Also 3 independent girls' schools; 1 parent board girls' school; Receipts, $05.
† Hospital and Records burned. ‡ One worker sent here at close of Conference year. ‖ Two workers under appointment. § Estimated.

cut to rebuild. Dr. Hall is anxiously awaiting this money so that she may go on with the building. She has held some clinics in the Men's Hospital and has attended out-calls. She has also been enabled to do a little more country work than she could have done if the hospital had been in operation. Miss Hallman is having a better opportunity to acquire the language for the same reason.

The city day school has had an enrollment of 332, and an average daily attendance of two hundred. It has necessarily taken a greater part of Miss Robbins's time, as well as that of three native teachers. A class of seven were graduated this spring. No class of American girls was ever more enthusiastic over examinations and grades than were these seven girls. The graduation exercises were notable for two reasons. First, this was the first class of Methodist girls to receive diplomas in Korea; second, it was the first time in Korea that girls appeared before an audience of men and women to carry out an entire program. The program consisted of three essays on such subjects as "Christian Education for Korean Women," two Chinese readings, and two English recitations. The men were amazed to find out that girls could do as well as boys, even in reading Chinese. The Presbyterian Mission asked us to join them in their Girls' Higher School by furnishing them one Korean teacher and by having one of our ladies teach a certain number of hours each day. The experiment has proven a success. Many of the young men of the academy are planning to send their wives next year.

There are on the district six day schools, with an enrollment of 460, which are supported by our treasury; besides this there are three others supported entirely by the natives. Urgent calls come from every direction for more schools, but we are unable to open them for want of funds and of teachers.

YENG BYEN DISTRICT.—The return of Miss Estey from the homeland and her appointment to this district was a cause of great rejoicing to Mrs. Morris, who has been carrying on work among the women. The call for day schools was so urgent and no teachers were available that Mrs. Morris instructed the two Bible women for some weeks and then set them to work teaching the girls every forenoon. The natives furnished the schoolrooms and all running expenses except the salary of the teacher. Country people sent their daughters to town to attend the school, paying board for them and buying their books. The number of women at the fall class was double what it had been the year before.

The urgent needs of Korea are at least *six* new missionaries, three new missionary homes, money to complete the Lillian Harris Memorial Hospital in Seoul and to rebuild the hospital in Pyeng Yang, a building and equipment for a Bible-woman's Training School and the support of at least six more Bible women and a larger number of day schools. Larger and better buildings than the natives can possibly put up are also needed for two or more of our largest day schools. Who will make it possible to answer one or more of these calls?

JAPAN CONFERENCE.

Woman's Work commenced in 1874. Organized as a Conference in 1884.

Official Correspondent, Carrie J. Carnahan.

The Japan Mission includes the northern part of the Empire of Japan.

MISSIONARIES AND THEIR STATIONS.

HAKODATE.—M. S. Hampton, Augusta Dickerson, *F. E. Singer, A. B. Sprowles.

HIROSAKI,—Mary B. Griffiths, B. Alexander.

NAGOYA.—R. J. Watson, E. M. Soper, M. Lee.

SAPPORA.—L. Imhof, A. V. Bing.

SENDAI.—E. J. Hewett, *C. A. Heaton, Frances K. Phelps, Georgiana Weaver.

TOKIO.—M. A. Spencer, Amy Lewis, *H. S. Alling, Ella Blackstock, E. Bullis, Miss Russell.

YOKOHAMA.—*Mrs. C. W. Van Petten, M. N. Daniel, A. B. Slate, G. Baucus, E. Dickinson.

The past year has seen some important Christian Conferences and Conventions in Japan which can not fail to leave a helpful imprint upon the nation at this important epoch in its history. In April the World's Student Christian Federation received an enthusiastic welcome from the people who, with true Japanese bounty and mastery of detail, provided for the comfort of the six hundred delegates, representing twenty-five nationalities which were present.

Later in the spring was held the General Conference of the three Methodist bodies contemplating Church union—the Methodist Episcopal Church, the Methodist Episcopal Church, South, and the Canadian Methodist Church. Representative men of the three denominations were present. The Conference lasted seventeen days and the union was happily consummated. The official title of the new organization is the Japan Methodist Church. Dr. Yoitsu Honda, formerly president of our Anglo-Japanese College in Tokio, was elected bishop. Bishop Harris was made bishop emeritus. The new Church has two Conferences, the East and the West. The latter includes Nagoya and all west and south of this. The male members of the Mission Boards remain members of their home Conferences, but the Japanese have given them full rights and equal standing with themselves. The missionaries of our Woman's Foreign Missionary Society are not affected by the union, but will have their separate Conference at the same time and place as the General Society, with probably one or two sessions, when both bodies will meet together. The new Church is planning an aggressive evangelistic campaign.

HAKODATE.—This station has been visited by two disastrous fires. On the evening of June 14th the almost completed dormitory building on the new property, two and one-half miles from the heart of the city, was destroyed by fire. The origin of the fire remains a mystery. Every precaution had been taken to prevent such an occurrence. Misses Hampton, Dickerson, and Sprowles bravely planned to open school for the winter in the old, crowded quarters when, about August 31st, a great fire swept over Hakodate, destroying most of the city. The mission homes of the General Board and the Woman's Foreign Missionary Society and the old school buildings were burned, and our missionaries lost practically everything, even their personal effects. The American consul, Mr. King, who has always been most kind to our workers, gave them shelter, and missionaries from Hirosaki and elsewhere shared generously with them such clothing, etc., as they could spare.

Our new buildings being on the outskirts of the city, escaped in this last great fire, but can not be rapidly pushed to completion because all

---

*Home on leave.

carpenters and other workmen are in great demand to provide shelter for the hundreds of families left homeless by the fire.

HIROSAKI.—Miss Alexander reports a year of varied experiences in the school. The loss of some of their experienced teachers has made things hard at times, but they go bravely forward.

Of the kindergarten, she writes: "This has been a good year in the kindergarten, for things have fitted in so nicely. Our hearts were made glad last December when word came from New England Branch telling us, that by special gift of a friend, our kindergarten in Hirosaki could be provided with a home of its own. This was very opportune, for we knew we would have to give up our present rooms in the school at the end of December, and had been looking around for new quarters. A lot suitably located was found and on it an old Japanese house. By putting four rooms in one and making some other changes, this made a temporary home for our little folks, and the term's work began there, the inconveniences being lightened by the thought of the new building we were going to have when spring came. When Miss Griffiths and I began to discuss plans for the building, who should happen home from Manchuria but Mr. Sakuraba, the Christian architect who was so helpful in the building of our Home. He was as interested in planning for the best building at least cost as if it were his own personal affair, and so greatly lightened our responsibility. He was not here long, business recalling him to Manchuria, but he was here long enough to have all plans practically settled and the work entrusted to a carpenter whom he could recommend as one who had faithfully fulfilled previous contracts for him. And so under such favorable conditions our new building is commencing."

SAPPORA.—Miss Bing reports a prosperous year for the district evangelistic work, and Miss Imhof writes of encouraging city evangelistic efforts.

SENDAI.—In this station Miss Ella Hewett is in charge of our Girls' School, and writes very encouragingly of the work there. She also looks after the Sunday-schools scattered about through the city. These little schools are certainly doing very much to win the hearts of the children to Christ. The Orphanage, which has been the outgrowth of the recent famine in Japan, now has 249 children under its care. Miss Phelps, who is in charge, writes: "The blessing of God upon this work has been very apparent from the beginning, and we rejoice to be co-workers with Him. Here Christian teaching is unrestrained, and with no opposing influences from the home, these children are growing up in a Christian atmosphere, the fragrance of which can hardly be lost in a lifetime. Simple hearts receive the truth gladly and naturally, and we ask you to pray with us that the feet of every one of these children may be found in the way of righteousness."

Miss Hewett, in charge of the Girls' School, tells of many changes in their staff of teachers, caused by the marriage of some and the leaving of others to pursue higher courses of study.

The Kings' Daughters Circle and Temperance Society, whose membership is made up from among the school girls, continue their helpful meetings.

Miss Hewett, with the help of some of the school girls, does quite a little city evangelistic work, such as the superintending of street Sunday-schools and conducting of the children's meetings.

The district evangelistic work and the work in the Military Hospital are under the faithful care of Miss Weaver.

TOKIO.—There is maturing a plan for raising the Anglo-Japanese

College to University grade, with departments for Koreans, Chinese, Indians, and others. The carrying out of this plan will necessitate the moving of our Girls' School to another site where we can have more room and where the desire, which has been growing in the minds and hearts of our missionaries for some time, namely, the raising of this School to full college grade, can be carried out. Our School has had a very successful year, but the fact is recognized that a well-equipped college is necessary if we are to be able to train young women in all that is required to make them workers of the highest efficiency.

At the Conference, Miss Amy Lewis, an alumnus of the Woman's College of Baltimore, was appointed principal of the school. She will enter upon the duties at the opening of this fall term. Miss Spencer, who for several years has been acting principal, will take a well-earned furlough. There is need for at least five new missionaries for Central Japan, and it was a real delight to our ladies on the field when Miss Elizabeth Goucher, who with her father and sisters was visiting the mission fields of our Church, decided to remain in Tokio to the end of the school year, next March, to teach in our Aoyama Girls' School.

YOKOHAMA.—The transfer of Miss Lewis to Aoyama and the necessary furlough of Mrs. Van Petten leaves our work in Yokohama very shorthanded. One of the five new missionaries asked for is needed at once for the Yokohama Day School. Another is needed for evangelistic work to relieve Miss Slate.

NAGOYA.—Last May the building containing the Girls' School and Ladies' Home in Nagoya was destroyed by fire. Through the presence of mind and heroism of Miss Watson and others all the pupils were gotten safely out of the building, which was a complete loss.

This is the third serious fire to visit our work in Japan this year. All the properties were insured, but in no case is the insurance sufficient to rebuild—the cost of labor and materials having risen frightfully since the war.

Miss Watson and Miss Lee soon had the school opened and hard at work in a rented building, which, though very poorly adapted to the need, has been made to serve until a new building could be provided.

We regret that illness has laid Miss Soper aside for a time, preventing her carrying on her dearly loved evangelistic work.

SOUTH JAPAN CONFERENCE.

Organized as a Mission Conference in 1899.
Organized as a Conference in 1905.
Woman's Work commenced in 1879.
Official Correspondent, Mrs. R. L. Thomas.

The South Japan Mission includes the island of Kiushiu and the other islands, south and east of the main land, including Formosa and the Loochoo group.

MISSIONARIES AND THEIR STATIONS.

FUKUOKA.—*Leonora M. Seeds, *Mabel K. Seeds, L. Alice Finlay.
KAGOSHIMA.—*Jean M. Gheer, Lida B. Smith, Hortense Long.
NAGASAKI.—Elizabeth Russell, *Mary E. Melton, Marianna Young, Lola M. Kidwell, Hettie A. Thomas, Mary A. Cody.
WIVES OF MISSIONARIES IN CHARGE OF WORK.—Mrs. J. C. Davison, Mrs. F. N. Scott.

---

*Home on leave.

FUKUOKA.—*Ei-Wa Jo Gakko.*—This school, with Miss Mabel K. Seeds as principal and Miss Alice Finlay as associate principal, has had a successful year in all its departments. They have reached the limit in their capacity to accommodate girls, having had a total enrollment of 150, of whom 119 are Christian girls. The boarding students almost without exception have accepted the Christian faith, and at the close of the year only thirteen of the girls in attendance were not Christians, three of whom have expressed their desire so to become, but are forbidden by their parents.

A few special meetings were held each term, resulting in several converts in the outside meetings, which are always held for those who desire to be Christians. Among the inquirers were two of the gentlemen teachers, one of whom has taught in the school for sixteen years. Twenty-five girls have been baptized and have joined the Church. There are four regular class-meetings held in the school, two for the boarding students and two for the day students. Also a students' Friday evening service, led by themselves; all of these the Christian girls attend and are ready to testify and lead in prayer at any time. Miss Seeds says: "We prize the growing reputation our students have of beauty of character and unquestioned morals, more than that other which we continue to enjoy among the people of high scholarship and general education, for by the former we can see more clearly the ultimate accomplishment of the primary purpose of the Mission school. It is universally known that the Bible and the Christian religion are taught, and that our standard of morality is based upon them. We always mention the fact that we are a Christian School to all who enter, and we tell the parents and friends bringing girls to the school for entrance that most of the girls become Christian in time.

The year has brought us some changes of teachers, but on the whole our strength in the teaching corps has been increased. At the first of the year we lost two valuable teachers because we could not pay their price, and we fear this may be repeated again and again unless we can meet the growing demand for the same wages that are paid for the same work in the government schools. We were especially fortunate, however, in securing other teachers in place of those who left.

We have been pleased to note the proportionate decrease of the irregular students and the increase of those taking the regular preparatory and academic courses, which is the result of greater confidence in the course of study. All of the new students necessarily enter the preparatory course, but such has been the faithful attendance that the preparatory and academic students number almost the same.

Of the four academic graduates last year three went to Kwassui in September, two of whom entered the freshman year of the College, and one the Kindergarten Training Department. The other one in the class went to the Southern Methodist Bible School in Kobe, preferring that school only because it was close to the home of her parents. This has been a great delight to us, for we deem it best for them to continue their education elsewhere, according to their higher ideals, in preparation for their life work. This is a remarkable incident in the history of the school, it being the first time an entire class exhibited such a worthy ambition.

This next June five girls will graduate. All of the class have had some city Sunday-school work for two years, and this opportunity for outside and definite Christian work has been used to great advantage, and has proven to us the possibility of their future usefulness in our Christian work. We realize that the workers already in the field are almost without exception from the Christian schools, by which the worth of Christian education toward the evangelization of Japan can not be gainsaid. Three girls will be graduated in June from the Japanese Sewing Department, all of whom are Christians. To have a part in helping to mold the character of the future Christian womanhood in Japan is a privilege that angels might envy; their and our prayer is that God may count us worthy of that great blessing."

NORTH KIUSHIU DISTRICT.—*Evangelistic Work.*—Miss Mabel Seeds also had charge of this evangelistic work and her district trips were each necessarily made at the close of a busy week in school and for which she had little time to prepare. But God wonderfully helped her and gave her both the message and expression in many instances, so she had the joy of returning each time with the assurance that He had used her to help others nearer to Him. Of this work she writes: "The part of the evangelistic work we could do in connection with our school work has naturally been the most successful, that is. the City Sunday-school work of Fukuoka and Hakata. The Fukuoka Sunday-schools, six in number, have increased greatly. The one in connection with our native Church, numbering more than two hundred little children, has been moved over into the school chapel for greater accommodation, the other adult classes occupying the church. The other five City Sunday-schools in different parts of Fukuoka have each gone beyond the one hundred mark. All of these Sunday-schools are taught by the older girls in the Mission School, thirteen girls in all, two or three going to each Sunday-school on Sunday afternoon. We meet these teachers one hour each week to study the lesson and pray for this special work. The six Hakata Sunday-schools are conducted on the same order as those in Fukuoka, and in all the twelve Sunday-schools are no less than twelve hundred children in attendance. The City Sunday-school Christmas exercises this year surpassed previous years in interest. Although two of the Sunday-schools were not represented on account of the distance, more than three hundred children attended the Hakata Christmas exercises, to each of whom were given cards, sent us by American children, and oranges as a gift. The sight of their happy faces was no less inspiring than the program they rendered. Six hundred and fifty children were present at the Fukuoka Sunday-school exercises, and to get them in the Church it was necessary to take out the seats, seating the children on the matting on the floor. The sight was wonderful, and amid the necessary confusion of so many children so closely crowded together, not one of the thirty children who took part forgot his recitation or song. A bag of cakes was given each as they passed out of the door. On the district at other points there are eleven other Sunday-schools conducted by the Bible-women, some of whom have two under their charge. These Sunday-schools often number more than fifty, and to all of which we send Sunday-school supplies. No work of the district is more encouraging than the Sunday-schools.

"We are able to report work in two more points than was reported last year, one of which, at Nogata, is an old work reopened, and the other, we believe, a new one, at Wataze.

The year's results of the Bible-women's work shows by actual count 26 baptisms, 19 probationers, and 188 definite inquirers. But figures do not count all the seeds that have taken root in the hearts of the many, with whom these faithful Bible-women have labored.

In all the work throughout the district we feel that it has been a prosperous year, and our hearts rejoice that God thus permits us in all our work to measure some growth and to count some results."

SOUTH KIUSHIU DISTRICT.—*Evangelistic Work.*—Miss Lida Smith, who had this work in charge, was sick and not able to do any work until the middle of October; during this time Miss Gheer and Miss Long had the oversight of the district. Added to the other difficulties, they had to move the home and it was January before they found a house suited to their needs. Of the work Miss Smith writes: "The work is growing everywhere; we need more Bible-women and more foreign helpers. We shall greatly miss Miss Gheer, who has gone home on furlough, not only in the work, but in our family life. Our foreign force will be reduced one-third in number. The work is making ever increased demands."

NAGASAKI.—*Kwassui Jo Gakko.*—Twenty years ago the school, which had been started ten years before by Elizabeth Russell, in the old city of Nagasaki, was changed to college grade. The first girl graduated in 1889. What a record and what a growth this college has made since! It has fought the battles for higher education of women in Japan and has won a national reputation, so that even its undergraduates can get positions in government schools at a good salary. The Inspector of Education, who visits the high schools for girls, says he has found nine of the graduates of Kwassui in government schools—all doing excellent work. Miss Russell, the founder of Kwassui, celebrated her seventieth birthday this year and is still doing the work of three people.

No more devoted, conscientious, hard-working missionaries labor for Christ anywhere than the six whose names compose the foreign part of the Faculty of Kwassui Jo Gakko. At present they are very much in need of new helpers. Miss Davison, who had charge of the Music Department, was married in January, and this department is without a head or even an assistant, as Miss Shibata, the music teacher, had left in June. Miss Melton had to come home on account of her health, and is longing for the time to come when she can return. Miss Kidwell, whose furlough is due, has had to go to Fukuoka to help Miss Finlay with that school, and Miss Cody has been very ill and will not be able to resume her work for some time; thus they have had to commence the new term with three missionaries to do the work, which was hard for seven. They must have help soon. 'The school has had the best year of its history, the enrollment being 422, of whom 146 are boarding pupils, 276 are day pupils. Twenty-seven foreigners are included in these. One hundred new girls were enrolled last spring, and many were refused entrance from lack of room. While the preparatory grades are overcrowded, there is still plenty of room at the top. The president, Miss Mariana Young, writes: "It will interest those who for so many years have supported the girls in this institution, to know that the scholarship girls are the backbone of our work, for we have no claim upon the self-supported girl. She is free from the day she graduates to go where she wishes, and if we employ her we must pay advanced salary, equal to what the Government Schools pay. Our scholarship girls would not have an education without help, and when one is granted the privilege of a scholarship, she not only pledges herself to complete the course, but also to give us four years of service on reduced salary, but annually increased, and in this way we can keep our schools partially supplied with the best teachers.

The Biblical Department is in charge of Miss Melton and there have been eleven girls in it this year. The eighteen city Sunday-schools in connection with the Bible training course have some eight hundred enrolled and afford an excellent opportunity for seed sowing. The Christmas mass-meetings are among the most interesting events of the whole year, and a sight to gladden the eye of the most earnest evangelist. About seven hundred met together this year. About seventy-five girls and teachers are engaged in this city work.

Nearly eighty girls have specialized in Industrial work; Japanese and foreign drawn work, embroidery, and lace making. The Gymnasium, *alias* the barn and the shed, is a reality, and is a real satisfaction as a room for physical drill as well as a play room; one-third of the money was raised among Kwassui girls and friends. A coat of paint on it and the school building, too, would assist greatly in adding to the durability, but that is only a dream at present.

The spiritual tone of the school is perhaps the best in a number of years. During the year twenty-five girls received baptism and twenty-one are on probation. At the close of the term almost every boarder in the school was a Christian. Special series of services have been held from time to time. The week of prayer was observed; also the day of prayer for colleges, which was followed by group and mass-meetings for two weeks. The group-meetings were especially helpful, doing special personal work. As a result of that last series of meetings twenty girls were taken into the Church, more than half of whom were day pupils. This is the most encouraging feature; for so many years the day pupils were hardly touched at all. One girl, whose mother is connected with the temple, was happily converted. She was much prejudiced against the Christian religion when she first entered the school, but after her conversion was very happy and exceedingly earnest. She had such joy that she was willing to bear persecution from her family for Christ's sake, and was earnestly praying that her family might be brought to know the same Christ, and we have faith to believe that in time this whole family will come into the Church as a result of her efforts, as many another family has come in through the efforts of a daughter who became a Christian in our school. It is no small thing to come into daily contact with four hundred girls. So if our work does seem routine and we can not see great results, each day we know that we are putting in the bricks that are building up the great structure, Christian character.

That this school has some influence in transforming character as the Japanese think, was evidenced a few days ago, when a step-mother brought her incorrigible step-daughter here, urging us to take her as a boarder, hoping she would become a better girl; her own inability to change the girl's nature was manifested by the mute, despairing look on her face. Another case shows the reputation the school has for this kind of work. A student was expelled from a Government School for bad conduct. She immediately said she would come to Kwassui and perhaps she would become a good woman.

But it is not only the four hundred that are touched and helped; the influence goes to families out in the country and to many of the people of a village through one or two who have entered the school here, and eight or nine hundred are touched in the City Sunday-school, in all perhaps fifteen hundred people are annually helped through this one school. Is it a small, a narrow sphere do you think?

The Kindergarten in Kwassui was started in 1895. It was continued under difficulties until the arrival of Miss Cody, since which time it has made great progress. This year there has been an enrollment of eighty children. Miss Cody has also established a Training class, which has had eight girls, though two dropped out; the remaining six are earnest Christian girls. Miss Takamori, Miss Cody's assistant, is a genius with children and quite clever in translating songs into Japanese for the work. The kindergarten is getting quite a standing and it is hoped will be an important factor in breaking down prejudice. In November, Miss Cody opened a new kindergarten in the Y. M. C. A. building. The kindergarten in the school needs a piano; what kind friend will supply this great need?

Of these two kindergartens Miss Cody writes: "The number of children that we can reach in the older kindergarten is necessarily limited on account of the size of the room, which will not accommodate more than thirty children comfortably. We closed last term with over forty on the roll; ten of them received little certificates and have gone to school.

"The new kindergarten we have named Tamanoye, the old, poetical name for Nagasaki. We feel privileged to have these pleasant rooms in the Young Men's Christian Association building. They will not always be available, so we earnestly hope some day to have a building of our own. The work has been a financial burden this year, but we expect it will be self-supporting in time. We charge an entrance fee of one yen and monthly fee of one yen. We began with thirteen children and now have twenty-nine. The mothers' meetings here are very satisfactory. At our first meeting twelve mothers were present, ten of whom had never been to anything Christian before. The work of visiting in the homes has been very pleasant. We are urged to come in and are given the place of honor in the parlor. A mother of a very frail child came to us to tell us that since her child had been coming he had had no fever and now has a good appetite, and how glad she was that she had sent him, though against the doctor's advice. We had a very merry Christmas. We certainly have most responsive, lovable children. It is a privilege to work for them."

KWASSUI JO·EN.—Miss Russell reports for the Girls' Home that all has gone well the past year; there has not been much sickness; the school has had half-day sessions as usual; the children have played, sang, and had good times, and the teacher has been faithful. The curriculum corresponds to the curriculum of the Government Primary Schools. Miss Russell writes:

"A new matron has been employed who understands the needs of children and knows how to keep house and prepare food after the most approved manner. The children like her and are obedient. The baby grows. She has eight teeth, climbs up about the screens, and tries to walk. I have been asked if the Orphanage is self-supporting. The children are not, but the hens are, and they do all they can to supply the children with eggs besides. In these latter days, when special days are set apart for special purposes, it seemed good to have an Orphan's Day; so the second Sunday in May was suggested and enthusiastically sanctioned by the preachers of the Conference. A program was prepared and sent out to the various pastors, who preached for the orphans and took up a collection. Already about twenty yen has been received from those collections, and our faith is that another twenty will come, making the amount that is required to support an orphan a year. This is the object of Orphan's Day, and the child supported will be known as the child of the Conference. Thirty-six children now enjoy the privileges of the institution, and I would have thirty-six more if I had room and money. Two girls are past twenty years of age, and prefer staying at the Orphanage. They are valuable assistants. There are four girls between twelve and sixteen, ten between eight and twelve, and others are all ages down to Baby San, who is sixteen months. There are twenty-five Christians, about all that are old enough."

LOO CHOO ISLANDS.—Because of Miss Smith's illness she has not been able to visit this work this year, but good reports have come of the work of the Bible-woman, Miss Hoei, and Miss Russell writes, July 20th:

"News has come to us of a great revival in the Loo Choo Islands. The revival began in April and continued till July 1st. One hundred and fifty people have been baptized. This has been the greatest movement that has yet been seen in Japan in any Church. They have no church building on the islands, and a gentleman gave the Methodist Episcopal Church $2,500 to build a church and parsonage. The contract has been given and the church is being built in Naha City, but so many conversions have taken place in Shusi, the old capital, that they need a church there, too. The largest room they could rent is 16 x 24 feet and they could not get all the people in to baptize them, so they baptized fifteen one day and sent them out, and the next day fifteen, and so on, until all received baptism. They have estimated that they can build a church here for $400, because the people have volunteered to give their services toward the work without pay."

MEXICO.

Woman's Work commenced in 1874. Organized as a Conference in 1885.

Official Correspondent, Carrie J. Carnahan.

The Mexico Mission includes "the Republic of Mexico, except the States of Chihuahua and Sonora and the territory of Lower California."

MISSIONARIES AND THEIR STATIONS.

GUANAJUATO.—Effie M. Dunmore.
MEXICO CITY.—Harriet L. Ayres, Laura Temple, Grace A. Hollister.
PACHUCA.—Helen Hewitt, Blanche Betz.
PUEBLA.—*Anna R. Limberger, Caroline M. Purdy, Ella E. Payne.

The growth of our work in Mexico during the past year, shown in the prosperity of our schools, marks a new era in our history in that country.

Prejudices against our schools—the result of the untiring efforts of the Roman priests—have been destroyed in the large cities, as well as in not a few towns, by the undeniable fact of the good work our missionaries have done in seeking to elevate Mexican womanhood to the high standards of genuine Christian morality. The mistrust of our schools by the liberal men of the country has also been dispelled on seeing that the aim of our work is not to proselyte, but to uplift.

The breaking down of prejudice and overcoming of mistrust have brought about the extraordinary increase in numbers and self-support of some of our schools. But this very popularity has created another difficulty; we are not able, under existing conditions, to properly accommodate these increasing numbers. We must have better facilities or lose our opportunities.

MEXICO CITY.—The second year of the Sarah L. Keen College has been marked by growth and development along all lines. The enrollment reached two hundred. Of these, fifty-six are boarders. As only fifteen of the entire number were in the school in the former location, this large matriculation shows the school's good standing. The self-support amounted to $7,000 (silver), an increase of $2,000 over the previous year.

*Home on leave.

The gifts of Mrs. Sarah Cochram, of Dawson, Pa., New York Branch, and other friends, have enabled Miss Temple to complete the chapel and to substitute for the old adobe wall a fine iron fence, which has greatly improved the appearance of the beautiful building.

The Industrial Institution, planned one year ago, for the benefit of the many poor girls who are unable to enter the school because they can not pay the cost of living, has not been begun for lack of funds. There is great need for a training that will elevate the idea of the home life among the poorer classes, and this Industrial School will, in time to come, prove to be an excellent means of, enabling the poorer girls to gain a livelihood and of teaching them the sweet message of Christ's love to mankind.

PACHUCA.—Our school in Pachuca is steadily growing in spite of many hindrances. The congested condition of all departments in this school shows that its present quarters have long ago been outgrown. An enrollment of five hundred eloquently speaks of public favor.

The number of teachers is altogether out of proportion to the number of students, nevertheless the High School Department sends to Puebla Normal School more·advanced pupils each year. The Puebla Alumnæ Scholarship was voted, last year, to one of the Pachuca graduates.

Mrs. Fannie Gamble paid for the support of a girl during the year.

The attention given by Pachuca Faculty to the students' spiritual development is shown in the growth in membership of the Epworth League and in their larger fields of service. The Junior League has had a most successful year, with an enrollment of 250 and an average attendance of two hundred. Both the Senior and the Junior Leagues contribute regularly to the support of the Church.

Our Pachuca School has also a very successful Auxiliary to the Woman's Foreign Missionary Society.

Miss Bohannon writes: "Our opportunities are greater than ever before. If we could grasp them our work could be extended to a class we do not now reach. How we long to help them all!"

This school is in great need of enlarged quarters and better sanitary conditions.

GUANAJUATO.—The total enrollment for the year was 127, with a very gratifying average attendance. Of those enrolled, thirty-two were boarding pupils. The self-support amounted to $1,399 (silver).

Deaconesses are very much needed in the work of evangelizing Mexico, and for this reason the Bible training department of this school is a very important one. There were three students in this department last year. Miss Dunmore's return to take charge of this part of the work is the promise of a larger number of students and higher ideals in the course of study.

We sympathize with the Misses Cook, of Guanajuato, Mexico, because of the ill-health of Miss Celinda Cook, which makes necessary their resignation.

PUEBLA.—Because of the absolute necessity for more room in our Puebla Normal Institute, it was voted at last Executive Meeting to purchase the property of the General Board immediately adjoining ours.

Mrs. Fannie Gamble, of Cincinnati, having seen the need, helped us with a very generous gift of $5,000. For this gift the Woman's Foreign Missionary Society wishes to express its most sincere thanks to Mrs. Gamble.

The Philadelphia Branch has been working hard to raise its share, and it is hoped that this year, with the help of the other Branches, the debt will be wiped out.

To show conditions and needs in the Puebla Normal Institute, we quote from Miss Palacios, one of the teachers:

"The Puebla Normal Institute has more than outgrown its actual premises during the present year. To accommodate eighty-seven boarders in a building that can hold hygienically only fifty has been the problem as well as source of anxiety to the Faculty. Class-rooms and damp store-rooms have been turned into dormitories; corridors as well as dining-rooms are used as class-rooms. Some of the teachers, after a hard day's work in a class-room filled to overflowing with pupils, do not even have the comfort of their own room, but must share it with a companion who is ill.

"Parents come bringing their daughters to become pupils, only to hear these words: 'Our house is already over full; next year we will have the adjoining property, but just now we have all the pupils we can accommodate.' Nevertheless, they insist in leaving their daughters, many of them having come from long distances.

"The boarding pupils of the Puebla Normal Institute represent twelve of the twenty-seven States of the Republic; some have come to us from the border line on the North, some from far-off Yucatan, traveling a distance of nine hundred or one thousand miles.

"The boarding and the tuition fees have been raised considerably and, although admission has been refused to more than one hundred girls, the enrollment for the year is 376, with a daily attendance of 325.

"The congested condition of the school has made it necessary to greatly increase the amount spent to improve sanitary conditions in order to prevent epidemics. This has also meant a great deal of care and vigilance from the very busy Faculty.

"Last July the Mexico State Normal School sent a large delegation to Puebla to visit the educational State institutions. The papers published very interesting articles about Puebla schools. Our Normal School was mentioned in these articles as one of the leading factors in Puebla development in educational lines. It is well to note here that Puebla Normal Institute is the only private school in Mexico that has the privilege of having its diplomas acknowledged by the Mexico City Board of Education.

"This is due to the fact that our Normal School has always striven for thoroughness in its courses. As the Government schools in large cities are very good, only high moral ideas and first-class instruction could have given Puebla Normal Institute its prestige in the city and in the country.

"This year's self-support has been $17,200.82 (silver), an increase of 43.7 per cent over self-support of last year.

"As yet the school can not be entirely self-supporting because it has to compete with first-class Government schools and it must needs have a large, competent Faculty and good equipment. The self-support money has been used to furnish the schoolrooms, to provide for very much needed physical and chemical laboratories—which, as yet, are far from what they ought to be; to buy desks, two pianos, a set of models for the art departments, and to give the girls the advantages of a good eight hundred volume library. Besides, the self-support money pays for one-half the twenty members of the Faculty.

"The Puebla school tuition and boarding fees are moderate. The pupils come from the middle classes, some very few from rich homes. The aim of this school is to develop Christian character, not to make money, and for that reason it has never striven to reach the wealthy classes, whose love of ease and luxury and eagerness to enjoy privileges

12

which money can buy, would be out of place in the Puebla Normal Institute, where love of work and perfect equality for all students have developed harmony and fellowship.

"Out of these two conditions have grown organizations which are a characteristic feature of the Puebla School: the Alumnæ Association, the Society for Character Development, and the School System of Self-government.

"The Alumnæ Association supports a scholarship in the school; conducts night schools, organizes temperance and savings associations—thus working to uplift the poor, degraded Mexican women of the lower classes; all this helps to enlarge the Puebla Normal School influence. Besides, this year the Alumnæ Association raised $1,000 to help to purchase the new property.

"The Society for Character Development is the fruit of the Christian influence of the school. It is a very well-known fact that a Christian student can influence a fellow student in ways that a teacher can not; hence, the aggressive Christian students forming this society have a great influence throughout the whole school. As a result of the eagerness of the members of this society to live according to Christ's teachings, the Puebla Normal Institute has the self-government system. It is the only school in the country where such system is practiced.

"The development of the Epworth League, Senior and Junior, is satisfactory; the membership increases every year.

"If we must judge of our love to Christ by our desire to help and serve others, and by our eagerness to extend the kingdom of God on earth, it can be truly affirmed that Puebla School has borne fruits that speak of its Christian influence. The majority of Puebla graduates are teaching in Mexico City, Pachuca, Puebla, and the towns and villages where our mission is established. As a rule, they help in Sunday-school and Church work and are the leaders of the Epworth Leagues and Woman's Foreign Missionary Auxiliaries.

"The Puebla School is the center of the missionary spirit in Mexican Methodism. The Missionary Society, formed largely by the students, works to enlarge its membership, provides literature for the other Auxiliaries, strives to have other Auxiliaries established, and it is due to the efforts of this society that Puebla Church raised last year $200—missionary collection—twice as much as the appropriation. God has certainly blessed our work in Puebla; without Him, the Woman's Foreign Missionary Society work there would not have succeeded. To Him we give praise.

"The crisis through which Puebla School has passed during the present year, for lack of adequate quarters, has made it a very trying one for missionary teachers and students; nevertheless, the work has been carried on regularly and successfully. The graduating class of 1907—eight young ladies who will consecrate their lives to God's service—is a fit prize for the year's labor.

"The news of Mrs. Gamble's gift of $5,000 was received by students, teachers, and missionaries with hearty thanks to God expressed in a service of prayer held at the regular chapel hour.

"Secretary Root's visit to Puebla gave us opportunity to know what is the standing of the school with the civil authorities. Miss Limberger was appointed on the reception committee; the girls were officially invited to take part in the festivities, and the mayor expressed his opinion of our work in the following words, 'I will tell Secretary Root that this school has been a blessing to the city.'"

The day schools in towns and villages have also had a prosperous year. Enrollment and self-support have increased, and all our teachers have worked successfully.

STATISTICS OF THE WORK IN MEXICO.

NAMES OF STATIONS.	Puebla	Mexico City	San Vicente	Ayapango	Guanajuato	Pachuca	Miraflores	Tetela	Tlaxcala	Apizaco
F. M. S. Missionaries	3	3			3	2				
es of Mis'aries in Active Work,										
ign or Eurasian Assistants	4	4				1				
ive Workers	11				6	11				
MEN IN THE CHURCH—										
ull Members	49	40			220	146				
Probationers	6	5			140	76				
Adherents					700	300				
nen and Girls B'zed during y'r										
Chris'n Women under Instr'n.										
-Chris'n Women under Inst'n,										
Bible-woman Employed		2				1				
OOLS OF COLLEGE GRADE—										
No Schools		1								
No. Foreign Missionaries		†								
Foreign or Eurasian Teachers..										
No. Native Teachers										
Self-Supporting Students										
Wholly-Supported Students										
Partly-Supported Students										
Total Enrollment										
Receipts for Board and Tuition,										
Govern't Grants & Donations,										
NACULAR AND ANGLO-VER-										
.CULAR BOARDING SCHOOLS—										
No. Schools	8	1			1	1				
No. Foreign Missionaries	3	3			3	2				
Foreign or Eurasian Teachers..	4	4				1				
No. Native Teachers	11	13			4	11				
Self-Supporting Students	32	12			13	7				
Wholly-Supported Students	23	18			7	11				
Partly-Supported Students	18	25			14	3				
No. Day Students	252	170			120	509				
Total Enrollment	325	225			154	530				
Receipts for Board and Tuition,	*$6,142 03	$3,495 00			$1,121 69	$1,083 08				
Govern't Grants & Donations..										
SCHOOLS—										
No. Schools			1	1			1		1	
No. Teachers			1	1			3		2	
Total Enrollment			45	50			298		58	
Average Daily Attendance			40	60			280		40	
Receipts for Tuition			$25 00	$11 00			‡$31		$81 00	$2(
Govern't Grants & Donations...										
DERGARTENS—										
No. Kindergartens	1	1				1				
No. Foreign Kindergartners										
No. Native Kindergartners	1	1				1				
Nat. Kinder'ners in Training										
Total Enrollment	34	19				265				
Average Attendance	30	13				150				
Receipts for Tuition	$111 05	$45 00				$201 12				
Govern't Grants & Donations...										

* Self-Supporting.   † Students only in preparatory department.
‡ Given by Factory, $1,200; Special Gift, $80, total, $1,280. Given by school, 31 gold.

SOUTH AMERICA.

Woman's Work organized in 1874. Conference organized in 1893.
Official Corespondent, Mary E. Holt.

MISSIONARIES AND THEIR STATIONS.

BUENOS AYRES.—Eleanor Le Huray, Susie A. Walker.
ROSARIO.—Mary F. Swaney, Bertha E. Kneeland.
MONTEVIDEO.—Lizzie Hewett, Jessie L. Marsh.
LIMA.—Elsie Wood.
CALLAO.—Alice McKinney.

BUENOS AYRES.—Last December, after sixteen years in the same
rented building, the school was moved, as the property had been sold.
As the notice came during vacation time, there were two months in
which to look for a new location. The rents being so high, it was found
necessary to go to the other end of the city, leaving the beautiful part
overlooking the river and going to a crowded district in the heart of the
city. Miss Le Huray was in the United States at the time the property
was sold, but returned to take up the direction of the school in the new
home in March. She writes that the house now occupied has twenty
rooms and is surrounded by a large garden.

Notwithstanding the assurance on the part of the owner that the
building was in perfect condition, it was found necessary to make many
repairs in order to satisfy the demands of the School Board, thereby
incurring large expense. Because of the long distance from the homes
of the pupils, none of the day scholars followed and self-support was
thus decreased. One thousand circulars, announcing the opening of the
school in new quarters, were printed and distributed in the neighborhood.
During the first month twelve children came, and in the second month
fifteen more were added. In Buenos Ayres there are one million inhabit-
ants. The people hesitate about sending their children to an unknown
Protestant school when Catholic and Government schools are free. Until
our school becomes known the number of pupils will not increase greatly.
The rent appropriated by our society is only one-half the amount required, and therefore it is necessary to secure pupils who can pay tuition.
The actual moving expense, $165, formed but a small part of the entire
cost of making the change. As this house can be rented for only three
years, another move faces the school. A new building of our own is
surely an imperative need if we are to do effective school and religious
work in this important and growing city. Miss Le Huray thinks that
a beginning could be made with a small amount of money which would
purchase land and erect a small building.

She reports that even with the large expense incurred in moving,
and with the falling off in attendance, the income from the school has
been sufficient during the five months to meet all expenses. There are
now forty children in attendance, of whom one-half are boarders and
scholarship girls from ten to twenty years of age. The rest are little
children living in the immediate neighborhood. Both among boarders and
day pupils there are children of Roman Catholic parents, who at first
refused to go to our meetings or open a Bible. Now they join in the
Bible lessons with perfect willingness, if not with pleasure, which is
really a step forward. It is thought than an English department would
help in self-support by increasing the patronage of the school and, for
this reason, the salary of an English teacher is put into the estimates.
Next year Miss Le Huray finishes twenty-five years of service in our

society, and she earnestly desires that, in the near future, this school may have a home of its own. The sale of the lease on the old property brought $5,000, which is being sacredly held as the nucleus of a fund for a new building, for which $10,000 is urgently needed.

Miss Walker is working temporarily for the Missionary Society in, the Boca Missions, where she has a class of thirty-three girls in English. She also has charge of a Sunday-school in which are over two hundred children. She makes visits among the children in their homes, holds mothers' meetings, and is doing good evangelistic work ·in this section. During the absence of Mr. and Mrs. Batterson in the United States, she has kept the Church people together and has had general supervision of all departments of work in this section.

ROSARIO.—Miss Swaney reports the number in the school as equal to those of last year. She has been obliged to refuse applications for places in the charity school on account of crowded quarters. The new owner of the San Luis building raised the rent repeatedly, until it was necessary to leave the place which our day school had occupied for over twenty years. Here also had been held a Sunday-school and weekly services of prayer. A location six squares farther South was secured. This is in a .thickly populated district, where such a school must have a good influence, but the house is not large enough to accommodate all the children that would come.

The teachers are the same as last year, all good Christian girls. The head teacher, Miss Paulina Schuster, underwent a serious surgical operation, but she was mercifully spared to resume her work and to .be a blessing to the pupils. Her place, during her illness, was supplied by Miss Maria Schuster and Miss Hoffman, with the aid of another of our Swiss-Argentine girls. There has been an unusual amount of illness in the other school, both among teachers and pupils, but the work has been carried on, although with difficulty and much anxiety. Early in the year a former day pupil was called from earth after unspeakable suffering. She was a lovable girl and became a woman of brilliant mind, one who was coveted for the Lord's work. She sought and found the Savior during her illness and she went away trusting in her Lord. Of the girls who have gone from the schools good reports are received. - A boarder in the home in 1890 sent a request to Miss Swaney to admit her twelve-year-old daughter to the school. The new building still waits for more money. Plans have been cut down again and again. At present it is suggested that a one-story structure be erected, for which $5,000 more than the funds now in hand is needed. Miss Swaney dares not crowd the girls in the present quarters through fear of typhoid fever, cholera, and bubonic pest, with all of which she has had sad experience in the past. In all these years the drinking water used in the home has had to be boiled, filtered, and cooled, imposing a burden of care upon cur workers. There is no more needy field in·all our mission work at present than in this city of Rosario, where we have a fine site, but not enough money for a suitable building. Miss Kneeland will probably go to the relief of Miss Swaney before next spring.

MONTEVIDEO.—This school, in its attractive new building, is doing fine work. The past year has shown the largest enrollment of day pupils ever recorded. The whole number of day pupils and boarders is 182. Of the eleven boarders, eight pay their own way and three are on scholarships. Conditions in the city have so changed that it is impossible to find good teachers for the salaries which we can pay. The most desirable of our own graduates will not remain as teachers for what was

SUMMARY OF WORK IN SOUTH AMERICA CONFERENCE.

NAMES OF STATIONS	Buenos Ayres, Argentina	Rosario, Argentina	Montevideo, Uruguay	Total
W. F. M. S. Missionaries	1	1	2	4
Wives of Missionaries in Active Work				
Foreign or Eurasian Assistants				
Native Workers				
WOMEN IN THE CHURCH—				
Full Members	*	95	*	95
Probationers		51		51
Adherents				
Women and Girls Baptized during Year				
No. Christian Women under Instruction				
Non-Christian Women under Instruction				
No. Bible-women Employed	1		2	3
VERNACULAR AND ANGLO-VERNACULAR BOARDING SCHOOLS—				
No. Schools	†1	†1	†1	3
No. Foreign Missionaries				
Foreign or Eurasian Teachers				
No. Native Teachers				
Self-Supporting Students	7			7
Wholly-Supported Students	8	7		15
Partly-Supported Students		1	*	1
No. Day Students				
Total Enrollment	15	8		23
Receipts for Board and Tuition				
Government Grants and Donations				
DAY SCHOOLS—				
No. Schools	1	2	1	4
No. Teachers	6	9	12	27
Total Enrollment	68	205	172	437
Average Daily Attendance				
Receipts for Tuition	¶ $1,922	¶ $500	$1,716	$4,138
Government Grants and Donations				
KINDERGARTENS—				
No. Kindergartens			1	1
No. Foreign Kindergartners				
No. Native Kindergartners				
Native Kindergartners in Training			1	1
Total Enrollment			20	20
Average Attendance			18	18
Receipts for Tuition				
Government Grants and Donations				

* No report. † Combined with Day School. ¶ Includes Board.

and Miss Hewett pleads that the full amount in the estimates be granted. In the spring Rev. F. E. Clark, D. D., of the Christian Endeavor Society, visited Montevideo and delivered an address in the hall of our school, which was most helpful and inspiring. Sunday-school work, devotional meetings, temperance, and other lines of special work have been faithfully pursued. Miss Marsh fits into the work splendidly and has made good progress with the language. She has a fine voice and affords much pleasure in the hospital, where she sings to the patients. Both of these missionaries are very busy and happily so in their work. They are full of enthusiasm over the good results in the school.

LIMA.—Last April Miss Wood wrote expressing her gratitude to the Branches who, by appropriating for rent, had made it possible to hire quarters for a new school, and she feels that this is the beginning of what will, in time, be the greatest thing for girls in the whole Republic. At first it seemed doubtful about securing good accommodations, as rents were very high, but, fortunately, some rooms in the house in which Miss Wood resides became vacant, the first time in many years. These were engaged at a less sum than that granted by the Society, and the balance was used to purchase the necessary furniture and equipment as the needs arose.

Last spring there were eleven children enrolled from six to sixteen years of age. A registration fee is charged, and Miss Wood hopes to save this towards the out-going passage expenses of a teacher. In order to charge large fees it is necessary to give each girl such teaching as she desires—drawing, fancy work, Latin, or German.

Miss McKinney went to Callao last winter and has been very busy in the school. The classes are large and the work is heavy. Financial help is needed in Peru, but more than all this Republic, directly under the control of the Vatican, needs our prayers that religious liberty may be granted to this people. Miss Wood earnestly asks for our prayers that this liberty may come, and that without revolution.

BULGARIA.

Woman's Work commenced in 1884.
Constituted a Mission Conference in 1892.
Official Correspondent, Mrs. F. P. Crandon.

MISSIONARIES AND THEIR STATION.

LOVETCH.—Miss Kate B. Blackburn, Miss Dora Davis.

Miss Blackburn writes that it is the best year yet known. "The new pay pupils were from families whose patronage will do honor to the school, and the new scholarship girls were a constant source of delight, not merely because they proved such bright, promising students, but because of their exemplary deportment and the benefit they seemed to derive from the instruction given and the influences thrown around them. One girl was received into Church membership and ten were taken into the Epworth League membership. A majority of these were from Orthodox homes, their parents allowing them to join the League ranks, though not yet ready to consent to membership in a Protestant Church. Not a few of our young people have thus been trained for future activity in the Church itself. More and more do we appreciate our streopticon, that valuable gift of Bishop Vincent some years ago. formerly paid. Money for repairs on the old building is much needed,

Each year we manage to purchase a few new slides, selecting with special reference to value in astronomy, botany, hygiene, and Bible. The monthly exhibits of these views are not only an oft-recurring pleasure, but a real benefit from an educational standpoint as well. The past year the girls have shown unusual interest in the monthly rhetorical exercises. The large attendance and spiritual fervor of the weekly class-meetings is good evidence that the religious side of their character is being touched and influenced. The Commencement exercises of June 26th were a fitting close to a satisfactory year. We were so glad to have with us on that occasion both Mr. and Mrs. Count, as well as a number of our Bulgarian pastors. Mr. Count preached an excellent baccalaureate sermon the Sunday preceding Commencement. The announcement that the school would henceforth have a seven years' course of study instead of six was received with enthusiasm by the students, alumnæ, and by the Conference. When the new catalogues were printed, a copy was mailed to each alumna and responses came in thick and fast, expressing interest and rejoicing and with assurance of hearty co-operation on their part. A member of the class of 1905, Lovetch Auxiliary, has found "Christus Redemptor" a most interesting study, for are not two of our former members (Mrs. Lydia Diem Wenzel and Miss Hanna Diem) now in missionary work in the islands of the South Sea? Their occasional letters, telling of the people, their customs, needs, etc., make those distant islands seem very real to us. In addition to its monthly missionary meetings, Lovetch Auxiliary holds weekly cottage prayer-meetings in the homes of the members of other friends who invite them. Frequently these prayer-meetings are held in Orthodox homes. One of these Orthodox women had attended the cottage meetings and other Church services until she became thoroughly interested and then, with the consent of her husband, she invited the meeting to her own home. About this time the parish priest, who claimed her as one of his flock, evidently thought she needed pastoral attention and proceeded to her home with "holy water" to expel the "devils" as he expressed it. Upon his approach she met him at the door with the announcement that her house did not need sprinkling, that if there were devils they were in her heart, and that sprinkling would be of no avail, for only the power of Jesus could cleanse her heart. Finally the priest was obliged to leave without accomplishing his mission or even entering the house, and was much annoyed over the effect of Protestant teaching and influence. This same woman has succeeded in awakening her husband to such an extent that he, too, is an earnest inquirer after the truth. Not a few are the taunts and persecutions endured by some of these women, but they are persistent in their efforts to win husbands or parents, as the case may be, to see the truth as they have found it in the Word of God.

"An event of importance, and one which afforded much pleasure, was a visit from Hon. J. G. Knowles, recently appinted Envoy Extraordinary and Minister Plenipotentiary from the United States to Roumania, Servia, and Bulgaria, with official residence at Bucharest, Roumania. He made an official visit to Bulgaria in August, and you may imagine our delight when he proposed to include Lovetch in his tour, and still further to enhance our joy, he was accompanied by Mrs. Knowles."

Miss Davis adds a few more items to show advance: "This year a large proportion of our girls were new in school, and, as usual, from Orthodox homes. They proved a fine company; some of them especially seemed so open to conviction, frankly giving their views in regard to religious matters, and almost without exception attended the weekly class-meeting regularly. One of them, soon after returning at the close of school, wrote to us that the weeks of vacation seemed long to one living in a town where there was no church. In Berkovitz, her home, there is no Protestant Church, and she evidently does not consider the others as Churches at all. And she is an Orthodox.

"One of our girls who graduated a year ago came to Commencement. She is making a fine record. She secured work in a family of high rank living in Sofia. The family has removed to another city and taken her with them, and so well has she pleased them that they will this coming year allow her to make her home with them and at the same time attend the pedagogical gymnasium. The certificate that she will secure from that school will entitle her to permission to teach. Another girl, graduated from the school in the class finishing last June, is also employed by a Sofia family. She also finds it a matter of advantage that she has acquired the English language. Her employer is also in the army, of the rank of general, and has been till recently Minister of War in the Government. The family this fall will go to Russia on a mission that takes them to St. Petersburg for a stay of three years, and she accompanies them.

"I mention these cases as examples of the opportunities that come to our girls. Where employment for girls is extremely difficult to secure, as here in Bulgaria, it is of immense value to us to have some girls independently supporting themselves, and serving as a continual incentive to those not yet through school. The first of the girls just mentioned is also helping to pay the expenses of a younger sister in the school.

"I think that the girls are themselves more than ever before finding out how much depends on themselves. The Oriental idea here seems to be never to do anything for one's self that another can possibly be induced to do for one. One of our steady, never-ending tasks is to develop the opposite idea in their minds, and it has proved of practical benefit in the establishment and continuance of our work here.

"I am afraid that Miss Blackburn will not herself tell you how very useful and helpful her sister, Ella Blackburn, was all throughout the year. From the very first of her arrival just after the opening of school last fall she won the love of every one, teachers and pupils, and you can readily imagine what her influence was in the school. She did not intend to become homesick and so at once undertook school work almost equivalent to that of a regular teacher. This in itself was an education to our people, the disinterested interest in the work itself that would induce any one to work so hard for nothing was a practical demonstration of something difficult for a Bulgarian mind to grasp. Of course she could not take classes requiring knowledge of Bulgarian, but the English classes thrived under her care, and she also took several others. The girls swarmed around her like bees around a honey-pot and the mischief that free hours often brings was no longer a thing to be dreaded.

"Her assistance in class work was a big material aid, too, as otherwise we would have had to employ one more additional teacher.

"As for Miss Blackburn and myself—our health continues good and we love our work as deeply as ever, more and more, in fact, the longer we are in it. We have so much to be grateful to our Heavenly Father for, so many blessings; and we never forget to be grateful, too, for all the friends at home whose prayers and steadfast faith help us so much to do our best for our Bulgarians."

SUMMARY OF WORK IN BULGARIA MISSION.*

NAMES OF STATIONS.	Lovetch	Hotantsa	Gabrovo	Rustchuk	Varna	Tirnovo	Sistov	Voyodovo	Hiblee	Orchania	Serlievo	Vratza	Lom	Pleven	Shumen	Viddin	Total
W. F. M. S. Missionaries	2																2
Wives of Missionaries in Active Work.																	
Foreign Assistants	1																1
Native Workers	4	1	1														6
WOMEN IN THE CHURCH—																	
Full Members	17	12	2	15	18	11	7	47	12	3	6	1	7	8	7	2	170
Probationers	3		2	4	5	6		3			2	1	2	15	3		46
Adherents	50	1	5	10	20	5	2	10	3	3	6	3	3		5		126
Women and Girls Baptized during Year.								4	2					5			11
No. Christian Women under Instruc'n	25		4		18	17		40				2	9		22		137
Non-Christian Women under Instru'n	25		5		20	5	2	24	10			8	8		25	1	123
No. Bible-women Employed			1														1
VERNACULAR AND ANGLO-VERNACULAR BOARDING SCHOOLS—																	
No. Schools	1																1
No. Foreign Missionaries	2																2
Foreign Teachers	1																1
No. Native Teachers	3																3
Self-Supporting Students	6																6
Wholly-Supported Students	6																6
Partly-Supported Students	8																8
No. Day Students	16																16
Total Enrollment	36																36
Receipts for Board and Tuition	$934 00																$934 00
Govern't Grants and Donations																	
DAY SCHOOLS—																	
No. Schools		1															1
No. Teachers		1															1
Total Enrollment		22															22
Average Daily Attendance		18															18
Receipts for Tuition																	
Govern't Grants and Donations																	

* Charges without paid workers reporting to Bulgaria Mission Conference of Woman's Foreign Missionary Society.

ITALY.

Organized as a Conference in 1881.
Woman's Work commenced in 1886.
Official Correspondent, Mrs. F. P. Crandon.

MISSIONARIES AND THEIR STATION.

ROME.—Edith M. Swift, Edith Burt, Eva Odgers.

ROME.—*Crandon Hall.*—We have so long associated Miss Vickery and Miss Llewellyn with Crandon Hall that we have hardly yet realized that others have taken the place which they so ably filled; but in our two Ediths, Miss Swift and Miss Burt, we have admirable successors.

No special changes have been made in the list of teachers, all having returned to their accustomed positions. But there have been added to the Faculty two teachers from America, Miss Hill, a graduate of Vassar College, and Miss McFall, of Boston University, both of whom are supported from the income of the school. The class work is progressing with commendable excellence, owing to the faithful interest of the teachers and the good spirit of the pupils. The girls in the home have entered into the spirit of benevolence and now spend many of their leisure hours in working for a bazaar for the benefit of the needy poor. Nearly three hundred girls are in attendance. All are required to attend daily prayers, and by the personal association with their teachers and the Bible study, the prejudices which have been instituted into their minds against Protestantism are gradually disappearing and they are coming little by little into a knowledge of the truth as it is in Jesus Christ.

On the 20th of December many prizes for good work were distributed by His Excellency, Sig. Hector de Castro, United States Consul, and by Presiding Elder Dr. N. Walling Clark. Sig. Castro remarked on the wonderful growth of the school, and how favorably it had impressed outsiders in its short history. We were glad to have such favorable comment from an observant onlooker.

The quiet influence of our Italian workers is largely responsible for the lively interest in our Sunday-school, which has developed most satisfactorily. In the report made for the Italian Conference by Miss Burt, she wrote: "The preliminary duties which occupied us prior to the opening of the school last year made us realize how much we were going to miss Miss Vickery and Miss Llewellyn, how much their experience and labor in this work from its beginning had counted in the smoothness with which affairs moved, and how grateful we are to them for the splendid organization which they bequeathed to us and without which it would have been impossible for us to have carried on as successfully as this year has proved that we could. We wish to express here our appreciation and gratitude to both these noble women for all they have done for Crandon Hall, not only by their administration and influence, but financially, and for us as well as for the Methodist Episcopal Church in this country.

"Notable visitors have come to us this year and we are glad to have them carry over the world the impression of our school. Among our visitors were Mrs. Butler, Miss Butler, and Dr. Butler, of Mexico, en route to the India Jubilee festivities.

"At the World's Sunday-school Convention held last May in the Methodist Episcopal Church in Rome, Miss Italia Garibaldi, a granddaughter of the great liberator of Italy, for some years one of the students of Crandon Institute, made one of the addresses of welcome. A reception was tendered to the delegates by Misses Swift and Burt, which was largely attended. Many other visitors thronging the city of Rome during the year have visited the institute. Many of the cab-drivers need no instructions as to the beauties of the school.

"Dr. Parkhurst, editor of *Zion's Herald*, and Dr. Spencer, of the *Central Christian Advocate*, visited us, and we are much indebted to them for their kindly notices of the school in their respective papers."

The very last news from Miss Burt is as follows:

"During the past week I have received many applications for next year, and the prospect of things in general looks promising. On account of marriage and illness, we have lost two of our teachers, but I trust we may be able to fill their places with good substitutes. Have you seen anything in the American papers about what has been going on this summer in Italy in several convent schools? Scandalous doings have been brought to light and cases of ill-treatment have been proved. This has so aroused the Italian people and officials that, after inspection, many convent schools have been closed. The papers have been full of the subject. The great cry is for lay schools. The following is a translation. from a notice which was published in several Italian papers. The writer, Signor Galantra, was accused of having brought up his two daughters in an English convent. They attended 'Crandon Hall' as day pupils for five years, and so he thus answers the accusation made against him: 'L'Avvenire d' Italia (an Italian paper) publishes in a prominent place an attack against me for having educated my two daughters in a convent in the Ludovisi quarter. I wish, therefore, to state that they attended during five years, that is to say, during their entire elementary course, "Crandon Institute," an American school placed in above said quarter. This institution not only is not a convent, but, being lay and anti-clerical, is constantly attacked by the Vatican.' This was a good advertisement for us. The opportunities are great; may we be given strength to meet them and wisdom to use them to God's glory!"

We have been very busy getting our duties into line and learning what must be done to keep this work up to its former high level. We have great hopes and plans for the future and shall expect and desire your co-operation in perfecting them. Each day we meet the day's work with high courage and strong determination, trusting not to ourselves alone, but to the blessing of God in Christ, through whom we can do all things in His strength!

VIA GARIBALDI.—Miss Odgers reports: "We have had an excellent school year, notwithstanding sickness among the pupils for over a month. Two of our pupils have graduated from the Normal School. One returns to Via Garibaldi as assistant teacher next year, and the other takes a Government school near Acquita. There are three vacant places for next year, as we are limited to fifty pupils, but have any number of applications, and so far not one who does not offer to pay something that their child may enter our school. Two have come to-day asking for a half place for their children. I know some of them are making a sacrifice to do this, and it only shows how anxious parents are to have their children come under Protestant influence. One of the presiding elders has just written us a beautiful and encouraging letter thanking us for the care of his two children who were in our school during the past year and giving much encouragement for the work and school and asking that they may return another year. I am glad to have his influence among the pastors, and it will be a help to the school in many ways to have him our friend.

"On acount of prejudices that have arisen against the converts in various places in Italy, Miss Odgers has been flooded with applications to the number of nearly a hundred people who are ready to place their children in Protestant schools, and as our prices are reasonable we could have any number were there places for them."

Thus surely, thought it may seem at times slowly, the little leaven is affecting the great mass of Italian Catholicism, and some day the sweet Gospel will be known throughout the pagan world.

GERMANY AND SWITZERLAND.

Official Correspondent, Miss Louise Rothweiler.

An appropriation of $375 is used to assist in the support of live Bible readers or visiting deaconesses in as many different cities in the North Germany and the Switzerland Conferences. The Churches in connection with which they work also help in their support. These women have done good work among the sick, the poor, and the Christless ones. In Berlin and Chemnitz, in the former place especially, numbers have been led to Christ. In Adlisweil, Lausanne, and Zurich in the Switzerland Conference, much house-to-house visitation has been done; 1,200 or more families have been visited, Christian counsel and instruction has been given, the sick nursed, and the poor helped. Christian literature has been distributed and many have been won to the Church and to Christ. At Lausanne the work in the Home for Girls had so grown that Miss Roetlisberger asked to be relieved from outside work that she might devote herself entirely to the Home, but for some time it was impossible to find a suitable woman who could use both the French and German languages, which is a necessary qualification for such a worker in that city. Finally one was found, but for a good part of the time she was ill and unable to carry on the work.

The contributions are a little in advance of last year. A few new places have been added to the lists of contributors. One patron who had for some years supported a Bible-woman in India died at the close of last year, but her husband continues the payments. Several enthusiastic Standard Bearer Bands have been organized. They are very anxious to be put in touch with the particular missionary whom they are helping to support. Our women in Europe feel very anxious to have some arrangement by which it may be possible for young women from our Churches there, who feel called to the foreign service, to be accepted and sent out by our Society. They have formulated a plan which we hope may be acceptable to our ladies here.

We here can scarcely understand the self-sacrifice represented by the something more than $1,000 which comes annually from our German sisters in Europe. If they could know that some one or more of their own number were being supported by their gifts it would increase their interest and their contributions many fold.

Is not Bishop Burt right when he says that perhaps the time is nearer than we have thought when from Switzerland and Germany we may get women who can learn the language of heathen peoples as well as those who speak the English tongue? Can they not be used of the Master in this service as well as those from this land? May God grant wisdom to solve this and many other problems in connection with the German work!

AFRICA.

Woman's Work opened in 1899.
Official Correspondent, Mrs. S. F. Johnson.

MISSIONARIES AND THEIR STATIONS.

QUESSUA.—Susan Collins, Martha A. Drummer.
OLD UMTALI.—Sophia Jordan Coffin.

Our woman's work has been established at only two points in the great continent of Africa, one being on the east coast, at Old Umtali, in Rhodesia, and the other on the west coast, at Quessua, in the province of Angola.

QUESSUA.—Miss Collins, who labored here so long and so faithfully alone, has been rejoicing for more than a year in the companionship and helpfulness of Miss Drummer, who now takes charge of the school, while Miss Collins still cares for the many other needs of the girls to whom they are giving a home and careful Christian training. Miss Drummer writes: "I am getting hold of the language and I enjoy the school work so much that I am often sorry when the time comes to close for the day."
The fact that the greatly needed new building for school and home is now being built is cause for much rejoicing. The Northwestern Branch is supplying the money, and our two missionaries, with the help of the presiding elder, are supervising the work. Miss Collins writes: "Our temporary house has answered very nicely for the children. True, the three rooms are pretty well crowded, but we have coarse wire nailed over all the windows (they are without glass) and we can have the shutters open, so there is good ventilation. The children have all kept well the past year." Thus is the bright side of life shown, while we know that living in three rooms with twenty-five girls must entail many discomforts. The new building will provide a good home for all, and we are thankful to secure not only the greatly improved social conditions for the girls, but a reasonably good home for our missionaries.

OLD UMTALI.—Here, also, we have a brighter picture to present, for through the generosity of a friend in the New England Branch, who gives for this purpose $3,500, a commodious school and dormitory is being built. This will greatly accelerate the growth of our work, which has made positive advances this year under the care of Miss Sophia Coffin. Miss Coffin is still greatly helped by Mrs. Swormstedt-Coffin, who was married a few months ago to Rev. S. D. Coffin, the pastor of our Church in Old Umtali.
At the close of 1905 there were nine girls in our school, while a year later forty-three were in attendance. We own thirty-five acres of land here, which was transferred to us by Bishop Hartzell. Eight acres are now under cultivation, including an orchard of seventy-two trees. The products of the garden have contributed over $300 toward the support of the school this year.
Mrs. Coffin writes: "Our greatest joy is in knowing that real character has been developed in these girls in so short a time, and there is not one girl here who does not want to grow better."
Six of these girls have recently been married to native pastors of our Church, and as they are really doing Bible-woman's work for us

we are urged to assume their partial support. They visit the homes, the Kraals, read the Bible and pray with the mothers, hold meetings for women and girls, and earnestly try to lead the people to Christ.

Miss Sophia Coffin, our new missionary, who has been in charge of Hartzell Villa, Old Umtali, since the marriage of Miss Swormstedt, writes as follows: "The more advanced classes in our school have been held in the morning from eight o'clock to ten-thirty. The girls make their own dresses and do as much of the necessary sewing about the house as their abilities allow. Some of them sew rather neatly, though they can not see why one long stitch will not do the work of two or three shorter ones. The other girls work in the gardens in the morning and come in for classes in the afternoon, while the morning girls work outside.

It has been my pleasure and privilege lately to visit some of the Kraals in which there are native schools conducted by mission boys from Old Umtali. Most of these boys have married girls from this school. It was interesting to see their homes and note the improvement in their manner of living. They eat from tables, have white tablecloths and suitable dishes. They have civilized beds, and flowers in every conceivable place. They dress neatly and are very influential in their Kraals. Some of them preach in the absence of their husbands and help in the teaching every day.

Our chief object is to train these girls for Christian homes and to instil in them an earnest desire to spread the Gospel among their own people. We realize very deeply that Africa must be saved by the Africans, and the few whom we personally touch must carry the story to the many who are beyond our reach.

Thus far we have not been able to improve the manner of eating among the girls. They hold to the belief that fingers were made before forks. When the dormitory is built, we shall have a proper dining-room, with tables and benches, and will introduce the girls to plates, spoons, and cups. Napkins and finger-bowls are dreams for the future. Our present ambitions are modest."

Bishop Hartzell urges us to begin work at St. Paul de Loando, where he offers to give us the necessary land. A missionary, and money with which to erect a building there, are the next things we ask for. Who will go, and who will give the necessary money?

Let us talk much to our people here about Africa's needs. Let us work for Africa and pray for Africa. The opportunities for our work are so large and we are doing so little.

WORK IN THE EAST AFRICAN MISSION.

NAMES OF STATIONS.	Old Umtali Hartzell Villa
W. F. M. S. Missionaries	1
Wives of Missionaries in Active Work	2
Foreign or Eurasian Assistants.	
Native Workers	4
WOMEN IN THE CHURCH—	
Full Members	5
Probationers	17
Adherents	30
Women and Girls Baptized during Year	3
No. Christian Women under Instruction	3
Non-Christian Women under Instruction	3
No. Bible-women Employed	
BIBLE INSTITUTES OR TRAINING CLASSES—	
No. of Institutes	
No. Missionaries Teaching	
No. Native Teachers	
Enrollment	
SCHOOLS FOR TRAINING BIBLE-WOMEN—	
No. Schools	1
No. Missionaries	1
No. Native Teachers	
Enrollment	3
Receipts for Board and Tuition	
VERNACULAR AND ANGLO-VERNACULAR BOARDING SCHOOLS—	
No. Schools	1
No. Foreign Missionaries	1
Foreign or Eurasian Teachers	
No. Native Teachers	1
Self-Supporting Students	
Wholly-Supported Students	25
Partly-Supported Students	
No. Day Students	5
Total Enrollment	30
Receipts for Board and Tuition	
Government Grants and Donations	
DAY SCHOOLS—	
No. Schools	3
No. Teachers	3
*Total Enrollment	
Average Daily Attendance	5
Receipts for Tuition	
Government Grants and Donations	

* Women in kraals won't enroll, hence no record yet.

EXPLANATORY NOTES TO TABLE ON FOLLOWING PAGES.

INDIA—a. Lucknow College.
b. Godhra.
c. Sitapur.
d. Bedar. -
e. Baldwin Girls' School—Bangalore.
f. Hospital at Calcutta.
g. Raichar.
h. Raipur.
i. Budaon.
j. Moradabad.
k. Dwarahat.
l. Kolar Rest Home.
m. Asansol.
n. Cawnpore Building.
o. Haiderabad Repairs.
p. Vikarabad Building.
q. Sironcha.
r. Tilonia.
s. Nadiad Home.

t. Borneo.

u. Malaysia Building.

v. Manila Building.

CHINA—a. Chentu.
b. Foochow Boarding School.
c. Dibhua.
d. Yen Ping.
e. Kiu Kiang—Ellen Knowles Training School.
f. Sztzkuan—Cripples Bungalo, Cora Bell Rawley's Memorial
g. Iong Bing Training School.

h. Famine Fund.
i. Building—Central China.
j. Tschieo Building.
k. Lotadi Training School.
l. Kiu Kiang Hospital.
m. Fish Memorial.
n. Ngu Ching Hospital.

KOREA—w. Seoul Hospital.
x. Konju.
y. Chemulpo Gate House.

JAPAN—a. Hirosaki.
b. Nagoya Emergency Fund.
c. Tokyo.
d. Nagasaki debt.
e. Aizana.

MEXICO—a. Guanajuato.
b. Pachuca.
c. Land for Mexico City Industrial School.
d. Puebla.
e. Buildings.

MISCELLANEOUS—
a. Endowment.
b. Annuities Invested.
c. Mite-boxes.
d. Return to Bequest Fund.
e. Zenana Paper Fund.
f. Medical Education Fund.
g. Famine Relief.
h. General Treasury.
i. Transferred to Special Accounts.

SUMMARY OF DISBURSEMENTS FOR 1906-1907.

STATIONS.	Columbia River	Pacific	Topeka	Minneapolis	Des Moines	Northwestern	Cincinnati	Baltimore	Philadelphia	New York	New England
*INDIA—											
For General Work	$6,581 00	$11,782 00	$23,516 86	$4,333 00	$32,040 00	$45,943 10	$25,279 18	$7,706 50	$15,860 29	$33,050 00	$14,976 91
Bareilly Roof		20 00			50 00			30 00			60 00
Poona		500 00	435 00	300 00	800 00	2,175 00	3,497 58	1,000 00	2,088 00		1,150 00
Pakur		280 00	300 00		510 00	647 35				200 00	156 00
Brindaban	k 12 00; s 2,100 00	n 25 00; q 35 00	35 00; 50 00; r 830 00; e 4,000 00; q 500 00	q 35 00	k 72 00; n 50 00; o 25 00; p 2,500 00	m 600 00	226 98; i 500 00; j 400 00; k 824 00; b 5,000 00	g 365 00; h 138 88	d 1,000 00; c 500 00; f 100 00	300 00; c 300 00	a 414 00; b 3,000 00
Total for India	$8,693 00	$12,542 00	$28,616 86	$5,568 00	$35,372 15	$49,365 45	$35,227 60	$9,300 38	$19,548 29	$33,150 90	$19,756 91
MALAYSIA—For Gen'l Work	$945 00		$193 00	$7,381 18	$200 00	$2,405 00; u 120 00	$1,618 75		$769 00; t 30 00	$350 00	$2,395 00
Total for Malaysia	$945 00		$193 00	$7,381 18	$200 00	$2,525 00	$1,618 75		$799 00	$350 00	$2,395 00
PHILIPPINES—	$490 00	$690 00	$1,730 00	$1,809 00; v 3,500 00	$950 00	$1,510 00	$927 50	$35 00	$50 00	$49 94	
CHINA—											
For General Work	$1,388 50	$3,698 00	$4,065 00	$5,106 51	$16,173 00	$30,613 12	$11,753 52	$3,869 00	$5,425 17	$17,411 99	$10,844 70
Pekin School debt		60 00			225 00	883 00	400 00		400 00		650 90; 400 00
Nanchang		b 8,000 00; e 100 00	1,500 00		f 100 00; d 1,000 00; n 50 00	b 3,500 00; m1,375 00; a 4,975 00; n 400 00; g 1,000 00	i 860 00; j 1,500 00; k 1,000 00		h 169 72	e 1,075 00; f 1,000 00; g 28 88	a 3,000 00; b 1,000 00; c 1,500 00; d 546 00
Total for China	$1,388 50	$6,858 00	$5,565 00	$5,106 51	$17,548 00	$42,746 12	$15,003 52	$3,869 00	$6,054 89	$19,513 87	$17,941 60
KOREA—											
General Work		$115 00	$70 00	$280 00		$1,150 00	$5,689 55; 100 00; a 8,371 00	$1,142 39	$2,724 51	$9,475 71	$1,500 00
Peng Yang Hospital							x 87 00		1,000 00	2,000 00	
Yeng Byen Home							y 900 00			501 00	
Total for Korea		$115 00	$70 00	$280 00		$1,150 00	$14,657 55	$1,142 39	$3,724 51	$11,976 71	$1,690 00

JAPAN—											
General Work	$3,875 00	$12,119 21	$8,817 02	$2,329 50	$13,167 20	$11,800 00	$4,030 00	$2,943 00	$3,408 00	$1,225 00	$585 00
Hakodati	105 00 / 1,000 00 / a 1,500 00	b 300 00		850 50 / c 80 00	b 280 00 / d 1,187 41	2,600 00 / e 73 50 / b 540 00	500 00 / a 25 00 / b 190 00	400 00	500 00	300 00 / b 80 00	b-e 50 00
Total for Japan	$5,480 00	$18,419 21	$8,817 02	$3,259 50	$14,584 61	$15,013 50	$4,745 00	$3,848 00	$3,908 00	$1,605 00	$585 00
MEXICO—											
General Work	$2,040 00 / a 1,000 00 / b 500 00	$3,800 00 / c 725 00	$6,769 00 / d 13,554 00 / c 100 00	$100 00 / e 30 00	$4,550 30 / d 5,000 00 / c 975 00	$7,067 50 / b 300 00 / c 1,100 00	$1,395 00 / c 65 00		$40 00	$105 00 / c 425 00	
Total for Mexico	$3,540 00	$4,525 00	$20,423 00	$180 00	$10,525 30	$8,467 50	$1,460 00	$75 00	$40 00	$530 00	
SOUTH AMERICA—											
General Work	$1,821 00	$5,148 20	$947 00		$15 00	$6,400 00		$300 00	$3,000 00		
Montevideo debt	222 00	586 00	1,200 00								
Total for South America	$2,043 00	$5,734 20	$2,167 00		$15 00	$6,400 00	$360 00		$3,000 00	$1,415 00	
AFRICA—											
West Central	$40 00	$20 00				$180 00	$40 00			$1,415 00	$1,415 00
East Central		1,283 42									
General Work	3,500 00										
Buildings			$17 00		$607 00	600 00					
Total for Africa	$3,540 00	$1,253 42	$17 00		$607 00	$780 00	$40 00			$1,415 00	$1,415 00
ITALY—	$251 00	$1,020 00	$328 00	$130 00	$240 00	$4,165 00	$200 00	$25 00	$25 00	$20 00	$20 00
Buildings	33 00			50 00		2,817	45 00				
Total for Italy	$284 00	$1,020 00	$328 00	$180 00	$240 00	$6,482 00	$245 00	$25 00	$25 00	$20 00	$20 00
BULGARIA—Total	$570 00	$530 00	$200 00			$2,600 00	$45 00			$50 00	
SWITZERLAND—Total						150 00					
NORTH GERMANY—Total						125 00					
NORWAY—Total											
MISCELLANEOUS—											
Folts Mission Institute	$3,466 34	$622 00	$475 10	$4 00		$302 50	$681 92			$1,305 81	$236 71
Contingent Funds	429 50	4,626 82 / 415 50 / a 100 00	2,016 53 / 201 25 / b 3,000 00 / c 80 00 / d 600 00	1,075 79 / 350 00	$3,785 80	6,410 27 / 991 83 / e 220 16 / f 400 00	391 50 / g 172 95	$251 73	$251 73	125 69 / i 2,784 00	
Interest on Annuities, etc.					42 92	h 588 00					
Total for Miscellaneous	$3,895 84	$5,764 92	$6,872 88	$1,429 79	$3,828 72	$8,414 76	$1,859 25	$251 73	$251 73	$4,215 00	$236 71
Total	$60,836 85	$97,288 17	$68,586 59	$19,396 06	$97,285 64	145,729 33	$62,394 52	$29,381 94	$43,399 59	$28,040 00	$12,288 21
Grand Total											$662,526 40

* Notes of explanation on page 198.

Appropriations for 1907-1908.

NEW ENGLAND BRANCH.

NORTH INDIA.

Naini Tal, Schools, conveyance and teachers (one-half)....	$110
Dwarahat, First assistant......	280
Three scholarships..........	60
Home (building)	52
Pithoragarh, Miss McMullen...	300
Conveyance ....·.......	60
Two scholarships	40
Bhot, Bible-women	24
Medicines	33
Itinerating	34
Moving	17
Expenses to Conference......	33
Bareilly, 16 scholarships.......	240
Hospital wall	45
Shahjahanpur, 4 scholarships..	60
Repairs on roof............	88
Moradabad, First assistant......	300
Fifty scholarships..........	750
Two Agra medical scholarships.	80
Twelve city schools	168
Inspectress	60
Conveyance ....·......	84
Bible-women	200
Mrs. Parker's itinerating....	33
Assistant for city work......	300
Rent	120
District work	1,160
Mrs. Core's itinerating.......	33
Miss E. M. Ruddick........	650
Bijnour, Second assistant......	220
Twelve scholarships	180
City workers	160
Conveyance	66
Circuit Bible-women and teacher	84
District work	800
Lucknow, Miss F. L. Nichols...	600
Miss Ada Mudge	600
Two memorial scholarships...	80
Two high school scholarships.	60
Budaon, Miss C. M. Organ....	600
Total	**$8,864**

NORTHWEST INDIA.

Phalera, Two scholarships......	$30
Cawnpore, Miss B. F. Crowell..	600
First assistant	240
Ten scholarships	150
Two one-half scholarships....	80
Meerut, First assistant	275
Muttra, First assistant	275
Conveyance	40
Thirteen scholarships	195
Total	**$1,885**

SOUTH INDIA.

Hyderabad, City schools........	$275
Assistant, Miss M. Elias......	260
Conveyance ....·.....	25
Four scholarships	80

Madras, Miss D'Jordan........	300
Miss Young ....·.....	300
Conveyance	80
Ten scholarships	200
Meenambal	100
Total	**$1,620**

CENTRAL PROVINCES.

Basim, Assistant	$240
Bible-women	275
Fifty-four scholarships	840
Rent	200
Raipur, Miss E. L. Harvey.....	650
Total ..·.............	**$2,205**

BOMBAY.

Telegaon, Five scholarships.....	$100
Baroda, Dr. Belle J. Allen......	600
Conveyance	100
Drugs	200
Water supply for Hospital...	700
Total	**$1,700**

BENGAL.

Calcutta, High School (property)	$350
Darjeeling, Miss E. L. Knowles.	300
Pakur, Building..............	300
Total	**$950**

MALAYSIA.

Malacca, One scholarship.......	$25
Singapore, Seven scholarships..	175
Miss Meyer	250
Rent, Teluk Ayer...........	200
Conveyance	125
Teacher	100
Kuala Lumpur, Miss E. A. Hemingway	600
Two Scholarships	50
Conference transit ....·..	40
Contingencies	120
Support of conveyance.......	150
Penang, First teacher.........	200
Debt (partial)	20
Total	**$2,055**

NORTH CHINA.

Peking, Miss E. G. Young, (home salary)	$350
Miss G. Gilman	650
Tartar city school..........	60
Hospital, current expenses...	500
Thirty scholarships	900
Ch'ang-Li, Dr. E. G. Terry.....	650
Miss E. E. Glover..........	650
Miss C. P. Dyer............	550
Day schools	100
Training-school	300

Hospital and dispensary.....	275
Mrs. Ti Tsao	40
Conference reports	25
Nineteen scholarships	570
Total $5,620	

CENTRAL CHINA.

Nanking, Seven scholarships....	$175
Day school	45
Total $220	

WEST CHINA.

Chung King, Bible-woman......	$40
Chentu, Miss C. J. Collier......	650
Miss M. A. Simester.........	650
Insurance	25
Itinerating	70
Ten scholarships	250
Total $1,685	

FOOCHOW.

Foochow, Twelve scholarships...	$240
One orphan	30
Ku Cheng, Ten scholarships, Woman's School.............	150
Bible-women	50
Day school	30
Repairs	25
South Yen Ping, Miss M. C. Hartford	600
Four scholarships	80
Hai Tang, Ten scholarships, Woman's School	200
Three day schools	90
Bible-women	50
Conference Minutes	10
Total $1,555	

HING HUA.

Deh-hua, Miss A. M. Todd......	$600
Miss J. A. Marriott.........	600
Bible-women	75
Conference expenses	10
Messenger	25
Total $1,310	

KOREA.

Seoul, House steward.........	$50
Fuel	200
West Gate day school........	50
Repairs, Scranton Home.....	50
Gateman, Mrs. Scranton	50
Keesou, Mrs. Scranton......	50
Twelve scholarships	420
Chemulpo, Miss Josephine O. Paine	700
Total $1,570	

NORTH JAPAN.

Hakodate, Teacher of literature.	$270
Teacher first and second grades	115
Seven scholarships	280

Hirosaki, Teacher third and fourth grades	100
Assistant	60
Bible-woman	90
Total $915	

CENTRAL JAPAN.

Tokyo, Aoyama, Science teacher.	$235
Eight scholarships	320
Two industrial scholarships..	80
Yokohama, Preparatory teacher..	75
Ground rent	60
Insurance and taxes.........	200
Fuel and lights	75
Mrs. Inagaki	90
Yamabukicho day school.....	650
Seven scholarships	280
Blind School	25
Literary work.............	40
Nagoya, Translation teacher....	150
Sewing teacher	200
Matron	100
Total $2,580	

SOUTH JAPAN.

Nagasaki, Seven scholarships...	$280
Conference reports	10
Debt..................	60
Total $352	

MEXICO.

Mexico City, Three scholarships.	$150
Bible-woman (in part)......	50
Children's building	150
School supplies	100
Industrial school land.......	487
Miraflores, A. Y. Ortis........	240
J. Ramirez	240
Pachuca, Miss Drozco........	250
Miss A. Martinez	200
Water tax and repairs.......	80
One scholarship	50
Puebla, Miss J. Palacios......	500
Three scholarships	150
Total $2,647	

SOUTH AMERICA.

Buenos Ayres, Rent..........	$200
Assistant teacher	200
One scholarship	80
Rosario, Assistant...........	400
Repairs and taxes	200
School supplies	30
Fuel and lights	50
Furniture	50
Miss B. E. Kneeland........	900
Two scholarships	200
Montevideo, Taxes...........	160
Insurance	40
School supplies	100
Total $2,610	

ITALY.

Rome, via Garibaldi, Five scholarships	$250
Total $250	

BULGARIA.

Lovetch, Matron and other service	$220
Taxes	35
Two scholarships	90
Total	**$345**

AFRICA.

Old Umtali, Two scholarships...	$40
Total	**$40**

SUMMARY.

North India	$8,864
Northwest India	1,885
South India	1,620
Central Provinces, India	2,205
Bombay, India	1,700
Bengal, India	950
Malaysia	2,055
North China	5,620
Central China	220
West China	1,685
Foochow, China	1,555
Hinghua, China	1,310
Korea	1,570
North Japan	915
Central Japan	2,580
South Japan	352
Mexico	2,647
South America	2,610
Bulgaria	345
Italy	250
Africa	40
	$40,978
Contingent	2,000
Total for New England Branch	**$42,978**

NEW YORK BRANCH.

NORTH INDIA.

Naini Tal, Bible-woman	$64
Mrs. Newman's Bible-woman.	50
Rent for Bible-women homes.	33
Dwarahat, Four scholarships at $20	80
Medical scholarship	40
Pithoragarh, Eight scholarships, at $20	160
Support of women	100
Industrial work	320
Miss Annie Budden	600
Assistant, Miss Ellen Hayes..	300
Two village schools, at $20..	40
Training-school	64
Six Bible-women	125
Repairs	20
Conveyances	80
Itinerating	125
Mrs. Newman's Bible-women.	100
Bareilly Orphanage, First Assistant, Miss Ramsbottom	300
Second assistant	240
Third assistant	220
110 scholarships, at $15	1,650
City schools, five at $20	100
Mohulla and village work, five Bible-women	165

Special Bible-women	25
Bible-women and conveyances.	320
Itinerating (Sadar Bazaar)	40
Woman's School, assistant (half)	100
Woman's School, teachers (half)	120
Books and incidentals	12
Hospital bed	20
Shajahanpur, Miss English, salary	600
Five scholarships, at $15	75
Shahjahanpur West, Bible-women	72
Mrs. West's district, itinerating	50
Shahjahanpur East, Four Bible-women and conveyance	200
Widows	64
Repairs	20
City schools	40
Katra Circuit	48
Khera Bajhera Circuit	62
Faridpur Circuit	67
Gahrwal District, Pauri, six scholarships	120
Pauri, Mrs. Newman's Bible-women	100
Moradabad, Five scholarships...	75
Evangelistic work, conveyance.	75
Bible-women	140
Medicines	25
Budaon District, Bible-women and summer school on seven circuits	950
Bijnour District, Boarding-school, two scholars	30
Mrs. Gill's assistant (half)..	120
Mrs. Gill, itinerating	50
Keep of Tonga	40
Pilibhit District, Bible-women and summer school on ten circuits	1,062
Hardoi District, Twenty scholarships	300
Bible-women and medicines..	180
Bible-women and summer school for eight circuits	630
Lucknow, Home for Women, conveyances	100
Caroline Richard	40
Bible-women and rent	145
Conveyance	80
Circuit Bible-women	60
Sitapur, Miss Ida G. Loper	600
Ten scholarships, at $15	150
B. W. Georgiana Dempster...	40
Gonda District, Circuit work Bible-women Ellenpur and Mankipur	100
Baraich, Schools, Bible-women, etc.	368
Kaisarganj Circuit, Bible-woman.	63
Bhinga Circuit, Bible-women....	84
Total for North India	**$12,643**

NORTHWEST INDIA.

Phalera, One scholarship	$15
Allahabad, Twelve scholarships, at $15	180
Assistant	220
Tilonia, Sanitarium, medical assistant	140

Cawnpore, Thirty-five scholar-
ships, at $15 525
High School, two scholarships. 160
High School, repairs 50
Seventeen Bible-women and
itinerating city and district 430
Meerut, Eight Bible-women and
itinerating 200
Agra, Assistant 240
Four Bible-women and con-
veyance 200
Day school 25
Jinrickshaw 35
Medical scholarship 40
Brindaban, Zenana, assistant ... 200
Two Bible-women 85
Bengali evangelist, Miss Dass
(half) 120
Muttra, Miss Agnes Saxe 600
Training-school, five scholar-
ships 100
Boarding-school, five scholar-
ships 75
Two district Bible-women 50

Total for Northwest India. $3,690

SOUTH INDIA.

Kolar, Eighteen scholarships, at
$20 .... $360.
Assistant, Miss Gladys Curties. 260
Conveyance 90
Two Bible-women 50
Hyderabad, Assistant, Miss Mary
Smith 260
Village school 40
Conveyances (partial) 50
Industrial work 25
Secunderabad, Bible-woman 40
Bowenpalli school 80
Madras, Taxes (half) 65
Seventy-one scholarships, at
$20 1,420
Matron 200
Three city and nine village
schools 468
Miss Clare Betreen 200
Munshi 20
Zenana work, Miss Lydia
Lewis 220
Four Bible-women 160
Conveyances 160
Pony and conveyance for ze-
nana work (half) 75
Raichur District, Bible-women
with Mrs. Ernsberger 25
Three Bible-women with Mrs.
Cook 75
Five scholarships, at $20 100
Gulbarga, Mrs. Garden, Bible-wo-
man "Martha" 50
Bible-woman 25
Belgaum, Mrs. Scharer, convey-
ance 15
Marathi Girls' School 100
Boarding-school, Miss Woods,
assistant 240
Matron, Miss Smith (in part). 80
Munshi 25
Fifteen scholarships, at $20 .. 300

Total for South India... $5,278

CENTRAL PROVINCES.

Narsinghpur, Six Bible-women
and conveyances $250
Raipur, Two scholarships 40

Total for Central Prov-
inces $290

BOMBAY.

Bombay, Miss Elizabeth Nichols. $650
Miss Reelly 280
Mrs. Binjibhoy 160
Agnesbai Silas 80
Mrs. Nathan 95
Bible-women and conveyances. 230
City schools: Miss Robinson's
passage and home salary ... 650
Teachers and rent (half) 280
Itinerating 25
Taxes and insurance 160
Telegaon-Dabhada, Miss O. H.
Lawson 600
Assistant matron 52
Nurse 60
Scholarships 660
Keep of conveyance 140
Miss Durant, salary 340
Two Bible-women 100
Taxes and insurance 25
Drugs 50
Well 200
Poona, Miss Files, home salary .. 300
Eleven scholarships, at $20 .. 220
One scholarship with Soon-
derabai 20
(Conditional) Debt on school,
interest 300
Gujarat District, Ahmedabad,
three Bible-women 90
Baroda, Twenty-four scholarships 480
Industrial work 50
Godhra, Thirty-one scholarships,
at $20 620
Miss Kate O. Curts 600

Total for Bombay $7,517

BENGAL.

Asansol, Six scholarships, at $20. $120
Bolpur, Bible-women 120
Pakur, Ten scholarships 200
Bible-woman Rebecca 40
Bullock cart 20
Calcutta, Five orphans, at $40 .. 200
Miss Elizabeth Maxey 400
Deaconess Home, rent 400
Hindustani Bible-woman ....:. 40
Two teachers 64
One teacher 40
Rent for schools 60
Kidderpur, Bible-woman 40
Bengali Work, Four Bible-women, 180
Seven scholarships 175
Nogendro and Shoju 50
Horse and gharry keep 150
Tamluk, Miss Moyer, home sal-
ary 300
Three teachers and jhee 140
District and Sunday-schools .. 80
Bible-women and scholarships. 55

Total for Bengal $2,874

BURMA.

Rangoon, Emma Kunzl	$80
Total for Burma	$80

MALAYSIA.

Kuala Lumpor, Six scholarships, at $25	$150
Matron	144
Insurance	45
Malacca, Missionary salary	600
Penang, Debt on C. S. Winchell Home	50
Tamil, Girls' Orphanage, teacher	87
Total for Malaysia	$1,076

PHILIPPINES.

Manila, One Bible-woman	$75
Total for the Philippines	$75

NORTH CHINA.

Peking, Mrs. C. M. Jewell, salary	$650
Mary P. Gamewell School, Twenty-two scholarships	660
Roudout day school	50
Bible-woman Phoebe Li	40
Bible-woman Mrs. Hsieh-Chao	40
Training-school teacher	40
Nurse	40
Miss Alice M. Powell	650
Tientsin, Bible-woman, Mrs. Kuo-Wei	40
Bible-woman, Mrs. Yang-Hsu	40
Ch'ang Li, Fourteen scholarships, at $30	420
Bible-woman, Mrs. Ch'in Yang	40
Bible-woman, Mrs. Wang-Chou	40
Training-school teacher	40
Shantung, Bible-woman, Old Lady Wang	40
Bible-woman, Clara Wang	40
Bible-woman, Mrs. Liu Chi Hsien	40
Publishing Conference Reports (partial)	25
Total for North China	$2,935

CENTRAL CHINA.

Chinkiang, Dr. Lucy Hoag	$650
Drugs and supplies (partial)	100
Nurse	50
Fourteen scholarships	400
Mrs. Longden's Bible-woman	50
Nanking, Four scholarships, at $30	120
One Bible-woman	20
Wuhu, Two Bible-women	100
City evangelistic work	50
Two day schools	100
Gateman	25
House rent	100
Itinerating	40
Kiukiang, Miss Jennie V. Hughes	650
Woman's School, 9 scholarships at $25	225

Woman's school teacher, Mrs. Mei	60
Woman's school, 3 Bible-women	150
Woman's school rent	75
2 day schools	100
Hospital, 5 nurses	250
Hospital, free beds, 4 at $25	100
Boarding school, 16 scholarships	480
Nanchang, Miss W. B. Honsinger	650
17 scholarships at $30	510
Medical assistant	70
3 day schools	150
Printing Minutes (in part)	15
One new missionary	1,000
Total for Central China	$6,290

FOOCHOW.

Foochow, Woman's training school, 3 scholarships at $20	$60
Romanized school, 3 at $20	60
Miss Phebe Wells, home salary	350
Return to Foochow	300
Four Bible-women	100
One day school	30
Special for old B. W.	12
Miss Florence Plumb, salary	600
Girl's school, 7 scholarships at $20	140
Nine orphans at $30	270
Miss Elizabeth Strow, salary	600
Repairs, Tai Maiu Home	50
Mingchiang, Dr. May E. Carleton	750
Four medical students	125
Medical assistants	75
Hospital expenses	500
Annie Fealing bed	30
Watchman	25
Repairs	50
Kucheng, Miss Grace Travis, home salary	350
Woman's training school (half)	150
Girls' boarding school, 7 at $20	140
Girls' boarding school repairs	50
Messenger	50
Kude Dist., Eight day schools	200
Eight Bible-women	200
North Iong Bing, Miss Linam	600
Messenger	50
Woman's training school	200
Two Bible-women	50
Repairs	50
Ngucheng, Dr. Li Bi Cu	250
Hospital expenses (in part)	350
Hospital assistant	75
Hospital student and nurses	120
Hospital matron	25
Hospital Bible-woman	25
Hospital watchman	25
Hospital gateman	25
Repairs	50
Haitang, Scholarships, 4 at $20	80
Furnishings	40
General Work, Business agent's expenses	50
Insurance	100
Foochow total	$7,432

HINGHUA.

Hinghua, Leper work and day schools	$50
Two Bible-women	60
Sieng Iu, Isabel Hart school, two scholarships	40
Total for Hinghua	$150

KOREA.

Seoul, Ewa Haktung, 16 scholarships	$560
Eunmum teacher	75
Industrial teacher	60
Chong Dong, B. W. Theresa	60
B. W. Delia	50
Hospital, Dr. Mary Cutler	700
Eight free beds at $35	280
Repairs and incidentals	165
Drugs and instruments	300
Sang Dong, Mrs. M. F. Scranton.	500
B. W. Hannah Chung	50
B. W. Alice Barr	50
B. W. Sarah Kim	50
B. W. Lucy Pak	50
Sang Dong day school	50
Muchinai day school	50
Fuel for day school	40
School supplies, books, etc.	40
Kong Ju, Itinerating	50
Day school	50
Pyeng Yang, Miss Robbin's home salary	350
Miss Robbin's passage home	300
Miss Robbin's B. W.	60
Miss Irene Haynes's salary	700
Miss Haynes's itinerating	75
Miss Haynes's B. W.	60
Woman's Hospital, R. S. Hall, M. D.	700
Drugs and instruments	150
Hospital and dispensary assistant	200
Hospital B. W.	60
Hospital matron, Susan Noe.	60
Hospital fuel	150
Hospital in-patients	100
Blind class	60
Blind class teacher	40
Insurance on home	75
Running expenses of academy.	75
Ham Chong day school (cond)	100
Chinnampo, Day school, fuel and supplies	75
Yeng Byen, Miss Estey's salary.	700
Miss Estey's itinerating	250
Bible-woman	60
Day school	60
Two Bible-women	120
Chemulpo, Miss Miller, home salary	350
Miss Lulu Miller's return passage	300
B. W. Helen	50
B. W. Helena	50
Kang Wha B. W. Frances Nary	50
Medical traveling	75
Freights and duty	100
Printing and reports	30
(Conditional)	200
Total for Korea	$9,005

NORTH JAPAN.

Hakodate, Caroline Wright Memorial School, Miss M. S. Hampton	$750
Hampton-income tax	30
School taxes	90
School insurance	100
School repairs	100
Fifteen scholarships at $40	600
Teachers, Chinese, Mr. Uno	350
Teachers, music and English	145
Matron	115
Dickerson Memorial Kindergarten, second assistant	100
Industrial and blind school teacher	60
Industrial and blind school rent	25
City work, B. W. and teachers' house rent	40
B. W. Tern Orikasa	90
Tracts and city work	25
Hirosaki, Teachers, assistant first and second grades	60
Teachers, eighth grade	365
Teachers, sewing	110
Teachers, first assistant	100
Teachers, second assistant	60
Teachers, drawing	60
Mary Alexander Memorial Kindergarten, head teacher, Toku Yoshizawa	220
B. W. at Aomori	90
Nurse girls' school	75
Yoshida children's meetings	30
Monthly meetings (travel)	30
Total for North Japan	$3,820

CENTRAL JAPAN.

Sendai, Evangelistic work, Miss G. Weaver	$700
Income tax	30
B. W. Hirabayshi	90
Repairs	50
Tokyo, Insurance	150
Four scholarships at $40	160
Harrison Memorial Industrial School, two scholarships	80
Yokohama, Higgins Memorial Training School, two scholarships at $40	80
Blind school	25
Bible-woman, Tokyo Central Church	90
Bible-woman at Mita	90
Bible-woman at Kamekura	90
Literary work, "Tokiwa"	150
Day schools, Miss Anna Atkinson	700
Income tax	30
Nagoya, Teachers, history and geography	300
Teachers, intermediate department	160
Teachers, two assistants	150
One scholarship	50
Bible-woman at Second Church	90
District travel (partial)	70
Total for Central Japan.	$3,335

SOUTH JAPAN.

Nagasaki, Fifteen scholarships at $40	$600
Teacher Japanese literature..	250
Teacher music (half)......	350
Treasurer's stationery, postage, etc.	15
Debt on play-ground	135
Fukuoko, Two scholarships	80
South Kiushiu, Miss Lida Smith.	700
Miss Hortense Long	700
Miss Jean M. Gheer, home salary	350
Bible-woman, Mrs. Ohima at Kumamoto	130
Bible-woman, Mrs. Matsunobu, Yatsushiro	105
Bible-woman, Mrs. Yamáki, Omura	115
Bible-woman, Mrs. Tsuchihashi, Kagoshima	115
Bible-woman, Mrs. Kubo, Kagoshima	65
Bible-woman, Mrs. Nakamura, Kagoshima	55
Bible-woman, Miss Hori, Loochoo	115
Bible-woman, Mrs. Yoneyama, Loochoo	95
Bible-woman, Miss Ito, Loochoo	35
Bible-woman, Mrs. Matsunobo, Kokubo	95
Tracts, literature, etc.	50
Sunday-school and supplies...	50
District and city travel and work	300
Kagoshima house rent, taxes and repairs	315

Total for South Japan.. $4,820

MEXICO.

Mexico City, Miss Laura Temple	$750
Miss Allen	500
Normal department, Prof. Cervantes Imaz	300
French, Prof. Mons. Gouthier.	200
Insurance	75
Seven scholarships at $50...	350
Mrs. Newman's Bible-woman.	50
Treasurer's expenses	60
Pachuca, Elisa Salinas	220
Kindergarten assistant	200
Three scholarships at $50....	150
Mrs. Newman's Bible-woman..	50
Puebla, Miss M. Tovar	160
Miss Manriquez	190
Matron	210
Four scholarships at $50	200
Repairs	70
Guanajuato, Matron	100

Total for Mexico $3,835

SOUTH AMERICA.

Buenos Aires, House rent	$750
Miss Eleanora Le Huray	750
Assistant teacher	400
Servants	275
Taxes and repairs	300
Physician	75

School supplies	200
Mrs. Newman's Bible-woman.	50
Eight scholarships at $85....	670
Matron's assistant	50
Montevideo, Mrs. Newman's Bible-woman	55

$3,570

NORTH ANDES CONFERENCES.

Peru, Lima, Miss Elsie Wood...	750
School rent (in part)	50
Miss Alice McKinney (half).	375

$1,175

Andes Conference, Santiago, Bible-women	150

Total for South America. $4,895

BULGARIA.

Lovetch, Teacher of mathematics	$240
Miss Leona Vasileva	240
Scholarship	45
Taxes	35

Total for Bulgaria $560

ITALIAN MISSION.

Rome, Isabel Clark crêche	$150
Via Garibaldi School, five scholarships	250
Via Garibaldi School, matron (part)	200
Via Garibaldi School, day teachers	100
Via Garibaldi School, repairs.	100
Crandon Hall, Mary Barratt.	150

Total for Italy $950

AFRICA.

Old Umtali, Miss Sophia J. Coffin.	$500
Five scholarships at $20	100
Corn mill	50

Total for Africa $650

SUMMARY.

North India	$12,643
Northwest India	3,690
South India	5,278
Central Provinces	290
Bombay	7,517
Bengal	2,874
Burma	80
Malaysia	1,076
Philippines	75
North China	2,935
Central China	6,290
Foochow	7,432
Hing Hua	150
Korea	9,005
North Japan	3,820
Central Japan	3,335
South Japan	4,820
Mexico	3,835
South America, Buenos Aires...	3,520
Montevideo	50
Peru	1,175

Santiago	150
Bulgaria, Lovetch	560
Italy, Rome	950
Africa, Old Umtali	650
Contingent	3,000

Thank-Offering:

North India, Shahjahanpur roof.	500
Sitapur (add.)	1,000
Bengal, Calcutta Girls' High School	750
China, Kiukiang Training School (add.)	1,200
Korea, Pyeng Yang Hospital	2,000
Yeng Byen Home (partial)	1,575
Japan, Hakodate School	1,000
S. America, Rosario School	375
Mexico, Puebla School	1,200
Industrial School (King's Heralds)	200

Grand total -New York Branch	$95,000

PHILADELPHIA BRANCH.

NORTH INDIA.

Dwarahat, Scholarships	$60
Building	80
Labha circuit work	25
Pithoragarh, Scholarships	100
Support of women	100
Bible-women	50
Bareilly, Scholarships	135
Assistant	100
Students' wives scholarships	100
Kindergarten	72
Itinerating	13
Wall about hospital	70
Shahjahanpur bungalow roof.	126
Pauri, Scholarships	300
Assistant	240
Medical scholarships	40
Miss T. J. Kyle, passage and salary	900
Village schools	100
Bijnour, Scholarships	105
Hardoi, Scholarships	150
Lucknow, Miss K. L. Hill, salary	600
Miss I. T. Blackstock, salary	600
Medicine and doctor	125
Schools and conveyances	150
Gonda, First assistant	240
Scholarships	150
Conveyance	35
Bible-women	175
Conveyance	80
Balrampur, Circuit work	130

	$5,151

NORTHWEST INDIA.

Phalera, Support of widows	$45
Telonia, Consumptives' hospital (6 beds)	120
Allahabad, Scholarships	90
Assistant	160
Conveyance	75
Bible-women	250
Itinerating and wheel tax	50
Cawnpore, Scholarships Hindustani School	225

Margaret Peale scholarship	80
Bible-women	90
Agra, Repairs	100
Brindaban, Bengali evangelist	120
Muttra, Bible-women	350
Itinerating	70
Conveyance	85
Lahore, Bible-women	150

	$2,060

SOUTH INDIA.

Kolar, Scholarships	$80
Partial support of Linda Lewis	60
Day schools	100
Bidar, Miss Fendrich's salary	600
Assistant	260
Munshi	30
Bible-women	180
Purchase of conveyance	75
Itinerating	50
Keep of conveyance	50
Hyderabad, Bible-women	230
Conveyance	50
Industrial work	25
Scholarships	100
Belgaum, Scholarships	60
Raichur, Scholarships	40
Conveyance	50

	$2,040

CENTRAL PROVINCES.

Jabulpur, Chindwara School	$24
Evangelistic work	48
Conveyance	30
Bible-women	120
Assistant	120

	$342

BOMBAY.

Baroda, District school scholarships	$600
Head teacher	100
Taxes and current expenses	100
Miss Williams's home salary	350
Miss Crouse's salary	600
First assistant	200
Second assistant	180
Matron	240
Pundit	40
Scholarships	2,300
Rent	120
Taxes and insurance	200
Industrial work	50
Medicine	50
Miss Nunan's salary	320
Nurse Shaw's salary	100
Bombay, Miss Forbes's salary	280
Poona District, Bible-women	75
Mrs. Stephens's itinerating	100
Godhra, Scholarships	200

	$6,205

BENGAL.

Calcutta, Lee memorial scholarship	$75

BURMA.

Rangoon, Scholarship	$20
Thandaung, Scholarship	120
Salary, Miss Illingworth	600
Printing Conference Minutes.	15
	$755

MALAYSIA.

Malacca, Rent on Bible Training School	$180
Singapore, Contingencies	50
Salary of Miss Fox	280
Chinese Bible-woman	80
Scholarships	200
Repairs	10
Penang, Debt on Winchell Home	30
	$830

PHILIPPINES.

Manila, Deaconess Home light and fuel	$25
Lingayen purchase of land....	500
	$525

NORTH CHINA.

Peking, Scholarships	$120
Tientsin, Bible-woman	40
Gate-keeper	40
Shan Tung, Scholarships	450
Dr. S. L. Koon's salary......	650
Dr. Benn's home salary......	350
	$1,650

CENTRAL CHINA.

Chin-Kiang, Scholarships	$170
Nanking, Scholarships	120
Kiu-Kiang, Scholarships	210
Miss White's salary	650
	$1,150

FOOCHOW.

Foochow, Watchman	$50
Repairs	50
Orphans	150
Conference Seminary scholarships	150
Medical students	80
Dr. Hu's salary	450
City Hospital expenses	500
Medical student	40
Assistant	50
Instruments	50
Matron	25
Repairs	50
Watchman	50
Ku Cheng, Scholarships	180
Scholarships deaf and dumb schools	50
Hai-Tang, Scholarships	40
School furnishings	40
Printing Conference Minutes.	10
	$2,015

KOREA.

Seoul, Scholarships	$280
Bible-woman, Hanna	50
Bible-woman, Drusilla Li....	50
Bible-woman, Hester	50

Assistant in dispensary	60
Nurses' Training School	210
Pong	50
Kang Syo Day School and supplies	75
Laura Arner School and supplies	75
Dr. Pak's salary	240
Bible-woman	60
Bible-woman's Institute	40
Chemulpo, Miss Snaveley's salary	700
Miss Snaveley's itinerating...	150
Miss Snaveley's Bible-woman.	50
Organ	75
Gateman	50
	$2,265

NORTH JAPAN.

Sappora, Bible-woman	$90
Hakodate, Miss Dickerson's salary	700
Miss Dickerson's income tax.	30
Miss Sprowles' salary.......	700
Miss Sprowles' income tax..	30
Miss Singer's home salary...	300
Scholarships	360
Kindergarten teacher	215
Assistant	110
Blind School	150
Insurance	100
Repairs	50
Hirosaki, Teacher	65
Repairs	25
Tracts and Gospels	30
	$2,955

CENTRAL JAPAN.

Sendai, Miss Hewett's salary..	$700
Miss Hewett's income tax...	30
Repairs	50
City evangelistic work	25
Mothers' meetings	20
Tracts and Sunday-school rent	30
Tokyo, Aoyama scholarships....	480
Teacher	250
Assistant	60
Asakusa Day School	400
Day school teacher	90
Travel of school teacher	10
Bible-woman	90
Mrs. Bishop's travel	100
Mrs. Bishop's assistant	30
Miss Spencer's home salary and travel	675
Miss Slate's salary	700
Income tax	30
Bible-woman	90
Bible-woman	90
District Superintendent's travel	100
District Superintendent's assistant	30
Tokiwa and literature.......	100
Nagoya, Miss Soper's salary....	700
Income tax	30
Assistant	60
Bible-women	90
Travel	30
	$5,090

SOUTH JAPAN.

Nagasaki, Debt on land	$90
Scholarships	200
Orphanage	40
Bible-woman	95
Bible-woman	90
	$515

MEXICO.

Mexico City, Miss Isabel Gamboa	$250
Professors of science and literature	360
Matron	250
Scholarships	250
Puebla, Miss Limberger's salary	750
Miss Purdy's salary	750
Miss Payne's salary	750
Miss Duarte's salary	250
Bible-woman	105
School supplies	80
Scholarships	250
Book-keeper	75
Guanajuato, Salary, Miss Dunmore	750
Teacher	250
Water tax and repairs	80
Scholarships	150
School supplies	66
Light	50
Bible Training School scholarships	100
San Vicenti Day School	200
	$5,766

SOUTH AMERICA.

Buenos Ayres, Scholarship	$80
Rent	200
Teacher	200
Lima, Peru, Rent	50
Half salary Miss McKinney..	375
	$905

BULGARIA.

Hatautse, Teacher	$90
Bible work	140
	$230

ITALY.

Rome, Via Garibaldi scholarships	$200
The Creche	125
	$325

AFRICA.

Quessa, Scholarship	$20
Furnishing	13
	$33

SUMMARY.

North India	$5,151
Northwest India	2,060
South India	2,040
Central Provinces	342
Bombay	6,205
Bengal	75
Burma	755
Malaysia	830
Philippines	525
North China	1,650

Central China	1,150
Foochow	2,015
Korea	2,265
North Japan	2,955
Central Japan	5,090
South Japan	515
Mexico	5,766
South America	905
Bulgaria	230
Italy	325
Africa	33
	$40,882
Contingent	2,500
	$43,382
Conditional	2,000
	$45,382
Thank-offering	15,000
Total for Philadelphia Branch	$60,382

BALTIMORE BRANCH.

NORTH INDIA.

Dwarahat, Scholarships	$80
Bible-women	140
Itinerating	25
Home	32
Pithoragarh, Bible-women	50
Itinerating	25
Bareilly, Scholarship	150
Wall	26
Shahjahanpur, Roof	50
Moradabad, Scholarships	120
Lucknow, Miss Ruth E. Robinson, salary	600
Scholarship	26
Gonda, Scholarships	120
Total	$1,444

NORTHWEST INDIA.

Tilonia, Nurse	$40
Cawnpore, Repairs on compound wall	25
Muttra, Bible-women	88
Conveyance	30
New conveyance	25
Total	$208

CENTRAL PROVINCES.

Sironcha, Scholarships	$80
Conveyance	30
Land tax	16
Repairs	25
Jabalpur, Scholarship	20
Raipur, Miss Manuel (school assistant)	260
Scholarships	500
Bible-women	100
Conveyance	60
Finishing the buildings	1,000
Mrs. Gilder's itinerating	50
Bible-women	160
Total	$2,301

SOUTH INDIA.

Kolar, Scholarships	$260
Miss Linda Lewis's salary	65
Day schools	100
Hyderabad, Conveyance	25
City schools	80
Miss Murray (assistant)	260
Bible-women	80
Miss Elias (assistant industrial work)	180
Matron	100
Scholarships	80
Miss Ross (assistant)	260
Vikarabad, Bible-women	168
Madras, Taxes	65
Scholarships	700
Elizabeth (evangelist)	56
Guilford Avenue School	40
Bible-woman	40
Miss Marston	200
Sooboonagam Ammal	124
Purchase of pony and conveyance	75
Miss Grace Stephens's salary	600
Belgaum, Bible-woman	25
Scholarships	100
Rent	300
Total	$3,983

BOMBAY.

Poona, Medical compounder and Bible-woman	$50
Scholarship	40
Drugs	100
Itinerating	25
Rents	60
Bible-woman	65
Keeper of cart, etc.	65
Gujarat, Bible-woman	24
Talegaon, Scholarships	120
Total	$549

NORTH CHINA.

Peking, Mary Porter Gamewell memorial	$589
Scholarships	180
Total	$769

CENTRAL CHINA.

Chinkiang, Scholarships	$120
Drugs	100
Nurse	50
Hospital bed	40
Nanking, Scholarship	30
Kiukiang, Scholarships	150
Total	$490

FOOCHOW.

Foochow, Romanized school	$40
Hospital Bible-woman	25
Leper work	50
Miss Wallace's salary	600
Girls' Boarding School scholarships	240
City Hospital students	80
City Hospital expenses	100
City Hospital student	40
City Hospital Bible-woman	25

Mrs. Tippets's salary	300
Miss Edna Jones's salary	500
Orphans	360
Kindergarten	75
Ming Chiang, Training School	200
Hospital expenses	50
Matron and Bible-woman	25
Ku-cheng District, Day schools	200
Bible-women	50
South-Iong-bing, Women's training class	80
Haitang, Girls' Boarding School	80
Furnishing girls' school	20
Treasurer's expenses	20
Publishing Conference Minutes	10
Insurance	65
Total	$3,235

HING HUA.

Hing Hua, Hamilton Boarding School	$20
Juliet Turner Woman's School	300
Isabel Hart Girls' School	60
Total	$380

KOREA.

Seoul, Scholarships	$315
Matron	50
Aogi Day School	50
Two hospital beds	70
Pyeng Yang, Chili San Li Day School	60
Miss Sarah B. Hallman's salary	700
Hospital	400
Total	$1,645

JAPAN.

Hakodate, Scholarships	$160
Sewing teacher	60
Hirosaki, Bible-woman	90
Total	$310

CENTRAL JAPAN.

Tokyo, Amy G. Lewis's salary	$700
Income tax	30
Scholarships	240
Harrison Industrial School	40
Teacher of penmanship	65
Teacher of embroidery	75
Yokohama, Fuel and lights	50
Simon Memorial	300
Tan Ogasawara, salary	200
Poor School	60
Day School visitor	80
Taxes	25
Nagoya	100
Total	$1,965

SOUTH JAPAN.

Nagasaki, Kindergarten assistant	$135
Scholarships	120
Conference reports	10
Play-ground	36
Total	$301

ITALY.

Mrs. Fraisse, Bible-woman.....	$95
Rome, Isabel Creche	35
Total	$130

MEXICO.

Scholarships	$100
Children's thank-offering	25
Total	$125

PHILIPPINE ISLANDS.

Manila, Scholarships	$80
Summer board	20
Total	$100
Calcutta conditional	200
	$18,135

SUMMARY.

India	$8,485
China	4,874
Korea	1,645
Japan	2,576
Italy	130
Mexico	125
Philippines	200
Conditional Calcutta Girls' School	200
Total for Baltimore Branch	$18,135

CINCINNATI BRANCH.

NORTH INDIA.

Naini Tal, Teacher and conveyance	$110
Pithoragarh, Miss Mary Means..	600
First assistant	240
Special Bible-women	25
Four village schools	80
Two Bible-women	50
Dwarahat, New Home	104
Bareilly, Orphanage-scholarships..	195
Pukka roof and thatch roof..	75
City and village work, city school	33
Assistant, Mrs. Tucker	300
Shahjahanpur, First assistant...	240
Second assistant	200
Sixty-two scholarships.......	930
Roof on Bungalow	145
Bareilly District Work, Tilhar Circuit	92
Jalalabad Circuit	68
Powayan Circuit	68
Panahpur Circuit	52
Mohamdi Circuit	44
Moradabad, Miss Alice Means..	600
Miss Nora B. Waugh	600
Twenty-six scholarships	390
Normal scholarships	15
City and village work, three Bible-women	75
Rent for Ladies' Home	120
Evangelistic work, assistant..	240
Itinerating	100
Medicines	25

Budaon, First assistant	260
Nine scholarships	135
Bijnour, Scholarships	225
District work, Bible-women..	125
Lucknow, Persian teacher	100
College scholarship	60
High School, first assistant..	300
Second assistant	300
Scholarships	400
Secretary's salary	220
Repairs	100
Home for Homeless Women, Miss Hardie, home salary..	350
Traveling expenses	300
Assistant	240
Conveyance	50
Matron and teacher	225
Scholarships	75
Repairs	40
Sitapur, Boarding School, first assistant	220
Second assistant	180
Sixty-two scholarships	930
Zenana and Circuit work, assistant	200
Conveyance	120
Bible-women	190
Oudh District, Bara Banki, ten Bible-women	250
Lakinipur, nine Bible-women..	225
Sidhauli, seven Bible-women..	175
Gonda, Boarding School, Miss Hoge	400
Miss Frances Scott, home salary	300
Scholarships	435
Circuit work, repairs and medicines	16
Village conveyance	53
Marietta Bible-woman	25
Day School	20
District work, Colonelganj Bible-woman	40
Total for North India....$13,100	

NORTHWEST INDIA.

Phalera, Circuit Bible-woman...	$20
Cawnpore, Second assistant ...	220
Brindaban, Medical work, Dr. Emma Scott	600
Medicines	345
Assistant	200
Compounder	45
Nurse and servants	65
Six beds	120
Conveyance	90
Itinerating	35
Dispensary debt and interest.	200
Rescue work	90
Muttra, Training School, four scholarships	80
Boarding School, 15 scholarships	300
Evangelist teachers and summer schools	1,275
Contingent fund ....:	35
Total for Northwest India $3,720	

SOUTH INDIA.

Bangalore, Baldwin High School,
two scholarships $80
City and village work, Miss R.
Davids, assistant, Canarese. 200
Miss F. Davids, Tamil assist-
ant 200
Two Munshis 40
Conveyance 60
Kolar, Boarding School, twenty-
four scholarships 480
Zenana and village work, Miss
B. Smith 260
Day School 50
Bidar, Two day schools 50
Hyderabad, Ten scholarships.... 200
Secunderabad, Bible-woman 24
Vikerabad, Girls' School, eleven
scholarships 220
Land tax 60
Evangelistic work, Bible-
women 236
Day School 24
Conveyance 60
Belgaum, Girls' Boarding School,
seven scholarships 140
Raichur, District work, Mrs.
Ernsberger, intinerating .. 50
Evangelistic work, two Bible-
women 50
Primary Boarding School, one
scholarship 20

Total for South India... $2,504

CENTRAL PROVINCES.

Nagpur, Bible-woman $25
Sironcha, Miss Galbreath 600
Eight scholarships 160
Two widows 30
Six Bible-women 150
Repairs 35
Raipur, Matron 240
Six scholarships 120
Assistant, Miss Thomas 260
Pundit 40

Total Central Provinces. $1,660

BOMBAY.

Poona, Taylor High School, Mrs.
Eddy $600
Three scholarships 60
Gujerat, Four Bible-women 100
Godhra, Two scholarships 40
Baroda, Seventeen scholarships.. 340
Poona, Marathi evangelistic work 300

Total for Bombay...... $1,440

BENGAL.

Asansol, One scholarship $20
Darjeeling, Queen's Hill, Miss
Wisner 600
Calcutta, Bengalic work, teachers 120
Day schools 225
Three Bible-women 150
Medicines 20
Pakur, Seventeen scholarships.. 340
Two Bible-women and convey-
ance 160

Dispensary and servants..... 150
One Bible-woman, Rampore
Haut 40
Four village schools 110
Tamluck, Miss Blair, return and
home salary 650
Land rent and taxes 25
Two scholarships 40
Bible-women 120
Conveyance 60

Total for Bengal $2,830

BURMA.

Rangoon, Two scholarships $40

Total for Burma........ $40

MALAYSIA.

Malacca, Training School scholar-
ship $35
Singapore, Taxes and insurance. 36
Deaconess Home, 12 scholar-
ships 300
Evangelistic, Miss Norris..... 180
Methodist Girls' School, re-
pairs 10
Telok Ayer, Miss Anderson,
salary and travel 900
General work 200
Kuala Lumpor, Three scholar-
ships 75
Penang, Contingencies 100
Debt on land of C. S. Win-
chell Home 35
Boarding School teacher 200
Tamil Girls' School scholar-
ships 250
Matron 72

Total for Malaysia $2,393

PHILIPPINES.

Manila, Miss Crabtree $750
Matron 30
Water 75
Light and Fuel 25
Scholarships 80

Total for Philippines.... $960

NORTH CHINA.

Peking, Dr. Margaret Campbell,
traveling and salary 1,000
Mary Porter Gamewell High
School, 26 scholarships...... 780
Tientsin, Day School 40
Bible-woman, Chao Wang.... 40
Watchman 20
Cheang Li, Lucy Alderman
School, five scholarships.... 150
Tsun Hua District, Day School.. 50
Bible-woman 40

Total for North China.. $2,120

WEST CHINA.

Chungking, Dr. Ketring, salary. $650
Furniture and repairs 50
Bedding and gowns 50

Nurses and helpers	40
Two charity beds	40
Evangelistic work, Bible-woman	40
Insurance	25
Chentu, Boarding School, four scholarships	100
Tsi-cheo, Bible-woman	40
District Evangelistic work....	50
Insurance	50
Furniture for Woman's School	75
Suiling, Evangelistic work, Bible-woman	40

Total for West China.... $1,250

FOOCHOW CONFERENCE.

Foochow, Woman's Training School, Miss Jewell	$600
Sixteen scholarships	330
Romanized School, five scholarships	100
Repairs	60
Nine Bible-women	225
Boarding School, Miss Bonafield, home salary	350
Thirty-three scholarships	660
Tai-main Home repairs	50
Liang-au Hospital, medical scholarship	80
Hai Tang, Two scholarships ...	40
Insurance	25
Dr. Hu's Hospital	1,000

Total for Foochow $3,520

HING HUA.

Hamilton Girls' School, eight scholarships	$160
Training School, 12 scholarships	300
Leper day schools	200
Day schools and traveling....	550
Fourteen Bible-women and itinerating	420
Miss Mary Thomas	600
Miss Lulu C. Baker	500
Sieng iu, Training School	550
Day schools and travel	300
Seventeen Bible-women	510
Itinerating	100
Miss Lebeus	600
Dr. Emma Betow	600
Dr. Draper	600
Isabel Hart, Girls' School, fourteen scholarships......	280
Two hospital beds	40
Nurse	25
Messenger and freight	15
Repairs (conditional)	50

Total for Hing Hua $6,400

KOREA.

Seoul, Eva Haktang, Miss Frey, salary	$700
Miss Marker, salary	700
Miss Albertson, salary	585
Scholarships	455
Gateman	50
Books and Stationary.......	50

Chong Dong, Bible-woman, Amanda	50
Bible-woman, Susanna	50
Training School, Miss Edmunds	700
Baldwin Dispensary, Dr. Ernsberger	700
Dr. Ernsberger's Bible-women.	100
Dispensary assistant	100
Dispensary fuel	100
Dispensary gateman	50
Dispensary repairs	75
Drugs and instruments	200
Insurance	50
Day School	40
Konj Ju District Work, Two Bible-women	100
Pyeng Yang, Mrs. Moore's Bible-women	60
Yeng Byen, Mrs. Morris's Bible-women	60
Chemulpo, Miss Ora Mary Tuttle, salary and travel	900
Bible-woman, Priscilla	50
Bible-woman, Elizabeth	50
Day School	60
Day School supplies	25
Insurance and taxes	40

Total for Korea $6,100

JAPAN.

Sappora, District evangelistic work, Anna V. Bing	$700
Income tax	30
Bible-woman's salary, Sappora District	90
Travel of District Superintendent	100
Taxes and insurance	35
Hakodate, Caroline Wright Memorial School, five scholarships	200
Hirosaki, Bessie Alexander, salary	700
Bessie Alexander income tax.	30
Tokyo, Aoyama Jo Gakuin, eight scholarships	320
Teacher, sewing and etiquette.	130
Teacher, drawing	60
Matron	75
Sunday-school work	30
Harrison Memorial Industrial School teacher, sewing teacher	80
Three Bible-women in Shinano	270
Travel	25
Bible-woman, Ida	40
Mrs. Alexander, mothers' meeting	20
Yokohama, Miss Leonora Seeds, salary and travel	1,000
Higgin's Memorial Training School, two scholarships...	80
Blind School	25
Nagoya, Teacher, drawing and penmanship	125
Evangelistic work, Bible-woman, Gifu	90

Total for Japan $4,255

SOUTH JAPAN.

Nagasaki, Kwassui Jo Gakko, Miss Russell	$750
Miss Young	700
Miss Thomas	700
Miss Kidwell	750
Miss Cody	700
Teacher, penmanship and art.	250
Science teacher	400
Industrial, Japanese sewing..	75
Industrial, drawn work and embroidery	75
Translation	115
Chinese literature	100
Twenty-three scholarships....	920
Ground rent	150
Insurance	200
Water rent	40
Dispensary	100
Repairs	300
Kindergarten supplies	50
Conference Reports	10
Fukuoka, Ei Wa Jo Gakko, Teachers' salaries	800
Miss Finlay	700
Six scholarships	240
Insurance	120
North Kiusiu District, Bible-woman, Miss Sada Tagagi..	85
Bible-woman, Mrs. Kato	120
Bible-woman, Miss Omura ..	120
Bible-woman, Mrs. Saruta..	120
Bible-woman in North District	75
Miss Finlay's assistant	50
City Sunday-schools	30
District travel	100
Tracts and Bibles	30
Omura, Kwassui Jo En, twenty-three scholarships	480
Teacher	60
Matron	40
South Kiusiu District, Bible-woman, Mrs. Watanabe....	100
Bible-woman, Mrs. Tokunami.	100
Bible-woman, Mrs. Uebara ...	60
Total for South Japan...	$9,815

MEXICO.

Mexico City, Sarah L. Keen College, Miss Hollister	$750
Miss Pilar Aragon	210
Miss Velasco	210
Porter	210
Sewing teacher	90
Street, water and property taxes	200
Cook	90
Five scholarships	250
Evangelistic work, Miss Harriet Ayres	750
Bible-women	150
Puebla, Miss Palacios	500
Music teacher	120
Porter	140
Taxes	240
School supplies	100
Orizaba, Miss Emily Magos	210
School supplies	60
Porter	60
Guanajuato, Bible-woman	50
Total for Mexico	$4,390

ITALY.

Rome, Isabel Creche, day nursery	$90
Via Garibaldi, three scholarships	150
Deaconess work	25
Total for Italy	$265

AFRICA.

Umtali, Twenty-three scholarships	$460
Man service on the farm....	60
Bible-women	125
Total for East Africa..	$645
Total for East African Conference	$645
Pro rata appropriations (conditional)	3,785
Special appropriations (conditional)	4,020
Total appropriations for Cincinnati Branch.....	$75,212

SUMMARY.

North India	$18,100
Northwest India	3,720
South India	2,504
Central Provinces	1,660
Bombay	1,440
Bengal	2,830
Burma	40
Malaysia	2,392
Philippines	960
North China	2,120
West China	1,250
Foochow	3,520
Hing Hua	6,400
Korea	6,100
Japan	4,255
South Japan	9,815
Mexico	4,390
Italy	265
Africa	645
Conditional appropriations	7,805
Total	$75,212

NORTHWESTERN BRANCH.

NORTH INDIA.

Naini Tal, Mrs. Worthington....	$400
Rent	100
Dwarahat, Second assistant	240
Scholarships	280
Bible-women	100
Bungalow	200
Pithoragarh, Assistant, Miss Tresham	240
Second assistant	200
Rebuilding home	400
Scholarships	320
Day schools	40
Repairs	100
Medicines	20
Bible-women	100

Bareilly, Scholarships	450
Dr. Gimson	600
Dr. Lewis, home salary	300
First assistant	160
Second assistant	140
Medical work and repairs	600
Hospital beds	240
Trained nurses	160
Scholarships	100
Bible-women	60
Conveyance	80
Hospital wall	185
New roof (conditional)	125
Pauri, Miss Wilson	600
Second assistant	220
Scholarships	220
Medical scholarship	40
District Bible-women	350
Medical woman	60
Medicines and itinerating	120
Moradabad, Second assistant	240
Scholarships	345
Training class	120
Circuit and village work	200
District work	420
Conveyance	130
Budaon, Miss Wright	600
Second assistant	200
Scholarships	240
School and zenana work	100
Bible-women and village work	280
Conveyances and itinerating	200
Repairs	25
New Conveyance	115
Shahjahanpur, New roof	340
Bijnour, First assistant	240
Scholarships	225
Medicine	20
Tonga and oxen	40
Bible-women	80
Teacher's room	500
Mrs. Gill's assistant	120
Assistant	50
Gonda, Zenana assistant	220
Scholarship	20
Lucknow, Miss Singh (partial)	300
Miss Northrup	300
Assistant	300
High school assistant	300
Winslow scholarships	75
Farewell scholarships	50
Blind women	75
New missionary's salary	600
Traveling expenses	325

Total for North India...$15,245

NORTHWEST INDIA.

Phalera, Miss Greene	$600
Miss Hoffman	600
Assistant	200
Scholarships	30
Repairs	100
Matron at sanitarium	200
Medicines	50
Allahabad, Scholarships	345
Cawnpore, Miss Logeman	600
Bible-woman and itinerating	170
Wheel tax and ekkas	75
Rent and taxes	50
Scholarships	495

English scholarship	80
Support for school	100
Day school	40
Meerut, Scholarship	20
Bible-women, itinerating and conveyance	500
Aligarh, Miss Kipp	600
Scholarships in boarding school	3,000
Assistant	240
Mrs. Matthews	400
Assistant	240
Second Assistant	200
Scholarships in industrial school	855
Women in industrial school	500
Muttra, Rent, repairs and incidentals	120
English scholarships	160
Munshis	60
Evangelistic band	50
Scholarships in boarding school	345
Second assistant	220
Zenana assistant	240
Bible-women	75
New missionary, outfit, furniture, and traveling expenses	1,000

Total Northwest India...$12,560

SOUTH INDIA.

Bangalore, Miss Benthein	$600
Kolar, Miss Holland	600
Miss Fisher, home salary	250
Miss Peters	260
Miss Harben	240
Miss Mann	200
Munshi	20
Mrs. Hall, matron	200
Scholarships	1,000
Bible-women	50
Brahmin day school	120
Madras, Pupil assistants	300
Miss Z. Doyle	300
Conveyances	100
Scholarships	400
Bible-women	160
Lingamah Nicodemus Home	40
Raichur, Bible-woman	50
Belgaum, Miss Woods	600
Miss Smith, matron	100
Bible-women	50

$5,620

BOMBAY.

Poona, Mrs. Grove	$300
Head mistress	350
Scholarships	80
Matron	100
Poona debt (conditional)	2,000
Taxes	175
Godhra, First assistant	220
Second assistant	200
Matron	240
Pundit	40
Scholarships	1,400
Repairs	100
Keep of conveyance	125
Medicine and doctor	100

Bombay, Assistant, Tungabai ..	160
Bible-women, conveyance and itinerating	260
Taxes and insurance	165
Telegaon, Assistant	220
High school teachers	360
Scholarships	800
Incidentals ....:...:...	50
Poona debt (conditional)...	2,000.
	$7,445

BENGAL.

Asansol, Miss Hoskins	$200
Miss Vernieux	160
Miss Clark	160
Miss Norberg	500
Traveling expenses and furniture	400
Miss Moore	180
Bible-women	225
Conveyance	100
Scholarships	1,260
Taxes and repairs	100
Pakur, Scholarships	240
Bible-woman	40
Miss Swan (partial)	200
Darjeeling, Miss Creek	600
Calcutta, Miss Bennett	500
Scholarships	360
Deaconess Home	400
Calcutta Girls' School	1,350
Bible-woman	40
Miss Johnson's Bible-woman..	100
Miss Lee's assistant	230
Mazefferpur, Miss Peters	600
Miss Bills	600
Scholarships	880
Assistants	320
Bible-women	200
Conveyance	150
Medical work	125
Day schools	180
Repairs	150
Taxes and land rent	65
	$10,555

BURMA.

Rangoon, Miss Stahl..........	$600
	$600

MALAYSIA.

Singapore, Matron	$100
Scholarships	175
Contingent	50
Mary C. Nind. Home	225
Taipeng, Miss Jackson	600
Traveling expenses (conditional)	300
Miss Toll	600
Teachers	120
Bible-woman	75
Conveyance	100
Contingent	60
Scholarships	250
Conference and finance expenses	80
First teacher	270
Painting	120

Publishing Minutes	25
Penang, Payment on building...	100
	$3,245

PHILIPPINES.

Manila, Dr. Parish	$750
Hospital conveyance	245
Hospital needs	750
Bible-woman	75
Scholarships	80
Miss Stixrud (partial)	375
	$2,275

NORTH CHINA.

Peking, Dr. Gloss	$650
Miss Wheeler	650
Miss Knox	650
Medical student	50
Nurse	40
Scholarships	450
Lettie M. Quine Day School..	60
Tientsin, Dr. Martin	650
Medical work	200
Chang Li, Evangelistic work...	100
Scholarships	90
Tai-au-Fu, Miss Martin	650
Scholarships	1,200
Bible-woman, Mrs. Li	40
Lettie M. Quine Day School..	25
Country day schools	50
Training school	75
School building	6,000
Home building	350
Expenses to Conference	50
Miscellaneous, Conference reports	25
New doctor	650
Outfit, traveling expenses and furniture	500
	$13,205

CENTRAL CHINA.

Kiu Kiang, Miss Merrill	$650
Miss Pierce's traveling expenses	300
Miss Pierce's home salary....	350
Scholarships	600
Wall S. A. R. Fish School....	500
Furniture for building	200
Training-school scholarships..	200
Lettie M. Quine Day School..	50
Esther Clark Day School....	50
Day School building	400
Drugs	500
Nurse	50
Beds	125
Nanchang, Miss Howe	750
Dr. Kahn	450
Assistant	70
Miss Howe, traveling expenses (conditional)	300
Dr. Kahn, traveling expenses (conditional) ....:...	300
Medical instruments	100
Chiu Kiang, Miss Crook	650
Scholarships ....:......	240
Bible-woman	50
New land and wall	600

Nanking, Miss Sarah Peters.... 650
Miss Alice Peters 650
Miss Shaw, home salary, one-
half year 175
Miss Shaw's traveling ex-
penses 300
Miss Peters' traveling ex-
penses 300
Scholarships 900
Women's Training School .. 300
Day schools 100
Bible-woman 50
Kindergarten furniture and
supplies 50
Miss Smith 550
Furniture 100
Wuhu, Miss Crane 650
                          _____
                          $12,260

WEST CHINA.

Chung King, Medicines and in-
struments $350
Furniture and repairs 100
Hospital beds 60
Incidentals 50
Bible-woman, Mrs. Tai 40
Bible-woman, Mrs. Dsang... 40
Chentu, Miss Jones 650
Miss Stout 650
Scholarships 475
Day School 50
Bible-woman 30
Hospital beds 80
Insurance 35
                          _____
                          $2,610

FOOCHOW.

Foochow, Hospital evangelistic
work $50
Seminary scholarships 50
Boarding school scholarships. 200
Day schools 480
Lettie M. Quine Day School.. 30
Dr. Lyon 600
Miss Simpson 500
Furniture 100
Dr. Hatfield 600
Traveling and furniture..... 400
Hospital expenses and repairs 1,130
Orphans 330
Ming Chiang, Miss Longstreet .. 600
Boarding School 240
Day schools and itinerating.. 240
Training School scholarships. 200
Bible-women 325
Repairs 100
Watchman and messenger.... 75
Ku Cheng, Miss Peters 600
Romanized School 300
Boarding School scholarships. 300
North Iong - Bing, Boarding
School scholarships 400
Training School 100
Day schools 180
Bible-women 100
South Iong Bing, Day schools.. 180
Ngu Cheng, Romanized School.. 100
Day school 20
Scholarships 40
Hospital expenses 200

Haitang, Scholarships 40
Building 500
Miscellaneous, Conference Min-
utes and insurance 110
                          _____
                          $9,420

HING HUA.

Hing Hua, Hamilton Girls'
scholarships $200
Juliet Turner Woman's School 100
Bible-women 300
Miss Wilson (conditional)... 300
Miss Westcott 600
Messenger 40
Sieng In, Scholarships 100
Hospital beds 100
Country medical work....... 100
Nurses 50
Repairs 25
Ing Chung, Miss Strawick 600
Woman's Training School ... 500
Day schools and traveling.. 125
Bible-women 200
Miscellaneous, Conference ex-
penses 25
New missionary 1,000
                          _____
Total for China $41,860

KOREA.

Seoul, Fuel, insurance and re-
pairs $675
Day School 50
Mrs. Hah 240
Visiting nurse 50
Hospital bed 35
Scholarships 420
Pyeng Yang, Day School teachers 100
Mrs. Moore's itinerating 50
Bible-woman 50
                          _____
                          $1,670

JAPAN.

Hakodate, Scholarships $240
Teacher, mathematics 320
Teacher, history 145
Teacher, preparatory 180
Hirosaki, Kindergarten assistant 125
Insurance and taxes 50
Sendai, Scholarship 25
Bible-woman 40
District work 100
Miss Heaton 700
Miss Heaton, traveling ex-
penses 250
New fence 25
Aoyama, Miss Bullis 700
Income tax 30
Repairs 150
Watchman 55
Scholarships 640
Teacher, Chinese 270
Teacher, literature 100
Teacher, translation 200
Teacher, English 200
Teacher, primary 115
Teacher, assistant 60
Teacher, normal 200

Miss Alling, traveling expenses and home salary	625
Fukagawa, Day school	400
Desks	150
Yokohama, Mrs. Van Petten, home salary	350
Fuel and lights	150
Special repairs	100
Books, tracts and travel	90
Training School scholarships..	280
Teacher, theology	330
Teacher, music	80
Teacher, sewing and etiquette	90
Aizawa and Kanazana, Day Schools	400
Rent and taxes	115
Day school, visitor and travel	160
Mothers' meetings	20
Nagoya, Insurance and supplies.	200
Teacher, mathematics and science	250
Teacher, literature and composition	200
Teacher, music	180
Teacher, assistant	75
Bible-woman, First Church...	90
Bible-woman, Toyohashi	90
City work	40
Miscellaneous, Literature work..	100
New buildings destroyed by fire	2,500
	$11,985

SOUTH JAPAN.

Nagasaki, Miss Melton, home salary and traveling expenses	$600
Teacher, mathematics	350
Teacher, primary	65
Biblical assistant	100
Scholarships	240
City work	150
Charity kindergarten	100
Orphanage scholarship	20
Payment on land	240
Treasurer	15
Fukuoka, Miss Mabel Seeds, salary and traveling expenses	525
Teachers	125
Scholarships	280
Repairs	120
Books, etc.................	50
Matron and watchman	100
Bible-woman, Mrs. Sakomato.	90
Bible-woman, Mrs. Saruta....	75
	$3,245

MEXICO.

Mexico City, Kindergarten teacher	$250
Kindergarten assistant	180
Scholarships	300
Pachuca, Miss Hewitt	750
Miss Betz	750
Miss Lopez	210
Miss Garcia	210
Miss Chagoyan	250
Miss Jiminez	175
Miss Miranda	275

School and dormitory supplies	225
Porter	120
Repairs	125
Scholarships	100
Puebla, Normal teacher	280
Kindergarten teacher	250
Dormitory supplies	25
Scholarships	250
Taxes	75
New building	2,000
Guanojuato, Miss Galvan	200
Kindergarten and sewing teacher	200
Scholarships	150
School supplies	125
Bible-woman	50
Porter	90
Miraflores, Miss Valverde	240
Rent and school supplies	70
Apizaco, Miss Marquez	210
Support of school	220
Haxcale Leon, Teacher and school	260
Bible-woman	60
	$8,675

SOUTH AMERICA.

Montevideo, Miss Hewett......	$750
Miss Marsh	750
Assistants	1,000
Scholarships	200
Porter, taxes and repairs....	500
Bible-woman	50
Debt	300
Buenos Ayres, Miss Walker	750
House rent	400
Scholarships	170
Rosario, Scholarships	500
Assistants	900
Property	2,000
Lima, Rent	150
	$8,420

BULGARIA.

Lovetch, Miss Blackburn	$600
Miss Davis	600
Miss Raichera	330
Miss Goulimanonva	240
French and Russian teacher.	280
Incidentals and repairs	200
Books and apparatus	50
Traveling expenses	50
Scholarships	270
Balance on property	235
	$2,855

ITALY.

Rome, Crandon Hall, Miss Swift	$700
Miss Burt	700
Mlle. de Lord	500
Scholarships	200
Via Garibaldi, New missionary..	700
Taxes and insurance........	500
Repairs	200
Scholarships	300
Teachers	500
Industrial department	200
Deaconess work	575
	$5,075

AFRICA.

Nuessua, Umtali, Scholarships.	$180
Tank	50
Bible-woman	25
	$255

NORTH GERMANY.

Bible-woman and work	$125
	$125

SWITZERLAND.

Bible-women and work	$150
Contingent fund	3,140

Total for Northwestern Branch $145,000

DES MOINES BRANCH.

NORTH INDIA.

Pithoragarh, Scholarships	$320
Bareilly,	135
Wall for Hospital	65
Shahjahanpur	300
Bungalow roof	120
Pauri, Scholarships	220
Moradabad, Third assistant	200
Scholarships	60
Budaon, Scholarships at $15	285
Lucknow, Miss Sircar	360

Total for North India... $2,065

NORTHWEST INDIA.

Ajmere, Miss Lawson	$725
Phalera, Scholarships	60
Cawnpore, Miss Pool	600
High School scholarships	560
Repairs	50
Boarding School scholarship	15
Kasganj District	700
Meerut, Second assistant	240
Scholarships, 5 at $15	75
Bible-women (4) and conveyance	90
Aligarh, Bible-women	88
Conveyance	100
Muttra, Miss Gregg	400
Assistant	275
W. T. S. scholarships	140
Boarding school scholarships	90
New conveyance	50
Miss McLeary	240
District Bible-women (17)	400
Punjab, Bible-women	125
Miss Bobenhouse	800

Total Northwest India.. $5,823

SOUTH INDIA.

Kolar, Miss Maskell	$600
Bible-women	144
Scholarships	320
Conveyance	100
Miss Lewis (in part)	75
Day School	50

Hyderabad, Miss Wood	600
Miss Smith,	260
Conveyance	75
Village school	40
Bible-women	80
Industrial work	25
Repairs	25
Miss Evans	600
First assistant	260
Miss Birt	260
Miss Zoe Murrey	260
Matron	100
Conveyance	50
Scholarships	1,000
Vikarabad, Miss Wells	600
Miss Simonds	600
Assistant	160
Scholarships	540
Evangelistic assistant	260
Bible-women	120
Day School	24
Conveyance	75
Property	5,000

Total for South India... $12,303

CENTRAL PROVINCES.

Jabalpur, Mrs. Holland	$600
Miss Reynolds	600
Scholarships	3,400
High School scholarships	125
Bible training assistant	200
Bible-woman	40
Evangelistic work, Bible-women	200
Conveyance	40
Gadarwara, Bible-women	120
Khandwa, Miss Lossing	600
Miss Liers	750
Miss Elicker	800
First assistant	200
Second assistant (conditional)	160
Scholarships	1,200
Evangelistic work assistant	100
Mrs. Abbott's itinerating	30
Bible-women (8)	160
Training class	50
Burhanpur, Bible-women (5)	100
Narsingpur, Bible-women (3)	100
Raipur, Miss Lauck	600
Miss Daniels	200
Teacher, city schools	24
Bible-woman	20
Conveyance	50

Total for Central Provinces............$10,469

BOMBAY.

Miss Davis, passage and home salary	$650
Poona, Property	765
Godhra	200
City schools	80

Total for Bombay $1,695

BENGAL.

Calcutta, Miss Henkle	$600
Miss Aaronson	300
Property	475
Furniture	50
Pakur, Scholarships	230
Property	225
Asansol, Scholarships	100
Bible-woman, Rebu	16
Bible-woman, Kunti	16
Total for Bengal	$2,062

BURMA.

Rangoon, Miss Stockwell	$725
Miss Rigby	700
Miss Robinson, salary and furniture	600
Itinerating	50
Sunday-schools	35
Village schools	25
Bible-woman	80
Lease	100
Scholarships	140
Thandaung	600
Scholarships	280
Conference Minutes	15
Total for Burma	$3,350
Total for India	$37,767

MALAYSIA.

Penang, Property C. S. Winchell Home	$30
Total for Malaysia	$30

PHILIPPINE ISLANDS.

Miss Crawford, salary	$750
Training school	80
Total for Philippine Islands	$830

NORTH CHINA.

Peking, Property	$800
Scholarships	360
Miss Wilson	350
Miss Boddy	950
Training school	150
Country work	140
Changle	210
Bible-woman	40
Shantung	60
Total for North China	$3,060

CENTRAL CHINA.

Kiu Kiang, Dr. Stone	$450
Nurses	100
Free beds	125
Rent	75
Scholarships	330
Bible-woman	50

Nau Chang, Scholarships	660
Bible-women	90
Conference Minutes	15
Miss Ogborn's salary and return	950
Miss Newby, home salary	325
Total for Central China.	$3,170

WEST CHINA.

Chung King, Miss Galloway	$750
Dr. Edmonds	750
Medical work, medicines	200
Beds	40
Bedding	10
Nurses and helpers	70
Incidentals	25
Miss Wells	650
Woman's Day School	75
Girls' Day School	75
Insurance	25
Chentu, Miss Hitchcock	650
Scholarships	300
Tsicheo, Miss Manning	650
W. Scholarships	50
District work	50
Simple remedies	25
Repairs	50
Freight (silver)	15
Land (conditional)	500
Total for West China	$4,960

FOOCHOW.

Foochow, Miss Sia	$250
Miss Hu	250
Scholarships	400
Orphans	60
Seminary	30
Yeu Ping, Emma Fuller Girls' School (conditional)	1,000
Ngu Cheng, Miss Allen	600
Miss Bartlett	600
Woman's School	400
Bible-women	425
Day schools and traveling	420
Boarding school	900
Repairs	50
Messenger	50
Haitang, Miss Trimble	600
Miss Glassburner	600
Woman's Training School	20
Romanized School	100
Bible-women	150
Day schools and traveling	330
Medical work	25
Messenger	50
Conference Minutes	20
Insurance	50
Boat	50
Total for Foochow	$7,430

HING HUA.

Sieng Iu, Scholarships	$180
One hospital bed	20
Total for Hing Hua	$200
Total for China	$18,820

NORTH JAPAN.

Hakodate, Scholarships	$120
Teacher, science	215
Teacher, translation	145
Teacher, Japanese	145
Hirosaki, Repairs	23
Miss Griffith's passage and home salary	650
Bible-woman, Kurvishi	90
Travel, assistant superintendent	75
Teacher, fifth and sixth grades	150
Teacher, seventh grade	360

Total for North Japan. $1,975

CENTRAL JAPAN.

Sendai, Scholarships	$500
Teachers and supplies	225
Interest and taxes	80
Insurance	40
Bible-woman, Yamagata	90
Miss Phelps	700
Income tax	30
Tokyo, Scholarships	280
Teacher, mathematics	235
District travel	25
Yokohama, Miss Daniels	700
Income tax	30
Yokohama, Bible-woman, Horimoto	65

Total for Central Japan. $3,000

Total for Japan $4,975

MEXICO.

Mexico, Scholarships	$200
Light	180
Puebla, Scholarships	200
Guanajuato	100
Ayapango, Teachers and supplies	360
Tezontepec	360
Orizaba, Rent	100

Total for Mexico $1,500

SOUTH AMERICA.

Montevideo, Property	$200
Lima, Rent	100

Total for S. America $300

AFRICA.

Scholarships	$40
Furniture	40

Total for Africa $80

ITALY.

Rome, Via Garabaldi	$200

Total for Italy $200

SUMMARY.

India	$37,767
Malaysia	30
Philippines	830

China	18,820
Japan	4,975
Mexico	1,500
South America	300
Africa	80
Italy	200
Contingencies	513

Total for Des Moines Branch $65,015

MINNEAPOLIS BRANCH.

NORTH INDIA.

Pithoragarh, Ten scholarships	$200
Bareilly, Eight scholarships	120
On roofs for buildings	30
Toward wall around hospital	27
Dwarahat, Toward bungalow	32
Shahjahanpur, Toward roof on bungalow	50
Pauri, Scholarships	80
Budaon, Scholarships	180
Bijnour, Scholarships	45
Lucknow, Deaconess Home medicines	25
Conveyance for English work	150
Gonda, Scholarships	120

Total $1,059

NORTHWEST INDIA.

Ajmere, Scholarships	$180
Allahabad, Scholarships	45
Cawnpore, High School scholarship	40
Muttra, Miss Ogilvie	220
Six native scholarships	120
New conveyance	25
Lahore, Four Bible-women	160
Conveyance and itinerating	60
Mussoorie, Two Bible-women and conveyance	68
Eight Bible-women	200
Roorku, Eight Bible-women and conveyance	200

Total $1,338

SOUTH INDIA.

Kolar, Five scholarships	$100
Two Bible-women	50
Madras, Two scholarships	40

Total $190

BOMBAY.

Bombay, City schools	$200
Mrs. Vardon's Hindustani work	125
Poona, Two Bible-women and itinerating	175
Summer school	25
Telegaon, Eleven scholarships	220
Assistant (in Miss Thoy's place)	240

Total $985

CENTRAL PROVINCES.

Jabalpur, Two scholarships	$40
Patan Circuit, Four Bible-women	80
Total	$120

BENGAL.

Pakur, Eleven scholarships	$220
Five widows	100
Matron's salary	120
Keep of horse and driver...	60
Day School	25
Debt on building	300
Calcutta, Girls' School (conditional)	200
Total	$1,025

BURMA.

Rangoon, Miss Whittaker	$600
Assistant	200
Two scholarships	40
Thandaung, Three scholarships..	120
Total	$960

MALAYSIA.

Singapore, Miss Blackmore's salary and transit	$600
Miss Rank, salary	600
Vernacular teacher	58
Miss Olson, salary..........	600
Vernacular teacher	58
Teacher	648
Repairs on school building...	50
Conveyance	72
Twelve scholarships	300
Repairs on Deaconess Home.	150
Contingencies	100
Conveyance	144
Penang, Transit to Conference.	60
Miss Martin, salary	600
Insurance	54
Bible-women	150
Conveyance	180
Matron	144
Scholarships	500
Teacher	144
Care-taker	72
Taipeng, Contingencies	60
Insurance	45
Matron	85
Bible-woman	75
Teachers, second and third standard	350
Conveyance	80
Malacca, Miss Pugh, salary	450
Furniture	100
Training-school teacher	72
Contingencies	100
Total	$6,701

PHILIPPINES.

Manila, Miss Stixrud, salary (in part)	$375
Training-school, light and fuel	50

Conveyance	175
Insurance	40
Matron	37
Scholarships, four	160
Bible-woman	75
Institutes	50
Lingayen, Furniture (conditional)	100
Keep of horse	25
Total	$1,087

NORTH JAPAN.

Hakodate, Scholarships	$120
Pupil teacher	60
Total	$180

CENTRAL JAPAN.

Tokyo, Miss Blackstock, salary.	$700
Income tax	30
Harrison Industrial scholarships	400
Ten teachers and matron.....	615
Insurance, repairs, watchman.	170
Publication	25
Nagoya, Miss Lee's salary	700
Income tax	30
Building fund (conditional)..	100
Total	$2,770

SOUTH JAPAN.

Nagasaki, Land	$36
Total	$36

KOREA.

Seoul, Three scholarships	$105
Chinese teacher	75
Bible-woman, Mrs. Kim.....	50
Pyeng Yang, Day School teacher, Helen	54
Total	$284

CENTRAL CHINA.

Chin Kiang, Four scholarships..	$112
Kiu Kiang, Four scholarships...	100
Four Bible-women	100
Nurse	50
Rent of medical home	75
Building new home (conditional)	1,000
Itinerating	60
Miss Tang's salary	400
Kindergarten building and land (conditional)	500
Printing Minutes	10
Total	$2,407

FOOCHOW.

Foochow, Boarding School, eight scholarships	$160
Woman's Training School, two scholarships	40

One orphan	30
Three medical students	100
Kucheng, Miss Lorenz's salary.	600
Two Bible-women	50
Boarding School scholarships.	640
Two deaf and dumb pupils..	50
Day schools	100
Repairs	50
Total	$1,820

HING HUA.

Sieng Iu, Miss Nicolaisen's salary	$600
Hospital beds, twenty-four ..	480
Isabel Hart Girls' School....	240
Hing Hua, Hamilton Girls' School	140
Messenger and freight	10
Total	$1,470

WEST CHINA.

Chung King, Hospital work, bedding and gowns	$40
Two helpers for nurses	40
Three charity beds	60
Chentu, Four scholarships	80
Tsi Cheo, Miss Brethorst's salary	650
Bible-woman	40
Day School	75
Total	$985

BULGARIA.

Loftcha, Scholarship	$45
Total	$45

SOUTH AMERICA.

Buenos Ayres, Pupil teacher....	$250
Rosario, Fuel and lights	25
Total	$275

MEXICO.

Mexico City, Children's thank-offering	$30
Total	$30

SUMMARY.

North India	$1,059
Northwest India	1,338
Bombay	985
Central Provinces	120
South India	190
Bengal	1,025
Burma	960
Malaysia	6,701
Philippines	1,087
West China	985
Central China	2,407
Foochow	1,820

Hing Hua	1,470
Japan	2,950
South Japan	36
Korea	284
Bulgaria	45
South America	275
Mexico	30
Contingencies	233
Total for Minneapolis Branch	$24,000
Of which amount the following sum is conditional	$1,900

TOPEKA BRANCH.

NORTH INDIA.

Pithoragarh, Scholarships	$100
Bible-woman	25
Salary of doctor to be sent.	600
Medicines	100
Conveyances	50
Hospital helpers	100
Dwarahat, The new home	40
Pauri, Scholarships	400
Bible-woman	50
Budaon, Scholarships	285
Lucknow, Miss Widney	600
Bible-woman	100
Rae Bareillie, Bible-woman...	250
Ite, Bible-woman	68
Shahjahanpur, Scholarships	150
New roof	75
Bareilly, Wall around property	40
	$3,033

NORTHWEST INDIA.

Ajmere, Scholarships	$1,020
Miss Nelson	600
Bible-woman	96
Conveyance	100
Teacher	40
Bible-women	400
Phalera, Scholarships	945
Tilonia, Dispensary	60
Meerut, Miss Livermore	600
Miss Nelson	600
Miss Winslow	300
Scholarships	1,095
Bible-women	810
Muttra, Miss McKnight	300
Scholarships in boarding school	270
Scholarships in training-school	225
	35
	$7,496

SOUTH INDIA.

Bangalore, Property and rent...	$4,000
Day School	125
Bible-women	270
Miss Montgomery	600
Miss Holland	600
Kolar, Scholarships	240
Assistant	60
Bible-woman	25
Bidar, Day School	60
Bible-women	180
Conveyance	40

Belgaum, Bible-women 150
Canarese Girls' School 60
Raichur, Bible-women 100
Gulbarga, Bible-women 50
Bible-woman 25

$6,585

CENTRAL PROVINCES.

Basim, Scholarships $200
Sironcha, Mrs. Turner 600
Assistant 240
Pundit 40
Bible-women 185
Conveyance 75
Delia Fuller memorial 500
Scholarships 140
Raipur, Bible-women 80
Scholarships 120
Mrs. Gilder's itinerating 50

$2,230

BOMBAY.

Baroda, Scholarships $240
Mrs. Parker's assistant 60
Nadiad, Miss Morgan 400
Assistant 220
Pundit 40
Itinerating 150
Godhra, Scholarships 800
Poona, Debt 435

$2,345

BENGAL.

Asansol, Scholarships $270
Bible-woman, ''Rachel'' 40
Calcutta, Girls' High School ... 300
''Grengli'' 15
Hindustani work 244
Bengali work 315
Beg Began 328
Pakur, Miss Swan 400
Scholarships 80
Bible-woman 40
Rampore Hat Bible-woman... 40
Sanlali Bible-women 80
Debt 450

$2,602

BURMA.

Rangoon, Scholarships $200
Miss James 600
Land lease 100

$900

MALAYSIA.

Penang, Matron $180
Taxes and increase 40
Debt on Charlotte Winchell
Home 18

$238

PHILIPPINES.

Manila, Scholarships $280
Bible-women 225
Cook 67
Furniture 50
Miss Driesbach 750

$1,372

NORTH CHINA.

Tientsin, Dr. Stevenson $650
Medical work 200
Scholarships 180

$1,030

CENTRAL CHINA.

Chin Kiang, Scholarships....... **$240**
Nanking, One girl 25
Bible-women 135
Itinerating 60
Kiu Kiang, Scholarships....... 300
Nanchang, Furnishing new home 200
Microscope (conditionally)... 100

$1,060

WEST CHINA.

Chungking, Miss Borg, out-going
and salary $900
One hospital bed 20

$920

FOOCHOW.

Scholarships $120
Kude, Bible-woman 25
Kucheng, Scholarships 400
Bible-women 200
Bible-woman (Mrs. Newman). 25
South Iong Bing, Bible-women. 100

$870

HING HUA.

Miss Varney $600
Scholarships 660
Sieng Iu, Scholarships 40
Hospital beds 240

$1,540

JAPAN.

Sappora, Miss Imhof $700
Income tax 30
Assistant 90
City work 10
Sunday-school 15
Oataru, Bible-woman 90
Hakodate, Scholarships 240
Sunday-school 25
Two pupil assistants 120
Tokyo, Scholarships 200
Miss Shibati 300
Penmanship 80
Yokohama, Bible-women 80
Nagoya, Miss Watson 700
Income tax 80
Supplies 60
Scholarship 40
Girls' School building....... 1,500

$4,310

SOUTH JAPAN.

$55

$4,365

SOUTH AMERICA.

Rosario, Miss Swaney	$750
Scholarships	400
Assistants	240
Matron	450
Repairs and taxes	200
Interest	500
	180
Furniture	80
Supplies	50
Miss O. Swaney	250
Peru, Lima, Rent	100

$3,200

KOREA.

Scholarships	$110

MEXICO.

Scholarship	$40

AFRICA.

Old Umtali, Scholarships	$60

SUMMARY.

North India	$3,033
Northwest India	7,496
South India	6,585
Bombay	2,345
Central Provinces	2,230
Bengal	2,602
Burma	900
Malaysia	238
Philippines	1,372
North China	1,030
Central China	1,060
West China	920
Foochow	870
Hing Hua	1,540
Korea	110
Japan	4,310
South Japan	55
Mexico	40
South America	3,200
Africa	60

$39,996

Contingent	1,964

Total for Topeka Branch, $41,960

PACIFIC BRANCH.

NORTH INDIA.

Bhabar, Bible-women	$120
Dwarahat, Scholars	80
Home	25
Pithoragarh, Scholars	200
Bible-women	100
Bhot, Dispensary	350
Repairs on Darchula bungalow	50
Bareilly, Miss Easton's salary	600
Scholars	225
Wall around hospital	30
Shahjahanpur, Scholars	120
Roof	55
Pauri, Scholars	160
Moradabad, Scholars	150
Bible-women	75

Budaon, Land for new buildings	700
Scholars	180
Bijnour, Scholars	135
Hardoi, Scholars	330
Mrs. Parker's itinerating	30
Lucknow, Inspectress	60
Sitapur, Scholars	150
Barabanki, Bible-women	50
Gonda, Assistant	200
Scholars	180

$4,355

KOREA.

Seoul, Training School, Miss Morrison	$250
Scholars	70
Day School	50
Chemulpo, Bible-women	100
Pyeng Yang, Five shares in support of students	50

$520

NORTHWEST INDIA.

Ajmere, Scholars	$975
First assistant	240
Second assistant	220
Water supply and taxes	40
Bible-women and itinerating	200
Phalera, Medical assistant	100
Medical itinerating	25
Medicines	50
Scholars	1,350
Matron	200
Widows	150
Bible-women	145
Tilonia, Sanitarium	45
Cawnpore, Scholars	540
(City) Bible-women	150
Meerut, Scholars	75
Bible-women and conveyance	135
Agra, Miss Holman's salary	600
Aligarh, Scholars	60
Muttra, Training scholars	40
Lahore, Bible-women	100
Roorku, Bible-women	200

$5,640

FOOCHOW.

Miss Elsie Site's salary	$600
Foochow, Orphans	120
Land and wall for college	500
Mingchiang, Scholars	260
Kucheng, Scholar	20
Bible-women	50
Day schools	120
Kude, Bible-women	145
South Iong Bing, Bible-women	150
Ngu Cheng, Scholars	100
Haitang, Scholars	80
Bible-women	100
Medical work	25
Building	500

$2,770

NORTH CHINA.

Miss Baugh's salary	$550
Peking, Scholars	60
Chang-li, Scholars	60

$670

HING HUA.

Hing Hua, Scholars	$120
Sieng Iu, Scholars	200
Hospital beds	40
Nurses	50
Repairs on Home	25
	$435

CENTRAL CHINA.

Dr. Taft's salary and home passage	$900
Chin Kiang, Hospital nurse	50
Hospital bed	40
Medicines	100
Scholars	170
Kiu Kiang, Scholars..........	120
Hospital Bible-woman	50
	$1,430

SOUTH INDIA.

Kolar, Scholars	$100
Day School	50
Hyderabad, Scholars	60
Madras, Scholars	140
Raichur, Bible-women	150
Belgaum, Bible-women and conveyance	75
	$575

BOMBAY.

Baroda, Scholars	$200
Godhra, Scholars	200
	$400

BURMA.

Rangoon, Charlotte O'Neal Hall	$3,000
Burmese School	200
Thandaung, Scholars	80
	$3,280

PHILIPPINES.

Manila, Training scholars......	$120
Bible-woman	75
Miss Decker's salary	750
Sea wall for hospital	500
Land lease	100
Fuel and light	50
Lingayen, Miss Parker's passage and salary	900
Furniture	50
Horse	75
Horse feed	25
	$2,645

NORWAY.

Christiana, Mrs. Newman's Bible-woman	$50
	$50

JAPAN.

Miss Russell's salary..........	$700
Tokyo, Bible-women	80
Nagoya, Bible-woman	90

Taxes	50
Hakodate, Buildings	500
Hirosaki, Sunday-schools	30
Tokiwa and other publications..	25
	$1,475

SOUTH JAPAN.

Nagasaki, Scholars	$80
Bible-woman	60
	$140

MEXICO.

Pachuca, Scholars	$100
Mexico, Children's offering for Industrial School	50
	$150

SOUTH AMERICA.

Montevideo, Building	$300
Scholars	100
Rosario, School and Home.....	1,000
	$1,400

AFRICA.

Miss Collins' salary	$500
Miss Drummer's salary	500
Quessua, Scholars	280
Furniture for new home	50
	$1,330

WEST CHINA.

Chentu, Scholars	$175
Woman's School	50
Tsi-cheo, Woman's scholarships.	50
	$275

BENGAL.

Asansol, Scholars	$100
Widows	100
Pakur, Scholars	400
Widows	100
Building and repairs	255
Santali Day School..........	25
Calcutta, Widows	45
Bible-woman	40
Girls' School	500
	$1,565

MALAYSIA.

Penang, C. S. Winchell Home..	$35
	$35

CENTRAL PROVINCES.

Kampti, Mrs. Butterfield salary.	$260
Bible-women	170
Day schools	190
Raipur, Bible-women	65
Nagpur, Bible-women	100
Mrs. Musser's itinerating....	25
New tonga	50
	$860

SUMMARY.

North India	$4,355
Northwest India	5,640
South India ....:	575
Central Provinces	860
Bombay ....-......	400
Bengal	1,565
Burma	3,280
Malaysia	35
Philippines	2,645
North China................,.....	670
Central China	1,430
West China	275
Foochow	2,770
Hing Hua	435
Korea	520
Japan	1,475
South Japan	140
Mexico	150
South America	1,400
Africa	1,330
Norway	50
	$30,000
Contingent	1,000
Day School Building, Wuhu China (conditional)	600

Total for Pacific Branch. $31,600

COLUMBIA RIVER BRANCH.

NORTH INDIA.

Dwarahat, Scholarships	$40
Pithoragarh, Scholarships	60
Lohagat, Bible-woman (cond.)..	80
Bareilly, Scholarships	75
Wall	12
Shahjahanpur, Scholarships	120
Roof	24
Budaon, Scholarships	105
Lucknow, Mrs. Ward	160
Rae Bareilli, Bible-woman...	25
Gonda, Scholarships	90
	$791

NORTHWEST INDIA.

Meerut, Scholarships	$600
Aligarh, Scholarships	180
Muttra, Scholarships	90
	$870

SOUTH INDIA.

Vikarabad, Bible-woman	$25
	$25

CENTRAL PROVINCES.

Jabalpur, Scholarships	$120
	$120

BOMBAY.

Baroda, Scholarships	$200
Miss Austin	600
Assistant and pundit	265
Itinerating	180

Nadiad, Miss Holmes	500
Assistant and pundit........	240
Itinerating	100
Rent	140
Taxes, insurance, etc........	135
Interest	50
Mary E. Whitney Home.....	1,500
Gujarati, Evangelistic work....	2,600
Godhra, Scholarships	240
Telegaon, Scholarships	100
Teacher, Bhimabai	60
	$6,910

BENGAL.

Pakur, Scholarships	$40
	$40

MALAYSIA.

Malacca, Bible Training School.	$54
Singapore, Scholarships	100
Teacher, Chinachie	72
Penang, Miss Lilly...........	600
Winchell Home	6
	$832

NORTH CHINA.

Peking, Scholarship	$30
	$30

CENTRAL CHINA.

Kiukiang, Hospital beds (cond.)	$125
	$125

FOOCHOW.

Foochow, Bible training	$20
Bible-woman	25
Boarding School, scholarships.	40
Miss Parkinson, home salary.	350
Seminary scholarships	100
Mingchiang, Scholarships	160
Kucheng, Scholarships	100
Ngu Cheng, Bible-woman	25
Haitang, Romanized class......	80
Boarding School scholarships.	200
	$1,100

HING HUA.

Sieng Iu, Bible-women........	$150
Scholarships	60
Hospital beds	40
	$250

CENTRAL JAPAN.

Yokohama, Bible training	$80
Literary work	25
Nagoya, Building	100
Tokyo, Industrial School	120
Teacher wood carving	40
	$365

NORTH JAPAN.

Hakodate, Building	$50
Scholarships	80
Hirosaki, Prize scholarship	40
Kindergarten teacher	60
	$230

PHILIPPINES.

Tarlac, Miss Dudley	$625
	$625

SUMMARY.

North India	$791
Northwest India	870
South India	25
Central Provinces	120
Bombay	6,910
Bengal	40
Malaysia	832
North China	30
Central China	125
Foochow	1,100
Hing Hua	250
North Japan	230
Central Japan	365
Philippines	625
Mexico	10
Contingent	677

Total for Columbia River, $13,000

SUMMARY OF APPROPRIATIONS FOR 1907-1908.

CONFERENCES.	NEW ENGLAND	NEW YORK	PHILADELPHIA	BALTIMORE	CINCINNATI	NORTH-WESTERN	DES MOINES	MINNE-APOLIS	TOPEKA	PACIFIC	COLUMBIA RIVER	TOTALS
INDIA: North India	$8,864	$12,643	$5,151	$1,444	$13,100	$15,245	$2,065	$1,059	$3,083	$4,355	$791	$67,750
Northwest India	1,885	3,690	2,060	208	3,720	12,560	5,823	1,338	7,496	5,640	870	45,290
South India	1,620	5,278	2,040	3,983	2,504	5,620	12,308	190	6,585	575	25	40,728
Bombay	1,700	7,517	6,205	549	1,440	7,445	1,695	985	2,345	500	6,910	37,291
Central Provinces	2,205	290	342	2,301	1,660		10,469	120	2,230	880	120	20,597
Bengal	960	2,874	75		2,830	10,555	2,062	1,025	2,602	1,565	40	24,578
Burma		80	755		600		3,350	960	900	3,280		9,965
Total	$17,224	$32,372	$16,628	$8,485	$25,294	$52,025	$37,752	$5,677	$25,191	$16,775	$8,756	$246,194
Malaysia	2,055	1,076	830		2,393	3,245	30	6,701	238	35	832	17,485
Philippines	75	75	525	100	960	2,975	880	1,087	1,372	3,145	625	10,994
CHINA: North China	5,690	2,985	1,650	769	2,120	13,205	3,060	2,407	1,080	670	30	31,089
Central China	220	6,790	1,150	490		12,260	3,170	985	1,000	1,430	125	28,602
West China	1,685				1,250	2,610	4,960	1,820	920	275		12,695
Foochow	1,555	7,482	2,015	3,285	3,520	9,420	7,480	1,470	870	2,170	1,100	40,567
Hing Hua	1,810	150		880	6,400	4,385	200		1,540	435	250	16,500
Total	10,390	16,807	4,815	4,874	13,290	41,860	18,820	6,682	5,420	4,980	1,505	129,443
Korea	1,570	9,005	2,295	1,645	6,100	1,670		284	110	520		23,169
Japan				310	4,255	11,985		2,950	4,810	1,475	230	25,285
North Japan	915	3,820	2,955				1,975					9,895
South Japan	352	4,820	515	301	9,815	3,245		88	55	140	365	19,279
Central Japan	2,580	3,335	5,090	1,965			3,000					16,385
Total	$3,847	$11,975	$8,560	$2,576	$14,070	$15,230	$4,975	$2,986	$4,365	$1,616	$595	$70,794
Mo.	2,647	3,895	5,766	125	4,390	8,675	1,500	30	40	150	10	27,168
South America	2,610	4,895	905			8,490	300	275	8,200	1,400		22,005
Bulgaria	345	560	230			2,845		45				4,085
Italy	250	950	325	130	245	5,075	200					7,195
Africa	40	650	88		645	255	80		60	1,330		3,098
Switzerland						150						150
North Germany						125						125
Norway										50		50
Contingent	2,000	3,000	2,500	200	3,785	3,140	53	233	1,964	1,000	677	15,027
Conditional			2,000							600		6,585
Thank Offering		9,800	15,000		4,020							24,800
Special Appropriations												4,020
Grand Total	$42,978	$95,000	$60,382	$18,135	$75,212	$145,000	$65,015	$24,000	$41,960	$31,600	$18,000	$612,282

REAL ESTATE

Belonging to The Woman's Foreign Missionary Society
of the Methodist Episcopal Church.

NORTH INDIA.

Almorah, Epworth Sanitarium..	$4,000
Bareilly, Hospital	15,000
Bareilly Orphanage	11,000
Bhot, at Dharchula, Flora Deaconess' Home	1,900
Chandra, Deaconess' Home	1,100
Bijnour, Boarding School	3,000
Budaon, ...	5,650
Gonda, ...	2,500
Hardoi, Boarding Home	3,000
Lucknow, Isabella Thornburn College and High School....	53,334
Moradabad	9,500
Naini Tal, Boarding-school.....	30,000
Wellesley Hospital	1,000
Pauri, Boarding School and Orphanage	11,000
Pithoragarh, Boarding School and Woman's Home.......	6,441
Shajahanpur, Bidwell Memorial School and Bungalow	7,000
Sitapur, Boarding School......	8,801
Total	**$174,226**

NORTHWEST INDIA.

Agra, Medical Home	$2,720
Ajmere, Boarding School and Marks Hall	13,335
Aligarh, Louisa Soule's Orphanage	12,528
Brindaban, Mabel Calder Home and Dispensary	4,600
Cawnpore, Hudson Hall and English School	23,300
Meerut, Howard Plested Memorial School	10,860
Muttra, Blackstone Institute...	16,800
Phalera, Orphanage and Industrial School	7,600
Total	**$91,743**

SOUTH INDIA.

Haiderabad, Stanley Home	$10,000
Zenana Home	6,000
Kolar, Wm. Gamble Deaconess Home	5,000
Orphanage and Darby Hall..	5,000
Widows' Home	2,103
Madras, Harriet Bond Skidmore School, Baltimore Memorial Home and Northwestern Memorial Home	33,333

Raipur, ...	500
Sironcha, Mary J. Clark Memorial	6,800
Vikarabad	1,000
Total	**$69,736**

BOMBAY.

Baroda, Orphanage	$22,000
Bombay, Boarding School and Home	25,000
Stevens Hall	16,666
Khandwa, ...	500
Jabalpur, Orphanage and Boarding School	12,000
Deaconess Home	5,000
Total	**$81,166**

BENGAL.

Asansol, Widows' Home	$1,500
Evangelistic Home	1,000
Darjeeling, Queen's Hill School (Crandon Hall, The Repose, Almira Hall and Pierce Building)	33,000
Muzaffurpur, Dispensary	3,516
Total	**$39,016**

BURMA.

Rangoon, High School.	$40,000
Charlotte O'Neal Institute...	30,000
E. Rangoon, Burmese Girls' School	600
Pegu, Mission	150
Total	**$70,750**

MALAYSIA.

Kuala Lumpur, School	$15,000
Penang, ...	7,000
Singapore, Mary C. Nind Home.	25,000
Singapore School	7,500
Taiping, School	10,000
Total	**$64,500**

NORTH CHINA.

Peking, ...	$19,000
Tientsin, Isabel Fisher Hospital	19,000
Tsun Hua	8,000
	$46,000

CENTRAL CHINA.

Nan Chang, Baldwin Memorial	$10,000
Dispensary and Home	8,000
Chin Kiang, Home, School, Hospital	13,916
Letitia Mason Quine Memorial	5,000
Dispensary at West Gate	1,230
Kiu Kiang, Elizabeth S. Danforth Hospital	7,850
The Home	3,500
Boarding School	2,500
Woman's Bible Training School	2,500
Kungling Day School	250
Rulison Fish Memorial School	8,000
Nan King, The Adeline Smith Home	5,500
High School	8,000
Amilla Lake School	1,638
Wuhu, Home	1,000
Total	$78,884

WEST CHINA.

Chung King, Flora Blackstone Deaconess Home	$6,000
Holt Country Boarding School	1,100
Wm. A. Gamble Hospital	6,700
Bungalow, Rest Cottage	1,500
Chang Li Hospital	1,250
Total	$16,550

FOOCHOW.

Foochow, Boarding School and Residence	$14,000
Woman's School and Residence	4,500
Liang-au Hospital and Woolston Memorial Hospital and Residence	11,100
Mary E. Crook Memorial Orphanage	3,100
Hok Chiang, School	4,500
Ku Cheng, School	3,950
Woman's Training-school	2,250
School compound	722
Total	$44,122

HING HUA.

Hing Hua, Juliet Turner Memorial School	$3,300
Hamilton Boarding-school	8,500
Packard Home	5,500
Bible-women's School	1,500
Anton	513
Sieng Iu, Isabel Hart Memorial School	5,400
Margaret E. Nast Hospital	10,000
German Memorial Home	2,000
Tek-Hoe, Woman's School	4,281
Total	$40,994

KOREA.

Seoul, Home and School	$13,000
Dispensary	600
East Gate, Scranton Home	2,000
East Gate Dispensary	300
East Gate Baldwin Chapel	250
Pyeng-Yang, Home, Hospital, and Dispensary	1,500
Total	$17,650

NORTH JAPAN.

Hakodate, School and Home	$13,500
Hirosaki, Home	1,000
Sappora	1,400
Total	$15,900

CENTRAL JAPAN.

Nagoya	$10,000
Sendai, Ladies' Home and Industrial School	7,495
Tokyo, Industrial School	3,000
Aoyama	20,000
Tsukiji	8,500
Asakusa Day School	500
Yokohama, Maud E. Simons Memorial	4,000
Higgins Memorial Home and Training-school	12,500
Yamabukicho School	1,200
Kanagawa, kindergarten	50
Don Tarbox School	200
Total	$67,445

SOUTH JAPAN.

Fukuoka	$15,000
Koga, Orphanage	5,000
Nagasaki, Home and School	50,000
Total	$70,000

MEXICO

Guanajuato, School	$10,000
Mexico City, Orphanage	50,000
Miraflores, School	1,000
Pachuca, School	20,000
Puebla, Normal Institute	25,000
Total	$106,000

SOUTH AMERICA.

Montevideo, School and Home	$22,700
Rosario, Home	9,300
Total	$32,000

BULGARIA.

Lovetch, School and Home	$6,500

ITALY.

Rome, Crandon Hall	$75,000
Home	20,000
Total	$95,000

AFRICA.

Hartzell Villa	$6,250

UNITED STATES,

Herkimer, N. Y., Folts Mission
   Institute $50,000
Endowment 70,000
Permanent fund 45,000

    Total $124,500

SUMMARY.

North India Conference.......$174,226
Northwest India 91,743
South India 69,736
Bombay 81,166
Bengal 39,016
Burma 70,750
Malaysia 64,500
North China 46,000
Central China 78,884

West China 16,550
Foochow 44,122
Hing Hua 40,994
Korea 17,650
North Japan 15,900
Central Japan 67,445
South Japan 70,000
Mexico 106,000
South America 32,000
Bulgaria 6,500
Italy 95,000
Africa 6,250
United States 124,500

    Total $1,358,932

MRS. WM. B. DAVIS,
MRS. CYRUS D. FOSS,
Committee on Titles of Real Estate.

QUESTIONS FOR MISSIONARY APPLICANTS.

1. Full name.
2. Residence.
3. Place and date of birth.
4. Have you an experimental knowledge of salvation through the atonement of Jesus Christ. our Lord? Answer this question somewhat in detail.
5. Are you a member of the Methodist Episcopal Church and a regular attendant upon its services, and are you fully in accord with its doctrines as set forth in Part 1, Division 1, of the Discipline?
6. Have you had special systematic study of the Scriptures?
7. Have you an earnest desire to win souls to Christ, and how has this desire been manifest in the past?
8. Do you trust that you are inwardly moved by the Holy Ghost to take upon you the work of a foreign missionary?
9. How long have you entertained this conviction?
10. Do you desire and intend to make this your life work, and are you willing to labor in any field?
11. To what extent are you acquainted with the work of the Woman's Foreign Missionary Society?
12. Have you any views which would prevent your cordial co-operation with the missionaries of the Methodist Episcopal Church?
13. Would you be willing to give up any personal habit which might grieve your fellow missionaries and lessen the influence of your example over the native Christians?
14. Are you a total abstainer from all forms of alcoholic beverages and from opium, cocaine, and other narcotics?
15. What is the condition of your health? (Answer question in Form II and procure testimony of a competent physician according to Form III.)
16. Outline the character and extent of your education. Name the institutions in which you were educated, the course or courses pursued, and date of graduation.
17. What languages other than English have you studied, and with what facility do you acquire them?
18. Have you a knowledge of music, vocal or instrumental?
19. Have you had business training, and in what line?
20. What positions have you held in business or professional life?
21. Executive ability. Provide testimonials relative to your success in teaching and in the management of financial matters.
22. Have you been married? If so, is your husband living?
23. Are you engaged to be married?
24. Are you liable for debt?
25. Is any one dependent upon you for support?
26. Gives names and addresses of at least ten persons, including pastors, instructors, and others who are able to give information relative to your Christian usefulness, your adaptability to people and circumstances, and your general fitness for the work.
27. A photograph should accompany your application.
28. Have you read the rules applying to missionaries, and do you promise to abide by them?

Signed....................................

Date................................

DIRECTORY OF MISSIONARIES.

APPOINT-MENT.	MISSIONARY.	FOREIGN STATIONS.	BRANCH.	HOME ADDRESS.
1872	Hoag, Lucy M. D.,	Kin Kiang, nd,	New York,	Ann, Mh.
1872	Howe, Gertrude,	Nan Chang, Ida,	Mn,	Lansing, Mich.
1878	*Easton, S. A.,	Nini Tal, India.	Self-supporting,	Washington, D. C.
1878	*Spencer, Ma A.,	Tokyo, Japan,	Ha,	Germantown, Pa.
1878-80	Swaney, Mry F.,	? Mo, Rosario, S. A.,	Topeka,	ta, Kan.
1879	* Gar, Jean M.,	Kagoshima, Japan,	New York,	Bellewood, Pa.
1879	Russell, Elizabeth,	Nagasaki, Japan,	Cincinnati,	Delaware, O.
1879	Budden, Annie,	Pithoragarh, India,	New York,	Almora, Hia.
1881	*Gallimore, Ana,	Agh, India.	Baltimore,	Bellevue, Ky.
1881	Hampton, Mary S.,	Kd, Japan.	New Yk,	lan, Mich.
1881	*Knowles, Emma L.,	Darjeeling, India,	New England,	Tilton, N. H.
1881	*Van Petten, Ms. Gine,	Yokohama, Japan,	td,	Neponset, Ill.
1882	tan, Ana P.,	Yokohama, Japan,	New York,	Cazenovia, N. Y.
1884	erll, Mrs. rtfite M.,	etg, China,	New York,	Etna Ms, Cal.
1883	Watson, Rebecca J.,	Nagoya, Japan,	Topeka,	Lincoln, Neb.
1884	English, Fannie M,	Shahjahanpur, India,	New York,	Senaca Falls, N. Y.
1884	*Harvey, Emily L.,	Raipur, ? Ha,	New England,	St. Johnsbury, Vt.
1884	Hewett, Ma J.,	Sendai, Japan,	tdhia,	Gd, Mich.
1884	Jell, afe I.,	Foochow, Ha,	Cincinnati,	ojo, Ill.
1884	Le Hy, Eleanor,	Buenos Ayres, S. A.,	New York,	Smit, N. J.
1884	Reed, Mary,	Chandag Heights, India,	Cincinnati,	ds, O.
1885	Gloss, Anna D., M. D.,	kg China,	Northwestern,	lan, Ill.
1885	Kyle, Ha J,	Pauri, India,	tdhia,	tMt Pant, Pa.
1885	Scranton, Ms. M. F.,	Seoul, Korea,	New York,	East Hartford, Conn.
1885	ih, Lida B.,	Kagoshima, Japan.	New Yk,	Binghamton, N. Y.
1885	Wisner, Julia E.,	Darjeeling, India,	Cincinnati,	Berea, O.
1886	Ayres, Harriett L.,	? Mo City, ? Mo,	Cincinnati,	Hillsboro, O.

* Home on leave.

DIRECTORY OF MISSIONARIES.—Continued.

APPOINTMENT.	MISSIONARY.	FOREIGN STATIONS.	BRANCH.	HOME ADDRESS.
1886	Hewett, Lizzie,	Montevideo, S. A.,	Northwestern,	Gilead, Mich.
1886	Lawson, Anna E.,	Ajmere, India,	Des Moines,	Ottumwa, Ia.
1887	Bing, Anna V.,	Sappora, Japan,	Cincinnati,	Painesville, O.
1887	Blackmore, Sophia,	Singapore, Sts. S.,	Minneapolis,	Sydney, Australia.
1887	Carleton, Mary E., M. D.,	Ming Chiang, China,	New York,	Elizabeth, N. J.
1887	Hartford, Mabel C.,	Yen-ping, China,	New England,	Dover, N. H.
1887	*Shaw, Ella C.,	Nanking, China,	Northwestern,	Moore's Hill, Ind.
1888	Terry, Edna G., M. D.,	Ch'ang Li, China,	New England,	Mt. Vernon, N. Y.
1888–1907	Allen, Belle J., M. D.,	Baroda, India,	New England,	Bellefontaine, O.
1888	Blair, Kate A.,	Tamluk, India,	Cincinnati,	Painesville, O.
1888	Bonafield, Julia,	Foochow, China,	Cincinnati,	Morgantown W. Va.
1888	Dickerson, Augusta,	Hakodate, Japan,	Philadelphia,	Philadelphia, Pa.
1888	*Files, Estelle M.,	Poona, India,	New York,	Brockport, N. Y.
1888	*Maxey, Elizabeth,	Calcutta, India,	New York,	Urbana, O.
1888	Peters, Sarah,	Nanking, China,	Northwestern,	Princeville, Ill.
1888	Sheldon, Martha A., M. D.,	Bhot, India,	Self-supporting,	Lordsburg, Cal.
1888	Sullivan, Lucy,	Pithoragarh, India,	Self-supporting,	Dayton, O.
1889	*Bender, Elizabeth R.,	Tokyo, Japan,	Baltimore,	Chambersburg, Pa.
1889	Blackstock, Ella,	Aoyama, Japan,	Minneapolis,	Lafayette, Ind.
1889	Griffiths, Mary Bell,	Hirosaki, Japan,	Des Moines,	Omaha, Neb.
1889	Imhof, Louise,	Sappora, Japan,	Topeka,	Lincoln, Neb.
1889	Phelps, Frances E.,	Sendai, Japan,	Des Moines,	Mitchell, S. D.
1889	*Scott, Frances,	Gonda, India,	Cincinnati,	Cincinnati, O.
1889	Sellers, Rue E.,	Naini Tal, India,	Self-supporting,	New Matamoras, O.
1889	Trimble, Lydia A.,	Ngu-cheng, China,	Des Moines,	Sioux City, Ia.
1889	*Wilson, Frances O.,	Tientsin, China,	Des Moines,	Corning, Ia.
1889	Wood, Elsie,	Lima, Peru, S. A.,	New York,	Greencastle, Ind.
1890	Baucus, Georgiana,	Yokohama, Japan,	Self-supporting,	Binghamton, N. Y.
1890	*Benn, Rachel R., M. D.,	T'ai An Fu, Shantung, Ch.	Philadelphia	Hydstown, Pa.
1890	Hall, Mrs. R. Sherwood, M. D.	Pyeng Yang, Korea	New York	Liberty, N. Y.

DIRECTORY OF MISSIONARIES.—Continued.

	MISSIONARY.	FOREIGN STATIONS.	BRANCH.	HOME ADDRESS.
90	*Limberger, ... R.,	... Mo.,	...	... R.
1890	Lyon, Ella M., M. D.,	...	...	..., Mh.
1890	..., ... A.,	Thandaung, ...	Des ...	..., ...
1890	..., ... H.,	...	...	... e, O.
90	*Stevenson, Ia M., M. D.,	...	...	... n, R.
91	..., Effie,	Guanajuato, Mexico,	...	Monroe, Wis.
1891	..., ...,	..., ...,	...	... a, Pa.
1891	..., ... L.,	Nan Chang, China,	Des ...	New ...
1891	..., ... M.,	Chin Kiang, China,	...	Philad ...
1892	..., ... B.,	..., Bulgaria,	...	Jacksonville, I.
1892	..., My M., M. D.,	..., ...	... rn,	... Rapids, Mich.
1892	..., Ella E.,	Ch'ang, Li, ...	New ...	... n, M
1892	..., ...,	..., ...	...	... e, O.
1892	Lawson, Ada J., ...	..., ...	New York,	Gen Island, N. Y.
1892	..., ... O.,	..., ...	Des Moines,	Roxbury, M
1892	..., ...	..., ...	New ...	Diagonal, ...
1892	..., ...,	..., ...	...	India.
92	..., ...	..., ...	Des ...	... n, ...
92	..., ... G.,	Peking, China,	New Engl ...	Waltham, M
1893	..., Hu E.,	Seoul, Korea,	...	... e, O.
1893	..., ... A.,	Sendai, Japan,	...	Seymour, ...
1893	*Singer, ... E.,	..., ...	...,	... e, Ind.
1893	..., Me E.,	..., ...,	...	
94	..., ...,	Ngu-cheng, China,	N	Chicago, Ill.
1894	..., ... S.,	..., ...	Des ...	Mt. Ayr, Ia.
94	..., Anna R.,	Khandwa, Japan,	Des ...	
1894	..., Hn R.,	Chung Kg, ...	Des ...	... e, ...
94	..., Lda My,	N ... i, Japan,	N	
1894			Cincinnati,	... City, Cal.

DIRECTORY OF MISSIONARIES.—Conti nd.

ENTR.	MISSIONARY.	FOREIGN STATIONS.	M.	HOME ADDRESS.
1894	N, de L.,	Nw, India,	New 1	Im, Ms.
1894	Es, Mary,	Kucheng, C,	Min,	we, Ill.
94	Wilson, Mary E.,	Bareilly,	Win,	d, C, Vt.
1895	Cdr, Cra J.,	1 te, ida,		Paterson, N. J.
1895	tG, Kate O.,	C Ga, India,	New 1	Russell, Id
1895	Evans, Ke A.,	beid, India.		New Yk C.
1895	*Hardie, Eva M.,	Khw, Ia,	Gi,	China.
1895	H, Sg Eng, M. D.,	C,	Ha,	Leesburg, H.
1895	Linam, de,	Foochow, C,	Ha,	l R,
1895	Purdy, Ge M.,	Yen-ping, Ga,	Ha,	ls As, Cal.
1895	Taft, Ge, M. D.,	Ch Kiang, China,		Boston, Ms.
1895	dh, Althea M.,	Boe Cty, China,	New 1 Hrl,	S. Chs als, N. Y.
1895	Vgt, Ira S.,	wl, China,	vn,	Washington, hd.
1895	thn, Zth M.,		Wl,	N, Ill
1896	*Fisher, He F.,	Bg, Cha,	Win,	Danville, Ill.
1896	C, Gertrude,	Nanchung, China,	New England,	C field, Vt.
1896	Kahn, da, M. D.,	Pithoragarh, I,	Mern,	Gi, O.
1896	Ms, Mary,	Kiu Kiang, Ha,	ndi,	ht, Eh.
1896	Mel, Clara E.,		Mern,	New Yk City.
1896	Ns, Eh,	Brindaban, I,		Gs, O.
1896	Se, Mary, M. D.,	Kn Kiang, G,	New York,	
1896	Wn, He,	Cd, S. A.,		Ga.
1897			Cincinnati, Ms,	Junction, N. J.
97	Daniel, N.	Tokyo, Fh,	Des Yk,	Ga, I
1897	Bs, Ma,	Sieng ln, Ga.	Des Ms,	Er, d
1897	Lilly, Ay B.,	ag, Sts. Settlement,	Self-supporting,	M, Wash.
1897	He, Melva A.,	Meerut, Ia,	Ca River,	Smith Center, Kans.
1897	M, Clara,	Penang, Sts. Settlement,	Ms,	He, Mn.

DIRECTORY OF MISSIONARIES.—Continued.

APPOINT-MENT.	MISSIONARY.	FOREIGN STATIONS.	BRANCH.	HOME ADDRESS.
1897	M, A,	Nagasaki, l,	Gi,	Akron, O.
1897	M, My E.,	Nagasaki, l,	Mn,	Jacksonville, Ill.
1897	Wig, M na, Eh A.,	Kda hr, Malaysia,	Gi, gl,	South Mee, Mass.
1898	llingworth, H,	Thandaung, Burma,	New Ha.	Me, O.
1898	Ingram, H,	Aw, l,	l,	Brighton, Eng.
98	Hs y G.,	do, l, Gina,	Self-supporting, de,	Wn, N. Y.
98	Longstreet, Isabella D.,	Ng Chiang,	N Wrn,	By Gy Eh.
98	Gr, la G,	Sitapur, l, G,	New York, Ea,	Ea, N. Y.
98	Varney, h W,	Hing L, G,	Ba,	do, G
1899	Ernsberger, Ea, M D.,	Seoul, Korea,	Gi,	Rice, O.
1899	Gregg, M Eva,	Muttra, da,	Self-supporting, M.	Danville, l
99	Manning, Ella,	Bo, China,	Des Mes,	G
1899	Ml, Florence W.,	Kolar, l,	Des Wk,	Ha.
1899	*Moyer, g,	Tamluk, India,	Mn,	Gl, N. Y.
99	m, Martha L.,	Gg l, China,	Nds,	Ga,
1899	in, Phoebe A.,	Aw, G,	Ga Rer,	Me, Wash.
90	As, an,	Aw, G,	g,	Pig, Pa.
90	s, lla R.,	Kda hr, Malaysia,	Gi,	Ada, O.
90	*Bohannon, l,	na, M,	Mn,	Dellon, Kas.
90	Davis, Dora,	Lovetch, l, ga,	wh,	Kao, Mh.
90	Es, la, Ml M.	l,	N	Ge, l
90	By, My C., Ge T.,	Gg Yang, Korea,	New York,	Be, N. B.
90	Hi,	Seoul, Korea,	Gi,	Mk, O.
90	Kd, Bertha E.,	Agra, l,	ac,	Be Wl Island.
90	Mn, h,	Bo, S. A.,	New England,	Sprague's M, Me.
90	in, ha, E., M D.,	Eg, Ga,	N Wrn,	Gn, Ind.
90	Gs, Eva,	Gn, China,	N vn,	Gn, O.
90	Organ, Clara M.,	Me, Italy, l,	Mn,	Chicago, l
		Ba, l,	New England,	Gi, Mass.

DIRECTORY OF MISSIONARIES.—Continued.

APPOINT-MENT.	MISSIONARY.	FOREIGN STATIONS.	BRANCH.	HOME ADDRESS.
1900	Pak, E dr K., M D.,	Pyeng Mg, Korea,	New York, Ba, Pa,	Seoul, Korea.
90	R y, 1a,	Rangoon, Ba,	Ms, Ms,	Fa, Ga. Ia.
90	* gn, Ren,	A, Ha,	B, Bn,	Ia.
90	* gn, Vi,	A,	Ha,	Ge G, a
90	rMs, Ma Agnes,	A, Ia,	Ma,	ogo, 1
91	B, Be A.,	A, Ga,	Tua	Bloomington, Ill.
91	Gs, Susan,	A, Ga,	N	Ba, Cal.
91	* Gs Agnes M., M. D.,	Chu 1g g, China,	a c, Ms,	Tina, Mo.
91	Gr, G,	Rangoon, Ba,	as Ms,	a, No.
91	* H, M	I a,	as Ms,	as M, a
91	*ell y, Ae,	I a, Iay,	Self- ng,	Shamokin, Pa.
91	Lewis, Ella A.,	Seoul, Korea,	Baltimore,	Ha, Ia.
91	* Ms, Margaret D., M. D.,	Bareilly, Ia,	Ba,	ogo, 1
91	Limburger, Ma R.,	A, Na,	(	Ie, R.
91	Mt, sal,	Tikhoe Cfy, China,	eW, Ba,	Osage City, M.
91	* Mt, Ja A,	M, a, Ca,	N Yk, 1gH,	Gothenberg, N b.
91	*Miller, Ja A, m May,	a, H,	N w Yk,	as, N. Y.
91	* Sa, Ma B,	a, an,	New England,	Eo, Kan.
91	* Ms, Mrs. Susan,	Yokohama, Ha,	a,	Wt, Pa.
1901	Ms, zath J.,	law,	Baltimore, Ba,	Bt, Ia. M.
91	* Ms, Gce M.,	eBd, Ia,	as Ha,	Ge, M.
91	Vs, H,	Mt,	Northwestern, di,	Morgan Park, Ill.
92	Eddy, Mrs. S. M.,	Belgaum,	as Moines, di,	cy, 1
92	Es, Margaret I,	Bombay, Ia,	N di,	ge, 1
92	Ka, C Ethel,	Po a, a,		Berea, O.
92	Montgomery, Urdell,	Seoul, Korea,	b, tn,	ho, O. Ge, Ind.
92		Taipeng, Masia,		Hastings, Neb.
		Bangalore, Ia,		

DIRECTORY OF MISSIONARIES.— Continued.

Appoint.	Missionary	Foreign Stations	Branch	Home Address
92	Pierce, Thirza M.,	Ku Kiang,	New York,	... Il.
92	...	... Hua,	New York,	... N. Y.
92	... n, MK.,	... y, ...		Ia.
92	*Spaulding, ...M.,	... Philippine Islands		Upland, Ind.
92	Swift, ...M.,	...		... ty, Ka.
92	Weaver, Georgiana,	Sendai, ...,	New York,	... Ms.
92	... Bessie,	... Hua, China,	...	Syracuse, N. Y.
93	... H.,	... India,	...	... Mich.
1903	... L.,	Seoul, Korea,		... Isl al
1903	... y,	...,		...
1903	Lee, ...,	Nagoya, ...,	Ms.,	... N. D.
1903	N ...	... w, ...,	...	Braceville, 1
1903	*Parkes, ...,	Penang, ..., The Islands		... Mi.
1903	..., ...,	..., Ila,	... c,	England.
1903	..., Lydia S.,	..., ...	...	... Ia.
1903	Soper, ...,	... o, ... y, ... Mo,	Ms.,	Japan.
1903	..., ...,	... o, ...,		...
1903	..., r A.,	Nagasaki, ...,	New	... N. J.
1903	..., Susan,	...h Cheng, ...,	... ci	... O.
1903	..., Maude S.,	... Ayres, S. A.,	New	Poughkeepsie, N. Y.
9	... M.,	..., ...,	N	...
94	...,	Ngu-	...	Lke ..., Vis.
94	..., J., M. D.,	Sieng ...,	...	Wall ..., Ia.
94	Crane, ... M.,	... China,	...	... Cy.
94	..., ... A.,	... Kiang, ...,	...	... Mo.
94	..., Mae F.,	Haitang, ...,	Pacific,	... Ia.
94	..., Mary	...,		San ... o, Cal.

DIRECTORY OF MISSIONARIES.—Continued.

APPOINT-MENT.	MISSIONARY.	FOREIGN STATIONS.	BRANCH.	HOME ADRESS.
1904				Ill.
1904	Mrs.			Ia.
1904	May L.,		Des	Pa.
1904	Sue L., M. D.	Tai		Germany.
1904	V.,			
1904	Lossing, M.			Kan.
1904				Ia.
1904	Ella E.,	M, India,	New England,	Ill.
1904				Ia.
1904		Mexico,		N. Y.
1904	Saxe, Agnes E... M.,		New York,	Jersey City, N. J.
1904	Strow,			Scandia, Kan.
1904	Swan, M.,			O.
1904	Mary M.,	Hing		Mn.
1904	Ite M.,	Taipeng,	Northwestern,	Ia.
1904	B.,		Cincinnati,	St. Ore.
1905	Ha A.,		Des	
1905	Laura F., da Thoburn			Englewood, Ill.
1905	M.,			Switzerland.
1905				O.
1905	A.,	Nagasaki		O.
1905	Creek,			
1905	F.,		New En	Cal.
1905		P. I.,		Los
1905				O.
1005	M. D.,			Mn.
1905	ine,		Self-supporting,	

DIRECTORY OF MISSIONARIES.—Continued.

APPOINT-MENT.	MISSIONARY.	FOREIGN STATIONS.	BRANCH.	HOME ADDRESS.
1905	Grove, Mrs. Harriet L. R.,	Poona, India,	Northwestern,	Chicago, Ill
1905	Hill, Katherine Byrd,	Lucknow, India,	Phila,	Newport, R. I.
19 50.	Hitchcock, Frances H.,	Chungking, China,	Des Moines,	Ade, Ia.
1905	Holland, Ary J.,	ape, India,	Topeka,	Abilene, Kan.
1905	Hollister, Grace A.,	Mexico City, Mexico,	Cincinnati,	Ea, O.
1905	Holmes, Ada,	Gujarat, India,	Ida Rr,	Ea, O.
19 50.	Hughes, Jennie V.,	Nan Chang, China,	New York,	Manchester, England.
1905	Ketring, My, M. D.,	Chungking, China,	H,	Ocean Grove, N. J.
1905	Logeman, Minnie V.,	Cawnpore, India,	Northwestern,	Ro, O.
1905	Long, Hortense,	Kagoskima, Japan,	New York,	Oa, Ill.
1905	Marker, Jessie B.,	Seoul, Korea,	Cincinnati,	East Syracuse, N. Y.
1905	* eNby, Alta,	Nanchang, China,	Des Ns,	Shipping Port, Pa.
1905	Simester, Mry A.,	Chentu, China,	New Engl nd,	Mt. Hrll, Ia.
1905	Shibati, Suye,	A yamaq Japan,	Topeka,	Boston, Mass.
1905	wSn, Hla,	Pakur, India,	Topeka,	Japan.
19 50.	nfr, Ws, Mid N.,	Sironcha, India,	Topeka,	Scandia, Kan.
1905	Wells, Annie My,	Chunking, China,	Des Moines,	Denton, Texas.
19 60.	Bills, Face Aa,	Muzzaffarpur, India,	Northwestern,	Shenandoah, Ia.
1906	Brethorst, Alice,	Tsicheo, China,	Minneapolis,	Evansville, Ind.
1906	Coffin, Sophia Jordan,	Old Umtali, Africa,	New York,	Lenox, S. D.
1906.	Crouse, Margaret D.,	Baroda, India,	Philadelphia,	Stanley, Alberto, Canada.
1906.	Draper, Frances L., M. D.,	Sieng lu, China,	Northwestern,	Reading, Pa.
19 60.	Drummer, Martha A.,	Sea, Ra,	Pacific,	di, Mh.
1906	Driesbach, Gale Ime,	iMa, P. I.,	Topeka,	Atlanta, Ga.
1906	Easton, Geste,	Bareilly, India,	Fc,	Roper, Kan.
19 60.	Bon, ith,	Kolar, India,	Aa,	Riverside, Cal.
1906.	ith, Elizabeth,	Sironcha, India,	Cincinnati,	Glag, Ill.
1906	As, Emily Ime,	Pyeng Yang, Korea,	New York,	Alliance, O.
1906	Hoffman, Carlotta,	Rl, India,	Northwestern,	Hornellsville, N. J.
1906	Holland, Harriet, A.,	Kolar, India,	N th,	Chicago, Ill.

DIRECTORY OF MISSIONARIES.—Continued.

MENT.	MISSIONARY.	FOREIGN STATIONS.	BRANCH.	HOME ADDRESS.
1906	Honsinger, Welthy B.,	Nanchang, China	New York,	Rome, N. Y.
1906	James, Phoebe,	Rangoon, Burma,	Topeka,	Burma.
1906	Kipp, Julia R.,	Aligarh, India,	N⸺,	1⸺n, Ill.
1906	Knox, Emma M.,	⸺g, China,	Northwestern,	⸺o, Ill.
1906	Marsh, Jessie L.,	Montevideo, S. A.,	Northwestern,	⸺e, Mich.
1906	Nelson, E. Lavinia,	Ajmere, India,	Topeka,	⸺d, Neb.
1906	Nelson, Lena C.,	Meerut, India	Topeka,	⸺d, Neb.
1906	Nolele, Edith,	Mexico,	Minneapolis,	Centerville, S. D.
1906	Parrish, Rebecca, M. D.,	Manila, P. I.,	Northwestern,	Logansport, Ind.
1906	Pugh, Ada,	Malacca,	Minneapolis,	England.
1906	Reynolds, Elsie,	Jabalpur, India,	Des M⸺ines,	Villisca, Ia.
1906	Rank, ⸺ie L.,	Singapore, S. S.,	Minneapolis,	Minneapolis, Minn.
1906	⸺ds, ⸺d,	Vikerabad, India,	Des ⸺Mines,	⸺o, Ia.
1906	Stixrud, Louise,	Dagupan, P. I.,	Minneapolis,	⸺s, Minn.
1906	Strawick, Gertrude,	Ing Chung, China,	Northwestern,	Butler, Pa.
1906	Sprowles, Alberta B.,	Hakodate, Japan,	⸺a,	Frankfort, Pa.
1906	Snavely, Gertrude E.,	Seoul, Korea,	⸺a,	Harrisburg, Pa.
1906	Tang Ilien,	Nanchang, China,	Minneapolis,	China.
1906	Wallace, Lydia Ethel,	Foochow, China,	Baltimore,	⸺th ⸺r, Canada.
1906	Widney, May C.,	Lucknow, India,	Topeka,	Lynden, Kan.
1907	Albertson, Millie,	Seoul, Korea,	Cincinnati,	⸺ths, O.
1907	Baker, Lulu C.,	Hing Hua, China,	Cincinnati,	Pittsburg, Pa.
1907	Baugh, EvelynB.,	North China,	P⸺fic,	Petaluma, Cal.
1907	Betz, Blanche,	Pachuca, Mexico,	⸺ern,	Denver, Col.
1907	⸺y, ⸺ie T.,	Tientsin, China,	Des Moines,	Winslow, Ill.
1907	Borg, Jennie,	Chung King, China,	Topeka,	⸺y, Neb.
1907	Brooks, Jessie,	Singapore,	Minneapolis,	Minneapolis, Minn.

DIRECTORY OF MISSIONARIES.—Continued.

APPOINT-MENT.	MISSIONARY.	FOREIGN STATIONS.	BRANCH.	HOME ADDRESS.
1907	Campbell, Margaret, M. D.,	Peking, China,	Cincinnati,	Troy, O.
1907	Crawford, Mabel L.,	Manila, Philippines,	Des Ms,	Sioux City, Ia.,
1907	Dudley, Ra E.,	Bc, Philippines,	Ha River,	Puyallup, Wash.
1907	Dyer, Ola B.,	Chang hi, China,	New England,	Providence, R. I.
1907	son, Estella,	Phalera, India,	Northwestern,	Flint, Mich.
1907	Hd, Sarah B.,	Pyeng Yang, Korea,	Baltimore,	Oil City, Pa.
1907	Hd, Lua, M. D.,	Foochow, Ha,	Northwestern,	Go, Ill.
1907	Jones, Edna,	Foochow, China,	Baltimore,	Folsom, Cal.
1907	Liers, Josephine,	Khandwa, India,	Des Ms,	Dubuque, Ia.
1907	Manderson, Melissa, M. D.,	North Ha	North ian,	South Bend, Ind.
1907	I Hy, Alice,	Callao, Peru, S. A.,	New York, ian,	Logan, Ia.
1907	Norberg, Eugenia,	Ink, India,	Go,	Go, Ill.
1907	Powell, Alice M.,	Peking, China,	New York,	Washington, Pa.
1907	Robinson, Alvina,	Rangoon, Burma,	Des Ms,	Huneston, Ia.
1907	Russell, Helen M.,	da, Japan,	Fac,	Poultney, Vt.
1907	Simpson, Cora,	Foochow, Ha.	N iari,	Guide Rock, Neb.
1907	Smith, Ha N.,	Big, China,	Northwestern,	I Se, Wh.
1907	Stout, Winifred L.,	Chentu, China,	N iatern,	uHey, S. Dak.
1907	Sutton, Me,	Singapore,	Minneapolis,	Alexandria, Minn.
1907	Tuttle, Ora M.,	Go, Korea,	Cincinnati,	Norwalk, O.

DIRECTORY OF MISSIONARIES.—Continued.

ACCEPTED BUT NOT APPOINTED.

APPOINTMENT.	MISSIONARY.	BRANCH.	HOME ADDRESS.
1904	Cantwell, ...h C.,	Cincinnati,	Delaware, O.
1905	...m, ...ce L.,	New York,	Passaic, N. J.
1907	Dutton, Mrs. M L.,	Cincinnati,	Bellefontaine, O.
1906	Frazey, ...t L.,	Topeka,	Nickerson, Kan.
1907	Gabrielson, Winifred,	T ...a;	Lincoln, Neb.
1907	...r, Minnie,	Topeka,	Baldwin, Kan.
1807	...r, ...a,	Minneap dis,	
1907	Richmond, Mary,	...a,	Toronto, Kan.
1907	Sante, ...n C.,	...a,	West Pittston, Pa.
1907	Search, ...e F.,	...a,	Wilkesbarre, Pa.
1906	Stallwood, Sarah E.,		Hagersville, Ont.
1907	...y, Aletheia M.,	New York,	Wellsville, N. Y.

Entered into Rest.

APPOINTMENT.	MISSIONARY.	FOREIGN STATIONS.	DIED.
1875	Miss ...a A. ...ell,	Peking, ...ia,	My 18, 1878.
1876	Miss L. H. Green, M. D. (Mrs. Cheney),	Bareilly, India,	September 30, 1878.
1878	Miss ...n B. Higgins,	...a, Japan,	July 3, 1879.
1881	Miss Emma Michener,	Monrovia, Africa,	December 11, 1881.
1884	Miss Ella Gilchrist, M. D.,	Kiu ...g, China,	April 23, 1884.
1871	Miss Beulah ...n,	Foochow, ...ia,	...r 24, 1886.
1878	Miss ...ia Guelf,	Montevideo, S. A.,	1886.
1881	Miss ...t Kerr,	...ly, I...ia,	December 11, 1886.

DIRECTORY OF MISSIONARIES.—Continued.

Entered into Rest.

Appointment.	Missionary.	Foreign Stations.	Died.
1880	Miss Fffe Nickerson,	ffi, India,	January 31, 1887.
1878	Miss Harriet Woolston, M. D.,	Moradabad, India,	1879.
1872	Miss Elizabeth M. fffz,	Moradabad, India,	N ', chr 5, 1887.
1883	Miss Emma J. Everding,	Nagasaki, Japan,	January 13, 1892.
1878	Mss M. E. ffn,	Cawnpore, India,	April 22, 1892.
1888	Miss M. E. V. Pardoe,	Tokyo, Japan,	August 31, 1892.
1887	Miss Mary A. Vance (Mrs. Belknap),	Tokyo, Japan,	September 27, 1892.
1880	Ms ffna B. Sears,	Peking, China,	December 4, 1895.
1884	Miss Clara A. Downey,	ffe, India,	January 4, 1896.
1888	Miss ffy E. ffi,	Bombay, India,	June 12, 1897.
1884	Miss Linna M. Schenck,	ffh, Bulgaria,	March 22, 1898.
1881	Miss Phebe ffe,	ffw, India,	April 13, 1898.
1889	Ms Maud E. Simons,	ffia, Japan,	July 29, 1898.
1874	Miss Mary Hastings,		August 15, 1898.
1876	Miss ffe ffi,	Pachuca, ffo,	1899.
1887	Miss Mary A. Hughes (Mrs. Frrisberger),	ffo,	1899.
1900	Miss Martha L. McKibben,	Madras, India,	ffr 12, 190.
1895	Miss ffe Sterling (Mrs. Leuth),	Mo Cffy, Mexico,	ffi, 190.
1898	Mss ffra Zentmire (Mrs. Brewster),	India,	January 8, 191.
1869	Miss Isabella ffi	Angola, Africa,	September 1, 1901.
1886	Miss Delia A. Fuller,	Lucknow, India,	November, 4, 191.
1884	Miss Mary De F. Loyd,	ffha, India,	November, 4, 1902.
1897	Miss ffn Harris, M. D.,	Mo Cffy, Mexico,	May 28, 1902.
1900	Miss Josephine ffson,	Pyeng Yang, Korea,	May 16, 1902.
1902	Mss ffi Sia,	Quessua, Africa,	July 5, 1902.
1903	Miss Ida May Cartwright,	Ngu Cheng, China,	November, 193.
1893	Mrs. ffna C. Davis,	Lucknow, India,	April 9, 194.
1904	Miss ffna Stone,	Nanking, ffa,	May 3, 194.
		Kiu Kiang, China,	ffh ff, 1906.

DIRECTORY OF MISSIONARIES.—Continued.

Entered into Rest.

Appointment.	Missionary.	Foreign Stations.	Died.
1884	Miss Mary C. Robinson,	Chin Kiang, China,	April 20, 1906.
1904	Miss Lois M. Buck,	Moradabad, India,	April 17, 1907.
1903	Miss Mary B. Tuttle, M. D.,	Pithoragarh, India,	June 22, 1907.
1902	Miss Susanna Stumpf,	Jagdalpur, India,	January 26, 1907.
1871	Miss Mary Q. Porter, (Mrs. Gamewell),	Summit, N. J.,	November 27, 1906.

RETIRED AFTER TWENTY-FIVE YEARS' SERVICE.

Missionary.	Foreign Stations.	Home Address.
Woolston, Sarah,	Foochow, China,	Mt. Holly, N. J.

RETIRED AFTER TWENTY-SEVEN YEARS' SERVICE.

Missionary.	Foreign Stations.	Home Address.
Swain, Clara A., M. D.,	India,	Castile, N. Y.

MISSIONARIES

Sent out from America or employed by the Woman's Foreign
Missionary Society since its organization.

m indicates Marriage; *s* Self-Supporting; *r* Retired; *dis*. Dismissed; *d* Deceased.
* Daughters of Missionaries. Name in italics is married name.
Abbreviations, in parenthesis, indicate Branch.

Date of App'm't.	Name and Branch.
1905	Aaronsen, Hilma. (Des M.)
1901	Abbott, Anna Agnes. (N.-W.)
1878 *r*	Abrams. Minnie F. (1898.)
1900 *s*	Adams, Jeanette.
1882 *m*	Akers, L. Stella, M. D. (*Perkins.*) (1885.)
1907	Albertson, Millie. (Cin.)
1908	Alexander, Bessie. (Cin.)
1888–1907	Allen, Belle J. (N. E.)
1894	Allen, Mabel. (Des M.)
1894	Alling, Harriet S. (N.-W.)
1900	Anderson, Luella R. (Cin.)
1882	Atkinson, Anna P. (N. Y.)
1888 *r*	Atkinson, Mary.
1905	Austin, F. Laura. (C. R.)
1886	Ayers, Harriet L. (Cin.)
1907	Baker, Lulu C. (Cin.)
1895 *m*	Barrow, Mrs. M. L., M. D. (*King.*) (1900.)
1904	Bartlett, Carrie M. (Des M.)
1890 *s.*	Baucus, Georgiana.
1907	Baugh, Evelyn B. (Pacif.)
1902 *m*	Beard, Bertha. (*Gasson.*) (1903.)
1900 *m*	Beazell, Laura E. (*Andres.*) (1903.)
1902 *m*	Beck, Edna L., M. D. (*Keisler.*) (1908.)
1889 *r*	Bender, Elizabeth R. (Balt.)
1890 *m*	Bengel, Margaret. (*Jones.*) (1892.)
1890	Benn, Rachel R., M. D. (Phila.)
1901	Bennett, Fannie A. (N.-W.)
1896	Benthein, W. (N.-W.)
1882 *m*	Benton, J. Emma. (*Elmer.*) (1885.)
1904	Betow, Emma J., M. D. (Cin.)
1907	Betz, Blanche. (N.-W.)
1906	Bills, Grace Ida. (N.-W.)
1888	Bing, Anna V. (Cin.)
1888 *r*	Black, Lillian A. (1889.)
1892	Blackburn, Kate B. (N. W.)
1872 *m*	Blackmar, Louisa. (*Gilder.*) (1900.)
1887	Blackmore, Sophia. (Minn.)
1889	Blackstock, Ella. (Minn.)
1905	Blackstock, Isabella Thoburn. (Phila.)
1888	Blair, Kate A. (Cin.)
1897	Bobenhouse, Laura G. (Des M.)
1900	Bohannon, Ida. (N.-W.)
1888	Bonafield, Julia A. (Cin.)
1907	Borg, Jennie. (Top.)
1897 *dis*	Boss, Harriet. (1898)
1888 *m*	Bowen, Mary E. (*Brown.*) (1898.)
1906	Bowman, M. Rebecca. (Top.)
1897 *m*	Bowne, Ida May. (*Manfre.*) (1903.)
1906	Brethorst, Alice. (Minn.)
1907	Brooks, Jessie. (Minn.)
1899 *m*	Brouse, Louise T. (*Cook.*) (1905.)

Date of App'm't.	Name and Branch.
1871 *m*	Brown, Maria. (*Davis.*) (1874.)
1891 *r*	Bryan, Mary E., M. D. (1897.)
1880 *	Budden, Annie. (N. Y.)
1904 *d* *	Buck, Lois M. (Cin.)
1905	Bullis, Edith M. (N.-W.)
1900 *m*	Bumgardner, Lucy E. (*Morton.*) (1903.)
1898 *dis*	Burman, Matilda C. (1903.)
1905 *	Burt, Edith. (N.-W.)
1879 *r*	Bushnell, Kate C, M. D. (1882.)
1894 *m*	Butcher, Annie. (*Hewes.*) (1896.)
1907	Campbell, Margaret, M. D. (Cin.)
1875 *d*	Campbell, Lettia A. (*Coleman.*) (1878.)
1876 *m.*	Carey, Mary F. (*Davis.*) (1880.)
1898 *m*	Carver, Margaret B. (*Ernsberger.*)
1888 *d*	Carroll, Mary E. (1897.)
1887	Carleton, Mary E., M. D. (N. Y.)
1903 *d*	Cartwright, Ida May. (1904.)
1874 *r*	Chapin, Jennie M. (1890.)
1904 *m*	Chisholm, Emma Mae. (*Brown.*) (1906.)
1884 *r*	Christiancy, Mary, M. D. (1891.)
1894 *m*	Christinsen, Christine. (*Ashe.*) (1896.)
1879 *r*	Clemens, Mrs. E. J. (1881.)
1904 *r*	Clippenger, Frances. (1905.)
1900	Cody, Mary. (Minn.) (1904)
1906	Coffin, Sophia J. (N. Y.)
1895	Collier, Clara J. (N. E.)
1901	Collins, Susan. (Pacif.)
1894 *m*	Collins, Ruth H. (*Thoburn.*) (1899.)
1873 *m*	Combs, Lucinda, M. D. (*Strittmater.*) (1878.)
1905 *r*	Cook, Celinda. (1907.)
1905 *r*	Cook, Rosalie. (1907.)
1884 *m*	Corey, Katherine, M. D. (*Ford.*) (1888.)
1905	Crabtree, M. Margaret. (Cin.)
1892 *m*	Craig, Frances. (*Smith.*) (1895.)
1904	Crane, Edith M. (N.-W.)
1907	Crawford, Mabel. (Des M.)
1905	Creek, Bertha. (N.-W.)
1904	Crooks, Grace A. (N.-W.)
1892 *dis*	Crosthwaite, Isabella. (1893.)
1895 *m*	Croucher, Miranda. (*Packard.*) (1903.)
1906	Crouse, Margaret D. (Phila.)
1905	Crowell, Bessie F. (N. E.)
1895	Curts, Kate O. (N. Y.)
1893	Cutler, Mary F., M. D. (N. Y.)
1880 *r*	Cushman, Clara M. (1889.)
1890 *r*	Daily, Rebecca. (1897.)
1888 *r*	Danforth, Mary S. (1893.)
1897 *s*	Daniel, N. Margaret. (Des M.)
1895 *m*	Dart, Jennie M., M. D. (*Dease.*) (1898.)

244

Date of App'm't.	Name and Branch.
1892 d	Davis, Mrs. Anna L. (1904.)
1900	Davis, Dora. (N.-W.)
1902	Davis, Joanna. (Des M.)
1902 m	Davison, Mabel. (Smart.) (1907.)
1888 m	Day, Martha E. (Abbott.) (1894.)
1896 m	Deaver, Ida C. (1897.)
•1903 m	Deavitt, La Dona. (Rosenberg.) (1907.)
1899 m	Decker, Helen M. (Beech.)
1905	Decker, Marguerite M. (Minn.)
1884 r	De Line, Sarah M. (1895.)
1891 r	De Motte, Mary. (Doering.)
1873 r	Denning, Lou B. (1890.)
1882 m	De Vine, Esther J. (Williams.) (1891.)
1888	Dickerson, Augusta. (Phila.)
1897 s	Dickinson, Emma E.
1893 r	Donahue, Julia M., M. D. (1897.)
1884 d	Downey, Clara A. (1896.)
1906	Draper, Frances L., M. D. (N.-W.)
1899 r	Dreibelbies, Caroline. (1906.)
1906	Driesbach, Gertrude I. (Top.)
1906	Drummer, Martha A. (Pacif.)
1907	Dudley, Rose E. (Col. R.)
1890 r	Dudley, Hannah. (1891.)
1891	Dunmore, Effie. (Phila.)
1907	Dyer, Clara B. (N. E.)
1894–06	Easton, Celesta. (Pacif.) (1900.)
1878 s	Easton. S. A. (Cin.)
1903	Eddy, Mrs. S. M. (Cin.)
1901	Edmonds, Agnes M., M. D. (Des M.)
1902	Edmunds, Margaret J. (Cin.)
1894	Elicker, Anna R. (Des M.)
1897 m	Elliott, Martelle. (Davis.) (1904.)
1879 m	Elliott, Margaret. (Wilson.) (1888.)
1895 d	Elliott, Mary C. (Stephens.) (1886.)
1886 r	Elliott, Mary J. (1890.)
1900	Ellis, Ida. (N.-W.)
1884	English, Fannie M. (N. Y.)
1906	Ericson, Judith. (Top.)
1899	Ernsberger, Emma, M. D. (Cin.)
1888 r	Ernsberger, I., M. D. (1900.)
1900	Estey, Ethel M. (N. Y.)
1895	Evans, Alice A. (Des M.)
1883 d	Everding, Emma J. (1892.)
1899 m	Ewers, Harriet C. (Lyons.) (1900.)
1903	Frenderich, Norma H. (Phila.)
1892 m	Ferris, Emma E. (Shellabear.) (1897.)
1887 r	Field, Nellie H. (1888.)
1888	Files, Estelle M. (N. Y.)
1887 r	Fincham, Ella B. (1894.)
1905	Finlay, Alice. (Cin.)
1884 m	Fisher, Elizabeth. (Brewster.) (1888)
1896	Fisher, Fannie F. (N.-W.)
1890 m	Forbes, Ella R. (Phillips.) (1894.)
1893 r	Foster, Eva M. (1895.)
1902	Foster, Carrie. (Des M.)
1898 m	Forster, Miriam. (N.-W.)
1889 m	French, Anna S. Freyer.) (1895.)
1891 r	Frey, Cecelia M. (1894.)
1893	Frey, Lulu E. (Cin.)
1886 d	Fuller, Delia A. (1901.) •
1906	Galbreath, Elizabeth. (Cin.)
1887	Gallimore, Anna. (1903.)
1894	Galloway, Helen R. (Des M.)
1879	Gheer, Jean M. (N. Y.)
1878 r	Gibson, Eugenia. (Mitchell.) (1882.)
1881 d	Gilchrist, Ella, M. D. (1884.)
1905	Gimson, Esther, M. D. (N.-W.)

Date of App'm't.	Name and Branch.
1896	Gilman, Gertrude. (N. E.)
1903	Glassburner, Mamie F. (Des M.)
1898 m	Glenk, Marguerite E. (Burley.) (1905.)
1885	Gloss, Anna D., M. D. (N.-W.)
1892	Glover, Ella E. (N. E.)
1900 m	Goetz, Adeline. (Guthrie.) (1901.)
1880 m	Goodenough, Julia E. (Hudson.) (1886.)
1895 r	Goodin, E. S. (1899.)
1905 s	Grandstrand, Pauline. (Minn.)
1894	Greene, Lily D. (N.-W.)
1876 d	Green, Lucilla H., M.D. (Cheney.) (1878.)
1899 s	Gregg, Mary E. (Des M.)
1889	Griffiths, Mary B. (Des M.)
1905 s	Grove, Mrs. L. R. (N.-W.)
1878 d	Guelphi, Cecilia. (1886.)
1903	Guthapfel, Minerva L. (Phila.)
1888 m	Hale, Lillian G. (Scott-Welday.) (1894.)
1905	Hall, Mrs. R. S., M. D. (N. Y.)
1885 r	Hall, Emma M. (1900.)
1907	Hallman, Sarah B. (Balt.)
1883 dis	Hamisfar, Florence N., M. D. (1886.)
1900 m	Hammond, Alice J. (Sharp.) (1908.)
1892 r	Hammond, Rebecca J. (1899.)
1881	Hampton, Mary S. (N. Y.)
1895	Hardie, Eva M. (Cin.)
1892 m	Harrington, Susan. (Cousland.) (1898.)
1895 d	Harris, Lillian, M. D. (1902.)
1891 m	Harris, Mary W. (Folwell.) (1894.)
1893 r	Harris, Nellie M. (1895.)
1904	Hart, Mary Ames. (Pacif.)
1887	Hartford, Mable C. (N. E.)
1884	Harvey, Emily L. (N. E.)
1874 d	Hastings, Mary. (1898.)
1906	Haynes, Emily Irene. (N. Y.)
1891 r	Heafer, Louise. (1907.)
1893	Heaton, Carrie A. (N.-W)
1892 m	Hebinger, Josephine. (Snuggs.) (1894.)
1884 m	Hedrick, M. C. (Miles.) (1890.)
1898	Hemingway, Edith A. (N. E.)
1901	Henkle, Nianette. (Des M.)
1904 dis	Henry, Mary. (1906.)
1884	Hewett, Ella J. (Phila.)
1886	Hewett, Lizzie. (N.-W.)
1904	Hewitt, Helen. (N.-W.)
1878 d	Higgins, Susan B. (1879)
1905	Hill, Katherine Ledyard. (Phila.)
1900 r	Hillman, Mary R. (1905.)
1905	Hitchcock, Frances H. (Des M.)
1872	Hoag, Lucy, M. D. (N. Y.)
1895 m	Hodge, Emma, M. D. (Worrall.) (1899.)
1906	Hoffman, Carlotta. (N.-W.)
1892	Hoge, Elizabeth. (Cin.)
1901 r	Holbrook, Ella M. (Pacif.)
1878 m	Holbrook, Mary J. (Chapman.) (1890.)
1900	Holman, Charlotte T. (Pacif.)
1906	Holland, Harriet A. (N.-W.)
1905	Holland, Ary. (Top.)
1904	Holland, Mrs. Alma H. (Des M.)
1905	Holmes, Ada. (C. R.)
1905	Hollister, Grace. (Cin.)
1906	Honsinger, Welthy B. (N. Y.)
1877 m	Howard, Leonora, M. D. (King.) (1884.)
1887 r	Howard, Meta, M. D. (1889.)

Date of App'm't.	Name and Branch.
1899	Parkinson, Phoebe A. (Col. R.)
1906	Parish, Rebecca, M. D. (N.-W.)
1890	Perkins, Fannie A. (Des M.)
1888 m	Perrine, Florence. (Mansell.) (1894.)
1904	Peters, Alice. (N.-W.)
1903	Peters, Jessie I. (N.-W.)
1894	Peters, Mary. (N.-W.)
1888	Peters, Sarah. (N.-W.)
1889	Phelps, Frances E. (Des M.)
1897 m	Pierce, Nellie. (Miller.) (1905.)
1902	Pierce, Thirza M. (N.-W.)
1900 *	Plumb, Florence J. (N. Y.)
1903	Pool, Lydia S. (Des M.)
1896 m	Porter, Charlotte J. (1901.)
1871 m d	Porter, Mary Q. (Gamewell.) (1882.) (1907.)
1906	Powell, Alice M. (N. Y.)
1886 r	Pray, Susan, M. D. (1887.)
1878 r	Priest, Mary A. (1880.)
1906	Pugh, Ada. (Minn.)
1872 d	Pultz, Elizabeth M. (1877.)
1895	Purdy, Caroline M. (Phila.)
1902 m	Pyne, Rosa M. (Berry.) (1906.)
1900 m	Rasmussen, Mrs. Helen E. (Springer.) (1905.)
1906	Rank, Minnie L. (Minn.)
1884	Reed, Mary. (Cin.)
1906	Reynolds, Elsie. (Des M.)
1900	Rigby, Luella. (Des M.)
1902	Robbins, Henrietta. (N. Y.)
1907	Robinson, Alvina. (Des. M.)
1902 *	Robinson, Helen. (N. Y.)
1884 d	Robinson, Mary C. (1906.)
1900 *	Robinson, Ruth E. (Balt.)
1889 m	Rodgers, Anna M. (Furness.) (1890.)
1887 r	Rothweiler, Louise C. (1898.)
1894 m	Rouse, Wilma H. (Keene.) (1905.)
1881 d	Rowe, Phoebe. (1898.)
1900 m	Rowley, Mary L. (Wilson.) (1904.)
1901	Ruddick, Elizabeth May. (N. E.)
1887 m	Rulofsen, G. M. (Thompson.) (1888.)
1879	Russell, Elizabeth. (Cin.)
1895	Russell, M. Helen. (Pacif.) (1897-1907.)
1899 m	Samson, Carrie J. (Sunder.) (1903.)
1904	Saxe, Agnes E. (N. Y.)
1884 d	Schenck, Linna M. (1892.)
1874 m	Schoonmaker, Dora. (Soper.) (1879.)
1889	Scott, Frances A. (Cin.)
1896	Scott, Emma, M. D. (Cin.)
1885	Scranton, Mrs. M. F. (N. E.)
1880 d	Sears, Annie B. (1895.)
1890	Seeds, Leonora H. (Cin.)
1902	Seeds, Mabel K. (N.-W.)
1889 s	Sellers, Rue E. (Cin.)
1879 dis	Sharpe, Mary (1883.)
1887	Shaw, Ella C. (N.-W.)
1888 s	Sheldon, Martha A., M. D. (N.E.)
1890 m	Sherwood, Rosetta, M. D. (Hall.) (1892-1896.)
1905	Shibati, Suye. (Top.)
1895 m	Schockley, Mary E. (Drake.) (1904.)
1902 d	Sia, Mabel. (1903.)
1903 r	Siddall, Adelaide. (1904.)
1905	Simester, Mary. (N. E.)
1906	Simonds, Mildred. (Des M.)
1889 d	Simonds, Maud E. (1898.)
1907	Simpson, Cora. (N.-W.)

Date of App'm't.	Name and Branch.
1898	Singer, Florence E. (Phila.)
1900	Singh, Lilavati. (N.-W.)
1891 *	Sites, Ruth M. (Brown.) (1895.)
1901	Slate, Anna B. (Phila.)
1885	Smith, Lida B. (N. Y.)
1907	Smith, Adelina. (N.-W.)
1906	Snavely, Gertrude E. (Phila.)
1896 r	Soderstrom, Anna. (1901.)
1903 *	Soper, E. Maud. (Phila.)
1900 r	Southard, Ada J. (1905.)
1870 r	Sparkes, Fannie J. (1891.)
1878 m	Sparr, Julia, M. D. (Coffin.) (1883.)
1902	Spaulding, Winifred. (Top.)
1896 m	Spear, Katherine A. (Collier.) (1900.)
1880 m	Spence, Mattie B. (Perrie.) (1883.)
1896 r	Spencer, Clarissa H. (1901.)
1878	Spencer, Matilda A. (Phila.)
1906	Sprowles, Alberta. (Phila.)
1892	Stahl, Josephine. (N.-W.)
1895 m	Stanton, Alice M. (Woodruff.) (1899.)
1900 m	Stearns, Mary P. (Badley.)
1889 r	Steere, Anna E. (N.-W.)
1892	Stephens, Grace. (Balt.)
1895 d	Sterling, Florence. (Leuth.) (1897.) (1900.)
1890	Stevenson, Ida B., M. D. (Top.)
1906	Stixrud, Louise. (Minn.)
1901 m	Stockwell, Emma. (Price.) (1908.)
1901	Stockwell, Grace. (Des M.)
1904 d	Stone, Anna. (1906.)
1896	Stone, Mary, M. D. (Des M.)
1907	Stout, Winifred. (N.-W.)
1906	Strawic, Gertrude. (N.-W.)
1904	Strow, Elizabeth M. (N. Y.)
1902 d	Stumpf, Susanna M. (1907.)
1888 s	Sullivan, Lucy. (Cin.)
1907	Sutton, Marianne. (Minn.)
1869 r	Swain, Clara A., M. D. (1896.)
1905	Swan, Hilda. (Top.)
1878	Swaney, Mary F. (Top.)
1902	Swift, Edith T. (N.-W.)
1903 m	Swormstedt, Virginia R. (Coffin.) (1907.)
1895	Taft, Gertrude, M. D. (Pacif.)
1906	Tang, Ilien. (Minn.)
1889 m	Taylor, Martha E. (Callahan.) (1893.)
1903	Temple, Laura. (N. Y.)
1887	Terry, Edna G., M. D. (N. E.)
1869 d	Thoburn, Isabella. (1901.)
1904	Thomas, Mary M. (Cin.)
1903	Thomas, Hester A. (Cin.)
1889 m	Thompson, Anna. (Stephens.) (1895.)
1890 r	Thompson, E.
1871 m	Tinsley, Jennie M. (Waugh.) (1876.)
1901	Tippet, Mrs. Susan. (Balt.)
1895	Todd, Althea M. (N. E.)
1897 r	Todd, Grace. (1898.)
1904	Toll, Evelyn. (N.-W.)
1874 m	Trask, Sigourney, M. D. (Cowles.) (1885.)
1908	Travis, Grace B. (N. Y.)
1889	Trimble, Lydia A. (Des M.)
1895 r	Tryon, Elizabeth. (1900.)
1890 m	Tucker, Grace. (Tague.) (1896.)
1905	Turner, Mrs. Maud N. (Top.)
1881 r	Turney, Mrs. L. M. (1882.)
1903 m	Turner, Sarah B. (Parker.) (1904.)
1908 d	Tuttle, Mary B., M. D. (1907.)

Date of App'm't.	Name and Branch.
1907	Tuttle, Ora B. (Cin.)
1889 m	Van Dorsten, Amelia. (Lawyer.) (1894.)
1887 d	Vance, Mary A. (Belknap.) (1892.)
1881	Van Petten, Mrs. Carrie. (N.-W.)
1898	Varney, Elizabeth W. (Top.)
1891 r	Vickery, M. Ella. (1906.)
1896 r	Waidman, Isabel. (1899.)
1906	Wallace, L. Ethel. (Balt.)
1903	Walker, Susan. (N.-W.)
1890 m	Walton, Ida B. (Multer.) (1891.)
1880 m	Warner, Ellen. (Fox.) (1885.)
1873 m	Warner, Susan N. (Densmore.) (1892.)
1883	Watson, Rebecca J. (Top.)
1904 *	Waugh, Nora Belle. (Cin.)
1902	Weaver, Georgia. (N. Y.)
1905	Wells, Anna May. (Des M.)
1901	Wells, Elizabeth J. (Des M.)
1895	Wells, Phebe. (N. Y.)
1902	Westcott, Pauline E. (N.-W.)
1881 *	Wheeler, Frances. (Verity.) (1893.)
1903 *	Wheeler, Maud. (N.-W.)
1891	White, Laura M. (Phila.)
1876 m	Whiting, Olive. (Bishop.) (1882.)
1904	Whittaker, Lottie M. (Minn.)
1906	Widney, May C. (Top.)
1896 m	Widdifield, Flora M. (Chew.) (1898.)
1892 m	Wilkinson, Lydia M. (Taft.) (1905.)
1901 m	Williams, Christiana. (Hall.) (1902.)
1900	Williams, Mary E. (Phila.)

Date of App'm't.	Name and Branch.
1896 m	Wilson, Fannie G. (Alexander.) (1900.)
1889	Wilson, Frances O. (Des M.) ·
1889 m	Wilson, Mary E. (Buchanan.) (1896.)
1898	Wilson, Minnie E. (N.-W.)
1894 *	Wilson, Mary E. (N.-W.)
1901	Winslow, Annie M. (Top.)
1885	Wisner, Julie E. (Cin.)
1905 m	Witte, Helena. (N.-W.)
1903 *m	Wood, Bertha L. (Robbins.) (1906.)
1892	Wood, Catherine A. (Des M.)
1889 *	Wood, Elsie. (N. Y.)
1901	Woods, Grace M. (N. Y.)
1880 m	Woodsworth, Kate. (Quinn.) (1883.)
1871 d	Woolston, Beulah. (1886)
1878 d	Woolston, Henrietta, M.D, (1879.)
1871 r	Woolston, Sarah H. (1896.)
1895	Wright, Laura S. (N.-W.)
1880 r	Yates, Elizabeth U. (1885.)
1892	Young, Effie G. (N. E.)
1897	Young, Mariana. (Cin.)
1898 d	Zentmire, Cora. (Brewster.) (1900.)

Missionaries	545
Medical	57
Married	115
Retired	76
Self-supporting	13
Daughters of Missionaries	21
Deceased	41
Dismissed	9

CONSTITUTION

OF THE

Woman's Foreign Missionary Society of the Methodist Episcopal Church.

ARTICLE I.—NAME.

This organization shall be called "THE WOMAN'S FOREIGN MISSIONARY SOCIETY OF THE METHODIST EPISCOPAL CHURCH."

ARTICLE II.—PURPOSE.

The purpose of this Society is to engage and unite the efforts of Christian women in sending missionaries to the women in foreign mission fields of the Methodist Episcopal Church, and in supporting them and native Christian teachers and Bible readers in those fields and all forms of work carried on by the Society.

ARTICLE III.—MEMBERSHIP.

The payment of one dollar annually shall constitute Membership, and twenty dollars Life Membership. Any person paying one hundred dollars shall become a Manager for Life, and the contribution of three hundred dollars shall constitute the donor a Patron for Life.

ARTICLE IV.—ORGANIZATION.

The organization of this Society shall consist of a General Executive Committee, Co-ordinate Branches, District Associations, Auxiliary Societies, to be constituted and limited as laid down in subsequent articles.

ARTICLE V.—GENERAL EXECUTIVE COMMITTEE.

SECTION 1. The management and general administration of the affairs of the Society shall be vested in a General Executive Committee, consisting of a President, Recording Secretary, Treasurer, the Corresponding Secretary, and two delegates from each Branch, the Literature Committee, Secretary of German Work and the Secretary of Scandinavian Work. The President, Recording Secretary, Treasurer and Secretaries of German and Scandinavian Work shall be elected annually by the General Executive Committee. The two delegates and reserves shall be elected at the Branch annual meetings. Said committee shall meet in Boston the third Wednesday in April, 1870, and annually, or oftener, thereafter, at such time and place as the General Executive Committee shall annually determine.

SEC. 2. The duties of the General Executive Committee shall be:
First—To take into consideration the interests and demands of the entire work of the Society as presented in the report of the Branch Corresponding Secretaries and in the estimates of the needs of mission fields; to ascertain the financial condition of the Society; to appropriate its money in accordance with the purposes and method therein indicated;

to devise means for carrying forward the work of the Society; fixing the amounts to be raised, employing new missionaries, designating their field of labor, examining the reports of those already employed, and arranging with the several Branches the work to be undertaken by each.

Second—To transact any other business that the interests of the Society may demand, provided all the plans and directions of the Committee shall be in harmony with the provisions of the Constitution.

ARTICLE VI.—PERMANENT COMMITTEES OF WOMAN'S FOREIGN MISSIONARY SOCIETY.

REFERENCE COMMITTEE.

1. The Committee of Reference shall be composed of the President of the Woman's Foreign Missionary Society and the Branch Corresponding Secretaries.

2. It shall meet immediately after the adjournment of the General Executive Committee and organize by the election of a Chairman and Secretary.

3. All cases of emergency that would come before the General Executive Committee, arising in the interim of its sessions, shall be submitted to this Committee, and decided by a majority vote.

4. The Chairman shall send each resolution that is submitted to the committee to each member, and when all have returned their votes, the Recording Secretary shall declare the result, and record both resolutions and votes.

5. The Committee shall present a full report of its action during the year to the General Executive Committee for approval and permanent record.

6. This committee shall hold a semi-annual meeting, at such time and place as shall be designated by the Chairman and Secretary. The expenses of this meeting shall be paid from the general treasury.

LITERATURE COMMITTEE.

There shall be a Literature Committee of three, whose duty it shall be to provide all literature of the Society, except the periodicals and the General Executive Committee's Report.

ARTICLE VII.—CO-ORDINATE BRANCHES.

SECTION 1. Co-ordinate Branches of this Society, on their acceptance of this relationship under the provisions of the Constitution, may be organized in accordance with the following general plan for districting the territory of the Church:

Name.	States Included.	Headquarters.
New England Branch		Boston, Mass.
	New England States.	
New York Branch		New York, N. Y.
	New York, New Jersey.	
Philadelphia Branch		Philadelphia, Pa.
	Pennsylvania and Delaware.	
Baltimore Branch		Baltimore, Md.
	Maryland, District of Columbia, Eastern Virginia, North and South Carolina, Georgia, and Florida.	

Name.	States Included.	Headquarters.

Cincinnati Branch ....Cincinnati, O.
    Ohio, West Virginia, Kentucky, Tennessee, Alabama, and
        Mississippi.
Northwestern Branch ....Chicago, Ill.
    Illinois, Indiana, Michigan, Wisconsin.
Des Moines Branch ....Des Moines, Iowa
    Iowa, Missouri, Arkansas, and Louisiana.
Minneapolis Branch ....Minneapolis, Minn.
    Minnesota, North and South Dakota.
Topeka Branch.......................................Topeka, Kan.
    Kansas, Nebraska, Colorado, Wyoming, Utah, Texas, New
        Mexico, and Oklohoma.
Pacific Branch ....Los Angeles, Cal.
    California, Nevada, Arizona, and Hawaii.
Columbia River Branch ....Portland, Ore.
    Montana, Idaho, Washington, and Oregon.

This plan, however, may be changed by an affirmative vote of three-fourths of the members of the General Executive Committee present at any annual meeting of the same.

SEC. 2. The officers of each Branch shall consist of a President, one or more Vice-Presidents, a Recording Secretary, a Corresponding Secretary, a Treasurer, an Auditor, and such other officers as shall be necessary for the efficient work of the Branch. These, with the exception of the Auditor, shall constitute an Executive Committee for the administration of the affairs of the Branch, nine of whom shall be a quorum for the transaction of business. These officers shall be elected at the annual meeting of the Branch, and shall continue in office until others are chosen in their stead.

SEC. 3. The Executive Committee shall have supervision of the work assigned to the Branch by the General Executive Committee, provide for all the needs, and receive reports from all forms of work carried on by the Society, which, by the plan of the General Executive Committee, are to be supported by the Branch,

SEC. 4. Each Branch shall appoint a Standing Committee of not less than five, of which the Branch Corresponding Secretary shall be Chairman, who shall investigate the case of any candidate within the limits of the Branch, and shall supply such candidates with blank for health certificate and constitutional questions, to be filled out and answered by her; and, when practical, a personal interview shall be had with the woman by two or more of the Committee before her papers are forwarded to the Reference Committee, or the Committee appointed at the General Executive meeting. The Corresponding Secretary of the Branch presenting missionary candidates shall have a personal interview with each woman presented before her final appointment to a foreign field.

SEC. 5. No Branch shall project new work, or undertake the support of new missionaries, except by the direction or with the approval of the General Executive Committee.

SEC. 6. Each Branch may make such By-Laws as may be deemed necessary to its efficiency, not inconsistent with this Constitution.

ARTICLE VIII.—DISTRICT ASSOCIATIONS.

District Associations shall be formed wherever practicable; said associations to have supervision of all auxiliaries within their limits.

ARTICLE IX.—Auxiliary Societies.

Any number of women who shall contribute annually may form a Society Auxiliary to that Branch of the Woman's Foreign Missionary Society of the Methodist Episcopal Church, within whose prescribed territorial limits they may reside, by appointing a President, one or more Vice-Presidents, a Recording Secretary, a Corresponding Secretary, a Treasurer, and Supervisor of Children's Work, who, together, shall constitute a local Executive Committee.

ARTICLE X.—Relating to the Missionary Authorities of the Church.

Section 1. This Society shall work in harmony with and under the supervision of the authorities of the Missionary Society of the Methodist Episcopal Church. The appointment, recall, and remuneration of missionaries, and the designation of their fields of labor, shall be subject to the approval of the Board of Managers of the Missionary Society of the Methodist Episcopal Church, and annual appropriations to mission fields shall be submitted for revision and approval to the General Missionary Committee of the Methodist Episcopal Church.

Sec. 2. All missionaries sent out by this Society shall labor under the direction of the particular Conference or Mission of the Church in which they may be severally employed. They shall be annually appointed by the President of the Conference on Missions, and shall be subject to the same rules of removal that govern the other missionaries.

Sec. 3. All the work of the Woman's Society in foreign lands shall be under the direction of the Conferences or Missions and their committees in exactly the same manner as the work of the Missionary Society of the Methodist Episcopal Church, the Superintendent or Presiding Elder having the same relation to the work and the person in charge of it that he would have were it a work in charge of any member of the Conference or Mission.

Sec. 4. The funds of the Society shall not be raised by collections or subscriptions taken during any of our regular Church services, nor in any Sunday-school, but shall be raised by such methods as the Constitution of the Society shall provide, none of which shall interfere with the contributions of our people and Sunday-schools for the treasury of the Missionary Society of the Methodist Episcopal Church; and the amount so collected shall be reported by the pastor to the Annual Conference, and be entered in a column among the benevolent collections in the Annual and General Minutes.

Sec. 5. Section 4 of this Article shall not be so interpreted as to prevent the women from taking collections in meetings convened in the interests of their societies; nor from securing memberships and life memberships in audiences where their work is represented, nor from holding festivals, or arranging lectures in the interest of their work.

ARTICLE XI.—Change of Constitution.

This Constitution may be changed at any annual meeting of the General Executive Committee by a three-fourths vote of those present voting, notice of the proposed change having been given at the previous annual meeting; but Article X shall not be changed except with the concurrence of the General Conference of the Methodist Episcopal Church.

BY-LAWS.

I.—OFFICERS.

The officers of this Society shall be a President, a Recording Secretary, and a Treasurer, who shall be elected by ballot at the annual meeting of the Society.

II.—DUTIES OF OFFICERS.

1. It shall be the duty of the President: (a) To preside at all meetings of the Society, and (b) with the Recording Secretary and Treasurer, in the interim of the General Executive and Reference Committee meetings, to have authority to transact all business that requires immediate action.

2. It shall be the duty of the Recording Secretary: (a) To give notice of all meetings of the General Executive Committee.

(b) To keep a full record of all its proceedings, placing the same in the safe of the Publication Office.

(c) To present a report of the year's work at the anniversary of the Society.

(d) To forward to foreign Treasurers a copy of the appropriations for each Mission as soon as practicable after the adjournment of the General Executive Committee.

(e) To prepare and print the Annual Report of the Woman's Foreign Missionary Society, including the minutes of the General Executive Committee.

(f) To prepare and present a quadrennial report for General Conference.

3. It shall be the duty of the Treasurer: (a) To receive all money from bequests, gifts, donations, or legacies made to the Woman's Foreign Missionary Society, and, unless otherwise specified by the donor, to pay the same to the Treasurer of that Branch within whose bounds the donor resides at the time of death.

(b) To receive all money paid into the General Fund by the several Branches, and disburse the same subject to the order of the General Executive Committee.

III.—BRANCH CORRESPONDING SECRETARIES.

1. The Branch Corresponding Secretaries shall superintend all the interests of their respective Branches, conduct the correspondence of the Society with foreign missionaries, be present at all Branch annual and quarterly meetings, and present a quarterly report of the work of the Branch and give to the public, or direct to be given, all communications and plans of the business of their respective Branches.

2. Each Corresponding Secretary shall furnish in her report to the General Executive Committee the following items: Number of Auxiliary Societies, members, life members, honorary patrons and managers, subscribers to the *Woman's Missionary Friend,* and the receipts of the Treasurer. In her report of the foreign work she shall include the number of missionaries, Bible readers, boarding schools, and orphans supported by her Branch.

IV.—BRANCH TREASURERS.

1. Branch Treasurers shall be required to furnish quarterly reports of moneys received for publication in the *Woman's Missionary Friend.*

2. The financial year of the Society shall commence October 1st. Branch Treasurers shall close their accounts for the year by September 30th.

3. The money received from annual memberships shall not be used to make life members, managers, or patrons. Life memberships shall be made by the payment of $20.00 given specifically for that purpose. If in installments, the final payment shall be made as soon as practicable, and the membership reported as conmplete only when that has been done; all the installments to be credited on the Treasurer's book and acknowledged in the *Woman's Missionary Friend.*

4. In case any Branch is unable to meet the obligations it has assumed, any other Branch may, by the action of the Executive Board, be permitted to use its surplus funds in aid of the Branch deficient.

V.—SECRETARIES OF LITERATURE.

There shall be a Secretary of Literature elected by each Branch, whose duty it shall be to assist the Literature Committee, through correspondence, by suggestions, by presenting the needs of their respective Branches, and aiding in any other way the Literature Committee may desire. It shall also be the duty of the Branch Literature Secretary to advance the interests and increase the circulation of our literature and publications in every possible way. She shall have charge, in connection with the Literature Committee, of the exhibition and sale of our literature at the various public gatherings and conventions throughout the country, the expenses to be borne by the Branch where the convention meets. When, as frequently occurs, the Epworth League, Student Volunteer, or other convention is held outside of our own country, this duty shall belong to the standing Literature Committee.

VI.—GENERAL SECRETARIES.

There shall be a General Superintendent of Young People's Work and a General Superintendent of Children's Work, who shall be elected annually by ballot by the General Executive Committee.

VII.—FIELD SECRETARIES.

Field Secretaries may be employed to travel throughout the Society for the promotion of the work. They shall be elected annually by ballot by the General Executive Committee.

VIII.—FOREIGN TREASURERS.

1. There shall be a Foreign Treasurer for each mission where the Woman's Foreign Missionary Society supports work.

2. It shall be the duty of each Foreign Treasurer (a) to forward receipt immediately upon receiving remittances from the Branch Treasurer.

(b) On January 1st and July 1st of each year to forward to the Branch Corresponding Secretary itemized statements, showing balance in United States currency.

(c) To apply the funds of the Society only to the purpose designated by the General Executive Committee. This rule shall be interpreted to mean that no expenditure shall exceed the appropriation.

(d) To pay appropriations for buildings and for salaries of missionaries on the basis of United States gold, and all other appropriations on the basis of the local currency of the country. Any surplus arising therefrom by exchange shall accrue to the Treasurer of the Branch remitting.

(e) To report in the semi-annual statements all surplus funds arising from unused appropriations, exchange, or other source, and hold said funds subject to the order of the Corresponding Secretary from whose Branch said funds accrue.

(f) To forward estimates which have been approved by the Field Reference Committee, and printed, to the Corresponding Secretary of each Branch, to insure arrival on or before September 1st.

(g) To pay money for buildings on presentation of properly audited bills only.

IX.—OFFICIAL CORRESPONDENCE.

The Branch Corresponding Secretaries shall correspond with the missionaries, so as to be able to present a full report of the work in each mission, such information to be presented to the General Executive Committee, the fields assigned to the several Secretaries to be arranged by themselves.

X.—MISSIONARIES.

1. Each missionary shall, on acceptance by the Woman's Foreign Missionary Society, be under the control of the General Executive Committee, directly amenable to the Corresponding Secretary of the Branch employing her.

2. She shall devote her entire time and attention to her appointed work.

3. When beginning service she shall be provided by the Society with not less than $100 for personal outfit, and also, if necessary, $100 for furniture, which shall be the property of the Society.

4. She shall consider the regulations of the Society named in the Constitution and By-laws as binding as the terms of the contract, and failure to conform to them on the part of the missionary shall release the Society from all financial liability.

5. She shall enter into the following contract by and with the Woman's Foreign Missionary Society through the Corresponding Secretary of the Branch employing her:

CONTRACT.

"I, —— ——, Corresponding Secretary of the —— Branch of the Woman's Foreign Missionary Society of the Methodist Episcopal Church, covenant and agree on the part of the Woman's Foreign Missionary Society to pay the traveling expenses of —— ——, a missionary in the employ of the ——Branch, from her home to her field of labor and her salary from the time of reaching the field at the rate of $—— for the first year, and thereafter at the rate of $—— per annum. I further agree to pay her return passage and home salary as provided in the By-laws relating to those matters."

"I, —— ——, a missionary, agree to give at least five years of continuous service as a single woman to the work of the Woman's Foreign Missionary Society in any field to which I may be sent, and, failing in this, to refund the amount of outfit and passage money. I also agree to conform to all the rules and regulations of said Society while in its employ."

6. The *salaries of missionaries* going to the field after October, 1901, either as new or returned missionaries, shall include all expenses hitherto classed as incidentals, and shall be, in Africa, $500; Bulgaria, $600; Foochow and Hing Hua, $600; North, Central, and West China, $650; India, $600; Italy, Japan, and Korea, $700; Malaysia, $600; Mexico, the Philippines, and South America, $750. The first year's work of a new missionary shall be so planned by the mission that the major part of her time shall be given to the study of the languages, and the first year's salary shall be one-sixth less than the full regular amount, except in the case of those whose full salary does not exceed $500. Medical missionaries shall from the first receive full salary.

7. Each missionary shall report each quarter to the Corresponding Secretary of the Branch employing her, and to the Presiding Elder of the District in which her work is located.

8. She shall furnish the Branch Corresponding Secretary, who is the Official Correspondent for that field in which her work lies, with all facts as required.

9. She shall report and credit in financial statements made January 1st and July 1st of each year, all sums received for the support of the work in her charge.

10. Medical missionaries shall keep an itemized account of all receipts and disbursements, and report them quarterly to the Treasurer of the mission. Medical outfit provided by the Society shall be the property of the Society.

11. Each missionary shall send annual communications for patrons supporting special work.

12. She shall keep a clear record of all special work, including Bible women, scholarships, etc., in her charge, under the Branches supporting, and on her removal or furlough, transfer it to her substitute or successor.

13. She shall incur no expense which has not been authorized by the General Executive Committee, and shall credit to the Society all donations received for the support of work, and annually report the same with her financial statement.

14. She shall not apply to private sources for financial aid without the sanction of the General Executive Committee. All solicitations for funds shall be made through the proper official authorities.

15. No missionary in the employ of the Woman's Foreign Missionary Society shall adopt any child as her own, or bring foreign-born girls or helpers to this country, except upon the recommendation of the Field Reference Committee of the Conference in which they reside, and with the permission of the General Executive Committee of the Woman's Foreign Missionary Society.

16. Each missionary shall present estimates and all other matters requiring the action of the General Executive Committee through the Field Reference Committee of the Conference in which her work is located.

17. She shall include in her estimates for Bible women and Zenana workers all expenses of conveyances, munshis and teachers, and in those for scholarships the cost of fuel, lights, medicines, and the minor expenses necessary in the maintenance of the schools.

18. Each foreign Conference and mission shall have a Field Reference Committee to be elected annually, whose duty shall be to consider all matters of general interest arising during the interim of their annual meetings.

19. (a) The Field Reference Committee of each Conference and mission shall consider the need of furlough or home leave upon the part

of the missionaries within its bounds, and shall, as occasion may require, forward its recommendations concerning individual cases to the Reference Committee, which shall fix the time of such furlough or home leave and notify the Secretary of the Field Reference Committee.

(b) In case of emergency, demanding immediate return home upon the part of the missionary, she shall bring a certificate of disability from a physician and from the Superintendent of the mission.

(c) A missionary returning from the field for any other reason than that of ill-health, shall secure permission from the General Executive Committee through the Corresponding Secretary of the Branch employing her, upon recommendation of the Field Reference Committee of her Conference.

(d) The liability of the Society for the necessary traveling expenses of furlough or home leave shall depend upon conformity to the regulations of this section.

20. In all cases where the relations of the missionary to the Society are harmonious her home salary the first year shall be $350. If her health requires her to remain longer in this country the second year's home salary shall be $300. If her detention for a longer period is necessary her case shall be in the hands of her Branch for adjustment.

21. Each missionary shall attend the first session of the General Executive Committee held after her return from the foreign field, and her traveling expenses to and from the place of meeting shall be paid from the same fund as those of members of that body.

22. The acceptance as missionaries of assistants or native workers shall be in the hands of the Reference Committee, which, in reaching a conclusion, shall take into consideration (a) the testimonials required in the regulations relating to candidates, including health certificates.

(b) A certificate showing three years of service under the Woman's Foreign Missionary Society.

(c) The recommendation of the Bishop in charge of the Conference.

23. When on furlough each missionary whose home is not in the United States shall receive full salary, in which case no furlough expenses will be paid by the Society. This provision shall apply only to missionaries in satisfactory relation to the Society, and for the term of furlough authorized by the General Executive Committee through the Branch employing her.

24. Each missionary shall accompany her application for return to the field after home leave with a new medical certificate, recommendation of the Corresponding Secretary of the Branch employing her, and a majority vote of the Reference Committee shall be authority for her return.

25. She shall, if proved manifestly unfit for missionary labor, receive three months' notice from the Reference Committee, at the expiration of which time the General Executive Committee may cancel its obligations to her. Return passage will be paid by the Society only at the expiration of three months.

26. All rules pertaining to the relations of the Woman's Foreign Missionary Society of the Methodist Episcopal Church with its missionaries shall be published in the Annual Report.

We accept the relation of the Woman's Foreign Missionary Society to the authorities of the Church, and to our workers in the field, as interpreted by the delegated Conference in India, in their session of 1881, as follows:

WHEREAS, Certain usages have grown up and been found acceptable and successful in connection with our older mission field in India, we deem it expedient to formulate the same in the following rules:

17

1. In general: The position of a lady missionary, placed in charge of work in connection with any of our circuits or stations, is the same as that of a second missionary or "junior preacher" to whom special work is assigned.

2. In particular: The general plan of work, such as establishing new schools, employing and dismissing head teachers, arranging terms of tuition, board, etc., and preparing a course of study, when these matters are not fixed by the Educational Committee, selecting classes of people among whom work may be more successfully carried on, arranging dispensaries and deciding the proportion of medical work to be given to natives and Europeans, Christians and non-Christians, etc., all such *general plans* shall be arranged by the lady in charge of the special departments of work, after free consultation with the Superintendent or Presiding Elder.

3. The lady missionary in charge of the work has full liberty to do the work assigned her in her own way, and to carry out the internal arrangement of her department in the manner which she deems best adapted to secure success.

4. The relation of the Superintendent or Presiding Elder to the work under the charge of a lady is the same as it would be were it under the charge of a member of Conference—he having a general advisory supervision, auditing the accounts (when not done by trustees), making suggestions, etc., exactly as with all the other work of his District.

5. Lady missionaries in charge of work, and all missionaries of the Woman's Foreign Missionary Society, are appointed by the President of Conference, at the same time and in the same manner that the appointments of Conference are made. Should, however, a President of Conference at any time decline to appoint, the Superintendent or Presiding Elder in Council will arrange the same.

6. All new buildings or expensive repairs or changes shall receive the sanction of Superintendent or Presiding Elder, even though no appropriations of money be asked.

7. A class of laborers is employed in our work, known as "assistants." In the employment or dismissal of these ladies, the consent of the Superintendent of Mission or of the Presiding Elder must be secured. They may be transferred by the Presiding Elder, with the consent of the lady in charge of the department in which they are employed. When these lady assistants, being members of our Church, by several years of faithful service, have come to be received as belonging permanently to our body of laborers, they may, on the recommendation of the Woman's Society, when such exists, or by Quarterly Conference, be formally recognized by Conference, and appointed the same as are women missionaries.

8. In case of a transfer of a woman missionary or an "assistant" from one Conference or charge to another, written permission shall be secured, signed by the Superintendent or Presiding Elder in whose jurisdiction the person may be employed, when, according to the condition in Rule 7, the engagement may be completed.

XI.—Missionary Candidates.

1. Each person who offers herself as a missionary candidate shall declare her belief that she is divinely called to the work of a foreign missionary, that she is actuated only by a desire to work in accordance with the will of God, and that she intends to make foreign missionary work the service of her effective years.

2. She shall be not less than twenty-five, nor more than thirty years of age. A special facility in acquiring languages, or a call to English work, may be considered a sufficient reason for deviating from this rule.

3. She shall fill out required application blanks and sign the contract in duplicate for file record with the ·Branch Corresponding Secretary and in the General Office.

4. When accepted she shall·be under the direction of the General Executive Committee, and if not sent out within the _yea_r her case shall be presented for reconsideration at the ensuing session of the General Executive Committee by the Corresponding Secretary in whose Branch she resides.

XII.—FUNDS.

1. All money raised under the auspices of this Society belongs to the Woman's Foreign Missionary Society of the Methodist Episcopal Church, and shall not be diverted to other causes.

2. Receipts from the publication office shall constitute the publication fund and be drawn on to defray the postage and traveling expenses of the Editors, Publisher, and the Literature Committee to and from General Executive Committee meetings.

3. The reserve ·fund, a capital of·$5,000, shall be retained in the treasury of the Society's publications, and in no case shall said amount be used in publishing interests or for any other demands.

4. Gifts, bequests, donations, and other moneys received from donors residing outside· of the United States, shall be paid into the general treasury and credited as received from the Society at large.

5. Proceeds on the foreign field accruing from rates of exchange, surplus from remittances made under appropriations, and other sources,· shall belong to the Branch supporting the work, and shall be reported January 1st and July· 1st of each year, and held subject to the order of the Corresponding Secretary from the funds of whose Branch they accrue.

XIII.—PUBLICATION DEPARTMENT.

1. The periodicals of the Woman's Foreign Missionary Society shall be known as the *Woman's Missionary Friend, Children's Missionary Friend, Der Frauen Missions Freund,* and *The Study.*

2. The literature of the Society shall ·include all other publications not specified in Section 1.

3. The Editors and Publisher of the periodicals and literature shall be elected annually at the General Executive Committee meeting, when their reports shall be received and a copy thereof submitted for publication in the Annual Report of the Woman's Foreign Missionary Society.

4. The Editors and Publisher shall be entitled to floor privileges on matters relating to their work.

5. The proceedings of the General Executive Committee shall be reported in the December number of the *Woman's Missionary Friend,* excluding appropriations and unimportant details.

.6. The territory of the Woman's Foreign Missionary Society shall be divided into three sections: The Eastern section to .be composed of New England, New York, Philadelphia, and ·Baltimore Branches; the Central section, Cincinnati and Northwestern Branches; the Western section, Minneapolis, Des Moines, Topeka, Pacific, and Columbia River Branches.

7. There shall be a Literature Committee of not less than three, whose duty it shall be to provide all the literature of the Society except the periodicals and Annual Report. ·

8. The Literature Committee shall be nominated by the delegates from the above sections, and elected by the General Executive Committee for a term of three years on the rotation plan. The Committee shall report to ₊the midyear meeting of the Reference Committee, to the· Annual Meeting, and to the General Executive Committee.

9. When the Epworth League, Student Volunteer, or other Convention is held outside our own country, the exhibition and sale of our literature shall be under the supervision of the Literature Committee, the expenses to be met from the treasury of the Woman's Foreign Missionary Society.

10. Sample copies of all publications issued by the Society shall be sent to the President, Secretary, and Treasurer of the Woman's Foreign Missionary Society, and to such other officers and to such exchanges as may be deemed essential to the progress of this department.

XIV.—ZENANA PAPER.

1. The Reference Committee shall take charge of the funds raised for the endowment of the Zenana paper and control of their investment and expenditure, and have the general supervision of the interests of the paper.

2. The Corresponding Secretary of each Branch shall have the control of the investment of the funds raised for the support of the Zenana paper within the bounds of her Branch, with the approval of the Reference Committee; the interest on investment to be paid semi-annually to the Treasurer of the Zenana paper.

3. The Woman's Conference in India shall nominate a Committee consisting of five persons, three ladies and two gentlemen, one of whom shall be the Publisher, to supervise the interests of the paper and arrange with the Press Committee for editing and publishing the Zenana paper in the various languages and dialects required; these nominations to be subject to the approval of the Reference Committee.

4. The Corresponding Secretary of the Woman's Foreign Missionary Society in India shall send an Annual Report of the Zenana paper to the Chairman of the Reference Committee, with the amount of circulation and items of interest, in time to be presented to the Annual Meeting of the General Executive Committee.

5. The Treasurer in India of the funds of the Zenana paper shall furnish the Reference Committee an Annual Report of the receipts and expenditures of said paper, in time to be presented to the General Executive Committee meeting.

6. A report of the Zenana paper shall be published in the Annual Report of the Woman's Foreign Missionary Society.

7. The Treasurer of the Zenana paper funds in America shall send the interest on the investments direct to the Treasurer of the Zenana paper in India, only upon order of the Chairman of the Reference Committee.

XV.—ANNUAL MEETINGS.

1. The General Executive Committee of the Woman's Foreign Missionary Society of the Methodist Episcopal Church is hereby authorized to hold its Annual Meetings either within or without the bounds of the State of New York, and at such times and places as said Committee may determine; and said Committee, at its Annual Meeting in each year, shall appoint a President, Treasurer, Recording Secretary, and other officers of the Society according to its best judgment.

2. The date and arrangements for the anniversary exercises of the General Executive Committee shall be made by the President and the Corresponding and Home Secretaries of the Branch within whose bounds the session of the General Executive Committee is to be held.

3. A majority of the members of the General Executive Committee shall constitute a quorum for the transaction of business.

XVI.—SECRETARY OF GENERAL OFFICE.

The Secretary of the General Office shall be nominated by the Committee on General Office and confirmed by the General Executive Committee.

The Secretary of the General Office shall be authorized to receive money sent through the Board of Foreign Missions to the Woman's Foreign Missionary Society, and forward the same to the Treasurer of the Branch to which it belongs.

XVII.—BY-LAWS.

These By-laws may be changed or amended at any meeting of the General Executive Committee by two-thirds vote of the members present and voting.

OFFICIAL RELATIONS OF LADY MISSIONARIES.

1. Definition of relations of the Woman's Foreign Missionary Society, as given by the Bishops in May, 1881.

"To the ladies of the Woman's Foreign Missionary Society:

"To your questions we respectfully reply as follows:

"1. We take the liberty to refer you to our action bearing date November 22, 1877, a copy of which is as follows:

TEACHERS IN MISSION SCHOOLS.

"1. In the judgment of the Bishops it is not within the right of the Superintendent of the mission to remove lay teachers from the schools to which they have been appointed, nor to interfere authoritatively with the internal arrangements of the schools, unless such right be expressly granted by the missionary authorities at New York.

"2. In case of difference between appointee and the Mission (including the Superintendent), which can not be adjusted between the parties without unreasonable delay, we recommend that such difference, with the papers and facts, be referred by the parties to the Bishop in charge for final decision.

"3. It is our judgment that the missionaries sent by the Woman's Foreign Missionary Society should be permitted to be present at the meetings of the mission and to speak on all matters relating to their work.   Most respectfully and sincerely,

"WILLIAM H. HARRIS."

BY-LAWS OF THE GENERAL EXECUTIVE COMMITTEE.

I. The General Executive Committee shall convene not later than the last week in October.

II. The annual meetings of the Woman's Foreign Missionary Society of the Methodist Episcopal Church shall be held at such places as the said Committee shall elect.

III. The President and Corresponding Secretary of the Branch within whose precincts the meetings of the General Executive Committee is to be held, shall fix the date of the meetings of said Committee, and arrange for the anniversary exercises.

18

IV. The Branch Corresponding Secretaries shall meet at least three days before the time of the meeting of the General Executive Committee for the purpose of nominating the members of the Standing Committees, and planning work for its session, and report the same at the opening of said Committee.

V. The traveling expenses of President and Recording Secretary shall be paid by Treasurer of the Woman's Foreign Missionary Society.

VI. The order of business shall be as follows:

1. Calling the roll.

2. Appointment of Standing Committees; i. e., Committee on Publication, Committee on Finance, Committee on Application of Missionary Candidates, Committee on By-laws.

3. Reception of Memorials and Petitions.

4. Reports of Corresponding Secretaries.

5. Report of Committee on Reference.

6. Report of Constitutional Publication Committee.

7. Reports of Editors and Publisher.

8. Reports of Official Correspondents and presentation of information from foreign work.

9. Fixing place for next meeting.

10. Election of President and Secretary, who shall continue in office until the appointment of their successors.

11. Notice of constitutional amendments.

12. Miscellaneous business.

13. Reports of Standing Committees daily; immediately after reading minutes.

VII. The rules of order shall be as follows:

1. Each session shall open and close with devotional exercises.

2. All resolutions to be discussed shall be presented in writing.

3. No member shall be granted leave of absence except by a vote of the entire body.

STANDING COMMITTEES AND THEIR DUTIES.

I.—On Publications.

1. To this Committee shall be referred all reports of Agents and Editors and of the Literature Committee of the Woman's Foreign Missionary Society.

2. This Committee shall carefully examine the receipts and expenditures of each department and as far as possible determine the source of any unnecessary and undue expense.

3. It shall nominate Agents and Editors and recommend amount of salary to be paid to each.

4. It may recommend the authorization of certain amounts considered necessary to secure satisfactory results in the issuing of periodicals and other literature, being always careful to observe the requirement in Article IX, Section 7, of the By-laws of Woman's Foreign Missionary Society.

5. As far as possible it shall consider the literary matter of all publications.

II.—On Missionary Candidates.

1. This Committee shall examine and report upon all the testimonials of missionary candidates that are presented at the General Executive session.

2. It shall consider all matters relating to native assistants and workers that may be brought before the Executive Committee.

3. All reports or memorials concerning Folts Institute shall be referred to this Committee.

III.—BUILDING COMMITTEE.

There shall be a standing Building Committee in each foreign mission and Conference, elected by a majority vote of the General and Woman's Foreign Missionary Societies.

IV.—REFERENCE COMMITTEE.

This Committee shall consist of the President and the Branch Corresponding Secretaries.

SUPPLEMENTAL.

All nominations not provided for in the duties of Standing Committees shall be made by the Committee of Reference, or be offered through a special Committee appointed at the General Executive Committee then in session.

CONSTITUTION FOR AUXILIARY SOCIETIES.

Auxiliaries are expected to labor in harmony with, and under the direction of, the Branch.

ARTICLE I.—NAME.

This organization shall be called The Woman's Foreign Missionary Society of..............Auxiliary to the ....Branch of the Woman's Foreign Missionary Society of the Methodist Episcopal Church.

ARTICLE II.—PURPOSE.

The purpose of this Society shall be to aid its Branch in interesting Christian women in the evangelizing of heathen women and in raising funds for this work.

ARTICLE III.—MEMBERSHIP.

Any person paying a regular subscription of two cents a week, or one dollar per year, may become a member of the Woman's Foreign Missionary Society. Any person contributing five dollars per quarter for one year, or twenty dollars at a time, shall be constituted a Life Member.

ARTICLE IV.—FUNDS.

All funds raised under the auspices of this Society belong to the Woman's Foreign Missionary Society, and shall not be diverted to other causes.

Remittances shall be forwarded quarterly to the Conference Treasurer.

ARTICLE V.—OFFICERS AND ELECTIONS

The officers of this Society shall be a President, one or more Vice-Presidents, a Recording Secretary, a Corresponding Secretary, a Treasurer, and Supervisor of Children's Work, who shall constitute an Executive Committee to administer its affairs. Managers and Superintendents of departments of work may be added as needed. These officers shall be elected at the annual meeting of the Society.

ARTICLE VI.—CHANGE OF CONSTITUTION.

This Constitution may be changed at any annual meeting of the General Executive Committee of the Woman's Foreign Missionary Society by a three-fourths vote of those present and voting, notice of the proposed change having been given to the Branches before April 1st of that year.

CONSTITUTION FOR YOUNG PEOPLE'S SOCIETY.

ARTICLE I.—NAME.

This organization shall be called The Young Woman's Foreign Missionary Society, or Standard Bearer Company of the Woman's Foreign Missionary Society of the..........Church, Auxiliary to the..........Branch of the Woman's Foreign Missionary Society of the Methodist Episcopal Church.

264

ARTICLE II.—Purpose.

The purpose of this organization is to interest young people in Foreign Missions and to support the work of the Woman's Foreign Missionary Society of the Methodist Episcopal Church.

ARTICLE III.—Membership.

Any person may become a member of this organization by paying not less than five cents a month, or may enroll as a Standard Bearer by signing the following pledge:

"In remembrance of our Father's love and in loyalty to the great commission of our King, I will give five cents a month as dues to the Woman's Foreign Missionary Society of the Methodist Episcopal Church to aid in sending the Gospel to the Christless millions."

The payment of fifteen dollars shall constitute Life Membership.

ARTICLE IV.—Badge.

The badge of this organization shall be the Church pennant pin. Members paying one dollar per year may wear the Woman's Foreign Missionary Society badge if preferred. Neither badge should be worn by any person not paying dues.

ARTICLE V.—Funds.

Funds raised under the auspices of this Society belong to the Woman's Foreign Missionary Society and shall not be diverted to other causes. Remittances shall be forwarded quarterly to the Conference Treasurer.

ARTICLE VI.—Officers and Elections.

The officers of this organization shall be a President, two or more Vice-Presidents, a Recording Secretary, a Corresponding Secretary, and a Treasurer, who shall be elected at the annual meeting of the organization and constitute an Executive Committee to administer the affairs of the same. Superintendents of departments may be added as needed.

ARTICLE VII.—Change of Constitution.

This Constitution may be changed at any annual meeting of the General Executive Committee by a three-fourths vote of those present and voting, notice of the proposed change having been given to the Branches before April 1st of that year.

CONSTITUTION FOR KING'S HERALDS.

ARTICLE I.—Name.

This organization shall be called the King's Heralds of the Methodist Episcopal Church, and be under the supervision of the Auxiliary of the Woman's Foreign Missionary Society in the said Church, if any exist; otherwise under the especial supervision of the District Secretary of the Woman's Foreign Missionary Society.

ARTICLE II.—Object.

The object of this organization shall be to promote missionary intelligence and interest among the children and to aid in the work of the Woman's Foreign Missionary Society of the Methodist Episcopal Church.

ARTICLE III.—Membership.

Any child between the ages of eight and fourteen may become a King's Herald by the payment of two cents a month. The payment of ten dollars shall constitute a child's life membership.

ARTICLE IV.—Officers.

The officers of this organization shall be a Superintendent, President, two Vice-Presidents, Recording Secretary, Corresponding Secretary, Treasurer, and Agent for the *Children's Missionary Friend*.

ARTICLE V.—Meetings.

Meetings of this organization shall be held on the..........of each month. The officers shall be elected semi-annually at the September and March meetings.

ARTICLE VI.—Badge.

The badge of this organization shall be a silver button with "King's Heralds" in blue lettering.

PLAN OF WORK FOR LITTLE LIGHT BEARERS.

Children under eight years of age may be enrolled as Little Light Bearers by the payment of twenty-five cents annually, receiving the enrollment card as a certificate of membership.

The payment of ten dollars shall constitute Life Membership.

DIRECTIONS.

The Superintendent elected by the Woman's Auxiliary shall have charge of the work for Little Light Bearers and plan for the collecting of dues, remitting and reporting quarterly through the regular channels, arrange for the annual public meeting, keep an accurate record in the Little Light Bearers' Record Book, and report regularly to the Woman's Auxiliary.

CONSTITUTION FOR DISTRICT ASSOCIATION.

ARTICLE I.—Name.

This association shall be called The .... District Association of the Woman's Foreign Missionary Society in the ....Conference of the Methodist Episcopal Church.

ARTICLE II.—Purpose.

The purpose of this Association shall be to unite the Auxiliaries of the District in an. earnest effort for the promotion of the work of the Woman's Foreign Missionary Society.

ARTICLE III.—Membership.

All members of the Woman's Foreign Missionary Society in ....
District shall be considered members of this Association.

ARTICLE IV.—Officers.

The officers of this Association shall be a President, three or more
Vice-Presidents, a Corresponding Secretary, a Recording Secretary, a
Treasurer, and Superintendent of Young Woman's Work and of Children's Work, who shall constitute the Executive Committee to administer
the affairs of the District.

ARTICLE V.—Meetings.

There shall be an annual meeting of the District Association, when
reports shall be received from all Auxiliaries in the District, missionary
intelligence be given, and necessary business transacted.

ARTICLE VI.—Change of Constitution.

This Constitution may be changed at any annual meeting of the
General Executive Committee of the Woman's Foreign Missionary Society
by a three-fourths vote of those present and voting, notice of the proposed
change having been given to the Branches before April 1st of that year.

ACT OF INCORPORATION.

State of New York,
City and County of New York, } ss.

We, the undersigned, Caroline R. Wright, Anna A. Harris, Sarah K. Cornell, and Harriet B. Skidmore, of the City of New York, and Susan A. Sayre, of the City of Brooklyn, being all citizens of the United States of America, and citizens of the State of New York, do hereby, pursuant to and in conformity with the Act of the Legislature of the State of New York, passed on April 12th, 1848, entitled "An Act for the incorporation of benevolent, charitable, and missionary societies:" and the several acts of the said Legislature amendatory thereof, associate ourselves together and form a body politic and corporate, under the name and title of "The Woman's Foreign Missionary Society of the Methodist Episcopal Church," which we certify is the name or title by which said Society shall be known in law. And we do hereby further certify that the particular business and object of said Society is to engage and unite the efforts of Christian women in sending female missionaries to women in foreign mission fields of the Methodist Episcopal Church, and in supporting them and native Christian teachers and Bible readers in those fields.

That the number of managers to manage the business and affairs of said Society shall be seventeen, and that the names of such managers of said Society for the first year of its existence are: Lucy A. Alderman, Sarah L. Keen, Ellen T. Cowen, Hannah M. W. Hill, Mary C. Nind, Elizabeth K. Stanley, Harriet M. Shattuck, Isabel Hart, Caroline R. Wright, Harriet B. Skidmore, Rachel L. Goodier, Annie B. Gracey, Harriet D. Fisher, Sarah K. Cornell, Anna A. Harris, Ordelia M. Hillman, and Susan A. Sayre.

That the place of business or principal office of said Society shall be in the City and County of New York, in the State of New York.

Witness our hand and seal this 20th day of December, A. D. 1884.
[Seal.]

CAROLINE R. WRIGHT,
ANNA A. HARRIS, •
HARRIET B. SKIDMORE,
SUSAN A. SAYRE,
SARAH K. CORNELL.

ACT OF INCORPORATION.

State of New York,
City and County of New York, } ss.

On the 20th day of December, 1884, before me personally came and appeared Caroline R. Wright, Anna A. Harris, Harriet B. Skidmore, and Sarah K. Cornell, to me known, and to me personally known to be the individuals described in and who executed the foregoing certificate, and they severally duly acknowledged to me that they executed the same.

[Notary's Seal.]

ANDREW LEMON,
Notary Public (58),
New York County.

City of Brooklyn,   } ss.
State of New York, County of Kings, }

On the 22d day of December, A. D. 1884, before me came Susan A. Sayre, to me known, and known to me to be one of the individuals described in and who executed the foregoing certificate, and duly acknowledged to me that she executed the same.

F. G. MINTRAM,

[Notary Seal.]   Notary Public of Kings County.

State of New York, } ss.
County of Kings,   }

I, Rodney Thursby, Clerk of the County of Kings and Clerk of the Supreme Court of the State of New York, in and for said county (said court being a Court of Records), do hereby certify that F. G. Mintram, whose name is subscribed to the Certificate of Proof, or acknowledgment of the annexed instrument and thereon written, was at the time of taking such proof or acknowledgment, a Notary Public of the State of New York, in and for said County of Kings, dwelling in said County, commissioned and sworn, and duly authorized to take the same. And, further, that I am well acquainted with the handwriting of said Notary, and verily believe the signature to the said certificate is genuine, and that said instrument is executed and acknowledged according to the laws of the State of New York.

In Testimony Whereof, I have hereunto set my hand and affixed the seal of the said County and Court, this 24th day of December, 1884.

[Seal.]

CERTIFICATE OF INCORPORATION, DECEMBER 27, 1884.

I, the undersigned, one of the Justices of the Supreme Court of the State of New York, for the First Judicial District, do hereby approve the within certificate, and do consent that the same be filed, pursuant to the provisions of an Act of the Legislature of the State of New York, entitled, "An Act for the Incorporation of Benevolent, Charitable, Scientific and Missionary Societies," passed April 12th, 1848, and the several acts extending and amending said act. Dated New York, December 26, 1884.   ABM. R. LAWRENCE, J. S. C.

State of New York,   } ss.
City and County of New York, }

I, James A. Flack, Clerk of the said City and County, and Clerk of the Supreme Court of said State for said County, do certify that I have compared the preceding with the original Certificate of Incorporation of the Woman's Foreign Missionary Society of the Methodist Episcopal Church, on file in my office, and that the same is a correct transcript therefrom, and of the whole of such original. Endorsed, filed, and recorded, December 27th, 1884, 1 hour and 25 minutes.

In Witness Whereof, I have hereunto subscribed my name, and affixed my official seal, this 12th day of November, 1888.

[Seal.]   JAMES A. FLACK, Clerk.

BOARD OF MANAGERS OF THE CORPORATION, 1896-97.

HARRIET B. SKIDMORE,	HELEN V. EMANS,	JULIA L. McGREW,
SUSAN A. SAYRE,	SARAH K. CORNELL,	ETTIE F. BALDWIN,
ELLIN J. KNOWLES,	MARY H. BIDWELL,	ANNA A. HARRIS.
ORDELIA M. HILLMAN,	ANNIE R. GRACEY,	

AMENDED ACT OF INCORPORATION.

CHAPTER 213.

AN ACT to Authorize the Woman's Foreign Missionary Society of the Methodist Episcopal Church to Vest its Management in a General Executive Committee.

Became a law April 12, 1906, with the approval of the Governor.
Passed, three-fifths being present.

The people of the State of New York, represented in Senate and Assembly, do enact as follows:

SECTION 1. The Board of Managers of the Woman's Foreign Missionary Society of the Methodist Episcopal Church is abolished.

SEC. 2. The management and general administration of the affairs of the said Society shall be vested in a General Executive Committee, to consist of the President, Recording Secretary, General Treasurer, Secretary of German Work, Secretary of Scandinavian Work, and the Literature Committee of said Society, together with the Corresponding Secretary and the two delegates from each co-ordinate Branch of said Society.

SEC. 3. The President, Recording Secretary, General Treasurer, Secretaries of the German and Scandinavian Work and the Literature Committee, now in office, shall be members of the General Executive Committee, which shall meet ou the third Wednesday in April, in the year nineteen hundred and six; and, thereafter, such officers and Literature Committee shall be elected annually by the General Executive Committee. The Corresponding Secretary and two delegates of each co-ordinate Branch shall be elected annually by such Branch.

SEC. 4. Meetings of the General Executive Committee shall be held annually, or oftener, at such time and place as the General Executive Committee shall appoint, and such place of meeting may be either within or without the State of New York.

SEC. E. This act shall take effect immediately.

State of New York, ⎰ ss.
Office of the Secretary of State, ⎱

I have compared the preceding with the original law on file. in this office, and do hereby certify that the same is a correct transcript therefrom, and the whole of said original law.

Given under my hand and the seal of office of the Secretary of State, at the City of Albany, this sixteenth day of April, in the year one thousand nine hundred and six.   HORACE G. TENNANT,

[Seal.]   Second Deputy Secretary of State.

FORMS OF WILL, DEVISE, AND ANNUITY.

FORM OF BEQUEST.

I hereby give and bequeath to the "Woman's Foreign Missionary Society of the Methodist Episcopal Church," incorporated under the laws of the State of New York, ... dollars, to be paid to the Treasurer of said Society, whose receipt shall be sufficient acquittance to my executors therefor.

FORM OF DEVISE OF REAL ESTATE.

I hereby give and devise to the "Woman's Foreign Missionary Society of the Methodist Episcopal Church" (describe land, etc., intended to be given to the Society) and to their successors and assigns forever.

Mrs. J. M. Cornell, 560 W. 26th Street, New York, is the Treasurer of the Woman's Foreign Missionary Society, with power to sign release to executors through whom the Society may receive bequests and to perform such other acts as are required by the Act of Incorporation, and which can not be legally executed by Branch Treasurers.

Note.—Prompt notice of all bequests and devises should be given to the Corresponding Secretary of the Branch within which the donor resides.

Note.—In each of the above forms the name of the Branch to which the bequest or devise is made shall be inserted immediately before the words, "Woman's Foreign Missionary Society," whenever such Branch is incorporated. The name of the State under the laws of which said Branch is incorporated shall also be inserted.

Incorporated Branches: New England under the laws of Massachusetts; Baltimore under the laws of Maryland; Cincinnati under the laws of Ohio; Northwestern under the laws of Illinois; Des Moines under the laws of Iowa; Minneapolis under the laws of Minnesota; Pacific under the laws of California; Columbia River under the laws of Oregon.

FORM OF ANNUITY.

Whereas, ..., of ...., has donated to and paid into the treasury of the .... Branch of the Woman's Foreign Missionary Society of the Methodist Episcopal Church the sum of .... dollars.

Now, therefore, the said Branch of the Women's Foreign Missionary Society of the Methodist Episcopal Church, in consideration thereof, hereby agrees to pay to said .... during .... natural life interest on the aforesaid sum at the rate of .... per cent per annum, payable semi-annually, said payments to cease on the death of said ...., and the said sum donated by .... as aforesaid is to be considered as an executed gift to said Society and to belong to said Society from this date, without any amount or liability therefor.

.... Branch of the Woman's Foreign Missionary Society of the Methodist Episcopal Church, by
....

RATES OF ANNUITIES.

Where it is practical, in the place of making a bequest, it is far better to convert property into cash and place the same in the treasury of the Missionary Society at once, on the annuity plan. By so doing all possibility of litigation is avoided, and a fair income is assured. The Woman's Foreign Missionary Society does not spend money so contributed while the annuitant lives, unless so requested by said annuitant, but invests it in good securities in this country.

The following rates are given:

To persons from 50 to 55 years of age.......................4   per cent.
To persons from 56 to 60 years of age......................4½ per cent.
To persons from 61 to 65 years of age......................5   per cent.
To persons from 66 to 70 years of age......................5½ per cent.
To persons 70 years and over.............................6   per cent.

Special cases shall be arranged for by the Branch Committee having in charge bequests and annuities.

This plan removes all risk of broken wills through skill of lawyers and uncertainty of courts.

AFTER DEATH BOND.

In consideration of my interest in, and love for the Woman's Foreign Missionary Society of the Methodist Episcopal Church, I hereby bind myself, my heirs, devisees, and representatives, to pay to the .... Branch, through the Treasurer of .... Conference of said Society, ... dollars, which said sum shall be paid at or before my death, without any relief whatever from valuation or appraisement laws.

[SIGNED.]
ATTEST:

MISSIONARY BENEFIT ASSOCIATION.

President—MRS. S. F. JOHNSON, 520 Oakland Ave., Pasadena, Cal.

Treasurer—MR. WILLIAM E. BLACKSTONE, Pasadena, Cal.

Financial and Corresponding Secretary—MRS. J. A. BURHANS, 2401 Magnolia Ave., Edgewater, Chicago, Ill.

Auditor—MR. F. P. CRANDON, Evanston, Ill.

This Society was organized November 6, 1901, in Park Avenue Church, Philadelphia, Pa., to take the place of another of the same name previously organized on a different plan.

The object of the Association is to "assist any of its members who may be in need," and any missionary regularly appointed by the Woman's Foreign Missionary Society of the Methodist Episcopal Church is eligible to membership on the payment of an annual fee of $10.

Total number on register February 16, 1907, 66. Total funds on hand January 1, 1907, $2,021.30.

All remittances and correspondence should be addressed to the Financial and Corresponding Secretary, Mrs. J. A. Burhans, 2401 Magnolia Ave., Edgewater, Chicago, Ill.

MEMBERSHIPS AND SCHOLARSHIPS IN THE WOMAN'S FOREIGN MISSIONARY SOCIETY.

The payment of one dollar a year, or two cents a week, constitutes membership.

The payment of twenty dollars constitutes life membership.

The payment of one hundred dollars constitutes an honorary life manager.

The payment of three hundred dollars constitutes an honorary life patron.

Bible women's salaries vary from twenty to one hundred dollars, according to experience in work and time given.

Scholarships vary from twenty to eighty dollars, according to the country.

Scholarships in India vary from twenty to forty dollars.

Scholarships in China are thirty dollars.

Scholarships in Mexico are fifty dollars.

Scholarships in Japan are forty dollars.

Scholarships in Korea are forty dollars.

Scholarships in South America are eighty dollars.

POSTAGE TO FOREIGN LANDS.

The rates of postage to Mexico are the same as in the United States. To all other points where our missionaries are stationed letters weighing an ounce are five cents; newspapers one cent for each two ounces; and on all printed matter the same as in United States; postal cards, two cents. Foreign postal cards may be procured at any postoffice. All foreign postage must be fully prepaid.

FOREIGN MONEY.

INDIA.—A pice is one-fourth of an anna, or about two-thirds of a cent. An anna is worth one-sixteenth of a. rupee. The rupee varies in value, and is worth about 33 cents.

JAPAN.—A yen, whether in gold or silver, is one-half the value of the gold and silver dollar in the United States. There are one hundred sen in the yen.

CHINA.—A cash is one mill. The tael is worth in gold about $1.15. The Mexican dollar is also used in China.

BEQUESTS AND GIFTS

TO THE

Woman's Foreign Missionary Society in 1906-1907.

NEW ENGLAND BRANCH.
BEQUESTS.

Names.	Residence.	Amount.
Mrs. Susan Poor,	Lynn, Mass.,	$70 00
Franklin Emery,	Lawrence, Mass.,	100 00
Miss Susan Peck,	North Woodbury, Conn.,	2,573 92
Rev. Michael A. Wicker,	Troy Conference,	950 00
Charlotte Remington,	Suncook, N. H.,	95 00
Celia Hitchcock,	Northfield, Vt.,	102 10
Mrs. Hunt,	Boston, Mass.,	1,000 00
Mrs. Willis P. Odell,		240 00

GIFTS.

A Friend,		3,000 00
A Friend of Missions,		37,700 00

NEW YORK BRANCH.
BEQUESTS.

Mrs. Emma A. Hill,	Medina, N. Y.,	$475 00
Mrs. Willis P. Odell,	New York City,	240 00
Mrs. Ordelia M. Hillman,	Troy, N. Y.,	1,000 00

GIFTS.

Mrs. Wm. Rawlings,	New York City,	
"Cora Belle Rawlings, Memorial Bungalow," at Sztzgnau, China,		1,200 00
"Marietta Hay Ward,"	Baroda, India,	1,100 00
A Friend,		500 00
Bishop Hartzell for Africa,		500 00
Mrs. W. J. Lewis,	Condersport, Pa.,	100 00

PHILADELPHIA BRANCH.
BEQUESTS.

Mrs. Mary H. Cooper,	Philadelphia,	$500 00
Mrs. Joseph H. Chubb,	Philadelphia,	500 00
Mrs. Helen M. Hill,	Pittsburg,	250 00
Miss Anna E. Peale,	Philadelphia,	2,932 33

BALTIMORE BRANCH.
BEQUESTS.

Mrs. B. F. Bennett,		$500 00

GIFTS.

Mrs. Mary E. Rice,		500 00
Mr. Fowler, in memory of a daughter,		400 00

CINCINNATI BRANCH.

BEQUESTS.

Name.	Residence.	Amount.
Mrs. Abbie A. Parish,	Cleveland, Ohio,	$1,118 63
Mr. Laban W. Haughey,	South Charleston, Ohio,	311 00
Mrs. Martha H. Brakefield,	Good Hope, Ohio,	4,200 00
Mrs. W. Singlewald,	Wheeling, W. Va.,	20 00

GIFTS.

Mrs. Lizzie H. Bitzer,	North Ohio Conference,	300 00
Mrs. Wm. A. Gamble,	Cincinnati, Ohio,	14,972 41

NORTHWESTERN BRANCH.

BEQUESTS.

Mrs. H. W. McFadden,	Illinois Conference,	$1,000 00
Mrs. Laura A. Calder,	Rock River Conference,	330 00
Mrs. Sarah Kirk Coe,	Rock River Conference,	200 00
Miss Lillian Hollister,	North Indiana Conference,	25 00
Mr. C. A. Cropper,	North Indiana Conference,	212 00
Mrs. Beamer,	North Indiana Conference,	155 80
Mrs. Jennie A. Betts,	Northwest Indiana Conference,	1,000 00
Miss Josephine Park,	Detroit Conference.	700 00
Mrs. Alice Chipman,	Michigan Conference,	262 50
Mr. Jerome A. Ormsby,	Michigan Conference,	309 01
Miss Elvira Elliott,	Michigan Conference,	100 00
Dr. C. C. Lathrop,	Michigan Conference,	200 00
Mr. Henry Dean,	Wisconsin Conference,	1,500 00
Mrs. Susanna Quayle,	Wisconsin Conference,	500 00

DES MOINES BRANCH.

GIFT.

Mrs. W. H. Knotts,	Kansas City, Mo.,	$5,000 00

MINNEAPOLIS BRANCH.

GIFT.

Mr. D. S. B. Johnston,	St. Paul, Minn.,	$3,500 00

TOPEKA BRANCH.

BEQUEST.

Mrs. Henry Jargenson,		$100 00

GIFT.

Miss Agnes Young,		75 00

PACIFIC BRANCH.

BEQUEST.

Mr. McElfresh,	Pasadena, Cal.,	$100 00

GIFT.

Mr. J. D. Payne,	Los Angeles, Cal.,	3,000 00

Total,		$95,719 70

SOME FIRST THINGS OF THE SOCIETY IN THE FOREIGN FIELD.

The Woman's Foreign Missionary Society Sent Out—
1869—The first woman physician, Miss Clara A. Swain, M. D., to non-Christian women, Lucknow, India.
1873—The first woman physician to China, Miss Lucinda Combs, M. D., Foochow.
1887—The first woman physician to Korea, Miss Metta Howard, M. D., Seoul.
1900—The first woman physician to the Philippines, Mrs. Anna J. Norton, M. D., Manila.

The Society Opened—
1874—The first hospital for women in Asia; Bareilly, India.
1875—The first hospital for women in China, Foochow.
1889—The first hospital for women in Korea, Seoul.

The Society Founded—
1887—The first Christian Woman's College in Asia, Miss Isabella Thoburn, Lucknow, India.
1890—The first Industrial Training School in Asia, Miss Ella Blackstock, Tokyo, Japan.
1892—The first Protestant Woman's College in Italy, Miss M. Ella Vickery, Rome.
1897—The first Christian woman's magazine in Japan, Miss Georgiana Baucus, Yokohama.
1904—The first Training School for Nurses in Korea, Miss Margaret J. Edmunds, Seoul.
1906—The first College for Women in Mexico, Miss Laura Temple, Mexico City.

AT HOME.

1870—District meeting first held Albion, Mich., Mrs. H. F. Spencer, Miss S. D. Rulison.
1871—Bequest; Sarah Kemp Slater, Grand Rapids, Mich.
1873—Proposed plan for Missionary Readings, Mrs. F. D. York.
1876—Conference Secretaries first elected, Michigan, Mrs. F. D. York, Mrs. Mary T. Lathrop.
1877—Missionary Leaflets, originated by Mrs. D. D. Lore and Mrs. J. T. Gracey.
1881—Thank-offering first observed, Lansing District, Mich., Mrs. H. E. Taylor.
1883—Thank-offering first observed by Branch, Northwestern.
1883—Missionary Lesson Leaf, Miss Sallie Ann Rulison.
1886—Children's Missionary Leaf, Frances J. Baker.
1889—Conference Treasurers first appointed, Northwestern Branch.
1890—Secretary of Home Department first appointed, Northwestern Branch, Mrs. M. Meredith.
1891—Little Light Bearers, Mrs. Lucie F. Harrison, Worcester, Mass.
1901—Standard Bearers, Miss Clara M. Cushman, Southbridge, Mass.
1905—College Department, Mrs. S. J. Herben, Northwestern Branch.

The Woman's Foreign Missionary Society

GENERAL OFFICE:

Room 611, 150 Fifth Avenue, New York City

Miss Elizabeth R. Bender, Office Secretary

PUBLICATION OFFICE:

36 Bromfield Street, Boston, Massachusetts

Miss Pauline J. Walden, Publisher

**Send all Orders for Periodicals to
the Publication Office**

DEPOTS OF SUPPLIES:

NEW ENGLAND BRANCH:

Miss F. Addie Farnham, · · · · · · · · Room 18, 36 Bromfield Street, Boston, Mass.

NEW YORK BRANCH:

Miss Anna L. Cole, · · · · · · · · · · · Room 401, 150 Fifth Avenue, New York City

PHILADELPHIA BRANCH:

Miss Hannah Bunting, · · · · · · · · · · · · · 1018 Arch Street, Philadelphia, Pa.

BALTIMORE BRANCH:

Miss Florence Allen, · · · · · · · · · · · · · · · · 516 Park Ave., Baltimore, Md.

CINCINNATI BRANCH:

Miss Alice M. Startsman, · · · · · 220 West Fourth Street, Room 84, Cincinnati, O.

NORTHWESTERN BRANCH:

Miss Francis Davis, · · · · · · · · · · · 57 Washington St., Room 808, Chicago, Ill.

DES MOINES BRANCH

Miss Mary Q. Evans, · · , · · · · · · · · · 105 North Mulberry Street, Maryville, Mo.

MINNEAPOLIS BRANCH:

Mrs. Fred. Noble, · · · · · · · · · · · · · 126 Orlin Ave., S. E. Minneapolis, Minn.

TOPEKA BRANCH:

Miss M. D. Thackara, · · · · · · · · · · · · · · · · · 1303 T Street, Lincoln, Neb.

PACIFIC BRANCH:

Miss Carrie M. Leas, · · · · · · · · · · · · · 531 West Fifth St., Los Angeles, Cal.

Miss Josephine Marston, · · · · · · · · · · · · 2534 Piedmont Avenue, Berkeley, Cal.

COLUMBIA RIVER BRANCH:

Mrs. L. C. Dickey, · · · · · · · · · · · 293 East Thirty-Fourth Street, Portland, Ore.

GERMAN WORK:

Miss Freda Cramer, · · · · · · · · 273 Southern Avenue, Mt. Auburn, Cincinnati, O.

Lightning Source UK Ltd.
Milton Keynes UK
UKHW041123290119
336365UK00005B/80/P